*Crossing
The Boundary*

Crossing the Boundary

Stories of Jewish Leaders of Other Spiritual Paths

Alan Levin

REGENT PRESS
Berkeley, California

Copyright © 2015 Alan Levin

PAPERBACK
ISBN 13: 978-1-58790-317-5
ISBN 10: 1-58790-317-2

E-BOOK
ISBN 13: 978-1-58790-322-9
ISBN 10: 1-58790-322-0

Library of Congress Control Number: 2015941821

All rights reserved under International and
Pan-American Copyright Conventions.
No part of this book may be used or reproduced in any manner whatsoever without the written permission of the publisher, except in the case of brief quotations embodied in critical articles and reviews.

Cover art by Michael Green

First Edition

1 2 3 4 5 6 7 8 9 10

Manufactured in the U.S.A.
REGENT PRESS
Berkeley, California
www.regentpress.net
regentpress@mindspring.com

Table of Contents

Dedication vii

Acknowledgments ix

Preface xi

Introduction xv

My Story 1

Father Paul Mayer / CATHOLIC PRIEST 31

Starhawk / WITCH 57

Pir Shabda Kahn / SUFI LEADER 79

Sharon Salzberg / BUDDHIST TEACHER (VIPASSANA) 105

Martin Lowenthal / BUDDHIST TEACHER (TIBETAN/BÖN) 125

Isaac Shapiro / ADVAITA TEACHER 147

Victoria Austin / ZEN BUDDHIST PRIEST 177

Krishna Das / CHANT MASTER 197

Allyson Grey / ARTIST 221

Tom Pinkson / MEDICINE MAN 237

Jonathan Goldman / SANTO DAIME LEADER 265

Nettie Spiwack / INTERFAITH MINISTER 303

Ken Cohen / TAOIST AND QIGONG MASTER 331

Sat Santokh Singh Khalsa / SIKH LEADER 369

Heresy / THE TALE OF AHER, ALISHA BEN ABUYA 389

Drawing Conclusions / THE JOURNEY WITH JEWISHNESS 401

Bibliography 413

DEDICATION

This book is dedicated to two Jewish men. Both tasted the fruit of the Garden and devoted their lives to bringing that beauty into the world.

RABBI ZALMAN SCHACHTER-SHALOMI (1924–2014)

Reb Zalman was ordained as an Orthodox Rabbi in the Lubivitch Hasidic world. After his introduction to LSD in the Sixties, he opened to a wider view of Judaism and spirituality. While he deeply honored all the world's religious traditions, he maintained a focus with Judaism and was the primary founder of the Jewish Renewal movement. Through his work, a whole new approach to Jewish spirituality (one that integrates mysticism, feminism, ecology, dance and meditation) has been embraced by people all over the world.

More than anyone I've met, Reb Zalman embodied the enlightening possibilities of Jewish spirituality and the loving heart of Yiddishkeit (the culture of European Jewry).

FATHER PAUL MAYER (1931-2013)

Father Paul converted to Catholicism at age 16 to become a Priest after escaping the Nazi onslaught in his native Germany. He was untiring in his advocacy for the poor and disenfranchised and for peace and ecological sanity. He marched in Selma in 1965 and participated in Occupy Wall Street demonstrations until shortly before his death. His boundary-crossing way of deepening his Christian faith included mediation, studying with a Native American shaman and practicing and teaching yoga. He always thought of himself as a Jew and attributed his social activism his Jewish heritage.

Father Paul was the first person I interviewed for this book. He continues to be a deep inspiration of what it means to be a mensch.

Acknowledgements

I am grateful to the many people who encouraged, supported and inspired me over the ten years of bringing this book to fruition.

I am especially thankful for the wisdom and compassion of those who served as my spiritual teachers: to Russell Schofield for his steadfast channeling of the teachings of Agni (light-fire) yoga; to Steven and Meredith Foster for teaching me the way of the vision quest and Earth-based rites of passage; to Angeles Arrien for her wise and endless generosity and commitment to walking the mystical path with practical feet; to Tai Situ Rinpoche for his diamond-mind clarity and penetrating understanding of the Dharma of the Buddha; to Rabbi Zalman Schachter-Shalomi for opening my heart to Jewish spirituality and for his devotion to healing the heart and mind of the Jewish people; to shaman and hierophant, Ralph Metzner, my friend and mentor, who introduced me to and nudged me through so many of the gates of consciousness expansion.

To the fourteen teachers who took the time from their busy activities to meet with me to be interviewed and put up with my follow-up messages and queries with patience and supportive replies. You inspire me with your wisdom and dedication.

To those who supported or advised my work through friendship and collaboration, thank you for helping me sustain my attention on the value of this project. To Shams Kairys for his wise and patient editing assistance, Lenny Grob for numerous readings and feedback, Rabbi Lynn Gottlieb, Rabbi Michael Ziegler and Rabbi Rueben Modek for supportive consultation on Talmudic references, Bharat Lindemood, Joseph Tieger, Bob Ressler, Johanna Luther, Teresa Johansing, Mike Lozoff, Wally Glickman, Ernie and Eva Sherman, Peter Schein, Michael Heller and Maria MacArthur for friendship and encouragement."

To the many folks who contributed financially to my Kickstarter campaign.

To Regent Press and the encouragement and technical help from Mark Weiman.

To my son and daughter, Brent and Tara, and granddaughter, Esther Joy, for their love and for the inspiration to act for the benefit of future generations.

To whoever it is that manages Wikipedia for constant, available information that was source for most footnotes.

To the one who broke and then opened my heart to the love that endures, for her great patience and encouragement, my dear wife and partner, Ginny Brooke.

There's a funny story that has circulated in various modern day spiritual circles about an elderly American woman, who, at great expense, and pushing through her aches and pains, flies to India aand enters the ashram of a famous guru. She asks to speak with the spiritual Master and is told that she must first fast for several days, do some purifying rituals, and then wait her turn in line with hundreds of other spiritual aspirants. She shrugs, does the fast and the purifying rites, and then waits in line. As she approaches the doorway to his chamber, she is told that she may only say three words to the Master. She enters, walks up to him, and in a loud voice, with a strong Yiddish accent, says, "Sheldon, come home!"

This story could relate to any of the people in this book. Unlike the mother in the story however, we ask these "Sheldons" not to come home, but to share with us from their new homes in which they have found strength, comfort, wisdom and peace.

Preface

In these challenging times of extraordinary change, many of us feel called upon to expand our awareness to a global perspective beyond the self-limiting identities of the past. The multiple world crises that we face present transformative opportunities for everyone. It is not an oversimplification to say that we need to evolve our ways of thinking and relating, or perish. Noting that the old paradigm is wreaking havoc on the life systems of our planet, His Holiness the Dalai Lama has called for a spiritual revolution, a transformative evolutionary leap in human consciousness and culture. What this spiritual revolution requires of us is in the process of unfolding. In my view, it must include the willingness to deeply engage and question the relevance of the teachings or transmissions from our ancestors.

At times like this we look for guides, those who have cultivated wisdom in action with a broad view of the challenges we face. I have selected fourteen spiritual teachers who have crossed over the boundary of their Jewish birth religion to other spiritual paths. Speaking with them has been a great privilege and learning experience for me, and it is my hope that this book illuminates concerns common to all human beings seeking happiness, wisdom, and compassion.

My journey in this life, beginning at the tail end of the baby boom, placed me in the context of a generation in conflict with the basic values and beliefs of the previous generation and the secular and religious institutions that were an expression of those beliefs. The counter-culture emerged and swept much of the planet into a maelstrom of existential doubt and optimistic searching for alternative answers to the basic questions of life. Who am I? Why am I here in this world? Who are my people? A significant part of those doing the rebelling and the questioning, a much higher percentage than found in the general population, were Jews.

In the realm of spirituality, many Jews became steeped in practices that look significantly different, even heretical, to the religious and cultural views of their parents. Likewise, many have become the leaders and core teachers of these other spiritual lineages and orientations. It seems important to me to take a deeper look at what is going on here. What are the stories of these people and what have they arrived at that can shed light on our own personal and collective journey?

What are the connections between being born and raised in a Jewish family, with Jewish values and perspectives, and choosing to become a Sikh, Sufi, Buddhist or Taoist teacher, an interfaith minister, a Catholic priest, a medicine-man/shaman, a Hindu chant master, a Pagan witch, or the leader of a branch of a syncretic Brazilian church? What is the meaning of being raised in a Jewish family with Jewish values and perspectives when you look through the eyes and heart of someone who has moved out of that world?

I believe these issues and questions are important not just for Jews, but for anyone seeking to find their own truth and their own path. To what degree does the way of our fathers and mothers inform and guide our way? How do we separate the wheat of generations of cultivated wisdom from the chaff of fear-based consciousness that separates us from our fellow human beings? How significant to our lives are the forms and language that our ancestors found for understanding and communing with the essence of life, with the sacred? How important to us are their forms of prayer, their ways of being good, or of being with God?

In addition to the interviews presented here, I offer my own musings on these questions and the understandings that I've developed in the course of my life. I do this in the Introduction and when I tell my own story in Chapter 1. I started writing this book to explore and better understand my own life journey. At various points along the way, as a secular humanist, in one or another phase of embracing Eastern or Western esoteric teachings, or participating with indigenous people in their spiritual ceremonies, I have asked myself, "Am I still a Jew?" This exploration led me to better understand my place in the human family, and beyond that in the web of life.

I've come to see this book as having universal significance beyond my initial questions. It is now my hope that it will be helpful to anyone struggling to understand who they are in the light of their ethnic or ancestral identity. It is my prayer that it will help people find the freedom to choose the path of their soul's calling. Though focused on Jews, the stories and wisdom of the spiritual explorers presented here provide keys for the survival and well-being not only of the Jewish people, but of us all.

Introduction

The Spiritual Quest and Jewish Identity

There is a mystery we experience in moments of grace, an awakening that brings us to embark on a spiritual journey. For some, there are glimpses in childhood of worlds beyond. For others, there are life-threatening or near-death experiences, mind-expanding psychedelic trips, vision quests, or an intuition to study with a spiritual guide or teacher. Whatever impels us to cross the threshold, moving forward involves choosing a path, finding a way of integrating the experience of the new-found realization with life in the "real world." The teachings of the world's religions and spiritual traditions offer disciplines and practices that guide us on the journey to explore the places of magic within and around us. They help move us toward enlightenment, wholeness, freedom, love, and being fully alive and awake.

Like other Jews of my generation, who by one means or another tasted the elixirs of the realms beyond, I was drawn to exploring my spirituality. The paths that spoke directly to this quest appeared to come from Eastern spirituality, Western esoteric traditions, or Native American teachings. Judaism never seemed an option. My Jewish identity had already diminished in its importance when the question of spiritual seeking came alive, and it had no bearing on what form of religious or spiritual practice I chose.

In the Sixties, waves of Jews began looking outside the boundary of the Jewish tradition. We immersed ourselves in the esoteric and mystical teachings of every part of the world (and beyond this world). We embraced practices from Buddhism, Hinduism, Shamanism, Sufism, Yoga, Christianity, Taoism, witchcraft and more. We traveled to lands that had never seen Jews and apprenticed to and became disciples of teachers who had never heard of Jews or the Torah. Some of us bowed down and prostrated ourselves before statues and gurus, or made the sign of the crucifix in sacred ceremonies, acts that were seriously taboo in the culture of our Jewish families and community.

The role of belief and heresy in tribal identity

As far as I know, none of my contemporaries were excommunicated for any of this. Although some Orthodox Jews may question the Jewishness of such spiritual explorers, (as they do of even Reform Jews),[1] the fact is that the practice of the Jewish religion has not been the core element of Jewish identity for some time, (in Israel or the U.S.). It seems that even when Jews take off the *tzitzis, yarmulke,* or *tallit,* when he stops going to Jewish religious services, when she stops lighting Shabbos candles, when he shaves his head and puts on Buddhist robes, when she kneels down before Mary and Jesus, when he bows his head on the ground facing Mecca and embraces Mohammed as his prophet, when she strips down in a sweat lodge or dances and drums in a Pagan ritual for the Goddess—they are still Jews. Although many of the foregoing behaviors might be considered heresy, few would say that the one who performed these acts was no longer a Jew.

Jewish tribal identification, once formed, seems nearly inescapable, much like one's gender or eye color. I am a man. I am a brown-eyed man. I am a brown-eyed, Jewish man. It seems that it doesn't really matter what I think, feel, believe or do; I am still a brown-eyed

---

[1] The Jewish religious world is segmented into four primary branches: Orthodox, Conservative, Reform and Reconstructionist. In the Sixties, the still rather small Jewish Renewal movement was initiated.

man and still a Jew. As beliefs, attitudes, feelings, and behavioral practices are all changeable, our identity associated with them is open to shifts and even radical transformations. One could say: "I am a Democrat," "I am a monotheist," "I am a pacifist," or "I believe in the sacredness of the Bible or Torah." It may seem that these are part of our identity, of who I am. Yet, while it is sometimes a wrenching process, people do change their minds and hearts, adopt contrary beliefs and different attitudes. When they do, they change that aspect of their identity. Democrats become Republicans; Catholics become Methodists, or even atheists; Trotskyites become neo-conservatives; and monotheists may become polytheistic Pagans.

It seems that being a Jew has a great deal more stickiness than other forms of identity associated with beliefs or behaviors. Yet, just how sticky is it? Does it persist beyond experiences of ego-transcendence? Deep spiritual teachings encourage us to let go of all forms of personal attachment and identity. Might such a radical letting go, even of Jewish identity, be an aspect or even a prerequisite to awakening and enlightenment?

Finding your own way

Literature and film offer a wealth of insight into the difficult journey of leaving the parental nest and finding one's own way in the world. As a father and a psychotherapist, I've witnessed what a huge transitional process it is when a young person leaves the matrix of their parents' physical, economic, and emotional shelter. Emotionally and somatically, it recalls the birth experience for both parent and child. The fierce energy required to move out from the womb/home through a gradually opening door is a Herculean struggle, a major passage in life's journey. As with birth in modern times, drugs are often used to alleviate or divert attention from the difficulty and pain of this passage. After leaving home, the struggle to individuate continues, with parental support or resistance, as the young adult clarifies his or her beliefs and values.

As adults, looking back at our lives we see that major life decisions were often made through unconscious acceptance of the ways of our parents, or an equally unconscious, rejection of them. When I became involved with radical political activism and then the hippie lifestyle, my choices involved the pull of powerful ideas and visions, but also the push from my discomfort with and rejection of the constraints of my family's way of seeing the world. Likewise, when I moved from the East Coast to California, I was drawn to the exciting lifestyle experiments and exploration of consciousness going on in San Francisco. But at the same time, there was the incentive to be 3000 miles away from my parents.

Not only parents, but cultural pressures, including community expectations and ethnic stereotypes, influence our decisions and the development of our personalities. For Jews, the journey into adulthood involves navigating various forms of Jewish identity that act as molds shaping who we become. Some are framed within the community while others are projected from outside. Yiddish and English colloquialisms offer us a Jewish typology: schlemiel, mensch, Jewish Princess, nice Jewish boy, loving Yiddishe Mama, controlling/clinging Jewish Mother, kind loving "Fiddler on the Roof" father, or cold and distant one as portrayed in the film, "The Chosen." These types have a gravitational pull on the psyche, drawing one towards a way of behaving, and eventually a cultural identity. We often struggle to avoid them, or find ourselves slipping into these molds as we try to find our own way.

From outside the Jewish community, Jews are often perceived on a spectrum that includes idealized expectations at one end and anti-Semitic hatred and ridicule at the other. While there is admiration for the *people of the book* as intelligent, generous, moral, high achievers, there is disdain for Jews as manipulative and selfish, crooked lawyers and bankers, greedy Shylocks, Judases and Christ-killers. These projected identifications from outside the community influence Jews to be attracted to or repelled from the Jewish community and can have profound effects on who we think we are.

It was only after years of spiritual practice that I could feel the confidence to open to a healthy relationship with my parents and not feel threatened by the thought of being reabsorbed into "their world."

INTRODUCTION

This book is a part of my process of clarifying for myself my relationship with the Jewish community. In Chapter One, I speak about my own journey from "good Jewish boy" through a series of rebirths and transformations. It is my hope that sharing my story, as well as the stories of the fellow travellers interviewed here, will shed light on the psychological and spiritual lessons of this very basic human quest, not limited to Jews—finding one's own way.

Not all who wander are lost — the wisdom of wandering

The adoption of a different spiritual path entails a change of identity. Humorous terms like "Jubu," or "Hinju," are often applied to Jews who have joined other religious paths. The personal stories of how the exemplars presented here navigate these changes are a major focus of this book. It is challenging for a family or community to see one of their own practicing strange rituals, wearing different clothing, speaking a different language, or espousing different beliefs. How did those in this book deal with Uncle Morris or Aunt Ida? Imagine the questions: "What's a nice Jewish boy or girl like you doing with a turban? Or a crucifix?!!"

Having come into their own as a teacher, each of those interviewed for this book has been recognized as a wisdom bearer with insights into life's fundamental questions. For the most part, their insights are shared within their own spiritual communities. Their contributions within this book will allow a wider audience to benefit from their teachings as we explore a range of issues with them—personal, cultural, and political, as well as questions related to consciousness and spirituality.

They have all wandered outside the boundary of the religious culture or their youth and adopted a different perspective from which to view the world. Our conversations take advantage of this in exploring the nature of group identity and its role in the world at this time. Ethnic and religious identity are involved in most conflicts raging on the planet today. We find people caught in collective competitive struggles over land, wealth and power. Even those distant from the conflict will often find feelings of loyalty or empathy for one side or the other determined by their group identity.

Since those in this book come from Jewish backgrounds, most of them were raised with strong feelings regarding Israel. They share how their view of the Israel/Palestine conflict and possibilities for a peaceful and just resolution has been influenced by their shift in identity. In more general terms, I inquire about how any individual seeking a healthy spiritual life can hold tribal identity in a world moving in the direction of a global society. Does tribal identity benefit the collective well-being of the people of the Earth, or is it no longer relevant for the evolution of human civilization?

Given their exposure to Jewish values and teachings as children, and their commitment and deep study and practice of another tradition as adults, these teachers see spirituality through multiple lenses. In the interviews, I encourage them to share their insights into many matters of interest to seekers of truth: spiritual practice, meditation, prayer, service, leadership, birth, death, and the meaning and purpose of our lives. Throughout, we explore how their perspectives may have been influenced by the blending of their present practice with their Jewish roots.

Stretching or dissolving boundaries

In doing research for this book, it occurred to me that the relative tolerance for heretical ways within the Jewish community may account for the tenacity of Jewish tribal identity. (there is a discussion of some exceptions to this in Chapter 16). At a perhaps overly simplistic level, tolerance keeps the "heretics" in the census count. There just aren't many "ex-Jews."

But delving deeper, though it seems counterintuitive, incorporating influences from outside the community also plays a direct role in the long survival of the Jewish people. The tribe itself learns and benefits from the knowledge of its wandering members. Jews who choose other paths may not fully return to the fold, but their new thoughts, attitudes, creative enterprises and consciousness seep back into the tribal field of knowledge and awareness. They help the whole group to learn new ways of adapting to changing realities in the world. For example, the rapidly expanding role of silent meditation in Jewish circles, sometimes introduced into the prayer services (especially within Jewish Renewal groups), clearly came from the experience of Jews who studied with Eastern spiritual teachers.

In the modern Jewish world, heretics, even those who proclaim themselves as atheists, are often seen as heroic and a source of pride for Jewish people, contributing to the resilience of the culture. Woody Allen and Lenny Bruce are examples of a vast array of irreverent Jewish comedians who stretched the limits of acceptability, but are honored members of the Jewish community. The same is true for iconoclastic, atheist writers, such as Phillip Roth, Norman Mailer, and many others.

The Dalai Lama, seeking to maintain the cultural and spiritual integrity of the Tibetan people, reached out to learn from the "survival of the Jewish people who were landless for two thousand years."[2] How did we do it? While there are many factors, part of the answer may lie in the radical tolerance for Jewish intellectual exploration. Indeed, many of the voices in this book extol intellectual curiosity as the major gift that they attribute to their family and "people of origin." Tolerance of creativity, variation and deviation creates an elasticity of the Jewish tribal boundary, providing flexibility, adaptability, and psychological and spiritual growth for the group as a whole.

Of course, things can only stretch so far before they break. The heresy of heresies is to question whether the tribe itself has any further purpose: Does Jewish identity need to persist? Is it important to me that my children, my children's children, my children's, children's, children, be Jews? Is it a moral imperative for Jews to preserve Jewish identity? Is it of benefit to Jews who are evolving spiritually to retain Jewish identity and pass it on? Is it of benefit to an evolving humanity to maintain this tribal identity?

A tribe, unlike a person, is not destined to die. Tribes seem to have built into themselves, into their codes and values, the intention to live eternally. They develop mechanisms to fight for their continuance.

---

[2] *The Jew in the Lotus* by Roger Kamenetz, Harper Collins, NY

However, it is worth considering whether we are moving towards a post-tribal period in human evolution, one in which global awareness, facilitated by enhanced methods of communication, heightens our human-family identity to the point that the tribal bond will dissolve or disappear. Still, another possibility is that we are experiencing a reshuffling of tribal identities wherein ethnicity, place of birth, and ancestry, will not be the defining aspects of one's sense of group identity. Tribal affiliations may continue to be valued as healthy and necessary forms for economic and cultural life, but commitment to shared values, mythology, and identity may involve more choice than in the past.

Individuals are born and die and the purpose and meaning of their life is not diminished because their life ends; what they contributed to humanity may be honored and passed on to others. Can it be the same for a group, a collective, a tribe? I find this to be a very compelling question, relevant to many real-world decisions we all make regarding who we marry, how we raise our children, and how we relate to events in the world. It is certainly one of the core questions motivating me to seek the counsel of those who have crossed the boundary of their tribe of birth.

Changing the lens of perception

As I spoke to friends while writing this book, I often received the feedback that my concerns and questions themselves seemed to come from my Jewishness. "It's very Jewish to think that way, to ask such questions," I'd be told. Is the very frame of reference with which I see the world, what I see as important, the questions I ask myself, determined by my Jewishness? Are even my deepest spiritual or mystical experiences "flavored" somehow by my Jewish roots?

Our mental conditioning ordinarily determines our experience of the world. Part of this conditioning involves seeing the world through the lens shaped by the collective understandings, agreements and worldview of "our people." This perceptual framing can come from our ancestors, parents, extended family and culture. However, spiritual teachers speak of the freedom of a transcendent view, a view free of any fixed set of perceptions or metaphors. As William Blake writes, "the doors of perception are cleansed and things are seen as they truly are."

A common metaphor for the awakened state is the garden. The garden evokes Eden in the mythic imagination of Jews, Christians and Muslims from the biblical tradition. More universally, it is seen as a mystical place of peace and harmony with all life; a place of being with God or divine Presence, beyond concepts and beliefs. While those of us who were raised as Jews will tend to see the world through "Jewish eyes," peak spiritual experiences or moments of awakening can reshape that lens. Entering and exiting the garden, we develop new eyes with which to see the world, new ways of understanding and being, new connections with that which guides us, a new freedom to choose which path to take.

Spiritual metaphors, however much they are connected to a specific path, can only point the direction. They help us make a shift in consciousness to a place beyond our ordinary mindset, some would say beyond the mind itself. Each of the people interviewed for this book has chosen a somewhat different map of the terrain of mind and spirit. They use different metaphors and different methods for the transformational process. Their core questions however, are universal: To what do we aspire? How does entering and exiting the mystery affect our awareness of the divine, God, the world of nature, and the good? They look through different lenses at the same Reality.

Encountering resistance, shadow or evil

As we approach the threshold of sacred space, there are great challenges. Carl Jung, in the Western tradition of depth psychology, coined the term "shadow" referring to those aspects of our individual and collective consciousness that are hidden from us, that are in the dark. Unless these aspects of ourselves are brought into the light of awareness and integrated, they sabotage our mental and physical health and wreak havoc on our relationships. The shadow stands in the way of experiencing our true nature or Self. To use the earlier metaphor, the shadow stands at the threshold of the garden and obstructs our entry.

In the East, fierce dragons and demonic faces are sculpted into the gateways of temples. They call attention to our inner demons, that which we fear or attempt to forget in our determination to be good. They remind us that there is powerful energy, divine in essence, in that which we tend to reject or fear. These reminders of the fierceness and importance of the dark on the spiritual journey are found in all spiritual traditions and reflect our experience of the inner and outer world. Advanced teachings address the state of mind or attitude that must be cultivated to understand and face these realities.

One of the ways that shadow forces manifest in our communities is through "us vs. them" beliefs and postures towards those outside the group with which we identify. We see those outside our group as other and project onto them our own group's shadow, essentially that which we can't see or don't like about ourselves. They become the enemy, hostile or evil. Jews have had centuries of being scapegoated and hated as the other in the Christian world, and many if not most Jews have a visceral imprint of this collective experience transmitted through their parents and through many generations, sometimes magnified by their own experiences of anti-Semitism.

This presents a great challenge: to not let fear control or distort one's view of the world. It is all too easy to fall into the "us vs. them" mindset, separating oneself from relationships with much of humanity, and thus much of the joy of this world. It predisposes one towards either defensive or aggressive postures and closes the mind to what may be learned from people with different worldviews.

Some of those interviewed for this book were required by their parents to go through "deprogramming" or psychoanalysis when they made the choice to follow a different religious or spiritual calling. Such was the intense fear and judgment when their family learned of their interest in an "alien" way. Confronted by their family shadow, they were forced to deeply question their sense of reality, discern light from dark, question the meaning of good and evil, and trust in their ability to choose their own path. Their stories are powerful lessons for us all.

INTRODUCTION

Conscious choice or pathology

We are each born to one mother and father who had their own mothers and fathers and so on back through the generations of our biological ancestors. For most, this ancestry defines what we call, "our people." We are taught to accept the worldview, values or spiritual perspectives of "our people" and most of us tend to take for granted a sense of loyalty to this group within which we were born.

Yet, with self-reflection, we may realize that much of this is a matter of choice. It is possible, for example, to find more comfort in the foods, music, literature, or even religious understandings of another people than the people of our birth family. Travel and communication on a planetary scale has made it easier to relocate oneself from the place into which we were born physically, psychologically and spiritually. It is possible that we may find that we prefer being in the company or living among other people than our own people.

Sometimes these choices bring condemnation from one's family and community. The term "self-hating Jew" is often used to condemn a Jew who strongly criticizes Israel, which is a modern day heresy for much of the Jewish community. But the "self-hating Jew" idea goes much deeper. It comes as a kind of diagnostic accusation, asserting that one has a pathological hatred of one's family, people, and self. Note the implication that the core nature of the self, by this understanding, is Jewish.

This pathologizing and related animosity is also directed at Jews who assimilate a bit too much into mainstream culture, who celebrate Christmas, eat ham, marry non-Jews, and especially those who convert to other religions. We must ask, however, whether doing any of these things, including the choice to find a place amongst another people than one's birth group, must arise only from some unprocessed wound or pathology? When it comes to religious or spiritual practice, may it not be an authentic calling stemming from a true connection to one's essence or Soul?

What makes Jews Jews?

Our personal psychology is just a thin skin, a ripple on the ocean of collective psychology. The powerful factor, the factor which changes our whole life, which changes the surface of our known world, which makes history, is collective psychology, which moves according to laws entirely different from those of our individual consciousness. — Carl Jung.[3]

There are several related expressions for the idea that consciousness, including what is "in our head," goes beyond the individual—collective psychology, collective mind, collective consciousness, group mind, collective unconscious. People in groups share thoughts, feelings and ways of seeing the world. How this plays out in the Jewish world has its own particular coloration, but sheds light on all human groups.

When sociologists use the term *collective consciousness*,[4] they are generally describing shared beliefs and attitudes of a clan or tribe which act as a moral force on individuals in the group, a kind of group conscience. We are raised to think that this or that is "not what our people do," or the opposite, "what we do." The term *group-mind* is usually used with a more negative connotation, referring to cults under the hypnotic influence of a charismatic leader or following unquestioned dogma. We think of Jim Jones or Charles Manson. Hitler was able to capture and nurture the already existing seeds of anti-Semitism in the group-mind of European Christians and focus it into rabid and vicious acts of hatred. We can see destructive manifestations of collective consciousness in all tribes or nationalisms, including those of the Jewish world.

While the above descriptions tend to call to mind the darker aspects of collective consciousness, Carl Jung used the term *collective*

---

[3] *Analytical Psychology: Its Theory and Practice:* The Tavistock Lectures (1935). In CW 18: (retitled) "The Tavistock Lectures"

[4] "The totality of beliefs and sentiments common to the average members of a society forms a determinate system with a life of its own....a collective consciousness." — Emile Durkheim Kenneth Allan; Kenneth D. Allan (2 November 2005). *Explorations in Classical Sociological Theory: Seeing the Social World.* Pine Forge Press.

unconscious to refer to the vast repository of forces and wisdom lying beyond the individual human mind. The *collective unconscious* includes the archetypes, universal patterns that influence all human beings whether they are aware of them or not. It is possible to imagine that a group or tribe can be defined by the archetypes by which its members are strongly influenced. In more ancient times, as Jung himself recognized, the archetypes were called gods and goddesses,[5] and tribes were defined by the different gods they worshipped. Much as it is blasphemy to most modern Jewish theologians, it is quite probable that the early Hebrews worshipped the god Yahweh, along with the goddess Asherah, and this was a defining aspect of their identity.[6]

Yet another view of the nature of collective consciousness can be derived from the theories of Rupert Sheldrake, the visionary biologist who coined the term morphogenetic field. Sheldrake hypothesizes that all things or creatures, such as crystals, plants, animals or humans, have a field of "pattern-related resonance" in which their structure, knowledge or behavior is embedded. All members of that category are influenced by that morphic field.[7] If we apply this to human groups, Jewish individuals may be connected with each other through the morphogenetic field that is constantly learning from and feeding into all members of the Jewish people. Alice Bailey[8] and other metaphysical writers offer the idea of "group-souls." These are entities existing in higher planes of consciousness that relate to collectives of individuals in families, tribes or nations. It is possible that all of the theories of Jung, Sheldrake and Bailey have a similar experiential basis even though they come from different perceptual frameworks and belief systems.

While these ideas will seem very far out or overly abstract to some, it is well to remember that Jewish religious beliefs include the

---

[5] "They (the archetypes) are the ruling powers, the gods, images of the dominant laws and principles, and of typical, regularly occurring events in the soul's cycle of experience." from the "The Psychology of the Unconscious", Carl Gustav Jung, 1928

[6] See: *The Hebrew Goddess*, Raphael Patai, Wayne State University Press.

[7] For a good review of Sheldrake's theory, see: http://www.co-intelligence.org/P-moreonmorphgnicflds.html.

[8] Alice Bailey is one of the most renowned writers of occult and metaphysical teachings. She authored many books which she attributed to telepathic transmission from a Master of Wisdom referred to as "The Tibetan," or Djwhal Khul.

existence of angels and archangels that watch over the Jewish people and are responsive to their prayers and communications. Every Passover, Jewish families pour a cup of wine and open the door to Elijah, the ancient prophet, who is said to continue to care for and protect the Jewish people.

Other ideas that may help explain group consciousness include the study of subtle, non-physical, energy fields connecting groups of people at mental, emotional, or spiritual levels. This might explain the sense of comfort or discomfort people experience with someone they encounter for the first time, as if there is some similar or resonant vibration between them. When and how these energy fields are formed is an area of exploration, but it is one possible explanation for the felt-sense of connection many Jews feel with other Jews.

When it comes to the Jewish people, as with all ethnic groups, there is a clear influence on the consciousness and conscience of individual Jews by their family and culture as knowledge and attitudinal orientation are passed from parent to child through the generations. Ethical codes about behavior are prescribed or proscribed by rules that are taught by families and Hebrew schools. The Jewish word "kosher," literally meant for dietary rules, is a code-word for "that which is allowed." At a deeper level, attitudes and core beliefs about human nature, and about nature Herself, are transmitted in this way. Even our perceptions and beliefs are to some extent determined by what is kosher, what we are allowed to see or believe.

But does it all come through ordinary physical and psychological communication? Is some of this transmission coming through from sources not related to direct parental and cultural messages? It stretches the boundary of Western scientific thinking to refer to the Jewish people having a collective mind, a group-soul, or a morphogenetic field that all Jewish individuals somehow participate in consciously or unconsciously. Yet within Jewish teachings there is an often expressed view that Jews are somehow linked in consciousness through a spiritually-based transmission of their collective history; the triumphs and tragedies of our people throughout history are our own triumphs, tragedies and sources of pride, guilt or fear. At Passover seders, we are told to imagine that we ourselves were freed from slavery in Egypt.

It's a hotly debated question, but numerous writers have asserted that there is a collective PTSD in the Jewish psyche as a consequence of the Holocaust and the centuries of pogroms in Europe.[9] The idea is that this is true of the entire Jewish community whether one had any direct experience of those events or not. Likewise, some Jewish teachings claim that the whole history of the Jewish people, even the perhaps mythical exodus from Egypt, the receiving of the commandments at Sinai, and the building and destructions of the Temple, are imprinted in the consciousness of all Jews.[10]

These reflections, though not always addressed directly, offer an important background to the issues discussed in this book. It seems to me that everyone has the job of sorting the wheat from the chaff of their own group consciousness. To do this, it helps to have a sense of how it works, how it is that we are connected to "our people," including our ancestors. It seems to me that such learning by folks in the Jewish community will shed light for those from other groups who are also seeking to sort out the collective wisdom or pathology they have inherited and to which they are tied.

The group ego — the wego as the source of suffering

The Buddhist teacher and writer, David Loy, coined the term wego for explaining the social causes of suffering.[11] Whereas the familiar term *ego* refers to an individual's sense of a separate self, the *wego* is the sense of collective identity, the absorption in and identification with a particular culture, ethnic group, or religion. Buddhists and Hindus alike describe our sense of being a separate self as the illusion at the root of all our anxiety, dissatisfaction and suffering. Wego, Loy suggests, is the sense of collective identity separating one group of

---

[9] See Leonard Fein, People-Wide PTSD published in the Berman Jewish Policy Archive
[10] For an intriguing account of this teaching and issues related to the theme of this book, see *Letters to a Buddhist Jew*, Akiva Tatz and David Gottlieb. Targum Press
[11] "Wego: The Social Roots of Suffering," by David Loy, in *Mindful Politics, A Buddhist Guide to Making the World a Better Place,* edited by Melvin McLeod, Wisdom Pub.

humanity from every other, creating an inevitable sense of competition between groups and ultimately leading to conflict, war and collective suffering.

Disputes between clans, tribes and nations involve enormous amounts of destructive psychic energy that lead to perhaps the greatest evil in human relations: war. The power of the wego to harness and enflame emotional reactions and distort thoughts and perceptions is immeasurable, leading otherwise rational and intelligent people to support unrestrained violence against other people.

Every spiritual seeker knows how challenging it is to step outside of one's egoic, seemingly separate, view of any given situation. Loy challenges us to look at what is often less obvious and equally difficult, stepping outside one's wego. As an example: the sense of victimhood experienced in a group wego, may bring about a compensatory righteousness felt by individuals in the group. An individual may internalize from their group's history, feelings of shame, blame, fear or anger, that then play havoc in their personal relationships. On a larger scale, this leads to chauvinistic and militaristic group or national behaviors. Loy and other spiritual teachers contend that even temporary experiences of transcendence could bring a clearer awareness of the destructive consequences of the wego's sense of separateness and offer us the possibility of life free of this tendency rooted in group identity.

Jewish people have for centuries been scapegoated and targeted for violence, especially in the Christian world. It's my view that this has left a strong victim imprint on the Jewish sense of self. Jews also have, in their stories and sacred texts, a strong wegoic sense of separateness and specialness, if not chosenness, which can lead to chauvinism and self-righteousness. Jews on a spiritual path, whether practicing Judaism or another tradition, will encounter these tendencies in themselves and be challenged to transform them.

On the other hand, suffering often has the consequence of bringing people to greater understanding, empathy and generosity, values and attitudes that are very strong in the Jewish community. Jewish prophetic and rabbinic traditions offer compelling wisdom about the importance of kindness and love towards the stranger.

INTRODUCTION

As I have been noting, experiences of awakening to one's essential nature provide awareness of both ego and wego transcendence, and bring a clarity that allows us to look more objectively into the roots and consequences of the patterns that are part of our tribal consciousness.

Into the Mystery

The people presented in this book have gone beyond the Jewish world, beyond the "people of the book." But they do not necessarily leave the Jewish people. As old forms dissolve, new forms appear that include aspects of the prior. So it may be with transformations of identity. Our journeyers have made new connections and opened to new sources of inspiration bringing them previously unknown fruits that add to what they received from their ancestors. The questions and speculations above serve as starting points for my dialogues with them. With deep respect for the individuals and the transmissions with which they have aligned, we will explore the paths taken by these "Jewish" teachers.

So, we embark.

My Story

SOON AFTER MY BIRTH, I was given a name and began absorbing the sound of that name and a number of other impressions and notions which gradually became who I thought I was, my sense of identity. Eight days after my birth, in accordance with an ancient tradition deeply embedded in Jewish tribal consciousness, an imprint was made on my body and psyche—I was ceremonially circumcised at a bris[12]. Through this ritual, a choice was made for me to enter into a contract, a covenant with God, as understood by the Jewish people.

I was taught and came to believe that I was one of the Jewish people. The "I" that I thought I was became identified with and bonded to the story, the heroes, the tragedies, triumphs, suffering, achievements,

---

[12] The *bris* (Yiddish) or *brit milah* (Hebrew) "covenant of circumcision" is a Jewish religious circumcision ceremony performed on 8-day-old male infants by a *mohel*, and is followed by a celebratory meal.

fears, hopes, anger, and pain of the collective experience of the people called "the Jews." Likewise, I was taught the Jewish way of devotion, understanding, and relating to "God." It all became a part of whatever I referred to when I used the words, "I," "me," "we," "mine," or "our."

Who am I? What am I doing here? Who are my people? The first two questions are at the core of all spiritual quests. The third speaks to the heart of human relationships. Most people take all three for granted—until they begin to wake up. When and if that happens depends on a lot of things, most of all grace.

My waking up began at the dawning of the Sixties. I stepped out of my place in a Jewish college fraternity and crossed a boundary into a multi-racial, politically radical, pot-smoking subset of college life. Questioning everything was a way of life among my new peers, quite unlike the folks with whom I'd grown up.

My growing up happened in a predominantly Jewish area of Far Rockaway, New York. My family moved from the Bronx when I was two to be near the ocean and chose this village in the borough of Queens. In my childhood mind, our neighborhood had homes that were bright and those that were grey; Jewish homes and those of the Goyim; friendly and scary. Well, that's not completely accurate. There were homes that were neither bright nor grey; not friendly, yet not scary. These were the homes of Orthodox Jews. These were not my people. My people were the assimilated Jews, those who went to *shul* on High Holidays and paid some level of attention to being kosher in our home. We avoided the uptight, very Orthodox Jews, but feared non-Jews. That's who we were. Who I was, was "a good Jewish boy." I believed and did what I was told.

My parents and grandparents spoke Yiddish when they didn't want the kids to understand. Occasionally, we'd hear mentions of "the old country," which was all I knew of where my grandparents came from. I later learned that they were from Eastern Europe—Russia, Poland, Lithuania. Our people were always on watch for signs of attack or disrespect from "them," (the Goyim), locally or afar. I heard about and feared "the Catholic kids" who would chase Jews and beat them up.

I heard of the Arab embargo, an evil plan aimed at destroying Israel (and us). Politicians were or were not "good for the Jews," or "good for Israel," which was essentially the same thing.

We watched the newsreels with footage from the concentration camps in silence; we cheered the great military victories of Israel; we were proud of the Jews who made it in the entertainment world, as scientists, athletes or businessmen. I learned that smart people had a "Yiddishe kop," and likewise, there were those with a "Goyishe kop,"[13] (usually said with a roll of the eyes).

Meanwhile, my home was a warm and safe place, often scented with the aromas of chicken fat and broiled beef. Our refrigerator was always filled with my favorite snacks. My friends and I played on the street and nearby fields. We walked to shul on the High Holidays and fasted on Yom Kippur, received lots of presents on Chanukah and sat through the long Passover story at our seders. Near the end of December we would drive through the nearby Christian neighborhoods to look at the Christmas lights. I felt, but didn't understand the discomfort in the car when we'd pass the homes with the mangers.

At certain times of year, after school, I walked through the neighborhood with a blue and white can, asking people to give to what I thought was the J&F, (actually the JNF — Jewish National Fund), which raised money for Israel. I didn't go up to the grey homes. I learned to count the money and was delighted to paste little paper leaves on a picture of a tree that represented a tree that would be planted in Israel to make the desert bloom.

Three times a week, after public school, I went to Hebrew School where we learned the Hebrew alphabet and they tried to teach us the Hebrew language. We read Bible stories in which Jewish heroes defeated giants and massive armies and we learned about our holidays, which seemed mostly about Jews defeating giants and massive armies. We sang the Israeli national anthem, Ha Tikvah, at gatherings of the school with the flag of Israel next to the American flag.

I can only remember one discussion that bordered on a religious

---

[13] Kop means head in Yiddish. Yiddishe (Jewish) meant smart; Goyishe (not Jewish), not smart.

question. A few of my friends and I challenged our teacher about the meaning of the universe being "infinite." We couldn't see that it made any sense, infinity. We'd say, "Well what's beyond the end of infinity?" He kept telling us, "It just keeps going, it doesn't end," showing us a great distance with his arms waving outward. This went on for several repetitions until we walked away feeling we had won the argument; it didn't make sense. It was only much later in life that I could begin to appreciate what that word points towards.

When I was thirteen, I was bar mitzvahed[14] singing the assigned prayers (the *haftorah*) in the synagogue and received great praise for my performance. But I was most proud that my reception (and my suit) was more expensive than any of my friends'. I beamed with pride about the ice sculptures, the fancy food and shmaltzy band. Relatives came up to me, shook my hand, pinched and kissed my cheeks and gave me envelopes which I put in my suit pocket. Later, counting the checks and bonds at home, I was told that my grandmother had died during the celebration; I shouldn't be counting the money now. In the midst of the glitz and glitter I felt little emotion, let alone anything spiritual.

Shortly afterwards, my family moved to Florida and our new neighborhood was a spread of ranch houses surrounded by grass and palm trees. There were shopping malls instead of a downtown village. It didn't feel Jewish. My mother was forever homesick for New York. I was on the swim team in high school, which had only a few other Jews. Being small in stature, the anti-Semitic barbs were thrown at me. They hurt in a way that I couldn't acknowledge to myself at the time, and I lived for many years with frustrated anger and the shame of not responding. The all-white school was mostly non-Jewish, and though there were only a very few encounters with anti-Semitism, and though I didn't admit them as such, they added to my already difficult adolescent discomforts.

Interestingly, it was the most virulent anti-Semitic swim team

---

[14] Bar Mitzvah literally translates as "son of commandment." The correct usage is to say, "I became a bar mitzvah," though among less Orthodox folk it is common to use it as above.

member who gave me a name that stuck with me through my high school and college years. He was teasing me and said my name, Levin, sounded like "Lenin." He said I was "Nikolai Lenin," the despicable communist. My friends heard of this and started to call me Nik and I adopted the nickname, much to my mother's horror. I soon forgot how it got started and liked the playfulness and non-Jewishness of the way it sounded. Sometimes I would be called "Nick the Greek," or even just, "Greek." In college, Nik fit well with my soon-to-be-adopted radical identity.

I didn't deeply question my good Jewish boy identity until my college years when I began to reconsider the whole package of cultural beliefs I'd internalized. In my second year at the University of Florida, in Gainesville, I began to get uncomfortable with the conformity and conservatism of fraternity life. At UF, you were either in a fraternity or a geek. If you were in a fraternity, you were either in a Jewish one (choice of three) or in one of the dozens that didn't accept Jews. The fraternity world was the grooming ground for future Florida politicians and business leaders and controlled all student government. When I chose to drop out of my fraternity, I wrote a series of articles for the school newspaper condemning the whole system and called for fraternities to be abolished. An independent editor agreed to publish the articles and I became, for a moment, a focus of campus buzz and a target of threats from some jock, fraternity guys. I felt the first rush of being a rebel in the spotlight and it felt good.

Leaving the fraternity freed me from the constraints of peer pressure and I found the courage to attend a meeting of the small, dedicated group of faculty and students who were picketing a local restaurant that refused to serve "Negro" students. This was 1963 and the agenda of the civil rights coalition locally was relatively conservative: they simply advocated that Negro students of the University be served in the restaurant across the street from campus. My fraternity brothers mocked these folks and saw them as very uncool, geeks.

Joining the civil rights group was a major psychological step for me, forcing me to face many fears and challenge my sense of identity. At the time, Gainesville was part of the deep South, with an active

Klan group in the area. As civil rights activists moved from the campus to deeper in the town and sought to desegregate racist strongholds, we met fierce opposition. The people in the movement were serious and dedicated. There were Jews and Gentiles, white and black. I was now in a very different scene and came quickly to see myself as part of this movement. I was now "an activist" and my people were "the movement." What we did was organize and protest against war and for social justice.

Right around that time, for a reason I can't explain, I felt a strong urge to go to Europe. I had fantasies of being with artists and writers in coffee houses in Paris. I convinced my parents that I would study for a year at the Sorbonne and they agreed to pay my way. A few months into it, I was bored and restless with the school program. So, when a good friend from Gainesville came to visit me in Paris, I dropped out of school and together we began a hitchhiking adventure through Europe. My parents came to refer to this as my "downfall," (although they would also use that word for several other non-conventional periods of my life). The year-long European adventure climaxed with a motorcycle trip from Belgium to Athens and then a boat trip to Israel.

Why Israel? My intention in going to Israel (I told myself and others), had nothing to do with being Jewish. I had, *in my head*, divorced myself from thinking of myself as a Jew. I wanted to see myself as a human being. My plan was to live on a *kibbutz*[15] and learn to establish something similar in the U.S.: a multi-racial, cooperative community in the South. The vision was that we would spark other such communities and heal the racial divisions in the nation. I told myself that my motivations and intentions were not related to the fact that these kibbutzim were in Israel and Jewish.

In my naiveté, I was unaware that one doesn't just show up in Israel and get to live on a kibbutz. You have to arrange it all in advance, apply through agencies, wait, etc. However (as with many transitional moments in my life), serendipity or divine intervention came into play. In Athens, I met an Israeli woman from a kibbutz who was hitching

---

[15] The early kibbutz movement was a network of utopian, collective communities that were primarily based on agriculture and explored radical ideas of communal living.

through Europe. She gave me a hand-drawn map and a letter of introduction to her kibbutz family living beside Lake Kinneret (also known as Lake Tiberias).

Until that point, although I now thought of myself as "a member of the human family," I'd been basted in the core belief that Jews were the good people and Israel was a nation steeped in that goodness. Although racism concerning Arabs had been instilled in my consciousness, it was stuffed below the surface of my awareness. Through Orwellian double-think, I could see myself as a universal citizen of the world, free from biases and stereotypes, yet hold visceral negative feelings towards Arabs. Likewise, as a liberal, I knew that Jews should make peace with the Arabs. Yet the basic narrative about the history of the creation of Israel and how the Arabs were out to kill us, (as told in the movie and book Exodus), was the gospel embedded in my heart.

Interestingly, in Israel, not everyone thought that way. Leftist literature there was as critical of the Israeli narrative as criticism of U.S. history was amongst the left in America. Such pamphlets and newspapers quickly came into my hands. I learned that Arabs were severely discriminated against within Israel and that peace opportunities were repeatedly spurned. More disturbing, however, was that most of the Israelis I spoke with expressed attitudes towards Arabs (even Arab Jews) that reminded me of white attitudes towards Blacks in the South from where I'd just come. The extremity of their views shook me to re-examine my understanding of what was going on and research further the history of the creation of Israel as a nation state.

Nevertheless, I loved my time on the kibbutz. I did whatever work they gave me with a hearty spirit and fell in love for the first time. Every day, after working in the fields or kitchen, I swam by myself in the lake. A mysterious feeling would overwhelm me in the water: a rush of excitement, strength and energy that had me jumping and swimming literally with joy. Much later, I came to appreciate that this lake, Tiberias, was the Sea of Galilee, where most of Jesus's ministry took place. At the time, Jesus was completely off the radar of my awareness. I'd never given any thought to him, the Sea of Galilee, or any of the Christian biblical teachings. It would never have occurred to me that there was any relevance of the Jesus story to me or my experience. That was for a later time and another identity.

I came home from Israel fully expecting to start the inter-racial commune plan. However, shortly after arriving and enrolling back in school, I found myself speaking at a meeting of the movement activists in Gainesville and was (quite willingly) pushed into running for student body president against the competing candidates from the fraternity blocs. I became the chairman of "The Freedom Party," and was now a full-fledged radical, (and full of myself).

I found myself behind a printing press or mimeograph machine into the late hours, attending and leading meetings, and organizing demonstrations. In retrospect, I see that I was trying to be someone by promoting an image of myself as strong and free. I wanted to be the leader of whatever radical group formed and was the chair of the Gainesville SDS (Students for a Democratic Society) and the somewhat similarly oriented SSOC (Southern Student Organizing Committee). I travelled to college campuses throughout Florida, where administrators had me marked as a professional "outside agitator," which I held as a badge of honor.

For many years I looked back on my student radical days with embarrassment. I felt that I'd been hiding my feelings and fear of intimate personal relationships behind a mask of the angry rebel or revolutionary. I argued for ideas based on whether they were the more "radical" position rather than whether I knew them to be true. I belittled people who disagreed with me and treated them with disrespect. Several decades later, when I was interviewed for *Struggle for a Better South*,[16] a book about the movement in the South, I had this to say about myself and how I felt about the emerging hippie movement of the time:

> *"I didn't get it. I didn't get it until I got it, and then I got it and ... left the movement. I really couldn't see a blending of the two worlds. I had such an 'either/or' mental type way of approaching the world. So it appeared to me, that the hippies were either putting us on or trivializing us, and I thought they*

---

[16] *Struggle for a Better South, The Southern Student Organizing Committee, 1964-1969*, by Gregg Michel.

were the ones being trivial. They'd go around painting their bodies green, with smiles on their faces and flowers in their hair and stuff like that. I thought we should be angry; we should be angry and we should be serious and we should be organizing and we should be demonstrating. And they just stopped—they thought our meetings were just boring as hell, (which they were). They would imply that I was on some kind of ego trip, (which I was). They would just smile and say, 'lighten up.' I didn't appreciate the message. I was too defensive."

Now, I have a gentler, more compassionate view of Nik. He saw the horror of the war, the awfulness of the injustice of segregation, the evil of the hatred that divides us, and in keeping with the deeper values of his ancestors, he gave all his energy to change things. He had real courage and fought for the good as he saw it. He was a warrior, albeit lacking awareness or appreciation of beauty, poetry, art or music, except as they contributed to the cause. All that would change and a transition to a whole new identity would come about with the ingestion of LSD, a trip which essentially brought about the death of Nik Levin.

Here is a journal entry about that experience in October, 1967:

"Deep into the trip, someone shared with me that people had surrounded the Pentagon and were lighting fires. There was a clear image in my mind of the fire, though at that point my mind was swirling in confused patterns. There was a thought that 'the revolution' was over, that something had completed or died. After that, I was in a state of total confusion about who I was and where I was for several hours."

For months I had helped organize for the massive demonstration planned for D.C. and I had coordinated busloads of people to go from Gainesville and other parts of Florida. But for some reason, I stayed home with my wife. We had decided to take LSD, something friends had encouraged me to do for quite a while, but which I kept putting off. A friend who was experienced with psychedelics offered to be our guide for this first session which turned out to be a life-changing trip. The experience went from being light-hearted, humorous, and fun, to confusion and darkness. After enjoying a period of euphoria and visual hallucinations in a park, we went to some friends' apartment and I became totally lost in what seemed to me to be "another world," or "realm" in which I couldn't understand who I was or where I was. ((Much later I learned about set and setting and their role in my experience.)

I had no preparation, language, or ability to integrate what I was experiencing. The only way in which I had used the term "consciousness" was politically, as in "radical consciousness." "Altered state of consciousness" was not in my vocabulary, so I had no words or concepts to contain, much less fully allow, the experience. Everything fell apart. Reality made no sense and my ego could not accept that that was a good thing. My guide, though well intentioned, didn't have a clue on how to help. I didn't know how to accept that with dying, something is born. I just tried to cling to what was.

After that experience, my movement identity had no heart. I drifted through being an activist in a hollow way. I printed and passed out flyers, attended meetings, organized demonstrations, but I was lost. Even on a trip to Cuba to see "the Revolution" as one of twenty U.S. student radicals honored by the Castro government, my mind was trying to figure out how that other world I'd glimpsed could exist side by side with this one. How did it relate to revolution? Who else knew about it? Why was it such a secret? I tried sharing my thoughts with people I thought would understand, but I couldn't even describe what I was thinking, what my questions were. Some of my wiser friends suggested that I needed to go to San Francisco. Some had been there and attested to the fact that, "it was really happening there." They seemed to have some kind of knowledge. But inside, I was wondering what they were talking about, what the "it" was that was happening.

Meanwhile, the Vietnam war raged on. My struggle with the Draft Board was coming to a head. Earlier on, I had received a I-0, conscientious objector status. But when I was called for my induction physical for alternative service, the local movement staged a major demonstration. My friends lay down in front of the bus and were arrested. At the induction center, I put on a wild protest performance, shouting out anti-war questions and wearing an "End the War" bumper sticker on my back. The events made it into the local and state newspapers and shortly afterwards I received notice that my C.O. status had been revoked and I was now re-classified 1-A, eligible to be drafted for active military duty immediately.

It's fascinating to me now how fearless I and many of us seemed to be at that time. With the power of the movement behind me, I could face threats from University administrators, police and FBI agents with a sense of invincibility. I chose to go on the SDS sponsored Cuba trip knowing I'd be there on the day that I was supposed to report for my induction into the military. From Havana, I sent a telegram to my draft board telling them that I was too busy working for "The Revolution" to report for their military.

Where was my Jewishness during all this? Certainly not in my thoughts. On rare occasions, some of the movement activists would notice, with a laugh, the significant number of Jews in the struggle. The moment would pass, perhaps with some embarrassment that it might have some meaning, and we'd go on with the fight. Much later, I saw the influence of hearing, year after year after year, the Moses story. Our family would read the same passages from the Passover Haggadah which told the tale of Moses's mission to free his people from slavery, helped by the Lord "with a mighty hand and an outstretched arm." Now, I am grateful for having received this powerful transmission that has so influenced my life.

While I was acting brave, I was scared inside. If I still held the certainty of my Nik identity I could have dealt with the fear, but my heart was no longer in the fight. I was facing a long legal battle to prove that the draft board had changed my status due to my political activity. Like so many others of my generation, I considered my options of escaping to Canada, going to prison, or going underground.

The angels of mercy (again) had other plans for me. A little child would save me, conceived without conscious intention, but lovingly welcomed by my wife and I. With mixed emotions, always worried about compromising with "the enemy," I signaled the draft board that I'd be willing to accept a deferment based on my wife being pregnant. Even though I'd already committed the crime of refusing induction, the board decided to avoid a protracted legal battle and the political heat. Or, maybe some invisible spirits waved their hands in front of whoever was in charge (like Obi-Wan Kenobi of "Star Wars") and said, "This isn't the lamb you're looking for." In any case, they agreed to let me off the hook. They reclassified me III-A (a permanent deferment), and I was now free to drop out of my life as a movement activist, head across the country to Haight-Ashbury, and begin life in the "other world." I was to become a new man, a father, and find my new people, the hippies, the flower children.

It was 1968, one year past the Summer of Love, and already the Haight had become infiltrated with Hate: hard drugs, guns, rip-offs, and greed. But there was still the deeper, positive side of the psychedelic culture that was growing and rocking the country (and not just musically): interest in the Tarot, I Ching, and other esoteric teachings; meditation; Eastern gurus; communal living; respecting our bodies as sacred; challenging political ideologies; sexual freedom; living on the land. Psychedelic experience and culture entered into media, medicine, education, business and politics. Views vary on how lasting the effects have been; whether establishment institutions merely co-opted the language and style, or were transformed. Certainly the former occurred, but I favor the latter view; "IT" is still happening and the psychedelic experience continues to influence our cultural evolution.

People embracing these interests started moving out of the city and onto the land, with neighbors who were often hostile to the outward appearance of hippies and our questionable lifestyle and behavior. The culture war was in full swing. With my wife and newborn son, Summer, we moved to the Russian River area north of San Francisco. It was like the screen image of pioneers moving into hostile Indian land, except we felt more like Indians moving into cowboy country. The hippie culture had its own version of us/them identity issues. Some bridged boundaries easily and found common ground with the "straight," "redneck" folk. Sometimes hands-on skills were the basis of mutual respect, softening the edge of our cultural differences. I was too self conscious to make such connections. Psychedelic experiences were slowly dissolving my hard shell, I was having genuine spiritual openings, but I was not able to fully surrender to being in my own skin comfortably and authentically. I knew this and felt it was clearly apparent to the bullshit detectors of people around me, which made me feel paranoid.

The bubble had burst on my harsh, radical identity, but I couldn't seem to fully form a new one. I felt half in and half out of the hippie world, constantly plagued by the feeling that I just wasn't getting it. My personal insecurities led me to idealize those who seemed confident in "having it together," as it was quite obvious to me that I didn't. This experience taught me a powerful lesson. It gave me a strong sense of empathy for people who fell in with the likes of Charlie Manson or other cult leaders, or found comfort in fundamentalist religious groups, paths that quite a few wayward hippies took.

Once again, a rescue from on high. As my second child, my daughter Tara was about to be born, a friend talked me into going to a retreat focused on "Maps of Consciousness" led by Ralph Metzner. We were both attracted to Metzner, the third, least prominent of the triumvirate from Harvard that pioneered so much of psychedelic culture. Tim Leary, Richard Alpert (Ram Dass), and Metzner were counter-culture heroes. They had notoriously been fired from Harvard (actually, Metzner was a graduate student and was not fired) where they had been researching LSD and other psychedelic substances. Their sacrifice of professional careers in order to spread the gospel of psychedelics was legendary.

I'd heard Leary speak at a series of lectures that he gave in Berkeley and I was astounded by his thoughts and his joyful and wild personality. I'd also seen Ram Dass, who appeared in San Francisco on his return from India. Ram Dass wore a white robe and beads, had a long beard and serene smile, and seemed to know what it was that we all wanted to know. I had wondered about this third hero. The blurb for the seminar said it was about Tarot, I Ching, astrology, alchemy and numerology; things that all good hippies were into. I guessed that he was involved with the more Western esoteric traditions.

I had no idea that attending this retreat would take my life in a whole new direction, initiating me into a disciplined spiritual practice and a new identity as, "light-worker." When I first met Dr. Metzner, I was so unimpressed that I nearly left. Clean shaven, short hair, looking like the archetypal straight guy, he spoke in a dry, mostly humorless tone with a slight German accent and an almost imperceptible edge of irony. He seemed to bristle when my friend and I lit up a joint.

After a day or so at the retreat, I decided to take a small amount of LSD before the next session in the series. It had become my way to really check something out, as I felt LSD enhanced my perception. (I realize, as I write this, that this is quite opposite to how most people view things, which is that "drugs" inevitably distort reality). Anyway, as I started to feel the acid come on, I heard Metzner say that he was changing the plan for the session. Instead of it being about numerology, astrology or whatever, he would introduce us to something called "AgniYoga," a kind of meditation teaching he'd been exploring. I right away felt disappointed; I wasn't interested in yoga and never could meditate.

But then something started to happen. I began seeing that he wasn't just speaking words to convey information. He was somehow emanating the very teaching he was offering. My mouth hung open as I saw, literally, an energy or light move from him through the room just as he was describing such phenomena with words. His physical presence changed and instead of seeming dry and hollow he was extremely alive, filled with energy and seemingly aware in a way that was beyond that of anyone else in the room. He appeared deeply wise, attentive and caring with those he addressed. He had my attention and I was able to go with his guided process.

This was my first introduction to the light-fire meditation practice that was to become the core of my spiritual life for the next 45 years. I wanted more right away, and after the group session I asked to talk with him. Instead of talking, he took me to his cabin and led me through a private session in which I felt all the negativity, doubt, fear, shame and pain that I'd been carrying cleansed from my body, cell by cell, cleansed by a stream of white light. I felt clearer than I'd ever felt, confident and certain that this was the path for me to follow.

I went home to our commune in the Haight and told everyone,

including my wife, that I was going to San Diego to study Agni Yoga at the School of Actualism. My destination was the home of Russell and Carol Ann Schofield. Ralph had informed me that these were his teachers; they had a school in which I could learn the transformative teachings of light-fire yoga. My ego was saying that I was going to get enlightened enough to come back and have a really cool shtick. My soul knew this was the end of hippie Alan and the beginning of true spiritual seeking. I took leave from my wife and two kids and set out hitchhiking down West Coast Hwy-1 with a backpack and lots of acid and pot. Everyone who picked me up would get a hit from a joint and a dose of the light-fire technique I'd just learned.

In my mind, the Schofields were monitoring my trip to Southern California telepathically and my consciousness was being evaluated as to whether I was a worthy candidate for the teachings. (I'd probably read too many esoteric books about the Brotherhood of Light, etc.). Every challenge, such as whether I was impatient and irritable waiting for a ride at a freeway entrance, or kept myself open to the inner Light and trusted the divine forces at work, was a test of my commitment and purity. It's hard to know, but it may have been this innocence and purity of purpose that allowed me, with my long hair, beads and psychedelic embroidered clothing (and my pack full of drugs) to make it through notoriously arch-conservative Orange County without getting questioned or hassled by police. I felt, and perhaps I really was, protected by the Light.

Russell and Carol Ann Schofield were warm and friendly, relatively straight looking people, but I believed they could read my whole story and all my thoughts just by looking at me. I was now convinced that the really high initiates, those who deeply knew the ways of the "other worlds," did not make themselves known by their appearance. For that reason and for the practical purpose of finding employment, I cut my hair, shaved off my beard, and began to dress like a normal San Diegan. I felt I was going underground in order to begin my immersion in the esoteric teachings of the School of Actualism. As a student and then teacher, this became my identity. I was an Actualist and my people were the Lightworkers. Our work was to do the great work:

transform ourselves and the planet by bringing the Light of Spirit (the energies of beauty, goodness and wisdom) into and through our bodies and then out into the world. We felt aligned with the great Tantric yogis, alchemists, and esoteric Western teachers such as Alice Bailey. Our path was to open to our true nature as Immortal Beings of Light and transform human consciousness.

When I arrived, the school had only a few students and was based in Valley Center, a rural area of northern San Diego County. Over the next decade, it grew to having teaching centers in Los Angeles, San Diego, San Francisco, Dallas and New York. We had teachers, including myself, offering the Agni Yoga light-fire methods in universities and college extensions to nurses and health care providers who wanted to learn the "Laying on of Hands," and others who wanted to learn about consciousness expansion.

One of the distinguishing features of "the work," was the regular use of hands-on bodywork. This involved very detailed focus on areas of the body, integrating the energy awareness practices with somatic experience and deepening the process that our teacher, Russell, termed "earthing," bringing the Light of spirit into and through the earth body. I believe it was this body-focused work that brought about some of the most valuable transformative experiences, for which I remain deeply grateful.

Students of the school lived in what could best be described as a decentralized ashram. The focus of our lives was the practice of the Agni Yoga techniques for transforming consciousness that we learned in weekly progressive lessons. Our social lives were insular and the group became our "real" family, our biological families taking a back seat, almost as if they were from a past life. Tribal associations, such as being Jewish, were looked on as unnecessary baggage from our earlier lives, a mind habit that we could eliminate as we would other toxic mental patterns gathered from the collective mind of the culture.

Though we spoke continuously of inclusiveness and unifying all beings in the Universal Light, a culture emerged that generally saw other spiritual groups as limited or false. Though we talked of opening to our own guidance within and not being caught in the "guru thing," we became overly reliant on the personal beliefs and opinions of the school's leaders. As a group, we tended to view ourselves as having the true understanding and way to experience Reality (or as we called it, Actuality). From within our world, it was almost impossible to see this slide into cult-like thinking and behavior. When confronted by family or others from outside the group, it was easy to laugh them off, seeing their thoughts as fear-based projections. From our perspective, they had no experience of the deep inner work we were doing and the personal transformations we were experiencing. They were the ones caught in a cult, the darkness of the collective mind; we were in a process of becoming free and we believed that our work was also freeing them.

Eventually the school largely fell apart, especially after Russell Schofield's death. It's only my opinion, but I interpret this as a tribute to the validity of the teachings and practices themselves. As the organizational culture failed to live up to the essential spiritual truths it was teaching, the spiritual forces that supported it withdrew. I wish the same were true for many religious institutions and cults that continue to mold minds into rigid belief structures and make lots of money doing it. Perhaps they have darker alliances in the spirit realm.

But before the school began to break down, the veils of my own rigidity and double-think started to dissolve as I became embroiled in a personal battle with the founder and primary teacher, Russell. This process ripped me apart emotionally and I found myself in a mythic, inner struggle of Light vs. Dark, good vs. evil, not knowing for sure which side I was on. On the one hand, I could see that I was opting for the freedom to make choices about my life. On the other, I wondered if my image of freedom was being manipulated by subtle, dark forces that aimed to keep me and the whole world captive to their influence. The latter was what I was being told by those I'd held as my teachers. How could I know what was true?

At the same time, my heart was broken over the ending of a brief relationship with a woman I'd fallen deeply in love with. She was the woman of my dreams and this was the time that my soul chose to shatter all dreams. It wasn't until several decades later that I came to understand the wisdom within the mystery of these events, the way such painful falling-aparts bring about our greatest transformations.

The confluence of personal heartbreak and my struggle with my spiritual teacher and group put me into turmoil. I threw the I Ching obsessively, sometimes asking the same question over and over, wanting more clarity on what the oracle was saying or just not liking the previous response and wanting a different one. I had to confront my identity, the one who believed that this group, with all its problems, was the essential carrier of the Light and healing power for the world (including myself), and that I was choosing the Dark side by separating myself from them.

Finally, after a year of emotional torture, I left. The struggle to decide was over. I let go of what had been my primary identity and my entire social network for ten years. With a heart filled with lead, I began a long period of healing the wounds of yet another self dying.

The Actualism community had been my tribe, my home, my sangha. It carried me through the death of my wife who was killed in a car accident in 1972. The community supported me as a single parent of two very young children. It comprised my whole social world and shaped my worldview. The only way I knew for processing the pain of separation from the community was to use the psycho-spiritual methods of Agni Yoga that were taught in the school itself. For those teachings I am forever grateful. They provided healing and the strength to move forward and that experience validated for me that no one individual or institution owns them. They are a part of the common heritage of humanity, brought through the centuries by yogis, shaman, alchemists and mystics of all faiths.

No longer Alan the "Actualism teacher," I was a guy with two young kids, without a job or career, in what I thought of as a strange world – a world in which people were not focused on spiritual development. I enrolled in a Masters degree program to study counseling psychology. My new plan was that I would teach the Light-work meditation methods under the guise of being a psychotherapist. I reasoned that whatever people came to therapy for, it could be cured by deep meditation processes along with whatever other techniques therapists used.

While in school, I became a counselor in a drug treatment program and was convinced that if I could just teach addicts these meditation techniques, they'd end their addictions. My naive assumptions about change and growth slowly dissolved as I began to recognize that: 1) heroin addicts, (and for that matter, most people), are not interested in learning the disciplines of spiritual practice; 2) even with significant dedication to meditation and transformative spiritual practices, changing deep-seated patterns comes slowly; and 3) personal growth occurs not simply as a result of spiritual practice, but from paying attention to and being willing to learn from life experiences.

This last notion dawned on me as, with more humility, I began to read and learn from those who had been focusing on exploring psychology while I had been meditating. I came to see in myself the syndrome of "spiritual bypass," a mechanism of denial in which you don't see your own negative patterns because you believe you have achieved a degree of spiritual freedom in which such negativity can't be happening. For example, "I'm not defensive and angry about what you said because (I believe) I have nothing to defend. I am Spirit, not attached and beyond such defenses." I had to face the humiliating fact that I still had an ego and needed to learn a great deal about human relationships.

As I was developing a more psychological eye, I also opened up to the many different worlds of spiritual teaching from which I'd been closed off during my time in the Actualism group. I began thinking of ways of integrating spirituality with psychology and soon learned through a book by Charles Tart[17], that there was already a movement called "transpersonal psychology" doing just that. In fact, graduate schools in Northern California were specializing in teaching these integral approaches.

As my field of attention expanded, I embraced the vision of the "Aquarian Conspiracy" (the term Marilyn Ferguson had coined in her book by that name). The "conspiracy" refers to a web or network of change agents weaving together expanded perspectives and holistic

---

[17] *Transpersonal Psychologies* by Charles Tart, Harper & Row 1975

approaches in the fields of education, science, health, ecology, feminism, consciousness, psychology, spirituality, brain research, and politics.

I recognized that a new world was being created within the structures of the decaying old one, but not through political revolution and not through solitary spiritual practice. I was inspired to re-engage with being an agent of change, social, political and spiritual change. The difference now was that I had a new attitude, more tolerant of different perspectives on the kinds of changes that would be helpful and the ways to get there. I could see from my own journey the danger of fixed perspectives and I had empathy for those so trapped. The integration of spiritual practice and political action became a primary focus of my life for these last thirty five years.

My new interests brought me back to Northern California and its consciousness of open exploration. My old friend and mentor, Ralph Metzner (who had left the Actualism group well before me) introduced me to shamanic practitioners and indigenous spiritual guides. This led me to go on a Vision Quest with the guidance of Steven Foster and Meredith Little. They had studied with Rolling Thunder, Sun Bear and other Native American teachers, as well as leaders in the emerging Western movements of personal transformation. Steven and Meredith were profoundly committed souls, living their lives with great integrity, totally dedicated to the vision of re-introducing wilderness rites of passage to our culture, adapting what they had learned from indigenous teachers to modern, Western folk. Their work found its fullest expression in the School of Lost Borders through which thousands have experienced transformative vision quest experiences.

On one of my earliest guided vision quests, I learned something that shifted my perspective on the whole issue of who I am, especially as it related to being a Jew. My work to this point had helped me to see both the shadow of the world's darkness mirrored within my own psyche, and the seemingly infinite openness, inner freedom, and complete connectedness of that which I called "me" with the web of life. The expansive and transcendent experiences, however, always involved a return to identifying with a limited self. I viewed this as a problem, a limitation to my spiritual development. The vision quest in the wilderness, described in a journal entry from 1982, helped me gain a more mature sense of the relationship of the personal self with the infinite.

> *(From a journal entry of a vision quest experience in 1982):*
> *".... with youthful intellectual idealism, I've considered myself not really a Jew, but a 'human being,' or a 'spiritual being,' no longer connected with the Jewishness of my parents. Here I am, guided by teachers into the desert wilderness, fasting on a vision quest. Into it a few days, feeling hungry, hot and tired, wandering with an internal sense of being lost, lost in life.*
>
> *I began to feel a tingling in my body, something familiar. Then a growing feeling, heart-warming, finally an insight. The thoughts were something like: 'This wandering, this being lost in the desert is familiar because I am a Jewish man! This is what my ancestors did!"*

This realization filled me with energy and strength. I literally began to dance around, no longer tired.

Granted, this realization that I was a Jew would have been perfectly obvious to anyone outside my head. But to me, it was life changing. I didn't feel a need to go to a synagogue or perform any of the *mitzvahs* every day prescribed by Jewish tradition (613, I later learned). What I felt made sense (in the way that the realization of self-identity makes sense); a knowing in the body and in the heart that "this is true" — perhaps not in the ultimate, but in the human realm, which now seemed to matter a great deal.

I came to feel that all of my life's learning, including what seemed so "outside" the boundary of the Jewish world, was now part of that world, by virtue of the fact that I, a Jew, was having the experience. My excursions, rather than crossing outside the boundary, had stretched that boundary, and the information and teaching that I had learned was now part of the Jewish collective experience.

It is often the case that visions are mixed with wishful thinking, and it's hard to distill what seems true at the time from what endures. But certainly this experience, and others, returned my attention to my Jewishness and to accepting my fate as a Jew. I use the term "return" advisedly. Returning to the fold is something much talked about in

Jewish circles. The term *baal teshuvah* ("master of returning"), refers to a Jew who has wandered away from religious observance and then returns with great or total commitment. There is also the "Law of Return" in Israel, which gives citizenship to any Jew who comes to Israel, with the understanding that he/she is returning to the land of her/his ancestors and the state of all Jewish people. I had neither inclination. However, I did start to pay attention to my sense of Jewish identity and Jewish ancestry. I started to struggle in earnest with what it meant.

While thoughts about my Jewishness had been mostly absent during the 60's and 70's, this was not true for many other counter-culture Jews. Many sought a spiritual home in Judaism. A small but growing movement had been working to reshape the Jewish religion into one that embraced feminism, ecology and meditation. This Jewish Renewal movement emphasized the mystical aspects of the religion (which had mostly been maintained only in the more rigid, orthodox world), but did so with a very open and inclusive spirit. One of the primary founders of this movement was Rabbi Zalman Schachter-Shalomi, whose life and teachings intersect with many of those in this book.

Reb Zalman had been ordained in the black-hat, ultra-orthodox Jewish world. While immersed in his Lubivitcher roots, he drank from the emerging rainbow counter-culture and the spiritual teachings that were coming from the East. He and his disciples and collaborators created a proliferation of re-translations of Jewish prayers, developed new rituals, feminized some of the ancient liturgy, and emphasized Love as the primary attribute of God. They infused what had seemed to most of my generation to be stultifying, dry and rigid rules of behavior (the mizvot), with a joyous new mindset.

Seeking to better understand the Jewish part of myself, I was drawn to Jewish Renewal and Reb Zalman. I had the honor and pleasure of attending several retreats with him and was deeply inspired to explore integrating Jewish practices into my life. I tried, but it didn't go very far. I attended a good number of workshops on Kabbalah and Jewish mysticism, read books, attended high holiday services with the Jewish Renewal groups in Berkeley, and brought some of the practices into my home life. But, it never truly felt like my path, my community, my tribe, my people. Something had deeply changed in me. What I sometimes experienced as the smoke of Jewish identity was still there, an ephemeral but palpable something. But it didn't lead me to practice the Jewish religion or see myself as part of that community. Gradually, my attempt with the practices and attendance at the Jewish rituals dwindled away.

Along with vision quests, sweat lodges, and looking into Jewish mysticism, I was reopening to psychedelics. In the School of Actualism, as in most spiritual schools, the use of drugs was forbidden if one was to advance in the structured practices and become a teacher. When I left these prohibitions, I was free again to explore. I was introduced to the use of what was now being referred to as entheogens[18], a term evoking the spiritual nature of the experience, in ritualized settings with a shamanic orientation. This opened me up to yet a whole new view of myself, the world, and spiritual practice. These were very profound experiences that shaped much of the development of my future path.

I began to weave together the experiences I was having in shamanic journeys with my increasing activism in the social and political realm. My Jewish identity drew me to feel strongly about the Israel/Palestine conflict, and I became active in Jewish/Arab dialogue and protests against the Israeli Occupation. The following experience describes some of my process regarding my Jewishness during that time. It is from a chapter I wrote for a book about the shamanic use of the psychedelic mushroom.[19]

"During this session, the shaman guided the group on a journey to the underworld. I became aware of the entanglements of many past relationships with roots like knots, tight and painful, being disentangled or untied. I felt weary and frustrated, as the healing work seemed endless. I felt heavy in my heart, but I remembered that in previous journeys my heart had been the doorway to greater visions and awareness. So I moved more deeply into the

---

[18] Entheogen translates as, "generating the divine within."
[19] Written under the pseudonym Abraham L., for *Sacred Mushroom of Visions, Teonanacatl*, ed. by Ralph Metzner. Park Street Press, Vermont 2005

experience with my breath and awareness. I became aware of my father and his father and the cold armor that separates us as men from certain emotions, especially painful emotions. I could see the stiff, defensive heart posture that prevents me from having deeper relationships with women, and I felt this armor dissolving and releasing.

I sensed my Jewish ancestors and became aware of the collective Jewish heart, connected to all Jews, including myself. I realized that part of my early disaffection from my family and the Jewish community was an aversion to the heart-pain of Jewish suffering. As a young person, I sensed that this unspoken pain was a cause of the separation of 'my people' from 'the other,' the Goyim. I had rejected or blocked out the feeling of this separation and the pain, but now I was feeling the agony of centuries of persecution, alienation and isolation, of being the stranger in a strange land, and of the Holocaust. I felt my connection to the collective Jewish experience.

For the first time I understood, felt empathy for, and accepted this pain in my heart. Instead of being overwhelmed, I felt expansion, ease, and comfort in accepting my place in the scheme of things. In accepting my connection to 'my people,' I was accepting myself as I am. I recognized that as a soul, I chose to be born a Jew and that there was a karmic purpose to this choice. Without any clear instance of past life memory, I felt that my own heart-path was in tune with the group awakening now going on amongst the Jewish people. I felt a merging of my karma with my people's experience. I recognized that my work as a Jew was more than utilizing Hebrew ritual or prayer; it was to hold awareness of this connection and to open my heart as an act of planetary importance.

The lesson of acceptance of my purpose and ancestry could not have been clearer, and I knew I could avoid it only at my own peril. I asked my ancestors what I could bring forth from this experience and I was told, 'Open your heart, open your heart, so that I and you and all our people and this planet may be healed.'

This vision has given me insight and empathy for the pain and fear at the root of Israeli behavior. I understand the primacy of healing the heart for peace in the world."

Several years later, another set of visions came to me in a similar process with a group journey, this time utilizing the Amazonian sacred visionary medicine, Ayahuasca.[20]

"I felt pain in my heart that seemed to relate to my father, who had died of a heart attack. I felt myself bringing healing energy into feelings of grief that had been unconscious. I remembered my ancestry, the long trail going back to the Jews of my lineage. I saw my association with being Jewish as anguished and sorrowful, a contraction in the heart, a deep, deep pain.

I saw masses of Jews clinging to something in their hearts. Clinging to grief, like an addiction. Holding onto it as though it was something precious, something that made them special or closer to God. It seemed related to the idea of being chosen, as if they felt chosen to carry this burden. My heart was getting lighter as I became more objective about it all. I saw people, Jews, pressing up closer to the Wailing Wall, straining and groaning with pain, pain being the ticket to get closer to God. Wailing was the song that carried the communication of the misery of the burden upward. The song says, 'We are doing what you have asked.'

I saw through this vision to a deeper vision. (I felt that) I had moved through the wall. There were great mystic rabbis laughing, dancing and singing in ecstasy and joyous celebration. They were celebrating God in nature and human experience. They were not at all judgmental, not even of the Jews wailing at the wall. They were celebrating that too: the struggle of those who wailed had its own purpose. I saw the long multifaceted journey of Jewish experience, with so many eras of suppression and bare survival, the marches through the desert. I saw a mouth reaching forward, totally dry, my own mouth, stretching out for a drop of some liquid that might satisfy. Knowing it is not physical water I need, knowing that only one drop, if I let it touch my mouth would wash through my whole body and quench this thirst. I would be blessed. Honey from the rock. I felt it come down; I swallowed and felt good.

(A bit later)

I saw many Jews, mostly old, some young, with their yarmulkes and

---

[20] I wrote this, also under the Abraham L. pseudonym for *Sacred Vine of Spirits - Ayahuasca*, ed. by Ralph Metzner, Park Street Press, Vermont

tallises, all in rows, praying. They were facing the Holy Ark where the Torah is kept, and the curtains were open and the Torah was streaming Light down into them. The Light was from God, and they were receiving it through their various levels of understanding and openness. It was nourishing them and allowing them to survive, giving them strength. I felt that Light move through me, and it felt very deep and good. It was healing and teaching me.

(Writing several months after this experience):

I've been very moved, angered and saddened by the current crisis in Israel, where Jews are relating with mean-hearted rigidity and cruelty toward their Palestinian brethren. I believe what was revealed to me points the way towards an understanding of this pattern of identification with suffering brought on by centuries of victimization. This identification is now a self-imposed suffering, attacking us from within. The feeling of being attacked reinforces the defensive walls that surround the heart. There is an inner battle that Jews need to wage to become free of their present conflict. I am experiencing my racial/ethnic karmic patterns and working to psychologically and spiritually process them. I'm also questioning what, if anything, I can do outwardly to help."

These transformative experiences deepened my acceptance of and freedom around Jewish identity. I felt a purpose in being born into my family as a Jewish family. The lessons were personal as well as collective; my awakening was part of the awakening process of this tribe and the human family. As might be obvious, these experiences played a significant role in motivating me to create this book.

As a whole new understanding of my relationship to the Jewish people was opening up, I continued to weave together what had once seemed to be the separate worlds of spiritual development and social/political involvement. Jewish theology and the evolving Jewish community has struggled with this very issue throughout its existence. I opened to and honored this aspect of my ancestral lineage.

From the teachings of Rabbi Gershon Winkler, I learned that early Jewish spirituality was indeed akin to the indigenous teachings of

Native Americans and other shamanistic, nature-based, spiritual traditions. The Torah story itself takes place mostly in the wilderness and involves repeated visions in and related to nature. This resonated and dovetailed with the work I was doing of leading people on group journeys into the desert wilderness for healing, self-awakening, and attuning to how they could serve in the world.

My experiences with Steven and Meredith Foster led me to apprentice with them, and I learned to guide groups into the desert for inner quest journeys. I helped people prepare for their time alone in the desert, teaching them meditative techniques and simple rituals for connecting more deeply with the energy and consciousness of the natural world. At the height of my efforts to connect with Jewish religious tradition, I led a group of young Jewish men on a wilderness quest during the Passover season. We made use of Jewish symbols and prayers to help deepen their personal healing and clarify their relationship to Jewish identity.

On a desert journey in Joshua Tree National Monument in Southern California, I had an experience which helped further clarify my own place in the complex schema of Jewish lineage. While the group was out on their four days of solo time, I would stay in our base-camp with my co-leader. At night, I would often drum and chant for long periods of time, praying for the safety and well being of the questers, praying for them to realize their intentions for themselves and their people.

It was a beautiful night, filled with moonlight and stars as we can only see far from the cities. There were thousands of Joshua Trees in the valley, standing as if their branches were arms stretching upward to the sky, all in different gestures, praying. I was drumming and singing chants and feeling myself in what I could only describe as a heavenly realm. I became quiet and knew that I was in a place where I needed to let go of all my prior concepts or beliefs about where I was. I was on holy ground and I was receiving a teaching.

My mind drifted to a story from the Talmud, the sacred tradition handed down by the Rabbis of the first several centuries of the common era. It speaks of four rabbis entering Pardes, the mystic garden.

Their mythic Presence was with me, teaching me, teaching me a lesson. "Letting go is not easy. Experiencing the infinite involves releasing even that which helped you to have the experience, whatever religious method or dogma, letting go of your attachment to the path itself. Just as the Joshua trees take many forms in praying, there are many, if not infinite ways to find truth, reality, heaven, awakening. At this last moment of realization, fear can lead to paralysis, shock. This is the teaching in the Talmudic story in which one rabbi goes mad and one dies."[21]

On the other hand, I realized, there is exhilarating wonder and awe at the freedom to choose any of the many possible paths on return from the experience of oneness. It is as if one is choosing where to be born again. I saw the two remaining rabbis, (Akiva and Elisha ben Abuyah), joyously recognizing that the Jewish path and the many other spiritual paths were equally valid, equally "kosher." Akiva chose to re-enter the forms and language of the emerging Jewish rabbinic tradition, recognizing his purpose to bring awakening to people in this way. He went on to help formulate the practices, laws and traditions that now define what we know as the Jewish religion.

Elisha ben Abuyah, made a different choice that led him to henceforth be called Aher ("the Other), and be shunned by the Jewish community. In my visionary state, it came to me that he sought out the mystical traditions of the Greeks, the Eleusiyan mystery schools, and the use of plant medicines for awakening consciousness, (the Talmud says, "he cut the plants.").

This vision gave me a deep sense of peace about my own path in life. For while I deeply honor those who maintain Jewish law and tradition as a religious or spiritual path, I chose a different way. While I honor my Jewish ancestors and remain open to their help and guidance, I primarily focus with the teachings that I've learned from non-Jewish sources of meditation, psychology, light-fire energy work, shamanism, and of promoting social justice. I do this for my people, all people, whatever their background or ancestry.

This journey of 70 plus years has taught me to deeply appreciate

[21] I explore this Talmudic story more fully in Chapter 16

the guiding hands that took me through the painful and joyful transitions and transformations. Everything had a purpose. The woman, Ginny Brooke, for whom my heart broke (open) as I was leaving the Actualism group, joined me in marriage when we re-discovered each other after thirty years apart. We'd learned enough in that period to know what love is.

I moved to New York to be with her, and we now work together through Sacred River Healing, named for the Hudson River near us and the river of life within us. Both rivers flow in two directions. The Hudson, known by the Iroquois as Muhheakantuck, ("river that flows two ways"), flows south from the upstate mountains and also in the reverse direction as the ocean pushes salty water northward 150 miles with the rising tide. The river within us, stream of life, flows downward from spirit/light to earth/matter and upwards from substance/form to formless/essence.

I'm now active in the ecology, peace and justice movements of the Lower Hudson Valley. My psychotherapy and teaching work is drawn from the many pathways I've explored and identities I've passed through. I teach a weaving together of shamanism, mindfulness meditation and Agni Yoga. I honor my Jewish ancestors for the many gifts that they continue to bring me. I honor my teachers, all my teachers along the way, for their part in passing on the transmission of bringing the Light of our spirit, compassion and kindness, to our earth body and all life.

This book is one effort to do just that.

Father Paul Mayer
CATHOLIC PRIEST

What happened? How did a good Jewish boy with your background become a Catholic priest?

I joined the enemy. (laughter)

A 6 year-old Jewish boy living in Frankfurt, Germany in the late 1930s is immersed in the fears of the Jewish community under the Nazis. He's had terrifying experiences of anti-Semitism, including being chased by Hitler Youth. As he passes a church, he spits on the ground. He doesn't know why exactly he hates this church, but he senses intuitively that this edifice of Christianity is somehow connected with the agony of his family and community. Within ten years, this boy, whose family has escaped to the U.S. and now lives in New York, chooses to be baptized as a Catholic. The church of his baptism, a half-mile from the synagogue of his bar mitzvah, is where he celebrates his first mass as a priest.

Father Paul Mayer was born in Frankfurt in 1931 and lived as a child under the Nazi regime until 1938. Within days of his family's escape from Germany, the synagogue he regularly attended with his father was destroyed during Kristallnacht[22]. Much of his extended family died in the ovens of the Holocaust. In New York's Washington Heights, the East side Irish Catholic kids would chase and beat up the West side Jewish kids in what Paul calls his "first experience of the Lay Apostolate" (he clarifies that he is being ironic – this being the term used by Catholics for the laity carrying out the mission of the Church).

I met with Paul Mayer in his apartment on the 11th floor of a building complex in East Orange, New Jersey, a predominantly Black neighborhood. A youthful 80 years old, he is relaxed, fit and energetic. He teaches yoga to residents of the building, mostly elderly African American women. He came to East Orange in 1972 after having worked in Latin America and founded the spiritual peace community Project Share, a mostly Catholic group that came together to pray, read scripture and discuss the implications of their faith for the economy, the

---

[22] Kristallnacht, also referred to as the Night of Broken Glass, was a series of attacks against Jews throughout Nazi Germany and parts of Austria on November 9–10, 1938. Jewish homes were ransacked, as were shops, towns and villages. Ninety-one Jews were killed, and 30,000 Jewish men were taken to concentration camps.

poor, and especially the war in Vietnam. A number of families and individuals decided to live in community, settled in East Orange, and for a time owned two apartment buildings comprising 12 units.

During this period he received a call from a local reporter letting him know that he was named as an unindicted co-conspirator in the Harrisburg conspiracy case, accused of planning to kidnap Henry Kissinger and place bombs in the heating tunnels at the Capitol. Eventually this was revealed to be a complete fabrication, the work of J. Edgar Hoover seeking to discredit the Catholic peace movement, including Paul's friends, the Berrigan brothers, and their actions at draft boards.

After Project Share, Paul stayed in East Orange. Pointing to the tree tops out his window and the hills in the distance, he tells me he feels blessed to be here.

Did you have religious experiences early on?

Even from my childhood, I had a religious inclination. I used to have this idea that I would go at night to the synagogue we attended and get into the Ark of the Covenant. I felt that there would be a sort of staircase there leading to the throne of God. I had that childhood idea. That synagogue was burned down by the Nazis.

Can you share more details about your conversion to Catholicism?

Basically, it was a kind of combination of adolescent schizophrenia and the descent of the Holy Spirit. I was going through a rather tumultuous adolescence, very insecure about my life, lots of inner turmoil, embarrassed by my parents, etc.. I guess not that unique. Somehow, I became friends with some of the Irish kids on the street and began to run with their gang. They were tough working class kids and I got to know them. I appreciated that many of the Catholics seemed devout, though I was quite aware of how they often didn't act that way in their lives.

One of them who was aware of my interest in religion invited me to meet his priest. I had never met one, and I said yes. I feel that higher powers were at work, using this imperfect human being to bring about something on a higher level. All of my dysfunction was used by the Holy Spirit to lead me to a higher understanding of religious reality. The priest was very open-minded and progressive, sympathetic to the Catholic Worker community. He wasn't trying to proselytize. He loved that I was Jewish. I always say that he was one of the few priests in the archdiocese of New York who wasn't anti-Semitic. Anyway, we began to meet fairly regularly and talk about all kinds of things.

How did your meetings with a priest play with your family?

They were in total shock. It became a state of constant shock. They sent me to a psychiatrist. He happened to be a Holocaust survivor and a very unusual man, very beautiful and wise. After seeing him for a year, he told my parents, "If Paul wants to become a Catholic, you should let him become a Catholic." He refused to see it as a psychotic disorder. So, at age 16, I was baptized at a church about a half mile from my bar mitzvah shul. Of course, my parents were very upset.

They didn't attend?

Oh no! And then two years later I told them I was going to be a monk. This was after my brother had died, so you can just imagine what those poor people went through.

Can you say more about the family dynamics involved in the conflict?

I was so shut down emotionally. My brother was very exceptional. When I was seeing the priest, my brother, who was then only 12, went by himself to talk with the priest to tell him about how upset my parents were. My parents went as well. The priest tried to reassure them.

My brother died shortly before his bar mitzvah. I found out later his full name was Franz Uriel. Uriel is the fourth Archangel. My parents, who were very enlightened intellectually, named him after Francis of Assisi, (that's where Franz came from). On a higher spiritual level, I believe he played some role in my entering the monastery. I felt he was close to God.

What were your parents like, especially as regards their connection to Judaism and Jewish identity?

They were liberal Jews in Germany, not Orthodox. My father took me to shul regularly, the one that burned down in Kristallnacht very shortly after we left. He was an intellectual and loved to recite Goethe. He was also a violinist; music was his life. He came from Strasbourg where he played with Albert Schweitzer, who was an organist. His parents were merchants. He was part of a study circle with Martin Buber and Franz Rosenzweig in Frankfurt. Both Buber and my father, by the way, advocated for a bi-national state in Palestine and were heart-broken at what happened.

My mother was from a prominent Orthodox family. Her father was a publisher, editor and writer. My grandfather was a successful businessman who was also the founder of many charities and raised money for the poor. There was a celebration in the Dresden Jewish community on the 100th anniversary of his death. I've also learned that six generations back, on my mother's side, there was a very famous cantor from Poland. I read in a history of the time that people felt it was a mystical experience to attend and hear him singing on the high holidays.

My parents married and, as liberal Jews, they had contempt for some of the Orthodox rabbis. But we had a kosher home and as I said, my father took me to shul. My mother was a nurse, and I was told that in caring for a dying child she lost her faith in God. Despite this, when we came to the U.S., my mother wanted us to be raised in a Jewish home in which we would welcome any relatives who might have survived the Holocaust. So we kept kosher and I went to Hebrew School.

For our first year in America, due to our poverty, I lived in the Israel Orphan Asylum and my parents lived with relatives. When we moved to Washington Heights our neighborhood was mostly German-Jews, and we jokingly referred to it as "the 4th Reich." Most everyone we knew and associated with was Jewish and there was a rich exposure to culture, especially musical talent.

I imagine you had the sense of a chasm between Jews and Christians and yet you chose being a Christian. Did it feel like a huge leap for you?

Maybe in the beginning, in my immature understanding. Later, I even dropped the idea of being a "Jewish convert," which is the classical way I would be described. That implies I had to desert my Jewish tradition to become a Catholic. I like to say that Jesus never stopped being a Jew and frankly I don't think I could stop being a Jew even if I wanted to.

Pragmatically speaking, whenever there's a Jewish persecution, they won't ignore any Jews, regardless of how safe we feel. When push came to shove in Germany, Edith Stein, a Jewish philosopher who became a Carmelite nun, died in Dachau. This can still happen, as with the Tea Party and some associated groups, which I fear is a move toward fascism.

Would you say you inherited some specifically Jewish values and traits that have influenced you positively or negatively?

I would say yes, enormously, genetically and psychologically. I'm a Jew and I think most of the positive and negative things I've been influenced by come from this. My childhood experience of oppression and persecution led directly to why I've spent a lot of my life identifying with the oppressed and the powerless. On the educational level, my parents gave me strong and clear progressive values: responsibility for other people; a sense of justice; a love for the poor. I'm happy for that now. When I was a child, my mother would embarrass me by asking me to give poor people clothes and money. I think the values that shaped my life are predominantly Jewish values.

These are also Christian values: charity, identifying with the poor and downtrodden. No?

Yes, but in my case they would have been colored by my experience. Anyhow, I do think they are also Christian values but I feel that as a Jew, I approach them in a particular way. I inherited some of the Jewish neuroses as well.

How would you describe those?

One of the most important is the feeling of victimhood, which I think screws up peoples' lives and minds, as we see in the Middle East. I think that's one of the basic ones. I remember this brilliant talk by a Palestinian psychiatrist who worked in Gaza. He felt that the worst thing that could happen to the Palestinian people is that they would take on this victim identity that has so perverted the Jewish path and psyche.

I've done a lot of work on myself regarding that sense of victimhood. I've had to deal with a sense of responsibility to the people I left behind, that I escaped and they didn't.

Guilt? Is that another of the negative Jewish transmissions?

Jews always have lots of guilt to go around.

You seem to have chosen another path also known for that.

(Laughs) Yes, right. What a combination.

Victimhood, guilt. Any other negative transmissions you associate with your Jewishness?

(Laughs) I would call it over-intellectualizing. Living too much on the cerebral level.

What about chosenness?

It's problematic. Jesus said, "You are like a city on a mountaintop; you are the Light of the world." That was the ideal of being a chosen people. But I think it turned out, and it's in the biblical literature, to mean contempt for the Goyim, animosity and feeling superior. I think those are perversions of a beautiful idea that have not served the Jewish people or their contemporaries well. Perhaps one could call it one of the greatest strengths and weaknesses of the Jewish people. Of course, Christianity has adopted its own form of chosenness, as being "the one true Church."

What would you say is the gift or essential truth of the idea of being chosen?

I think you will find this idea if you read Genesis, Exodus, God choosing Abraham; "I will make your descendants like the stars of the heavens." It's also there in the children of Israel being delivered from Egyptian slavery, all the mythological stuff that goes behind that. I think that their chosenness was to be reflected in their holiness and in their devotion to the divine and to higher moral values. That's why I feel, if one can generalize, that the Jewish community today is in tremendous crisis, tremendous moral crisis. Israel has really confused the situation tremendously. Mind you, I was raised in a Zionist home. My parents were Zionists, we almost emigrated to Israel. We would have, but it was not an option. I have many relatives in Israel.

You remember the Zionist fervor as a youth?

Yes. I remember the picture books my parents gave me. One was called, "The Deliverer of Chula," about a young Jewish boy who saved his village from the Arab attackers. I remember the little tin blue and white collection box [23].

When I was awakening politically, I avoided the issue even though I was a peace activist, a radical activist. Nobody talked about the Middle East in the peace movement in those days. That was forbidden territory. However, I went there with Dan Berrigan, who had given a very controversial speech about Israel. He received a lot of heat from the Jewish community, from many who had been his admirers until then. He invited me to join him for a month over there and it was very traumatic for me. We spent half the time in Israel and half in the occupied territories. This was in '73. We met with Palestinians, with Yasser Arafat, with people in the camps, and with progressive Israelis. I came back totally traumatized, but it became very clear. I saw what my people were doing and then I became very involved in the issue.

The Jewish soul is at risk today as never before.

What is the Jewish soul?

I'm being poetic. That term could simply mean the tradition of our people.

But do you believe there is some kind of soul or spiritual being that is specifically related to the Jewish people?

Undoubtedly. I've done a lot of work with Native Americans. I'm a multi-religious person, I practice Buddhist meditation, yoga, etc. The indigenous path is very close to me. I'll very soon go visit a medicine man who is very close to me, a Dine. But I think I could put it in a more dry way; what I'm referring to is the Jewish value system. It's the value system that is being distorted.

But I do believe that we have spirit guides that are connected to

---

[23] Most Jewish children in the U.S. (including the author of this book), were asked to go door-to-door with a blue and white can asking for donations for Israel.

the Jewish history, and of course we have these accounts of angelic beings. Whatever that spiritual connection is, which I do not fully understand, that mission, that Jewish psyche, that history – it is being largely compromised today, and I feel that the American Jewish community is in a tragic moment.

Primarily over Israel?

Yes. But of course it has a lot to do with how we have tasted generously of the *fleshpots of Egypt*.[24] Not that we're alone in that. Maybe it comes because I actually have this inappropriate expectation of the Jews being a chosen people and acting like one. I like to think that whenever I meet a Jew, I don't have to explain myself or why I've lived my life this way. I've lived my life this way because I've continued the tradition of my people. It's what I learned from my parents and my ancestors such as I know them, though I've done it imperfectly for sure.

Did you ever feel that you left behind being Jewish?

In the early stages of my becoming a Catholic, I think there was a part of me that just did not want to be part of a persecuted minority. I wanted to be accepted, and that has been one of the driving forces in my life, even though I've done so much that has caused me to not be accepted. So there was probably a sense of not wanting to be Jewish. But as I later evolved through my reading of scripture and with my contemplative life and prayer, I came to esteem and value my Jewish roots.

I do not feel I've left my Jewish identity behind me. I still feel very much a Jew. I've come to understand more and more clearly that Christianity is really a Jewish sect, and if there hadn't been anti-Semitism in the early church, Christians today would still have Jewish identity. Jesus never rejected Jewish identity or practice. I do believe that the Gospel teaching at its core is Jewish. You know Jesus and Paul were rabbinic figures.

---

[24] A biblical reference to the exodus from Egypt when the Israelites, suffering in their long trek through the desert, longed for the richer food and other material benefits of their time in Egypt, even though they were slaves there.

Do you feel that being Jewish is simply genetic?

It's more than genetic, but it's also that. It's a subtle kind of thing. It includes things like being a Chosen People, which as I've said is tricky when it turns like it has in Israel. I pray that something comes from the present peace talks, but I'm not very optimistic.

Have you ever felt a pull to return to the Jewish religion? There are quite a few people who chose to explore or become part of other religious paths and then had a vision or feeling that pulled them back to full religious identity with being Jewish.

Never in that full sense. I've become too universal a person. A lot of Catholics wouldn't consider me an orthodox Catholic. I've been married, and opposed many church policies.

I would and do feel very comfortable participating in Jewish ritual. I feel very at home there and usually attend seders with Jewish friends. I've led joint Christian/Jewish seders.

You also seem comfortable with going to Sufi or Buddhist or Native American ceremonies. Is there a difference for you?

It's not the same. The difference is that the Jewish tradition is my own. It's something deeper and more ancient. Just this year, I felt Rosh Hashanah very deeply. I felt my connection to my tradition, my ancestors, and the spirit of the Holy Day, coming to terms with wrongdoings and the beginning of a new year. I connected deeply with my ancestors though I know almost nothing about them. There is only the one cantor about six generations back. I found mention of him in a German book, how he drew people into deep devotional experiences. I feel really blessed to have this in my ancestry

So the notion of kinship and identity with the community, that still feels very real to you. Did you go though a period of feeling estranged in terms of how other Jews would react to you?

Well, there have been many experiences. One time it involved a close friend of my parents, Ernst Simon, an associate of Buber. He was a famous philosopher and Israeli German refugee, also one of the champions of a bi-national state, along with Buber. They were having a service and he said – though with great reluctance – that I couldn't be counted in the minyan[25]. That really hurt me. I felt this rejection as a wounding.

An important healing moment in my life occurred with Rabbi Zalman Schachter, who I met through Jean Houston's "Mystery School" in the 80s. He was leading a retreat on The Natural World and Kabbalistic Teaching, and he called and asked me to participate. I told him that I thought it would be inappropriate, that I would evoke a lot resentful and negative feelings. I thought that his students would hear of my background and that I'm a meshumed (an apostate). Zalman said, "Father Paul, most of us are born in one place or another and we stay there. We are in one tradition or another. Some of us find a way of connecting the two. You are a bridge builder and we want you here at this retreat." So I decided to go.

Zalman then told me that there was a nun attending who asked about Ascension Thursday, and that he had told her there'd be a priest there to lead a service. I really feared the reaction to celebrating mass at this Jewish gathering, but with very mixed feelings, I agreed. It turned out that the room was an "upper room[26]" and that the group, pretty much all Jewish, decorated it with flowers. More than half the retreatants came, along with Zalman and the sister. Zalman put his rainbow tallis on me and we celebrated Eucharist together. I explained how we were renewing the seder[27] of Jesus and friends and that everyone was welcome to communion, to celebrate the holy meal. I just began to cry. It was a very moving moment, a moment of being accepted again by my own people, a beautiful moment where these wonderful people who came to communion accepted me.

---

[25] It is a Jewish practice to only have a prayer service when there are at least ten Jews present. This minimum number constitutes a minyan.
[26] The place of the Last Supper was said to be the "upper room."
[27] The Last Supper is understood to have been a seder.

Reb Zalman helps dissolve boundaries.

Yes

What about prejudices from the Christian side? Did you have fears, especially with your history of anti-Semitism being directed at you from within the Church? Or did you ever find yourself feeling uncomfortable with ideas expressed about the Jews?

I often detected anti-Semitism in the Church. There were typical Irish New York attitudes towards Jews (even though this was not indigenous to Ireland). After all, "the Jews killed Christ."

How do you see this accusation?

As far as one can determine historically, undoubtedly the Jewish leadership of the time played a major role in getting rid of this prophetic rabbi. The Romans, of course, were in on it. But to make that generic statement that the Jews killed Christ is just like any racist, prejudiced attribution of one particular thing to a whole group of people. Overlooking of course the fact that Jesus was Jewish. That's why I have no trouble with identifying myself as a Jew. I always say at least that's one thing I have in common with Jesus, we both grew up as Jewish boys.

Because of my politics, both regarding Church reform and also the issues of the world, I was in a lot of trouble during my time in the monastery. I went to Selma with the only Black monk in the monastery. I received permission from the Prior (who was second in command), who didn't realize what he was doing. When I came back, I was just on fire. That was a mystical experience, the spirituality of the Black church interwoven with the freedom struggle. That was a profound spiritual experience.

Some of the older monks didn't approve of me – my theology and my politics. I would say I was marching to a different drummer. They thought it was Che Guevara, Elvis Presley, or Martin Luther. I thought it was Jesus.

You get a new name as a monk, and my chosen name was Elias. I consciously chose it for the prophet Elijah who was the precursor for the messiah, taken to heaven in a fiery chariot. I identified with him. I remember overhearing some of the critical monks saying, "the trouble with Elias is that he's nothing but a liberal Jew."

Did some of the monks feel there was something wrong with you because you were a Jew, even though you'd converted?

With some, undoubtedly, especially since I held such views. I was very much behind the Second Vatican Council, which many of the monks were not. Politically, I was against the war, and associated with the Catholic Worker, Dorothy Day, and so forth.

You spoke about the vision you had as a child, of the stairway to God in the Ark of the Covenant. Were there other awakening experiences that have been important in your life?

Within the course of being a monk, chanting the Divine Office five or six times a day, and in prayer and contemplation, I felt close to God. I can't say I had a mystical experience or vision there. I have had more mystical experiences especially with my Dine medicine man out West.

Did that involve peyote?

I did that in a Native American Church ceremony. I must say it didn't affect me psychedelically at all, but it was a very beautiful experience.

Was that your only experience with psychedelics?

I had some very profound spiritual experiences with mushrooms.

How else have you experienced visions?

A lot of my visions are connected with the natural world. Once, two hawks flew right by my window here in the inner city. The medicine man that I've worked with has taught me a lot. He's a remarkable man, a sophisticated intellectual, yet is a Dine with a pre-Columbian cosmology.

At first, he was skeptical of me, but gradually he took me in and did ceremony with me. One time, he said he wanted to do the Eagle Feather ceremony for my life journey. Then he gave me a little bag of the white corn meal and tobacco that they pray with and he said, "Don't ever think that you are a medicine man. You have a vocation to be a bridge between our world and the European world. So that's why I'm giving you these things to pray with." Then I went out to Shiprock in the desert, this amazing cathedral-like structure of stone that the Indians call "Eagle Feather About to Fly." I also went on a vision quest once, three days and nights fasting alone.

Is there something you can share that you brought back from the vision quest?

I felt I was getting information from the other side, and it was basically affirming my calling to be an Earth Guardian. I later co-founded an organization called the Climate Crisis Coalition. That's been my priority since having worked on peace and justice issues all my life. I feel that is now of the greatest importance, the issue that incorporates all other issues and that we must make our priority.

I feel connection to the natural world, and that this is my path. I've always loved nature and I'm happiest there, even though I live here in the inner city, God blessed me with this apartment where at least I can see the trees and the hills off in the distance. I started a religious peace community near here 40 years ago, and then found this apartment.

Any other important spiritual moments or experiences?

I was recently thinking of this wonderful woman, Judith

Thompson, who co-founded Children of War[28] with me. She told me of different experiences such as with Kundalini and other things. It made me think about being almost 80 and I've never had a really dramatic mystical breakthrough. I think it's either because, to put it simply, I'm not worthy of it and have not reached that level of spiritual evolution; or, maybe the Creator intends a sort of different type of experience for me. I've had amazing experiences in the natural world.

I've always had a great devotion to Crazy Horse, one of the great Lakota teachers and warriors. I love his spirit because he was a very humble man, a man of the people. I was going off to the First Earth Summit in Brazil, and wanted guidance. Larry Emerson said to me, maybe I can help you have a dream. He gave me this instruction. "Take a crystal and bury it in the earth for three days to purify it. Put it next to your bed and leave an offering for Crazy Horse, tobacco or whatever." It sounded pretty far out, but I trusted this man so I did it. Two nights, nothing happened. The third night I had this amazing dream, one of the most powerful dreams I've ever had. I dreamt I was in the midst of a great migration of indigenous people, mostly young people, and I was encouraging them to go on, not to stop, to keep on struggling, and it was in a very beautiful mountainous environment and there were many colors. Then I just woke up and sat up in my bed.

Later when Larry talked with me, he interviewed me very carefully, asking about the colors I saw in the dream, etc. The Navajo work with dreams very carefully in their tradition. I felt that this was Crazy Horse giving me the instruction. So, at the Earth Summit I insisted that the time had come for the Jewish and Christian members to take a humble step back and allow the indigenous traditions to step into the center of the circle because they know the way out of our crisis. If we don't listen to them, we'll be in big trouble. Some of the rabbis and priests didn't like to hear this.

Several times in Rio there were native people delegations not being admitted or listened to and I played a role, along with Oren Lyons, in advocating for them. So that was a vision that my medicine man

---

[28] A non-profit youth leadership organization that helped transform the lives of teenage survivors of international and domestic wars.

helped me to have that I put into practice.

Many people would argue that there is a very significant difference between the monotheism of Judaism, Christianity and also Islam on the one hand, and the shamanic traditions of indigenous people. Your thoughts on this?

I don't see such big distinctions and differences. The tendency to trivialize indigenous spirituality as animism, polytheism and paganism, all as pejoratives, is prevalent in the literature. I think from my study and experience of indigenous spirituality, what they call the Great Spirit is what Christians call God, even though they have a sense of the presence of the Great Spirit in a much more immanent way. Much of the Western interpretation of Biblical revelation emphasizes the transcendent. The treasure of indigenous spirituality and teaching is that in addition to the transcendent, which they definitely have, they also emphasize the immanent – the presence of the sacred in the trees, in the rocks, the animals, the sky and the wind. It's not pagan worship of rocks, that's just an interpretation by Western thinkers, what Larry Emerson would call "colonial thinking." Rather it is an enrichment, and it is precisely because we have lost that, that we have devastated this planet home, that we are committing ecocide. We have destroyed the tree nations; 90 % of the old-growth forests on this continent are gone. The deer and bear and other creatures have lost their habitat. We build shopping malls and the creatures have nowhere to go. We've poisoned the sky, poisoned the air, poisoned the food and water.

We try to survive in the midst of it all. That is why my calling is as an Earth Guardian.

When I was invited by a former priest to participate at the Earth Summit in Brazil, it was a powerful experience for me. I met some rather prominent rabbis and priests and nuns and I told them that I felt the time had come for those of us in the Abrahamic religions to take a step backwards and with humility recognize the centrality of the indigenous spiritual teaching about the Earth. They have so much to teach us and there is so much at stake, and if we do not listen to them but instead continue on the track we are on, it will not be good.

And what would we hear if we listened?

The basic central teaching, and this is an over-simplification, is that the Earth is holy, that the Earth is our mother, not as a poetic image. The Earth is a living reality and we need to recognize the sacred web of life, the inter-connectedness of all the living creatures. If you damage one strand of that delicate web, it has reverberations for the others. You can't damage the air without it affecting the trees. You can't cut down the trees without it affecting our oxygen. You can't affect the rain without it affecting the food chain. Those are the apparently simple but profound teachings for us from Native people. This is why I treasure my relationship with my Dine teacher and also the profound influence of Black Elk on my spiritual life. I consider Black Elk Speaks to be one of the revealed sacred books.

Is any of that different from Jewish or Christian reality?

Not in terms of what is authentic. Think of the Psalm (sings): "How great is your name Oh Lord our God in all the Earth." It's all there, but it's been buried. It doesn't fit with Western mercantilism, capitalism and worship of the scientific age. This is what has ravaged the planet.

In Jesus' parable, "Look at the lilies of the fields, they neither sow nor spin. Yet Solomon in all his glory was not adorned as one of these." He's calling forth the sense of the sacredness of nature in the rabbinic way of teaching. He was calling us to really look at the connections that we have lost: look at the lilies of the field; listen to them. There's a teaching there. I don't think there's a contradiction. We have tended to prefer Genesis 1, where it says, "subdue the Earth." That's the way it's been interpreted, though it may not be the original idea. That's why Father Thomas Berry[29], perhaps with tongue in cheek, said, "we need to put the Bible on the shelf and give the Earth a break for about 20 years." His point was that we have used the scripture as an excuse for devastating the Earth.

Thomas Berry was one of my most important teachers. He also said, "The Earth, our home and mother, the community of which we are a part, the primary revelation of the divine, is composed of subjects to be communed with, not objects to be exploited." And, "We probably have not had such participation in the dream of the Earth since earlier shamanic times, but herein lies our hope for the future, for ourselves and the entire Earth Community." Native people use the phrase, "all my relations" before they begin a sweat lodge or sun dance – it's all there.

What about differences between Jewish and Christian transmissions? What do you honor from your Christian lineage that is significant and different?

There is the issue of messianic reality. Even though that has been put forward as the main point of difference, it is really an aspect of the inter-connection of the two transmissions. The Christos is the anointed one, as is Meshiah. It seems like an organic development of Biblical teaching.

Ivan Illich was a friend of mine and my parents got to know him. We were on vacation in Puerto Rico together and sitting on a beach where he was the rector of a Catholic University. My father liked to be contentious on the issue of the Messiah. Ivan said that we both believe in the Messiah; Jews say we are still waiting and we Christians also say that we are waiting for him to come fully, when the teachings of the Gospel are fulfilled. The fact that the world is still filled with so much war and bloodshed says that we are still waiting.

I have come more and more to feel that the walls of separation are not so high as the theologians on both sides have made them. Now we have more Jewish theologians saying Jesus was a great rabbi.

---

[29] Thomas Berry, 1914 - 2009, was a Catholic priest, known as an ecotheologian. He was the author of *The Christian Future* and *The Fate of the Earth*, and a visionary leader of the deep ecology movement.

But beyond theology, is there a transmission of transformation, perhaps non-verbal, when someone accepts Jesus in the way Christianity holds him?

Yes. When we speak on the more spiritual and contemplative plane, it is the experience of Jesus as living reality, which Jews would say is their experience of the promised coming. I feel that one flows into the other.

This current Pope[30] is bringing back the prayer for the conversion of the Jews. I don't feel any need to convert Jews; that's probably considered heresy. I'm just a happy heretic.

Yet, beyond "not wanting to convert the Jews," given the benefit you feel from opening to Jesus, would that, in your view, be helpful to Jews in terms of healing the heart and relating to suffering?

Absolutely. In my own searching spiritual life, imperfect as it is, there is an experience of the words of Jesus, "I have come so that they may have Life" and "freeing the captives." There is also the first sermon of Jesus in his hometown synagogue, where he read from prophet

---

[30] We spoke before Pope Benedict abdicated the papacy. Father Paul did not live to see the advent of Pope Francis

Isaiah, "The spirit of the Lord is upon me and He has anointed me to bring good news to the captives, to bring sight to the blind, to bring justice to the poor, and to declare a new Jubilee year." It's such a powerful passage, and then he closed the book and said, "This day this scripture has been fulfilled in your sight," and sat down. They were in an uproar, and some in the crowd wanted to push him over a cliff.

There is another passage where he speaks so explicitly about freedom from the burden, burdens such as the paranoia that some Jews (understandably) carry within them. I don't begrudge them that, but it doesn't make our lives any easier. I've felt plenty of it in my life and still do sometimes. But it is the inner experience of the Light of which Jesus is speaking that frees us. I'm sharing my own experience with Jesus. This is the heart of my faith. It isn't based on something in a book or a doctrine.

What is your understanding of an experience that takes us beyond attachments, what some call, non-duality?

I've found the teachings of Eckhart Tolle, in which I've taken a strong interest in the past few years, to be a synthesis, in a purified and simplified way, of many things that I've been thinking and doing. I do find it very Buddhist, but also akin to Christian mysticism. What I really like about him is that without getting rhetorical, he's very connected to the political and social crisis of our time. If he didn't address that, I'd be very uncomfortable. I can't relate to disembodied spiritual teachings when people are dying, starving and killing each other. But he does this in a very powerful way; he says quite simply that we must "evolve or perish." The idea of living in the present, the sacredness of the present moment – he simply calls it Presence – which I think is in Christian Mysticism, is a very helpful vehicle. In that sense, I very much relate to letting go of the dualistic, especially since I am so addicted to dualism, as many are.

Is this the human condition?

Yes. I hold so many opinions, support so many causes – be they good causes – I have so many ideas about things. Of course, I'm always right. (laughs)

So how does one support causes, take positions, take sides, when there is this spiritual experience that involves non-attachment and letting go of agenda? How do you bring those two together?

One of my teachers is Thomas Merton, (points to a photo on his wall). He's had a big influence on my life. While I was in college, my good Jewish mother, at my request, got me his autobiography, *Seven Story Mountain*, and that had a transformative effect on me, ultimately inspiring me to be a monk. He has continued to be my teacher even though I never met him. That was one of the other mystical dreams I've had, one of the few I really remembered. After he died, I had a dream of him walking on an upward path, up into the stratospheres, and I remember him beckoning to me. That was it. He has continued to call me, and I still study him and read him.

There was this wonderful passage where he talks about the temptations of the activist. I feel very deeply about this, having been subjected to many of these temptations, and I say this not in a judgmental way, not even of myself, though it does very much apply to me. In order to have an authentic paradigm, there must be a radical political analysis and some connection to the world of spirit, but also it must include the healing of the heart. That last dimension is so often lacking in our political organizing. Spirit is also missing in much of it. But sometimes you find people who have the correct political analysis and are spiritual or have some vague Native American connection, but the emotional/psychological dimension has been gravely neglected. It is so necessary in our work of political, social and cultural healing, and without it we will go awry.

One of the great graces of my life was this project, Children of War (he points to a large framed photo on the wall of many faces of children of different ethnicities), bringing together teen youths from war-zones all over the world and helping them become leaders. It was most amazing. We found out very early that we couldn't just jump right into organizing, as was our tendency. These young people had been deeply wounded by seeing their parents killed before their eyes, or being in hiding underground in South Africa, Belfast, Israel, Palestine, Soweto, the inner cities, or the Cambodian genocide.

Fortunately we had some wonderful leaders there from the Re-evaluation Counseling Community, co-counseling, some brilliant people who really helped us get on the right path. We began by forming support groups and teaching young people to listen to each other, and I was affected myself. I finally had to deal with my own feelings, that I was myself a child of war, and I had not spent a lot of time dealing with my emotions. It had screwed up my life and relationships. I'm still working on it, but it was a big breakthrough and I realized that that was an essential component of activism that is usually lacking. The women's movement has been our model, but even there it's not sufficiently addressed. Without that, the spiritual dimension has a certain vacuous quality to it. It's about the healing of the heart; maybe I should write a book about it.

You mention the idea of "evolve or perish" that you quoted from Eckhardt Tolle. The Dalai Lama talks about a need for a spiritual revolution. There is also the notion of paradigm shift. What do you see as the role of continuing to maintain identities that are tribal, ethnic or national in relationship to that kind of shift or revolution? Do you see them dissolving or being helpful or what?

I think the shift from tribalism is an essential component of this transformation. Tribalism is one of the factors holding us back. But this can be a delicate dance. It doesn't mean denying the traditions or roots that we have grown out of. There are these wonderful teachings that are mostly ignored, like non-violence, turning the other cheek, etc. Just last Sunday, the reading from the Gospel was about when one of Jesus' critics challenged him on his saying, "Love your neighbor as yourself." The man said, "Who is my neighbor?" So Jesus told the story of the Samaritan, a man from the group that was hated by the Jews. In the story, there was this man who was on the road, beaten by robbers and left to die. Each of the Jewish leaders and priests who passed by, left him, and then the Samaritan came along.

Note that he didn't make the Samaritan the victim, but the one who took the victim and bound up his wounds and took him on his donkey to an inn. That's the way he told the story; it was precisely about breaking down this tribal separation. As long as we continue along paths that separate us, whether they be religious, political, intellectual or cultural, we will make things worse. Now we must find a way that these borders, or walls like the one in Israel/Palestine and the new one, on the Mexican border (people are still obsessed with walls), can be transformed.

And psychic walls?

Yes, these are even higher. That's what the physical walls symbolize — material walls are the material manifestations of the psychic and spiritual walls that we have in ourselves. They recently kicked out this woman rabbi who wanted to pray at the Holy Wall. A woman rabbi who was wearing her tallis, and they got horrified! And the Vatican has just come out with this incredible decree. In issuing a condemnation of the pedophile priests, they put anybody involved in the ordination of a woman in the same category as molesting a child! I, myself, participated in the ordination of a woman priest!

Have you been excommunicated?

Well, I don't know. They never wrote me a letter. Since I got married, they probably don't like me a lot.

Anyway, the walls: we have to find a way, but to say "dissolve them" is simplistic. Let them become the source of healing. Let them become our treasures. Let the richness of our respective traditions become the nourishment of the new tree of life. At the risk of our survival, we can no longer perpetuate them as a source of self-aggrandizement on any level, material or spiritual. We have to surrender that, and if we don't, the perils are enormous. All we have to do is look around at the world. We seem to thrive; the human animal seems to thrive on these walls of separation. Like the teabaggers, they just love that wall. It comes out of fear, our own deep existential insecurity. Many in the teabagger group may be people who have lost jobs or homes and are being manipulated by some folks with really big homes.

Do you see this Tea Party trend as coming from fear of loss of identity, the loss of being part of some superior group?

Yes, and this applies to Jews in a really big way.

Do you have a message to the Jewish people?

I feel presumptuous. I'm speaking to myself, to my own people, my flesh and blood, without whom I would not only not be here physically, but I would not be who I am. Whatever good I've accomplished, whatever modest good, much of it is surely attributed to those roots.

I make an appeal, a deep and fervent appeal, with love, to return to those roots in their purity. To void feelings of superiority and separatism, of victimhood identity, of reveling in one's suffering and history of persecution, always using that as a wall, a shield of self-righteousness and superiority over "the other." Return to that  ancient teaching of our forefathers and foremothers – that we have been given so much. That is what chosenness means: that we have been given so much by the Creator, by the world of spirit, and by our cultural and historical experience, that much is expected of us. This is what the world is awaiting from us, and this will not endanger us more, but really will be the greatest safeguard. We will not be acting out of fear and anger, but out of love and openness. It may sound simplistic, but I think that is the direction in which our healing lies, and through it we will be healed. That is where our own healing as a people lies, because we have a deep desire for healing because of our history of woundedness.

The healing will come through opening to others, taking down the barriers?

Yes, it's right there in Psalms: "Some trust in chariots and some trust in horses, but we trust in the Lord our God."

Thank You.

Starhawk
WITCH

As a young Jewish girl with an intuitive interest in religion, Miriam chose to go to Hebrew School even into her high school years. On her first visit to Israel however, she decided she was an atheist, taking the first of a long series of steps of rebellion regarding religion, spirituality, sexuality and politics. A number of years later, reflecting on the destructive, patriarchal, power-based relationships prevalent in the modern world, she would write:

"Estrangement is the culmination of a long historical process. Its roots lie in the Bronze-Age shift from matrifocal, Earth-centered cultures whose religions centered on the Goddess and Gods embodied in nature, to patriarchal urban cultures of conquest, whose Gods inspired and supported war. Yahweh of the Old Testament is a prime example, promising His Chosen People

dominion over plant and animal life, and over other peoples who they were encouraged to invade and conquer. Christianity deepened the split, establishing a duality between spirit and matter that identified flesh, nature, woman, and sexuality, with the Devil and the forces of evil. God was envisioned as male – uncontaminated by the processes of birth, nurturing, growth, menstruation, and decay of the flesh. He was removed from this world to a transcendent realm of spirit somewhere else. Goodness and true value were removed from nature and the world as well." [31]

The Jewish girl, Miriam Simos, had become Starhawk—Pagan, practitioner of "the craft," witch.

Does anyone still call you by the name Miriam Simos?

Only the authorities.

How did you come to be called Starhawk?

It came from a dream about a hawk that turned into a wise old woman. I started using it originally just for spiritual teaching. When The Spiral Dance was ready to come out I had to decide what name to publish it under and I chose that. I went back and forth for a while. This was around 1975.

"In a dream I looked up to see a hawk flying across the sky. There was a feeling to the dream that I cannot capture in words, as if the universe shimmered and split to reveal some underlying shining pattern of things. The hawk swooped down and turned into an old woman. I felt that I was under her protection.... I began using the name Starhawk, which I took from my dream about the hawk and from the Star card in the Tarot, which represents the Deep Self." —— from *The Spiral Dance* by Starhawk

In the mid-seventies, when I moved to San Francisco and got seriously into the Pagan practice and started to write *The Spiral Dance*, I

[31] *Dreaming the Dark,* Starhawk, Beacon Press, Boston 1982

went through some real soul searching about whether I wanted to be a witch, a rabbi, or someone who synthesized both. I seriously thought about going to rabbinical school, and my mother never quite gave up hope that I'd become a rabbi.

At one point I sat down and thought, "If I'm a rabbi I have to go to services all the time and I really don't like going to services; that's not the practice that takes me where I feel my deepest connection. I find the services really boring. I can't in good conscious become a rabbi if that's not really what I'm drawn to."

Was there anything else that you were not drawn to in Judaism?

At that time, it was still a battle for a woman to become a rabbi. I wasn't really thinking about the Israel question at that point. It was more of a question of do we want to battle the patriarchy inside the tradition or from outside and start our own path. It just seemed to me that trying to duke it out within the tradition felt exhausting and somewhat fruitless. It was simpler and cleaner and more creative to just step outside and say we'll do our own thing.

Did you always have a religious impulse?

I can't say I felt it was religious. My religious experiences were outside the institutional ones. They were Jewish in orientation when I was young. When I was about 12, I was sitting in the synagogue when everyone was singing and I felt a Presence. I felt it was God and it seemed that the Presence was generated by the people singing. It wasn't something from outside. I certainly thought of these things in a Jewish context.

Did you have a religious education?

My mother sent me to Sunday school when I was five or six, and I wanted to go to Hebrew School, which was even more of a commitment. I went from the time I was six or seven. I was Bat Mitzvahed and went on to Hebrew high school in the afternoons after public school. I then continued with classes for a year with the University of Judaism while I was still in high school. The University of Judaism was a college level program in Hebrew studies where one can just take classes.

Do you remember why you wanted to go?

I wanted to learn Hebrew, and even as a child I had an interest in spiritual things.

Was there any external influence regarding this?

My grandparents were religious but not spiritual. The religion was all about doing the right things, saying the right prayers, and following the right rules. I don't really know where it came from, possibly from my father dying when I was so young. Seeing that life was short gave me an interest in questions of life and death. I had a dream the night he died that he came back as an angel and talked to me. He said not to feel bad, that he was in heaven. I'm sure that was a factor.

Your mother didn't really transmit a sense of spirituality?

My mother was a psychotherapist and her belief system was in Freud and post-Freudian psychology. She believed that it was good to have religion in order to have an identity. She didn't really believe in it, but I think that her own sense of guilt for not believing and not following the rules made her think it was important for me to have that identity. We went to temple sporadically. We'd light candles on Friday night when she'd get a bee in her bonnet about it for a few weeks, and then she'd forget about it.

Did you have seders?

We had seders and celebrated Chanukah. We never had a Christmas tree. We weren't kosher, though my grandparents were. My mother was probably anti-kosher. We did the high holidays.

Did you feel that you were part of the Jewish community? Were your mother's friends all Jewish, Mahjong[32] and that sort of thing?

She never played Mahjong, being a single mom from when I was 5 and not interested in that sort of thing anyway. But, yes, most of her friends were Jewish. My parents were Reformed Jews. My father was really more of the Communist orientation, but since he died when I was so young, he didn't have the same imprint on me.

Were your parents involved with Jewish organizations?

Not specifically. They were professionals and worked for Jewish Family Services. Most people my mother associated with were Jews. I thought that normal was Jewish.

Can you talk about your lineage, your grandparents?

My grandparents on both sides always said they were Russian Jews, but now we would say they were from Ukraine. My grandmother was from Novohrad-Volynsky and I'm not sure about my grandfather's side, but not far away. They all immigrated in the early part of the 20th century, so I am third generation. They were all cousins; my father's mother and father as well as my mother's father and mother were first cousins. I'm highly inbred.

Do you know if that was unusual?

It wasn't in that generation. They thought it kept things in the family. I know my grandmother's story best, because she wrote it all out when she was in her 80's. She came here when she was 16. Her

---

[32] Mahjong originates in China, but according to Wikipedia, in the U.S., "The most common form, which eventually became 'American mahjong,' was most popular among Jewish women."

mother had told her, "You have to either move to America or get married—there's no other future for you in Europe." She didn't want to do either, so her mother moved out of the house and left her to starve until she agreed to do one or the other. She finally gave in and agreed to move to America. She came and stayed with her aunt in Duluth, and her cousin liked her and they eventually got married.

My mother was born in Duluth, my father in St. Paul. I was born in St. Paul. My father died when I was 5 and we moved around and landed in Southern California when I was about 10.

Did you have a strong sense of anti-Semitism?

I knew that my grandparents felt fear, and it was in the air—there were lots of discussions of anti-Semitism. I remember people talking about the war and seeing the concentration camp films on TV. My father worked in two institutions for disturbed children where he led therapeutic groups, and they still had kids who came from the war. I heard stories of hungry children in Europe and remember feeling ashamed.

What about yourself—did you have any personal experiences of anti-Semitism?

Not really as a child. In L.A. there were always so many Jews around. The first time I personally experienced it was when I was 15. I had a boyfriend, my first passionate boyfriend. After we started going together, his father forbade him to go out with me because I was Jewish. That was the first time I remember experiencing that. I was angry at him for obeying his father.

Was there a strong sense of connection to Israel?

There was a strong bond to Israel in the home. My mother's best friend was Israeli and it was in the atmosphere. No one had a critical word about Israel. Perhaps if my father had lived it would have been different. As it was, if there was anything said about Arabs at all, it would be critical. There was almost no mention of Palestinians. All of the history of the foundation of Israel was as if the Palestinians were not part of the picture.

Politically, there was a view that Jews were all liberals, pro-civil rights, etc. Our family had a kind of mythic story of my father getting up off his sickbed to go testify in a civil rights case involving kids he'd worked with. In synagogue, when the three civil rights workers were killed, there was pride in the two who were Jewish. But when it came to Arabs and Palestinians, they were in a different category; "Let's not even talk about them." To the extent it was mentioned, all blame was on the Arabs.

I went to Israel when I was 15 with the Ulpan summer-in-Israel program. As soon as I got there, I decided I was an atheist.

What was going through your mind?

Partly, it had to do with reading the existentialists, though I'm not sure I understood them. Partly, it was an excuse for not going to morning prayers, something I never liked. Partly, the atmosphere of Israel itself; it's very Jewish, but you didn't have to be religious to be Jewish and most Israelis weren't. Israel has had that effect on me several times—you either become a fanatic or an atheist, either believe everything passionately and rigidly or stop believing in anything.

Were you stepping into your more radical identity at that point?

Yes, it progressed from there. Going to Israel made me more independent and I saw a different side of life. When I got back, my mother and I were fighting a lot. She had this tendency to give me all the things she never had herself, the things she would have liked, and then get resentful about it. She sent me to Israel, but she'd never been there.

My girlfriend's family rented a house in Newport Beach and we, her sister's boyfriend and I, were going to hitchhike there. I'd gotten used to hitchhiking in Israel. So we hitchhiked, got arrested, and had to go to court, and my mother found out. I was always telling her plausible stories which she got furious about when she shouldn't have, except that the stories weren't true and what I was really doing was worthy of her fury. Looking back, perhaps she was psychic.

Also, when I came back from Israel it was 1966. I was 15 years old, and at my high school we had a strong group organizing against the Vietnam war. I wrote for our underground newspaper. One of my friends and I started reading Tarot cards, and we set up a booth at the Renaissance Fair where we met witches.

You got your own booth at the Renaissance Faire at 15?

In '66, it was a lot easier. We were just two 15 year olds and said we want to do card readings and we set up a tent.

Did you really have a sense of Tarot at that point, it's symbols and their meaning, or was it more of a game?

We got the cards, went to an esoteric bookstore and read the books. Very quickly, I got rid of the books and just read the cards and found that they actually told me things.

That spring was just before the Summer of Love. My friend Hilda and I wanted to go up to San Francisco and visit one of her friends living there. Our parents didn't know what was going on there and okayed our trip thinking we were visiting college students. It was the heyday of the Haight; we hitched to Berkeley, met poets in cafes, and had a great time. The week that we came home, Life magazine did a spread on the scene.

Did you take psychedelics?

No. But I came to two conclusions on that trip: one, that I wanted to take LSD; the other, that it was time to lose my virginity. By that next summer I went on to do both.

When I did take LSD during the school year, it was life changing. The first time, unwisely in retrospect, I took it on my own at home while I was grounded and not allowed to go out. I decided to take it in my room and listen to music. After about an hour I wanted to get out and managed to talk my mother into letting me go. I met up with friends and we went to a concert where The Incredible String Band was playing. It was mystical music and I felt a sense of incredible connection with everything; I felt like "this is it."

I really wanted to go to Haight Ashbury for the Summer of Love, but my mother wouldn't let me, knowing what was going on by then. The next year, when I was 17, upon graduating high school, my friend and I told our parents that we would take buses to the various campuses in California and look at colleges. What we really did was hitchhike around, live in the woods, and do all the things you don't want your teenage daughter to do.

Did psychedelics continue to play a role in your spiritual development?

I took LSD a number of other times. Not all were wonderful. I remember at one rock concert looking around and it was like I was looking into the pit of hell. I'm sure it had a huge impact on my spiritual life because it opened up a different kind of spirituality. I was reading Alan Watts, Herman Hesse, the *Tibetan book of the Dead*, all that stuff. That summer, I ended up in Big Sur, camping out with all these people by the ocean for a couple of weeks. I had a very profound experience of totally belonging to that place, never wanting to leave. I saw that everything is alive and I was part of that life. It was my primal experience of the Goddess. I'd had other spiritual experiences in Nature, but this one, because of living there and being out in the elements all the time and because of the LSD, was much more intense.

Did you have a language for it at the time: Goddess, mystical oneness, consciousness, or something like that?

I didn't really have a language at the time, but I knew it was outside the framework of what I'd been taught that Judaism was all about. When I came back that fall, I started UCLA. I took an anthropology class in which we had to do an independent project. My group decided to do it on witchcraft. We met a lot of people who thought that it was creepy or satanic, but finally we met with people who spoke of it as "the old religion of the Goddess," the pre-Christian religion from Europe and the Middle East. They suggested we read *The White Goddess*, by Robert Graves, and some of the Jungian books on the Goddess. Some were pretty difficult to read without a background in classical mythology. Graves' thesis is really that poetry is about the evocation of the ancient, pre-Christian Goddess, the White Goddess, who is Love and Death. We also read Joseph Campbell about the nature of mythology.

This was your first year in college. Would you say the Goddess became your path from then on, moving from an academic to a more experiential focus?

We started teaching a class in witchcraft at the experimental college, even though we didn't really know anything. It was the kind of anti-hierarchical do-it-yourself program that sprung up in the sixties; you could just study and learn. We started an experimental coven where we'd get together and spontaneously create rituals.

The people we connected with were the ones we had met originally at the Renaissance Faire. They were in the American Celtic tradition. They began training us, but after a while we drifted away. I think I didn't have the discipline to follow a training at that point. They did validate for us that witchcraft is a religion of the Goddess and that nature is sacred. That matched my experiences and gave a name and framework for them. They also talked about reincarnation, which I'd always believed.

You believed in reincarnation before you'd heard about the idea?

I remember when I was four or five years old, and there was a program on TV where they talked about dying and going to heaven. I thought, "That's stupid, everyone knows that when you die, you just come back as another person."

Did your mother have much reaction to your new spirituality?

Her reaction was all tied up with the issues of drugs, sex and lifestyle. My second quarter in college I moved from home into a co-op. Then a group of us formed a commune and I moved into that. I was living with my boyfriend in a large closet with nine others in the same room. By spring, I got very sick with a throat infection and my mother found out how I was living and started yelling. She never liked my boyfriend, who actually was a drug addict and not reliable or responsible or caring (again perhaps, her on-target intuition). Of course, the madder she got, the more I clung to him.

What would you say is your inheritance from your Jewish lineage?

What I take from it, culturally, is all those things that make you who you are: how you talk; the sense of humor; appreciation of intelligence and intellectual freedom; a sense of ethics and justice. Also, that religion is about what you do and not just about what you say or believe. What you do should be about creating a just world. I feel that that got ingrained in me.

Were there things you've struggled with?

I've had to struggle with the patriarchy. Partly, I have my mother to thank or blame for that. She would tell me of how she was jealous of her brothers being bar mitzvahed. She rejected the patriarchy, but I didn't understand all her complaining. For me, the problem was more the passive patriarchy; I didn't see a role for a woman to take any spiritual authority or do anything more interesting than be a Hebrew school teacher.

Things did start to change just a few years after this time we are talking about; women started challenging the system and seeking to have women rabbis. But in '66, that wasn't even talked about or thought about, at least as far as I knew. So, finding a religion in which women are leaders was like, "Whoa! this is what I've always intuitively believed in."

Second, it's saying, "God looks like me," and third, "I get to be a leader in this; this is for me."

It seems that you consciously saw the element of patriarchy in the Jewish world and rejected it. Were there things that you internalized as a child, but only later came to recognize as not healthy beliefs or behaviors?

Well, I had to learn not to just yell all the time. I do think Jews are much more comfortable with argument and yelling, in general. I've had to learn to sort of suppress that tendency, although it will come out under stress.

There's also the clubbiness of it, especially around Israel as I became more aware of that issue. There's, "we're all Jews together and it's us vs. them." I grew up thinking of Jews as smarter. I think there may be some residue of that. Going to Israel was somewhat of a wake up on that; there's a whole country of Jews, so there's not only the intellectuals but the dumb people as well. We also felt we had a special destiny and were morally superior.

In terms of how different groups embody different transmissions, would you say Jews have a particular way of relating to suffering?

Well, "nobody suffers like we do"—that's one of them.

In addition to suffering and martyrdom and worrying, we have complaining. In 1984, I went to Nicaragua with Witness for Peace. It was with a Jewish delegation, but Witness for Peace was primarily Christian. Part of the goal of the trip was to investigate rumors of the Sandinistas being anti-Semitic. We were also there to do non-violent peace witness work. There was the idea that if we Westerners were on the border, the Contras were less likely to attack villagers there.

There was this interesting cultural gap between the Jews and the expectations of the organization. The woman who led the trip happened to be Jewish by birth but had become a Quaker and was more steeped in that, including the idea of sharing the suffering of the oppressed. At one point, she informed us about a dilemma. At the border there was gunfire and some of the group wanted to get closer to the gunfire. The Sandinistas wouldn't let them go unless they were accompanied by soldiers with arms. Some of the Witness group were strict pacifists and they couldn't morally go together with armed soldiers and so they were wrestling with this. I saw the faces of the Jews going, "This is crazy. We aren't here to share their suffering. We're Jews and we've suffered enough. We're here to find out what's happening and go home and do good political work."

There was also a difference that would come up when things would go wrong. The Jews would all complain whereas from the Quaker/Christian perspective, you're not supposed to complain; you suffer in silence. If you're Jewish you've learned with 2000 years of suffering that when you complain, it feels better.

How about the wisdom transmission that especially comes through the Jewish lineage? Is there a way in which you feel your Jewish intelligence informs your being a witch?

Yes, I would say that there is a kind of skepticism and holding to the rational even when engaging the mystical; a practicality and down to earthness; the sense that mysticism is really embodied in what you do and what you eat and practice, not just in theory or rapture. Certainly also the strong belief in justice.

As for me, I believe anyone whom Hitler would have killed as a Jew is still a Jew, and I was raised with some core Jewish values I still hold dear and that inform my approach to Pagan spirituality and all of my actions.

The first is that real religion is rooted in justice. And justice is uncomfortable. True justice is not blind—it means facing those truths we often don't want to see.

The second is that the role of religion is not to comfort but to prod. True prophets do not congratulate us on our righteousness but rather point out our hypocrisies and challenge us to peer through our blind spots. They call us to account.

The third is that the divine transcends tribe and nations, that justice is for all, not "just us."

— From *Dreaming the Dark*, by Starhawk

It must have seemed, especially in your earlier days, that there was a big chasm between what you knew as Judaism and your path as a witch. I'm sure you are now familiar with those Jewish practitioners who see Judaism itself as very Earth-based and shamanistic. Do you continue to feel that there is a fundamental difference between Judaism and the Pagan way?

I do think Judaism started out as another place-based, Earth-based shamanic tradition, including there being a Jewish Goddess. If you start digging around, you see that. The Jews and the Canaanites weren't all that different. They might have been different tribes inhabiting the same place; there is a common ground there.

I had a really powerful experience when I was in Israel. I hadn't been back for 30 years and went back in '96 to do some Goddess work. I went with a friend and we went to Ein Gedi, a famous oasis on the shores of the Dead Sea. We went on a hike in the mountains to the ancient temple built around 2000 B.C. You hike up along a beautiful little stream on the edge of this bleak desert at the edge of the Dead Sea, and you get to this wonderful spring and forest and water. It was traditional to wash and bathe there and then you keep going up to the temple. I saw that this was Jewish ritual in the landscape. Jews still talk about going up: to the bema[33]; to Jerusalem; up the mountain, and washing your hands and doing the purification. It was all there and I believe the rituals came from the land. Arthur Waskow has written about the Pagan origins of the holidays and the foods. Even the holidays are still about the food more than anything, especially for the women.

In the more Eastern forms of spirituality, there is a focus on what people call non-duality and the experience of dissolving the ego and individual self-identity. In your work is there an aspiration to dissolve the ego? If so, what effect does that have on tribal identity?

Paganism isn't so much about dissolving the ego. It's more about embracing the oneness that's interwoven into the whole natural world and the diversity of the ways it expresses itself in the world. Also, we are polytheistic; we see many faces of Goddess or God. So tribalism is part of that diversity, and diversity creates resilience in an ecosystem. The more diversity you have, the more resilience you have. The thing about tribalism is, it can be a way of connecting more deeply with people. When I've done diversity work related to bridging gaps around ethnic, racial or cultural identity, I always start with having people tell their own story. When you tell your story and hear other people's stories, you hear differences but also common threads, and there's a richness to that which we can all share. I don't have to appropriate someone else's story. American culture tends to homogenize everything and tell us to forget your ethnic identity, that we are all the same. We are not all the same, and that's good.

At the same time, you can reify your story. Like what's happening now in Israel where it's, "We are the tribe and no one else is the tribe, and in the name of the tribe we have the right to do anything we want to anybody else. Nobody else really counts except the members of the tribe. Because we've suffered so much, we can't possibly be the aggressors. We are always the victims." It becomes tremendously destructive. It shifts from being simply a group identity to group-think.

---

[33] The elevated platform in a synagogue from which the Torah is read.

So you are not looking to dissolve the sense of individual identity but to immerse yourself into the web of the larger inter-connected universe. When one does that, does it have an impact on the tendency you describe as reification of the individual ego or group with which one is identified?

One of my witchy teachers used to say that in the craft we work for ourselves; you have a right to work for yourself, to pursue your goals and desires. But as you mature in the work for yourself, you begin to see that self is everywhere. Once you see that self is everywhere, you see that your self is just part of the ultimate. It's one facet of the multiplicity of selves.

Does that idea go back in Pagan understanding, or is it an idea that has been absorbed from some of the more Eastern ways of looking at "Self?"

I'd say it's probably both. We don't have a lot of intact Pagan mystical literature or writing for the last few thousand years, especially from the early period. We only have myth and imagery, artifacts. We don't have explanations of Pagan philosophy. But, I'm sure it's both.

When you say you are a Jew, does that also include what you consider to be the higher or deeper part of yourself? For example, in terms of your understanding of reincarnation, is the identity between death and rebirth Jewish?

No. We talk about the deep self or high self as the part that reincarnates. That is beyond the personality of the moment. That isn't bound by a tribal identity. It isn't man or woman; it goes beyond all those things. In this life, you can connect with that and that doesn't have Jewish or Christian or whatever identity—you are light, or sound. You could say Jewish is something I'm being in this moment, just as a woman or a writer is something I'm being.

It is often thought that a person who is Jewish looks through a Jewish lens. Is it possible for a Jew to not look through a Jewish lens?

I think you can learn to expand your lens.

How do you do that?

I think you have to learn about other cultures and traditions and other kinds of spirituality. It's useful to take off those lenses and look through different lenses at different times.

Is that through study or inner work?

I think it's both study and inner work—and experience. Crossing the line and going into Palestine and living with Palestinians and being in Palestinian refugee camps when they were under siege by Israeli soldiers, that was really putting on a different lens. It was really profound for me. It was probably the deepest spiritual experience I've ever had in my life.

Most Jews would say that they have a special relationship with other Jews in a way that's different from their relationship with other people. You grew up this way. Does that still operate—the affinity, commitment, loyalty?

I'd say there's a comfortableness. There are so many unspoken things. There were times when I've been on the border of Palestine having a screaming argument with an Israeli soldier. Though I'm trying to practice non-violent communication, I'm having this screaming argument: "Why don't you let these people through?" He'll be yelling at me and I'm yelling at him, and at the same time there is this underlying thing that we're both Jews who like to argue. We're having an argument and we're enjoying having an argument because we are Jews and like to argue.

I wouldn't say at this point that I feel more loyalty to Jews than to other people. I feel loyalty to everybody.

Do you feel that your activism regarding Palestine and part of your feelings about it, even though it is also an American and global issue, come from your being Jewish?

Definitely. I've felt a special responsibility to the issue because of being a Jew, because so much of that issue is bound up around the question of Israel, the land, and Jews going back to take the land, and what we as a people have done to another people in the name of taking back "our land."

You feel a particular responsibility because of that? There are so many other tragic issues around the world.

Yes, but this is the one that my people are doing. I guess in this case, I do feel that clan identity and responsibility.

In the course of your own spiritual or political awakening, when did you begin to see through the early teachings you received regarding Zionism and the whole issue of the invisibility of the Arab people?

It was a long process. For many years I was aware but not active, partly because it was too painful. I went there in '96 aware of it, but working in Israel mostly with Jewish Israelis interested in my spiritual work. I thought that maybe I should try to go over to Palestine, but my friends discouraged me and I didn't fight them.

I got active around 2002. I had been very active around global justice, Seattle, the WTO, and this threw me into a new phase of intense political activism. In the winter of 2001 or 2002, someone sent me something about Netta Goldman who was doing work with Palestinians. We corresponded and she invited me.

That Passover there was a suicide bombing in Haifa and the

Israelis went into Jenin and massacred the place. Another friend in the International Solidarity Movement sent an anguished e-mail from Jenin, and this brought me to go there. I went that summer with ISM and met with Netta for about ten days, ending up in a refugee camp in Balata under siege by the Israeli army. I went back to Jenin again with an affinity group when it was still under siege.

I went back again in 2003 when the US was preparing to go to war in Iraq. We thought the Israelis would make a major move against the Palestinians. I went also to be Netta's birth support twice. We did organizing work around the world. Since then I haven't been able to go back, since the Israelis won't let me in.

I understand quite well the wrenching emotional journey that many Jews must make to admit the reality of what Israel is doing. For those of us who grew up saving our pennies to plant trees in the Galilee, who, snowbound in blizzards, celebrated the New Year of the Trees timed to the blossoming of almonds in the Judean hills, who ended every seder with the prayer "Next year in Jerusalem," no other issue is so painful and sad.

I am a Jew who has spent her adult life as a voice for a different religion, a blatant Pagan whose spirituality is attuned to the Goddess of regeneration, not the God of my fathers. To Orthodox Jews, I'm a heretic, which gives me a certain freedom to say what I think. I was born into, raised in, and acculturated by the post-war Jewish community, but I have not been immersed in that world for many years. I speak from the margins of the Jewish community. But I am still a Jew, and the view from the edge can sometimes be clearer than that from the center.

From Starhawk's website:

http://starhawk.org/activism/activism-writings/israel_palestine/heresies.html

What do you make of the idea that being born into a family or group has something to do with the purpose of one's life?

In permaculture, we have this biological concept of "the edge"; the place where two systems meet creates a third system that is often more diverse and creative. Jews, from my perspective, are kind of an edge species in that we have, for thousands of years, been on the edge of multiple cultures. The land from which we were displaced is itself an edge where many different civilizations meet. On top of that, we were thrown out and wandered around.

Edges are places of creativity but also of tension and conflict. Being born a Jew is kind of being born an edge species. I think we are at our best when we are at the edge. In history, when we've become an empire we've gone wrong. Maybe in that sense, if you have a creative destiny, being born a Jew is a good thing, because you have a vantage point not totally immersed in any culture. This certainly seems true of a diaspora Jew in the U.S.

Please talk more about this "edge species" idea.

The place where the forest meets the meadow is a much richer zone than the deeper part of the forest or out in the meadow. If you're a deer, you live in those edges and you can get shelter in the forest and go out to graze in the meadow. Certain plants, certain trees or berries, are edge species; they like to live in the ecotones between two systems. You won't find them in the heart of the redwood forest or out in the middle of the meadow, but where those two systems meet. Of course, I'm not saying Jews are a different species—it's a metaphor.

Perhaps some of us Jews are an edge of the edge.

Yes.

Is it comfortable for you to say, "I am a Jew"?

Yes.

There's no "but"?

It's more of an "and" than a "but." For me, it's an ethnic and cultural identity as well as a religious identity, an ancestral identity.

A religious identity?

Well, I'm mixed on that. Religiously I'm Pagan, but I probably do as much Jewish practice as my mother did. I light candles sometimes. I used to go to high holiday services with the Jewish Renewal groups, Michael Lerner's synagogue, or the Gay and Lesbian one. We used to go until it got too crowded.

In many traditions, honoring the ancestors is significant. Do you feel that your ancestors would want you to spend more time with Torah or Jewish ritual? How do you hold that?

More likely, it's that they would have wanted me to marry a Jew and produce some nice Jewish children. Having failed to do that, the rest doesn't matter that much (laughs). The more recent ones perhaps would want more religious practice. But the further back, I don't feel that they are bugging me to do more Jewish ritual.

What about having Jewish children? Do you feel something is off because of not raising Jewish children?

I wanted to and I tried and couldn't have children. I feel that as a personal loss. I would have raised them as Jewish and Pagan.

Is it important to you that there be a Jewish people in a few more generations?

It would be a great loss if there were no more Jews.

By choosing witchcraft, do you choose non-monotheism or anti-monotheism? Is monotheism an enemy of Paganism?

We have a different perspective, but depending on who you ask it isn't all that different. We'll say firmly that we are polytheistic and some of us are staunchly polytheistic. But the truth is that underlying that sense of many Goddesses and many Gods, many powers, many names, at least for me there is an underlying oneness and unity of the fabric of the universe. I see less importance in insisting that there are many gods, but rather that there are many different truths or ways of framing truth and they all contribute to the richness of the diverse worlds.

Would you address the Jewish people?

There's nothing more Jewish than being a prophet, and mostly what the prophets were doing was complaining about the Jewish people, calling them back to themselves to be their best. I think the best aspects of Judaism are around the idea of justice; it's not *just-us*, it's universal. The real meaning of monotheism is that God is not just the tribal god for us but that everybody is a child of God. We would say that everybody is the Goddess. Everyone is called to step out of looking for only their own interests and really look at the world in a broader way. I feel really strongly that if we don't do this as a people, particularly around the issue of Israel and Palestine right now, that it will be devastating ultimately for Judaism. The real depth and richness of Judaism will get funneled into this rigid, autocratic, and often militaristic view of what Judaism is supposed to be. Such a view doesn't have the spiritual heart and depth that a religion needs to survive, and that will lead people to do things that are overtly cruel and unjust.

Thank you.

Pir Shabda Kahn
SUFI LEADER

Photo by Beverly Duperly

"I didn't turn my back on the Jewish religion. I didn't see the need to turn my back on it at all. I wanted to learn as much as I could from wherever wisdom was. But I didn't see any reason that a human being had to choose their spiritual practice based on their genetic bloodline. I think that is a curious notion in the world."

Please talk about your family background.

My parents were German-Jewish refugees. My mother made it out of Germany in 1932, and lived in Holland for some years as well as in Palestine. She came to America in 1936. My father had a business in Belgium that he sold in 1940. I was told about how he had his money sewed into his clothing. When France and Belgium were occupied, he was picked up and put in an internment camp from which he escaped and came to America. My parents met in New York and in 1947, I was born.

They gave me the name Peter, probably wanting me to have a moniker as far from Jewish as possible. They didn't want us to stand out. Whenever someone Jewish would do something bad they would think that there would be a big wave of anti-Semitism. If any Jew did something foolish, people would brand all the Jews. So I was born in Queens and named, Peter Kahn.

I also had the privilege of having my great aunt, my father's aunt, live with us. She had been underground in Holland through the war and was protected by two different families; they saved her life. In '47, she wrote to my parents that we were the only family she had left and asked to come live with us. The year I was born she moved in. So it was like having a mother and grandmother living in-house. I was treated very affectionately by her.

Your parents were Holocaust survivors. Would you say there was much trauma around that, fears that you had to deal with?

My parents were German Jews, but to paint them with the brush of "Holocaust survivors" would not really be accurate. My mother left in '36 at age 24 to come to America. Her family enjoyed their life in her youth; they were well to do. They didn't experience any extraordinary brutality to themselves. For my father it was a little different. There was some horrendous stuff, but he had an optimistic point of view. What he remembered was his getting out and how lucky he was, how lucky he was to meet my mother and have a really beautiful life. So that's how he dwelled on it, "How lucky I am."

As for me, I seem to have been born with an optimistic attitude. Also, I'm the second child, and I think my sister got more of the angst. Growing up in Queens, there were Jews all around; it wasn't Alabama. We didn't experience persecution. Later on, as I became eighteen, we were smoking pot, taking LSD and that put you in a different movie. You were part of a wholistic interdependent universe.

I was certainly very conscious of what happened and the extraordinarily horrific nature of it. It made me, like other Jews, naturally compassionate regarding human suffering that was based on foolishness of one kind or another. I went to the civil rights march on Washington. However, I was not inspired to be a radical or political activist. My calling was more music and harmony, working with people as a humanitarian.

Was your family religious?

They weren't religious in the sense of going to temple every day. They chose the Conservative denomination in America, the middle rung, for us to participate in. My father had had an epiphany during the war; he ended up living when he should have died, and somehow he connected with the idea that there is a guiding principle, some guiding force in this universe. So every day, when he'd get up in the morning, he'd stand at the window and pray. In that way, he was a very feelingful and prayerful person, but not in a ritual or organized way.

We celebrated all the Jewish holidays. I went to Hebrew school and was bar mitzvahed. I was a very bad bar mitzvah student, extremely poor. I only learned a smattering of Hebrew.

Did you have any experiences or feelings as a child that you would now consider spiritual?

I did have an optimistic and prayerful side, especially as a young child. My mother would always comment about my optimism, my confidence in prayer and inner connection.

Do you think that was from your father?

Probably. I was the second born and I think I was born an easy going and happy-go-lucky person. I don't think an extraordinary sense of spirituality arose until I had experiences with botanicals[34] and LSD. I had extraordinary experiences with LSD when I was about 20 years old. I started going on retreats in the woods. I'd take a tent and explore the inner world. LSD provided my first really profound experience.

I haven't taken any since '69 or '70. I don't have any objection to it. Everything comes with a bill. Certainly the revelations that opened with LSD are completely available without any ingestion of substances. In fact, where that might have been the first floor, there are quite a few floors above that. Though it seemed awfully spectacular at the time, now I might just need to take a little breath, be moved to tears, and *wow*.

Was that how you began your spiritual path? Was there any interest in Judaism?

It wasn't really until Baba Ram Dass had come back from India and I heard him talking on WBAI. I'd dropped out of McGill University and had transferred to City College in New York, staying at my parents' home for summer school. Ram Dass came on the radio and started talking about his experiences with psychedelics, and then his trip to India, meeting his teacher and being given guidance and instructions. It was the first time that I connected religion with the natural spirituality of the heart that I was experiencing. That was stunning. I realized at that moment what every religion was for, even though the people who were the caretakers of religion may not know it. It wasn't part of their experience. So then the religions of the world started to open their doors to me. But I didn't see any reason to be Jewish-centric.

I didn't turn my back on the Jewish religion. I didn't see any need to turn my back on it at all. I wanted to learn as much as I could from wherever wisdom was. But I didn't see any reason that a human being

---

[34] A reference to plant hallucinogens such as psilocybin mushrooms, peyote or cannibis.

had to choose their spiritual practice based on their genetic bloodline. I think that is a curious notion in the world.

Was that also clear to you at the time? Was it even a consideration to consider that your spiritual path could be Jewish?

I was only looking for the quickest method to awaken, the most profound and most deep. At that moment it looked like the yogic path. Ram Dass had come back. He'd been meditating, reciting sacred phrases in Sanskrit, practicing different aspects of yoga, and so I did that. That's where I started.

In New York in 1968, the whole circle of whatever you want to call us, "new age," "mystics" or whatever, the circle was very small. So we all attended everything that was going on. Swami Satchidananda taught classes at the Unitarian Church. Pir Vilayat Khan came to New York and I met him in 1968. He was having his first retreat in America in the mountains in Colorado; he invited me and I went. While there, I met twenty of Murshid Sam's disciples and was introduced to the Dances of Universal Peace[35] ; that's Murshid Samuel Lewis, (Sufi Ahmed Murad Chishti), who became my primary teacher.

Meanwhile, after the retreat in Colorado, I went back to New Hampshire and lived with Baba Ram Dass on his father's land and thought I'd be a yogi for the rest of my life. I did lots of meditating and fasting. We lived in cabins that we built, but when winter approached we were not prepared

[35] The Dances of Universal Peace and Walking Concentrations are spiritual practice in motion. Drawing on the sacred phrases, scripture, and poetry of the many spiritual traditions of the Earth. See: http://www.pwdonline.info/international/home.shtm>)

for the cold. So in the fall of 1969, I went to the West Coast and became a disciple of Murshid Sam. I have been ever since. Murshid Samuel Lewis and his teacher, Hazrat Inayat Khan, are the umbrella under which all my spiritual practice runs.

Was there any conflict with your family about your choice to become a Sufi?

There was more of a difficulty when I went exploring with Ram Dass. We were *bramacharya*, meaning celibate. My father was very concerned that I would miss the beauties of life. It made him very happy, later on, when he came to my wedding in 1976 and saw my many friends and the dignity, laughter and jubilant mood. My parents were very happy at that point.

They didn't understand it all at first, but they had ears, they didn't close off. My mother once said, "Why didn't you choose to be a rabbi?" I used to joke with her that the only difference between the rabbi and myself is that the rabbi has a better salary. But whatever thoughts they had in that direction, they always expressed them in a mild manner. They saw the change in me from selfish to more altruistic, to more kind, compassionate, more strong and tolerant; they saw that and they were very proud of it. My father didn't live long after my wedding. He died in '77, but he was happy to live to see my wife pregnant and give birth to a son. So it pleased my father that there was another Kahn to carry on the name.

I have two boys. The first was my wife's from before we were together, whom I inherited when he was 3. My father called him his instant grandchild. My wife wasn't Jewish and they probably would have been happier if I'd married a Jewish woman. But they loved her and saw how beautiful she was. It may have been an issue in the first instant, but in no time it was erased, human qualities being far more important than concepts.

How did you come to change your name to Shabda?

I went for an interview with Pir Vilayat Khan in 1972, to share with him that I had begun to study Indian classical music, in the same tradition as his father Hazrat Inayat Khan. I brought a tamboura and sang for him. He felt inspired and gave me the name Shabda. It means universal sound or sound current. In one way of understanding, the whole universe is sound, just as "in the beginning is the word." It is the essence of all that is.

Your last name being Kahn has a striking similarity to the names of your teachers; Pir Vilayat Khan and Hazrat Inayat Khan. Did you consider changing the spelling to Khan?

It just happened to be a delightful resonance, but there was never any thought of changing my last name.

Did you have any personal feelings that made it difficult to take on a Sufi path, it being a part of the Muslim religion?

Our specific Sufi tradition is completely universal, it has no boundary about religion. There was a question asked of Hazrat Inayat Khan, by Marmaduke Pickthall, one of first English translators of the Koran. Pickthall said that he thought that Sufis were Muslims. The answer to his question has been repeated many times. It is that our lineage has been universal for generations, for thousands of years. That doesn't mean that everyone in the lineage realizes it. Not everyone has a deep understanding of awakening.

Don't the practices you do have names that are Arabic, such as the dhikr[36]?

Absolutely, such as repeating the 99 Beautiful Names of God.[37] In

---

[36] Dhikr (or Zikr), "Remembrance of God," is an Islamic devotional act, typically involving the repetition of the Names of God, supplications or formulas taken from Hadith texts and verses of the Qur'an. Dhikr is usually done individually, but in some Sufi orders it is practiced ceremonially.

[37] *Physicians of the Heart: A Sufi View of the 99 Names of Allah*, by Wali Ali Meyer, Bilal Hyde, Faisal Muqaddam and Shabda Kahn, publ.: Sufi Ruhaniat International.

a way, it is a delicate question. We love being with other Sufis and Sufi lineages from around the world because they love the same practices and approaches. Yet, they don't all have this universal view in the same way that we have it. Hazrat Inayat Khan taught that Sufism doesn't have any founder or location. It's from the beginning of time.

So we were able to approach Sufism without having to say I'm this religion or that. But without a question, it took time to overcome feelings about Islam or make these feelings softer. I've had the privilege of traveling a lot and so I have the wider perspective. For me, it's kind of meaningless to say "Muslim" and wash everybody together into one pallet. The Turkish Muslim is so different than the Jordanian or Syrian Muslim or Sufi, Indonesian, Indian or Pakistani and so on; there are Chinese and also African Muslims. To paint a brush stroke and say one word for them, "Muslim," it doesn't work.

For most Americans, there is fear of Islam because there's been a thousand year campaign by the Church against Islam. There is rarely anyone brought up in a Western culture who hasn't been given a prejudice against Islam. It took time to develop a deep inner relationship with Prophet Mohammed. We didn't know anything about him. Not much in the English language. Martin Lings had a book called, *The Life of Prophet Mohammed*[38], which I found kind of dry when I first read it. Then I read Karen Armstrong's *Mohammad: A Prophet of Our Time*[39], a really good biography that helped a lot of people — a great blessing to English speakers. As my relationship developed inwardly with the prophet Mohammed, I then could re-read Martin Ling's book with deep delight and feel the connections which then graduated into an inner guidance relationship. That took time.

Was it ever a problem for you to not be passing on the Jewish lineage?

Never.

---

[38] Muhammad : His Life Based on the Earliest Sources, Martin Lings, Inner Traditions 2006 (Revised edition).
[39] Mohammad: A Prophet of Our Time, Karen Armstrong, Harper Collins/Atlas Books, 2006

Do you feel you have a Jewish identity?

How could I not? Oy! (laughter)

So what is that? How do you hold that?

It's a genetic inheritance and also a cultural inheritance. I think its naive to say Jewish heritage, because there are German Jews, Polish Jews, Moroccan Jews Spanish Jews, Algerian and Egyptian Jews.

I'd be interested to know what you feel you inherited as a German Jew, and also if you feel there is something more common regarding the Jewish identity of all Jews of different national origins?

I think there might be. I couldn't say without making a really deep study of it. Certainly, we are more familiar with European Jews, Ashkenazi. We don't know as much about Sephardic Jews and their training and their spiritual practice. From my experience, I'd say the inheritance includes: skillful means of behavior, kindness, strength, tolerance, compassion, and understanding. Those qualities will arise directly from living in the heart, if you can find your way to live in the heart. But before you get to that stage, it's wise that someone gives you some guidelines on how to behave. I think that in the culture I grew up in, a lot of those lessons were good.

I had good lessons in kindness, strength, honesty, sincerity and tolerance. I think a much higher principle is that that is the nature of the essence of your Being, of your heart as it manifests through the mental and physical planes. If you connect with it, there is extraordinary strength, extraordinary compassion and so on.

We had a strong sense of family, and there was affection in the family. We ate meals together, so there was rhythm. When you eat meals together you have rhythm. Rhythm brings health. Were those German-Jewish qualities? Or were those qualities from the level of education and the culture that my parents came from? I'm sure this didn't happen in every German-Jewish family, that everybody was kind to each other. I know that many people who came through the war were deeply wounded. When they couldn't deal with their own wounds, they projected them onto their kids. So which part of that is Jewish? Which part is being a war victim? Which part is having been tortured or abused? That's why I say it is different for Russian Jews or Polish Jews and so on, and each family within that.

I think that generally speaking Jewish people are family oriented. But so are Italian people. Jews are warm-hearted and have a sense of responsibility. But it would be hard to separate out whether that sense of responsibility came from the way my parents led their lives or whether it came from the particular period in which they came here with nothing and had to start out fresh. I remember, as an example, when the Vietnam War was going on and I was against that war, that was difficult for my father who felt that since this country gave him safety and haven, it would be our responsibility to fight its wars. But then later, when he saw more evidence, he said to me, "I was wrong, now I see that." He had that unique ability to be very strong about his opinions and later say, "I was wrong about that." So I would include responsibility and openness to what was passed on to me.

When you think of the Jewish transmission you've received from your family or the larger Jewish world, what has most impacted you, positively or negatively?

My current state is that I'm much more concerned about the human family and ridding us of any divisions that create a sense of superiority or inferiority. I'd like to rise above them. I don't deny they exist; they're all part of the causes and conditions that you have to unfold as you live, without question. I was born to German-Jewish refugees. On the one hand, they felt a false pride in being German-Jewish rather than being Polish; but they also had been persecuted, so there was a very conscious choice by all of them to not objectify anyone, not to do that to someone else.

When I was an active participant in the Civil Rights movement in the '60s, my parents supported that. When I had to face the military draft, I dealt with it by getting a 4-F[40]. I went in to the draft board and acted crazy so I wouldn't have to go in the army. I couldn't imagine serving in the army. It was beyond my conception. Somehow, I learned that.

Social justice was a strong theme?

Yes. It's not surprising that at this moment in time, more than 60 years since the Holocaust, Jewish people are very involved in social justice issues. There was also a strong standard of education, and you could probably make a generalization about European Jews having a stronger standard of education than the general public. Then also, you could draw the conclusion that there was an artistic "gene" that was passed on in the transmission of being Jewish, since you see so many Jews in the music and arts world. So much of the music in Europe shows evidence of that. I've been involved as a musician for my entire adult life.

Any negatives that you feel you inherited? Prejudices?

I was always turned off by the idea of "chosenness." Maybe that's why I never really sequestered myself in a Jewish identity.

I probably inherited from my parents a concern about anti-Semitism, about being judged disproportionately because I was Jewish. I certainly can't say I walked around being proud of being a Jew. I was wary about it. Yet, concern and paranoia are different. Concern may have been an appropriate form of discriminating wisdom. I'm sure I was somewhere in between. Without question, when someone else knows you are Jewish, it may affect the way they see you. It doesn't make you paranoid to recognize that.

You've encountered some of the mystics of Jewish Renewal. Did you ever feel drawn to return to Judaism as a practice?

---

[40] The rating of the American Selective Service System for unfit for service. Many young men sought this out as a way to avoid the draft during the Vietnam War.

No. I have, nonetheless, participated at High Holiday services with Reb Zalman Schachter. He became an honorary teacher in our Sufi lineage. Shlomo Carlebach was a friend of my teacher, Murshid Sam. There were retreats together, our Ruhaniat Sufi school[41] along with Reb Zalman. We'd do Easter and Passover together, bringing in the three religions.

My Sufi teacher, Murshid Samuel Lewis, received a Peace Plan for the Middle East that he reported came in a vision from Jesus in 1949, which centered around Muslims, Christian and Jews eating, dancing and praying together. This work is still being carried on in the Holy Land by devoted peaceworkers.

Up until 1977, I lived in a home called The Garden of Allah, a communal home north of San Francisco in Corte Madera, where Murshid Sam would come and teach. We had a group called the Sufi Choir that made five or six records, and Reb Zalman did a retreat with our choir. We remain close friends to this day. I'm in awe of what he's done to bring spirituality to Jewish practice; it's what I think every religion needs.

Religion to me is supposed to be a vehicle that helps bring humans closer to God, not some cultural process to create guilt, and divide, and make one group better than another. I'm completely against the idea that only by having the right beliefs are you okay. That's a really big mistake that society makes today. I think of religion as a vehicle, like what kind of car you drive.

Do you feel that different religions take you to somewhat different places or serve different purposes, or are they just different sets of ritual practices, different clothes, so to speak?

They might be different paths, but I feel they all lead to the same top of the mountain. Otherwise, there's going to be a Jewish God in the left corner and a Christian God in the right corner, and that whole concept is very unappealing to me. From my point of view, there is a thirst that everything alive has, and that is to fulfill the wish to be

---

[41] The Sufi school founded by Hazrat Inayat Khan's teachings on Sufism, along with the subsequent teachings of Murshid Samuel Lewis. See: www.ruhaniat.org

happy. That is the pursuit for which we do everything in our lives. In my opinion, kindness, meanness, brushing your teeth, eating chocolate, making love, killing people, all come from this thirst for something we call, "I want to be happy." When you investigate that, you enter the spiritual path.

The path to happiness, in my opinion, is to overcome a false notion of a separate self. So the spiritual journey on the one hand is deconstruction of the false notion of a separate self, and on the other side, affirmation of your true nature: deconstruction and affirmation. The end result is union. There's no longer you and a God. You've overcome this false sense of "I". The "I" doesn't go away, just the small "i". That's not a Jewish experience or a Christian experience. In that way, it doesn't work to say you are a Christian mystic, a Jewish mystic, a Buddhist mystic, etc. Once you are a mystic, you are not confined to any particular religion and this is what Sufism is for me. It can't be owned by any religion. Now I can be like Krishna stealing the butter.[42]

Mohammed said, "Seek wisdom unto China." In other words, look for wisdom everywhere. I think it would be very valuable for the world if the common person were to be educated in the universality of religious ideals. But it's also true that, if you can do any one thing thoroughly or well, you can awaken through that, whether it's gardening or music or religious practices and ceremony.

Each ritual and ceremony was developed for certain reasons, some good and some bad. Many were developed so that the general population wouldn't surpass the stage of priests, who were in control; otherwise the priests would lose their power. Many things were developed to keep people down.

However, especially when you go back to the founders, you find that the core experience is the same even if the method, the vehicle, is different. The prophets themselves, I feel, were all expressions of the same guidance stream manifesting in a particular time in a particular place to serve a particular purpose.

---

[42] It is said that in his childhood Krishna was fond of butter, and that he learned as a child to steal butter from everywhere. It is understood that the wisdom of life is butter so wherever he found wisdom he learned it, benefiting by everybody's experience.

What do you see as the source of the inclination to try to keep other people down?

The confusion about love and power in human beings. "I'll be happy if I'm in power." It's a mistaken view, misguided.

What causes that confusion?

When you have a false notion of a separate self, you feel that in order for you to be happy you need to maintain that false notion. So naturally, if you think that you are your physical body in its current incarnation, then you'd be very upset if something goes wrong with it. But if you contact the essence of your Being, then you will be happy to have a nice raincoat to wear (pointing at his body) and you'll wear it to the best of your ability. You do the most you can with it, but when it's time to give it back, you give it back with ease and keep going on your adventure.

It's not surprising that people have learned to abuse power, especially as we've grown up from more savage times where you had to be strong in order to protect yourself. It's quite understandable, the abuse of power, for power is very provocative, tempting. Here I am the spiritual director, the Pir of our lineage. Many people put me on a pedestal. Women may fall in love with me because of what they project on my position, and it would be easy to take advantage of that. You have to have a strong ethical standard and realize that when you abuse the trust people will be hurt, and you create havoc. But, shortsightedness is understandable, it's part of the confusion.

Do you find yourself being more sensitive or troubled by the problems of Israel than other trouble spots in the world?

When I look at the Jewish community in general, I see some of the wounds, the sense of superiority for example. It's very painful to see the behavior of Israel as a country towards the Palestinians. Certainly there is no simple solution. The Palestinians have been scapegoated by even the Arab world. Yet, regarding Israel, it's very painful to see what is happening. It's almost like, "This was done to us and now we will do this to someone else." You can't say this of all Israelis. We know so many who don't feel or act this way.

I am perhaps more sensitive to Jewish conflict than other conflicts in the world. But I also feel the plight of Muslims in India, as well as the Hindu side. We have in my lineage a connection with Rama and Krishna which links me to the Hindus. I've been in a Sufi music lineage and studying Indian classical vocal music since 1972. The lineage has been going on for 800 years and I have a very strong connection with that. I have a strong connection to my Tibetan Buddhist teacher, the 12th Tai Situ Rinpoche. So I am particularly attuned to the plight of the Tibetan people. As I grow, wherever I go I feel, "these are my people."

Do you have any thoughts on why so many Jewish individuals have chosen other spiritual paths?

Even the statement "other spiritual paths" makes an assumption—which is prevalent in the world today, so you have every right to make that assumption—that someone should confine themselves to the religion of their bloodstream, what they inherited from their parents.

When I communicate to my children, I don't tell them which way they should practice kindness; I try to model strength and kindness and compassion and tolerance and affection and community and service. Those are the qualities that I feel fulfill the purpose of life. It's not that they should practice their spirituality like I practice mine. I practiced every day in their presence. They saw me practicing meditation; they saw me practicing music, and saw the community events we had. Now it's their opportunity to continue on.

So I'm not that concerned about the form of practice. I recognize that there is no particular form necessary to realize God. Yet, I have nothing against forms, and have lots of forms of my own.

In your current understanding, is there a sense of identity prior to birth and after death, a continuity of the individual?

I don't have particular memories of my previous incarnations. Maybe I have feelings of them, but I had more feelings about them at age one or two or three, before the power of this very dense manifestation covered that over.

I have made a choice to make life my teacher. I recognize what awakening looks like; the awakened Being is a Being whose condition is no longer based on circumstance. That means that any circumstance that arises, that takes you out of your natural condition, has really come as your teacher to say, "How will you transform in this situation?" It may be said that the unconscious is the best "hiring agent" for the work you must do in the world. You find yourself in those circumstances that would be the best teacher that you could have. Even if that isn't the case, I see that the best strategy with whatever arises is to learn to be present, have as much equanimity as possible, and learn from the situation.

A metaphor I use regarding the Beloved, Self, or God, whatever you want to call it, concerns how it manifests in a variety of forms. In each of those aspects, God gets confused. God manifests and then God becomes confused in order to become God realized. In the confusion stage, uniqueness becomes the belief of a small self that is dependent on certain things: on a body, on good feeling, on bad feelings.

I find that the more I can go to the center of my Being, the essence of my Being, the more beautifully I can use this unique form to serve everything. In this way, it's also serving myself. For example, you take care of your hand. One may say that everyone takes care of their hand, so that's not special. As your vision expands, and you feel yourself in everything and everyone, it is natural to serve all, just as natural as taking care of your hand. When you go deep within, you find your Self in everything and everything in you. So, without question the relative and the absolute are inseparable; they're not two separate things.

Do you have the belief that there are reincarnations of yourself as an individual?

Yes, life lives and death dies.

It may not be a linear thing in the way it's often portrayed: "I've been Cleopatra," or all these famous people (laughs). It's not that important to me to know for certain. I certainly have some strong feelings about leaving the body and coming back into the body. It's very convincing, especially if you've studied some of the modern near-death experiences. There is some universality about that, and a connection between those experiences and scripture.

I know that my physical body will be returned to the elements it came from. You just give it back and it melts and is reused in a new way. It doesn't disappear; it just changes. I know that when the spirit is in the body, there's a Light that shines through it. When that spirit goes out, the body looks more dull, except on those rare occasions when it's been infused by a very strong presence, like a spiritual master. I have to assume that it may be so in every plane. If there is a mental body and an emotional body, then perhaps the mental body returns to the mental plane and the emotional body returns to the emotional plane. When you come back toward manifestation, by the magnetism of your needs, you collect what you need from each plane. You are given that opportunity to keep growing because the universe wants to realize itself.

One of the Hadiths[43] says, God speaking: "I was a hidden treasure and I wished to be known."

Given that there are these different planes, where does Jewishness come in? At what plane?

The human plane.

---

[43] Hadiths are regarded as a narration on the lived example of Muhammad. They include reported sayings, actions, and traditions of Mohammad and his companions.

What about the mental and emotional plane?

Yes.

Is there a realm that some call the Garden or Paradise that is beyond all that?

The Garden, for me, is in your heart, in the heart of all. If you can experience life on all the planes, you are in paradise.

What is that like?

It's unbounded joy. When you overcome the false notion of a separate self, you feel unbounded joy and bliss and union. It's paradoxical because it doesn't mean that you don't feel the suffering of the world. In fact, you could say that you move from feeling your own suffering to feeling the suffering of the world. You might end up crying like Avalokiteshvara.

Please explain.

In Tibet, there is a deity of compassion, Avalokiteshvara, which the Tibetans call Chenrezig, the holy Bodhisattva of compassion. In the modern world, Tibetans believe that His Holiness the 14th Dalai Lama is the incarnation of Chenrezig. In the mythical story, Chenrezig is there to relieve suffering, to bring compassion. He felt that he wasn't truly relieving suffering, so he cried and two tears fell to the ground. Where they fell, the White and Green Taras took birth. So even out of such despair comes extraordinary help; the feminine rays of the Taras are here to serve all planes of existence, to relieve suffering and bring awakening.

We need to take life in stages. First you take guidance from a teacher and you start to let go of your self-grasping with their guidance. It's about attunement and letting go of your own thought of self and getting the rhythm of the teacher. Then you graduate to an inner world with a guide or prophet, a spirit that trains you in the inner world. The guidance stream comes from the great masters, saints and prophets. You no longer need the outer part. For me, as an example, I felt attunement with Prophet Mohammed and other inner teachers.

Then the last stage that arises is that there is no longer any form. It's really merging with the whole universe. But another way of saying it is, there's nowhere to stand. Your heart has become so wide that you no longer need anywhere to stand. There is nothing left: no two, no lover and beloved, there is only Beloved. If we were just cast into that stage, we'd be terrified. Some people can't take the bliss when they don't have any place to stand.

It's like an electrical current. First you are a small wire, then as you develop yourself spiritually your wire gets bigger and more current can flow through it. For those who short circuit and go for the big current before they've got a big enough wire, you've seen it in this world, they can go crazy.

Some Jews would say your path is heresy.

So some Jewish people may be confused. Let it be.

I would say that I am following the path that I interpret of value in my ancestors' guidance. I'm not driving a Studebaker, even though my mother drove a Studebaker. Forms change. I feel I inherited something from my ancestors as well as from my teachers. I've made particular people my teachers, made life my teacher, and I'm also doing my best to make my genetic lineage my teacher. I think it would be a mistake to think that any human being doesn't have a mixture. You want to take the part that represents freedom, and not the part that represents confusion. My actions are still mixed; they're human.

I don't think of myself as selling a particular form any longer. The heart can't be confined to any color. The heart is universal: it's not Jewish, it's not Buddhist, it's not white or black, it's not woman or man. It's any and all of those. It's you and me. It's the essence of all. That's my assignment in this life, wherever I go: to emphasize the universal and be kind, be strong, be compassionate, be tolerant, be in tune with the infinite. Practice those qualities and you will be fulfilling the purpose of your life. Those qualities aren't confined to any particular method. I can study how to be strong in many different ways.

Some teachings emphasize attunement to one's ancestors, especially biological ancestors. Do you attribute any significance to this?

Honor thy mother and father. It's in all the traditions. To me, it is tied to the natural effulgence of the heart, but it has expressed itself through the mouths of all the prophets and into the traditions that have followed them. Those traditions have been used wisely or distorted throughout history. Certainly we see tremendous distortion in religion.

Many indigenous spiritualities seem much more focused on relating us to nature than the monotheistic ones. What can you share regarding how spiritual and religious traditions can help connect us with the natural world?

I can trace my own story. I went to summer camp and, having grown up in the city, I learned a love for the outdoors through that. Then, there was the psychedelic experience; I always went into nature with that. With LSD, I would see growing, living nature as a divine mother, and it was an automatic blissful state. Right away, I had a sense of what today is called "permaculture."[44] Then I became a disciple of Murshid Sam, who was a soil scientist, gardener and horticulturalist. Through that I became a gardener, and have been growing things all my adult life.

You develop a sense of permaculture through seeing the balance of life, the fragility and inter-dependence of life. It also came through my inner practices with Murshid Sam. Along with being a Sufi master, he was also a Zen roshi who practiced Zen for 50 years, as well as a Hindu master. Right from the beginning, we were practicing the Prajna Paramita Hridaya Sutra, commonly known as the Heart of Perfect

---

[44] Permaculture is a form of sustainable land use design for human settlements and agricultural systems modeled on the relationships found in natural ecologies.

Wisdom Sutra, which is the ultimate permaculture document, teaching the insubstantiality of any particular thing, with everything interconnected and interdependent. So my love for the natural world was supported everywhere I looked.

Do you regard the natural world as a teacher as is emphasized in shamanism?

I just feel very connected to the natural world. I want to find the Teacher everywhere, including my red-tail hawk friend on the ridge here where I live, the plants and the trees out there, and so on. I did spend a little time with some Hopi elders such as David Monongye and Thomas Banyacya[45]. They stayed at our home in '71-'72 and we visited them in Hotevilla. But I didn't take up a Native American path. Wherever there were elders, I was hungry. I didn't go to them to study native teachings per se, but to be with wise elders.

And now you are one.

Well, we are getting older.

While the path of the heart is to accept what is, do you feel any sense of urgency with what is going on at this time on the planet? Do you feel we are at a unique juncture?

It's easy for me to go back and forth. I wonder if at other times or any period in history there weren't people saying that. But I do feel we are at a particular stage in that we have the capacity to do grand damage. There is the weaponry we have now, and events such as what happened in Hungary where sludge flowed into the river that is so toxic that it burns.[46] I have solar panels on my house. We have a vegetable

---

[45] Thomas Banyacya and David Monongye were Hopi elders who were appointed to reveal Hopi traditional wisdom and teachings, including the Hopi prophecies for the future, to the general public in 1946, after the dropping of two nuclear weapons on Japan.
[46] On October 4, 2010, a large reservoir filled with toxic red sludge in western Hungary accidentally released 185 million gallons of caustic mud that killed animals and people and inundated several towns along the Marcal River.

garden and compost pile. In my own simple way, I live harmoniously.

I remember when I first drove through Sudbury in Canada where the steel mills had polluted and made the landscape barren. It's been part of my bloodstream to study that. I feel that way about nuclear energy, the inevitable nuclear catastrophe that awaits us if we don't stop using this method of developing power. It's a great way to produce a lot of energy, but it is a failure and we have to stop it or there will be more disasters and more people will suffer and more terrain will be sacrificed. The half-life of nuclear pollution is a lot longer than the sludge in Hungary. Even an oil spill can be repaired much more quickly than a nuclear catastrophe.

How does all that call you?

I sometimes wonder why am I even spending this time with human beings in this way. Why aren't I out there working for the environment? Because I feel that my assignment is to emphasize these lineage tools that have been passed on to me, this living method of spirituality that helps human beings waken to their heart and strength and kindness. I feel the world will change from that. I feel that that's my assignment.

One of my other Sufi brothers, Ahamed Jonathan Granoff, whom I feel in awe of, is the head of the Global Security Institute that was founded by Senator Alan Cranston and Mikhail Gorbachev for nuclear non-proliferation. Jonathan talks at the UN, to presidents and world leaders, and travels around constantly—totally powerful. That's what he's dedicated his life to. He doesn't have a bunch of students. I would study with him; he is a great teacher and a great heart. I'm in awe of him and people who have voices that can be heard far and wide to help change the way we treat this Mother Earth. But if we treat each other better, I think that will translate.

How does one find their assignment?

I love that question. The universal purpose is very clear to me;

that is to answer the thirst that every living creature has, which we could say outwardly is the wish to be happy. When we make the investigation into what will bring lasting happiness, we begin to see that it's not what we thought, it's something much more profound. We find it is to awaken to our true nature. In that way I feel that this is a universal purpose. Let's look at that Hadith: "I was a hidden treasure and wished to be known." I know its a silly metaphor, but you could say, God, the unmanifest, becomes manifest and confused,(that's us), in order to become God realized. That's universal.

But each of us is unique, there's no duplication. Each part of the universe has an opportunity to manifest in a unique way, and for us to fulfill that, that's the calling we feel. What am I supposed to be doing? My advice to myself and others is to practice being strong, tolerant, kind, compassionate, affectionate, and attuned to the infinite. If you practice those qualities you will be on the path of fulfilling the unique purpose you are here for. Some people have it luckier than others as far as professional life. The way that our society is structured, you have to have an income-producing method in order to sustain enough prosperity so you can do your work. At a retreat, HH the Dalai Lama was asked what he thought about prosperity and he said, "I think it's wonderful. If you don't have any prosperity, what will you give away?"

Will you speak from your heart to the Jewish people?

I feel that we aren't alone in this world, because from the inside out we are always connected to the whole universe. But the causes and conditions of our individual existence have got us to feel separate and separated. As a remedy, societies and religions have created community. A healthy community is a great boon in the life of a human being. If someone can find that community in their religious circle and it feeds them, that's fantastic.

Often times, people go to different religious expressions and find a mixed bag: beautiful ethical teachings and hypocrisy and abusive behavior. We have it in all of our spiritual families; people became teachers and tell their students to be celibate and screwed all the women.

I'm sure wherever human beings go there will be human mistakes; it's not confined to any particular religion.

But on the positive side, community is fantastic. Most cultures start with the community of your family. That's where you go when you really have a need. If all of a sudden I was in trouble financially, my blood family would most likely be the first in line that would care for me. Second would be, in my case, my spiritual community. Spiritual community should be nurtured and appreciated. We shouldn't be expected to just receive from it, but also give to it. What is the children's song? (He sings) "Love is something if you give it away, you end up having more." Life is like that. Whatever you give, you receive it before the giver gets it. If its kindness, you're infused with the joy of kindness. If its anger, you're poisoned long before the anger may reach the other. I think it's really good to be part of a community. In that sense, a Jewish community is wonderful for those who find they can drink from it and pour into it.

Yet, don't give up your common sense. One of our teachers, Joe Miller used to say, "There are only three things needed for the spiritual path: common sense, a sense of humor, and more common sense."

Regarding Israel and the situation there. In 1949 my teacher, Samuel Lewis, had a vision which he said came from Christ: a peace plan for the Middle East. It had two aspects. He told us that it was clear that all the physical problems like housing, food and shelter, were easy to solve, there was plenty to go around. The problems were emotional. As a program, he suggested that we help Muslims, Christians and Jews to eat, dance and pray together. We supported this very powerfully in the '70s when we would go over there and have activities like that. We also had them here.

We support others who are involved with those activities. I'm very inspired by the *Sulha* movement with Eliyahu McLean, Sheikh Ghassan Manasra,[47] and a number of Rabbis and Christian mystics. We must bring people together so they see that they have the same wishes, the same desires, and the same sufferings. We must overcome the crazy education that's given both in Palestine and in Israel. They

---

[47] See http://jerusalempeacemakers.org/

are taught to hate. It's difficult, but we need to bring them together to see, "Look, they are just like me." It's more difficult to bomb somebody you know.

I understood the purpose of the wall that Israel put up to separate the Palestinian towns from the Israeli towns and make it more difficult for suicide bombers to wreak their havoc, etc. But in the long run, I feel it's a failed strategy. Work on getting people together. Work on reconciliation. Reconciliation may mean giving something up, but work on it. Follow the golden rule; it's the basic tenet of every religious practice. It's clear in the Koran, the Bible, and everywhere else. It will be a long and challenging path. There is so much hatred. We have to overcome that. I'm not going to be a politician, so I use my influence in the way that I can, which is to help people be more tolerant and kind.

Thank you

Sharon Salzberg
BUDDHIST TEACHER WITH INSIGHT MEDITATION SOCIETY

"In Bodhgaya, at my first meditation retreat, I was like a newborn calf in my bright faith, and the Buddha's voice, full of love, promised to lead me home. The voice of the dharma was showing me how to get there, step by step. The voice of the sangha was reminding me that I wasn't traveling alone.

— from *Faith*, by Sharon Salzberg

Please share a bit about your childhood.

My parents divorced when I was four, and then my mother died when I was nine. After that, I went to live with my father's parents, who were from Poland.

My father left when I was four. He was mentally ill. He came back briefly when I was eleven when my grandfather died, but he didn't stay long. He ended up in psychiatric hospitals and nursing homes for the rest of his life.

Was there a very Jewish atmosphere in your grandparents' home?

They were pretty observant, Orthodox—no lights on Saturday and things like that. This was in Washington Heights in New York City.

Was your mother observant of the religious traditions?

Not really. There was, of course, cultural identity, but not really religious as far as I can recall.

Did you take on the religious attitudes of your grandparents? Did you identify with that?

I didn't have that kind of feeling that their way was the right way to live or anything like that. I didn't go to Hebrew School. I can recall having a kind of amorphous spiritual longing. I didn't find the resolution of that longing in the synagogue.

But culturally, with your neighborhood and friends, etc,; were you clearly identified with being Jewish?

Sure. Don't forget this was Washington Heights, full of Eastern European immigrants. Both my grandparents came from Poland, where my father was also born. They probably came over in the 1920s. They spoke Yiddish.

Do you remember how you saw the world outside the Jewish community? Did you fear anti-Semitism?

I don't remember fear of anti-Semitism for myself. There was a great guardedness in the community. My more distant cousins, who were Holocaust survivors, would talk about not wanting to buy a Volkswagon and that kind of thing. It was a very insular world. I felt the enclosure of that.

Was that a negative feeling or more a protective one?

Not really either. There was a strong feeling of separation as between the white people and the people of color who went to the same school. It just seemed that was how things were.

Was this also true of the relations between Jews and non-Jews who were white?

If someone lived in your building, there would be cordiality, but not a sense of deeper connection, like, "We're all in this together." Diversity wasn't on anyone's mind. No one was saying, "Let's find a different kind of person to spend some time with and make a community with."

I didn't hear fear or prejudice in a direct way, but there was this sense of "beware, be wary." It was amorphous. I didn't have the sophistication to call it anything. I didn't have a reason or moral argument to define it or argue with it.

There was a strong sense of Jewish identity and a sense of, "Be careful; take care; no one else is going to look after you."

Would you say there was a pride in being Jewish?

Not that I noticed as a child, but now, yes, certainly. There was a great deal of pride in being reasoned and scholarly, sophisticated.

Were your grandparents very interested in Israel?

They were Zionists.

How would you describe the way in which you took on Jewish identity yourself?

I think an example of that was an experience from my trip to Ireland where I went to teach several years ago. It is a very homogenous place, all the students were white and Catholic. At the end, an older woman came up to me and said, "It's so much fun to have someone here from New York." When I thought about that, I realized that "New York" might mean "Jewish." My humor, the way I express myself, my cadence of speech, but especially my humor.

On the other side of it, there is a more negative aspect. We did a diversity workshop at IMS and one of the African-American leaders of the workshop was saying something like, "Imagine how I feel when there's a robbery or other crime and I find out the perpetrator was African-American." One of my Jewish colleagues in the room said, "That's what I felt like regarding Bernie Madoff. I felt this kind of shame." But I said, "I don't feel that at all. That's not when I feel Jewish. I feel Jewish when I sense there is something to be afraid of from being Jewish." I see a kind of reflexive paranoia. When someone is threatening or implies a threat towards Jews, I feel acutely Jewish.

If someone said something derogatory about Blacks, I'd feel it was wrong, not moral. If it is about Jews, I'd feel it was immoral, but I'd also feel fear. I remember feeling that when someone critical of Israel, instead of saying Israelis, said "Those Jews."

Would you say that you are Jewish, that you are a Jewish woman?

I say different things at different times. You can also ask me if I am a Buddhist and I will say different things at different times.

If somebody asked me if I was Jewish, I'd say, "Yes," because I wouldn't know what else to say. It just doesn't mean that much to me in terms of actual spiritual practice. You could ask me if I were a Buddhist, and I'd say, "Yes," because that is the core of my spiritual life. But I don't think of Buddhism as an identity, as a religious identity. It is more practices and methods. So that's what I mean when I say it would depend on the context.

Someone could ask me if I'm Buddhist and I might say, "I don't think like that." If people were to ask me how much of my day-to-day spiritual life is rooted in Judaism, I'd say, "It's really not."

Other people would consider me Jewish, so there is that. One time I was returning from Nepal where I studied with a Tibetan teacher. At the airport in Bangkok, they pulled me back for extra security and one of the questions they asked me was, "Are you Jewish?" I answered, "Yes." Then, a few minutes later, my bags were going through the security scanners and all the Buddhas I had bought in Nepal that were in my hand luggage showed up. The woman said, "Are you Buddhist?" and I said, "Yes" (laughs). That was me answering differently about my religious affiliation within minutes.

I know some people say, "I was born Jewish," or "I'm Jewish on my parents side."

Would you say you were shaped at all by experiences of anti-Semitism?

I grew up in a rather narrow slice of the Jewish world and I went off to college and then to India. My whole world changed. Once in a while, people ask me if I felt discriminated against as a Jew. I say, "No, because I've made my own world." On the other hand, a week or two ago, I received an e-mail via the address on my website. The subject line was, "Stinking Jews," and the first sentence was something like, "We don't need any Jews in Buddhism." I was really stunned ....

And the fear came?

Yes, I had a rush of fear. I ended up reporting it to the Anti-

Defamation League[48], which I haven't agreed with in a long time because of our differing stands on a number of issues. I didn't know what to do with it. I thought, well, someone should know about these things. I got a second one the same day, some anti-Zionist website, or something like that. So I thought, I'll report it. I ended up talking to somebody there. She asked me if I felt personally in danger and threatened in any way and I said, "No, I don't really." She urged me to call the police if I felt that or if I received another one. She asked if there was anything in my website that identified me as a Jew, and I said, "No, just my name." I ended up writing about it in the Huffington Post.[49]

Are you drawn to some aspects of Jewish practice? Do you ever go to a synagogue?

Occasionally I go at a friend's invitation. In the last two years I've been to seders, which I haven't done in a long time. Both times we used a Jewish-Buddhist Haggadah.

Do you feel your sense of Jewishness is connected to the Holocaust?

I'm sure it is. I went to the Holocaust Museums in Jerusalem and in D.C. The second time I went, somebody said that they would have liked it more if there was more about other people who were killed besides the Jews. I realized that it hadn't even occurred to me. I had been raised with it being so singular, about the Jews.

Do you have much of a visceral connection to Israel?

Not much, no. I went to Israel to teach, and I did feel very Jewish while there. I was also very aware of the intensity and the level of

---

[48] The Anti-Defamation League was founded in 1913 to fight against anti-Semitism, and became active in the struggle against bigotry and for civil rights for all people. It has aroused controversy for its tendency to link criticism of Israel with anti-Semitism.

[49] http://www.huffingtonpost.com/sharon-salzberg/no-place-to-hide_1_b_856831.

security there. When I explored the Holocaust exhibits I thought, this is so traumatic, this is not a one-generation fix.

I also feel a lot of frustration with Israel. I have friends who have gone to Gaza and seen the conditions. They went without antagonism towards Israel, but they were horrified. So, now I do feel this frustration. But I don't think it would be different if I saw England behaving in this way. It's not a sense of it being bad because of it being done by Jews. Perhaps I do feel somewhat that because they're Jews and what they've been through, they should know.

Let's come back to your personal journey. When you turned 16, you went to college. Did you want to leave home?

I definitely wanted to leave home. I also had skipped two grades in the public school system. That was 1968.

Did you get involved with spirituality at that point?

Mostly what brought me to spirituality was taking an Asian philosophy course when I was a sophomore. I didn't pick it because of its spiritual dimension; that was almost accidental. I was curious and it was an easy elective. Certainly, it was the time; spiritual questioning was everywhere.

I had never meditated (until I went to India, later), so I didn't have a serious encounter. But it piqued my interest. From there, I applied to an independent study program at the university to spend a year studying meditation in India. They accepted the proposal, so I went in my junior year.

What were you looking for?

I was looking to really learn how to meditate. I was looking for some very practical tools that I thought might give me some peace of mind.

In your book, *Faith*, you speak of feeling a lot of turmoil, that you were in a great deal of pain and you knew you needed something to help with that.

Oh yeah. I knew it, but I didn't know the dimensions of rage, grief and fear. I didn't really know what I was feeling. I just knew that I was really unhappy and I had an instinct that meditation could help.

Your trip to India was planned to be for a year?

Yes, but I stayed longer and connected very deeply. First with some methods taught through intensive 10-day meditation retreats with Goenka[50], and then various other teachers, both Burmese and Tibetan.

Do you feel that you became a Buddhist then, that that's where you felt your comfort zone?

Yeah.

That became your identity?

Yes, but that sense of identity has changed over time. The first night of my first retreat, the teacher said that Buddha does not teach Buddhism, that Buddha taught a way of life. So for me, there's always been something almost like a secular context.

But if I had the time to learn a language, it would be Sanskrit. When I consider what I study, it is Buddhist teaching: the stories they tell; the examples they use, they're from Buddhist tradition.

Did you connect with other American seekers at that time?

---

[50] Satya Narayan Goenka (1924-2013) was a leading lay teacher of Vipassan meditation and a student of Sayagyi U Ba Khin. He trained more than 800 assistant teachers and each year more than 100,000 people attend Goenka led Vipassana courses.

At my first retreat, I met Krishna Das, Ram Dass, Joseph Goldstein, Daniel Goleman and Wes Nisker, (who coined the term Jubu). I just heard someone say Jufi the other night, for Jews involved in Sufism. (laughs)

So, with that circle of people, all Jewish, was there any talk of what that meant, that you were all Jewish, why that was happening?

It certainly was noticed. That's why Wes used that phrase. But, it seemed a really minor thing. All of our teachers were non-American, non-white. There was this explosion of interest in the world and many who responded were European who were not Jewish. We weren't all Jewish. It was just that particular group of Americans that were Jewish.

Would you say that your core group was Jewish because there was some magnetism or connectedness?

I think we did have a kind of common cultural reference. But our energy was not in the past. We were interested in learning from our teachers and forming very different kinds of relationships.

You describe in your book, that your experience in India was a mind-expanding and heart-opening process for you. Can you describe any of what you mean by that?

I don't know if there was a particular moment. There was this profound event of exploration which was so exciting. Every once in a while, I would be sitting down and meditating and I would be doing something very simple, such as going back to just feeling the breath, and it would be such a "wow" experience. I marvel at that now, when such simple processes were so profound. There was that sense of learning, of discovery, of understanding; it was so huge, like the biggest thing in the world.

When you were in India, you were quite young.

I was 18, the youngest in the group.

Was there ever a feeling along the way that you had stepped outside of the Jewish world?

Many of us felt alarm from our families. I got a letter from my grandmother asking if I was still Jewish. The interesting thing about this kind of Buddhism is that it's very psychological. You don't have to say you are a Buddhist, or become a Buddhist. You teach meditation methods and there are very scientific studies about the brain, releasing stress, etc.. This was true even back then, though it was no where near as laid out and elaborated as it is now. I could just say, "I'm just meditating, I'm not a Buddhist."

That's what you would say to your family?

Yeah, why cause them alarm? And also, it's true. We didn't use the word "guru." We'd say, "teacher." The phrase in the Pali language was "kalyana mitta," which means spiritual friend. So that's what your teacher is, your spiritual friend. The guru relationship is a very different kind of relationship.

Did it ever occur to you to try to find a spiritual path in Judaism?

I didn't feel drawn in the way my friend, Sylvia Boorstein (who is also an IMS teacher, and an observant Jew) did. It didn't occur to me that after India I should try to find a source of my spiritual life back within Judaism.

Of what you know of the Jewish tradition or transmission, do you feel it is somehow different from the Buddhist one, a different flavor of spirituality perhaps?

I don't think of it so much as a different flavor. Perhaps different methodology. I'm very into "method." The question for living our values becomes "How?" Clearly in Judaism, there is a huge wisdom tradition. The insistence on justice, social justice, acting on one's values, is so large in the Jewish community. That's a very beautiful thing.

Do you feel that in some way that those values were imprinted in you?

Certainly they're my values.
But I want to say, while we've been speaking, I've been mulling over whether I still feel Jewish and how. It's not only when I'm afraid, but when I see films on the freedom riders. One was on the other night on PBS. I see these young Jewish kids getting on those buses, and I feel very proud. Yeah, I do feel proud. Hey, cool!

Ok, so you feel fear and pride associated with being Jewish; not shame. Maybe that will come if we sit long enough?

(Laughter)

You have said that you're more focused on the method. But do you think there's an ultimate difference in different religions? Particularly thinking of your chosen path of Buddhism and the Jewish religion.

I don't know really. I mean when you read great beings like Heschel, I don't really see a difference.

Do you see the influence of an experience of non-duality in Judaism?

Oh, I would think so. There is Martin Buber and a great deal more. But the question of method is really important to me, because it also speaks to how exclusive or how inclusive that realization is felt to be. I was talking with Roger Kamenetz[51] after I had been to a

Buddhist-Christian conference. I shared with him my observation that for most of the Buddhists, when they were talking about spiritual life, or obstacles to spiritual life, or confrontation with those obstacles to spiritual life, they spoke of it as very much in the moment. Many of the Christians who spoke would quote a 15th century saint or other figure from the past, and leave it at that. I was very eager to hear about their own experiences of the path.

Both Roger and I wondered if the same wouldn't be true of most Jewish leaders. How ready do they feel to claim the possibility of real liberation for themselves? Or is that thought to be excessive pride or conceit, that it would be better to pay respects to the great ones who have gone before, not to even imagine that you yourself might accomplish anything like that. To the extent that's true, it speaks of perhaps a very great difference. Are we supposed to aspire to real freedom or to think, "Isn't it great, someone did it centuries ago?"

Even Jews who were born in families without relatives who were victims of the Holocaust, who were born in this country, somehow seem to tie into that sense of suffering. How does that work?

There does seem to be a kind of cultural inter-connectivity.

Do you see that as a negative thing?

I think it's potentially a limiting thing. I was teaching with Krishna Das and he was telling a story he often tells about Maharaji and Jesus. Somebody in the room took great exception to it. The person was Jewish and felt like she was being excluded and it became a very strong dialogue in the room. It took a lot of time and I think people got a lot from it and she was happy at the end, which was very important. She didn't come away feeling it was wrong for her to bring it up or anything like that. But, it was striking that someone would be in a room where a conversation is going on about the spirituality of Jesus and feel excluded or perhaps attacked.

[51] Roger Kamenetz is the author of *The Jew in the Lotus*, a book describing a visit with the Dalai Lama by several prominent Jewish leaders."

Do you have any frame of reference for understanding why she had that reaction?

Well, I'm not sure how prevalent such a feeling is in the Jewish community. I think that she was probably taught to be frightened, that if Jesus is upheld, you're being put down, and if Jesus is evoked, you're in danger?

You never felt that way yourself?

I think I had some degree of that. The whole Jesus idea was a bit scary. It was more alien than scary. It has turned out that Christianity is the religion I have explored the least.

Your path is called Theravada Buddhism. In addition to the practices and methods of Vipassana meditation, is there a set of texts with a theory and with a direction for what it promotes in the world?

There is a set of ethical teachings, like not harming anyone, including yourself. There is a sense of community and a sense of lineage and history, and a contemporary community with like-minded people. There is also a set of methods. One of my colleagues who grew up in the church of England spoke of how he loved the teachings as a child. You know: "Love thy neighbor as yourself. Do unto others...." He said the overriding question he had was "how?" How do you deal with your anxiety? How do you deal with hostility? How do you deal with the fact that you don't like your neighbor? How do you deal with.... like, HOW? For him, the answers came in Buddhism, the how. That's really the core of it all. It's that set of methods.

Is there also a cosmology?

Yes, there are descriptions of levels of existence and of rebirth, laws of consciousness and karma.

That's a set of beliefs. How does your mindfulness practice reconcile with beliefs?

Well one of my teachers was asked about other realms of existence within the cosmology. He said they are there although impermanent, even if they last a very long time. Some last longer than the normal human lifespan, though it is still said to be impermanent as we cycle around and around. He basically said, "You don't have to believe it; it's true, but you don't have to believe it." Maybe because I was so young when I got involved and it's been so long, I tend to think in those terms. When somebody dies, I think about rebirth. It's just the kind of milieu in which I'm used to being. But if a student came to me and said, "I don't really believe that stuff," I don't have a problem with that.

So it's not important for membership?

(laughter) No. I don't think it's important for membership. Which is why so many people of different faith traditions feel comfortable using the methodology within Buddhism and don't feel cut off by having somewhat different beliefs.

I was using the term "membership" kiddingly, of course. But in addition to people taking workshops and applying these practices as best they can in their lives, is their some kind of organizational affiliation that people come to identify with in the IMS world? Is there a kind of boundary where you are within it or not?

It's a little messier than that. But to some extent it's true. The other day, the full moon of May, is the Buddha's birthday in the Theravadan tradition; it's THE big day. I was reading something on Twitter and somebody said, "Happy Wesak," which is Happy Birthday, and it reminded me, it's the Buddha's birthday. I sent out e-mails, people sent me e-mails, it was a thing. Happy Birthday Buddha. That's the Theravadan Buddhist world. I think the Tibetans celebrate it on a different day. With the Zen Buddhists, it's celebrated on a different day yet. If I occasionally see a Buddhist monk, yeah, I have a rush of feeling. There is a sense of connection, community, sangha.

But I have friends who are much more identified with being Jewish or with being Christian, and what's very nice is that they still feel a home in IMS and in the methods.

In your understanding or experience, why is a person born into a Jewish world or a Jewish family. Is there anything significant about that?

I don't know the why. Sometimes, when we were speculating on why so many of our early group of seekers who were together in India were Jewish, we wondered if we had all died in concentration camps and been reborn with this intense need to understand life in a different way. Some people said that, while others thought it was related to how we all were raised with a premium on inquiry: "find out; figure it out; think."

But I can never really answer a karma question; who knows? Like, why was I born this or that? I don't really have an intuition about why I was born Jewish, but now that we're talking about it, it may relate somehow to the suffering question.

Whether it relates to past lives, I don't know. I went to Poland with Joseph Goldstein one year to teach. We were on our way to somewhere and all I could think of was dogs chasing me through the forest, tracking me down. So was that from my family? Or was that from a previous life? It was just for a short walk in the forest. "I don't like this. This is creepy." I don't know where it comes from, but there it is.

I didn't like looking at showerheads in the middle of the ceiling in Switzerland. There is this feeling, "I don't like this." I have never had an experience where I could say definitively, "that's a previous life." But these experiences did involve feelings of fear and repulsion and there were bodily reactions prior to any thoughts about it. I didn't look at it and say, "Gee, that's really like the kind of showerheads they had in Auschwitz."

I don't really know where it comes from, but it is very dreamlike, where you can almost be back there, walking down the street, carrying a suitcase during the war. There is this feeling, not unlike remembering a dream.

So I wouldn't be surprised if, within the context of death and rebirth (which I do believe in), that I was in Europe during the Holocaust. But, all those feelings: did they come from a past life, from my family, from stories I've heard? I don't know.

In Jewish thinking, there is the Garden, or Paradise. What is that in your understanding?

Well, it's the mind free of greed, hatred and delusion. It's a mind of boundless love, kindness and compassion. It's not a place in the world, but a place in consciousness.

Would you say that the method that you emphasize has the purpose of bringing you to that place?

Yes. You could say that we have achieved it in flashes, or in moments, but it tends to be unsteady or infrequent or certainly intermittent. So, the aspiration is to live there, to be there in a much more steady state – in this lifetime.

Is having a mind free of greed, hatred and delusion the same as what people call "God" or "God consciousness?"

I think it's very similar. That moment is not just introspective; it yields a sense of interconnection. Because there's no defensiveness, there's no agenda. So reality is seen very differently, and I think in a more true way. There is this vast sense of interconnection. It is related to what I would call "God consciousness," but it's not an elevated, removed, transcendent consciousness, disconnected and above everything.

How would you describe the feeling quality of the experience?

When a relationship to what's happening is free of greed, hatred and delusion, we open the door to seeing the truth of inter-connection. This opens the door to really boundless compassion, love and kindness. I usually say that's not a feeling. It can, of course, be seen as a feeling, experienced as a feeling. But the reason I say it's not a feeling in my teaching is because we may not be experiencing such a warm rush or a big emotional wave. Rather, we may be paying attention much more fully to someone, really listening or caring about them.

Even in seeking to help another person, there may not be much of an emotion; it might simply feel like the most natural thing in the world.

There is the question of how personal liberation relates to social consciousness. Ram Dass has described a significant shift when he went from strictly the path of self-liberation to becoming involved with social change causes, the peace movement, social justice – things like that. Has that been a part of your journey too?

Yes. When I went to India, my suffering was so acute that I had no time and space to care about anybody else. The context was there: you are taught to practice for everybody even if you think, "who cares about anybody else, really?" But over time, that shifted, and I felt much less personal internal stress and conflict. There was room to actually care about the situations of others. I think that shift naturally happens with practice.

Is it another shift that moves one from caring about others or the planet to taking time to be involved in actions that help transform the world?

Yes, I have felt that as well, but I think that takes many forms. What if a person is an artist? People don't necessarily find their manifestation of connection to others through working in a prison or trying to change social policy. But there will be a manifestation that's right for them. For me, I do get politically involved, and I write. When I got the "stinking Jews" e-mail, I knew I needed to write about it both to process it for myself and also because it makes a contribution to the collective consciousness.

Do you ever think that the part of your path involved in working for justice and peace could be attributed to your being Jewish?

Well, it could be. There's that prophetic voice in Judaism which is so strong. Did I just get it from Buddhists? Hard to know. In Buddhism, even in early Buddhism, there is a lot about engagement. Monks were always building schools; that's how kids got educated in Asia, through the monasteries. They also had dispensaries and were feeding people.

But there wasn't a sense of monks or nuns suddenly engaging in political or systemic change. They would focus more on feeding people than in changing the system or redistribution of wealth. Maybe I did get that from the Jewish thread. It's definitely in the air for me. I see the distinction very clearly between social work and social justice, feeding somebody and trying to change the way society is organized.

Lastly, what would you say to the Jewish people at this time in our human history?

I don't know if this is especially directed to Jewish people, but I would say that our ideas of what we need and what makes us happy are completely awry. We're lost and confused in general, and we would be a lot happier if we really took a look at some of our assumptions and realized how so many beings are living in poverty and how appalling it is. That really diminishes our own lives. We need to recognize the strengths and happiness we have without endless accumulation. We need to look and really see one another and be able to connect.

I was recently very moved by seeing the documentary on the Freedom Riders. I was young when it all took place, but cognizant. But I hadn't remembered quite the degree of violence, people in those buses, kids in those buses, and people setting the buses on fire hoping that they burned alive. Oh my God, and they went out and did it again.

It was just amazing, and I just realized that's what it took, for that kind of confrontation to happen, for change to come about. It wasn't that long ago. It's hard work trying to change the world. It's very hard work.

I think about the Israelis and Palestinians who come together after they've each lost a child to violence.[52] I imagine what it takes for them to communicate with one another and that they actually do. We can reach beyond those identities and see what we share. We all want a sense of belonging, but what if the belonging isn't that kind of tight, enclosed, self versus others? We have to realize that we're not so different.

Thank you.

---

[52] The Parents Circle - Families Forum (PCFF) is a joint Palestinian and Israeli organization of over 600 families, all of whom have lost a close family member as a result of the prolonged conflict. http://www.theparentscircle.com

Martin Lowenthal
BUDDHIST TEACHER
(Tibetan/Bön Lineage)

"Being Jewish, and never abandoning that identity while incorporating other teachings, I cannot take the view that there is one right way. I try to be inclusive and take the value of all traditions, including Christianity and Islam...."

"I openened to a larger pantheon of heroes."

What kind of Jewish life did you have as a child? What kind of imprint did being Jewish have on you?

There was an important pro-Jewish imprint on me in my childhood. We identified with Jewish people as special in our hearts and the specialness of being Jewish. The heroes and people we talked about were nearly all Jewish—the artists, musicians, politicians or whatever, were Jewish ones. My parents were very involved with Israel and my father was a very active Zionist, chairman of a West Coast Zionist organization. There was an emphasis on the heroism of the Jews in the '48 and subsequent wars. David Ben Gurion, Abba Eban, and other prominent Israelis were all heroes.

Later on, I've come to see it was a filter or attitude in my psyche. Many of those things I'm still disengaging from to this day. Over time I have opened to a larger pantheon of heroes.

When you feel these impulses or tendencies towards the specialness of the Jews, do you try to let them go?

My approach is to examine them, to see how they operate in my own psyche.

Did you have experiences with anti-Semitism when you were growing up?

I grew up in a largely Catholic neighborhood of San Francisco but didn't experience any anti-Semitism. Interestingly, our home was on Mount Davidson where there is a very large cross on the top. As a young child, many of my friends went to the local parochial school and I went a few times to mass at the local church. The priests were very friendly.

My experience of anti-Semitism was largely related to the public activities of my father, who was a prominent attorney. He was active in many civic issues and took on controversial legal causes. For example, he won a number of legal actions in the 1950's on behalf of gays and lesbians, establishing their civil liberties long before such actions had any popular support. He was also involved in fighting censorship (along with the ACLU) and he helped redefine the way obscenity cases were decided.

My father and our family were targeted as Jews because of these public activities. We would receive anti-Semitic hate mail and occasional threats that came from outside our community.

Was there very much fear that you felt as a result of that?

We had a consciousness of what happened to Jews during the war. In the 40s and 50s, anti-Semitism was very active in our larger society. We were aware of it. When I was growing up, nearly every family I knew had money in reserve or special bank accounts in order to leave on short notice.

When I moved to the East Coast, I noticed more institutional anti-Semitism. As late as the early 1970s, when I moved to the Boston area to teach at Boston College, the neighborhood club where we lived did not allow Jews or Blacks to be members. Over the following decade, these kinds of restrictions mostly disappeared.

How did that become part of you, the fear or imprint of fear?

It did not become a significant part of my life or my psyche.

Did you have any sense of aversion to Christianity from your Jewish upbringing, the Cross for example?

I did have some aversion to the Cross in terms of its association with the persecution of Jews, the inquisition, and its use by the KKK as part of the violence against African Americans.

At the same time, I respect and admire much of Christian theology, particularly the modern and more liberal theology, as well as many Christian philosophers. Christianity in its mystical and mature forms brings emphasis and elements that are different than Judaism and Buddhism and that inform and influence my teachings.

In some Christian theology, the life of Jesus points to the idea that a human being can embody divinity, not just the spark of divinity as you might find in Judaism. Other Christian thinkers argue that Jesus was a man who became divine after the resurrection when he becomes a part of the Christian collective imagination, a particular sacred consciousness. In this way, the Christian community becomes the body of Christ.

Did you ever feel much connection to the religious tradition of Judaism?

I had a very strong Jewish identity, but I was not particularly connected to the religion until college when I tried to be involved. I was unaware of any of the mystical tradition. Even in my youth, I knew that what I was looking for from a spiritual tradition was not based in my being Jewish.

What was it about Judaism that you were moving away from or what was it you were drawn to in other traditions?

I don't think I was moving away from anything. My spiritual journey started in my teens when I started reading books on Buddhism. I found an affinity there. When I first started meditation in my twenties, it felt like the most natural thing for doing the spiritual work that I was seeking. Also, I was drawn intellectually to philosophy, exploring what it means to be human and the different dimensions of life. Buddhism addressed that.

Later, the Tibetans I met seemed to embody their teachings as well as have a practice and an intellectual focus. I was also exposed to Indian kirtan and more devotional practices, but they didn't have the same resonance for me.

Was it having teachers who embodied what they were teaching and who had specific practices that seemed to be key for you?

I had a very humanist view of spirituality then. I believed that spirituality helped us to be more human, to develop our human potential, the spiritual being part of that. Over time, that has expanded to be not so homo-centric and not so focused on the personal journey. I see more of a collective element to it and my sense of the sacred is much broader than simply the realization of human beings.

"Service and spiritual work are sacred paths of the bodhisattva, a Buddhist ideal of becoming awake and being dedicated to the awakened happiness, growth and freedom of all sentient beings. The word 'bodhisatva' can be translated as 'one who embodies wisdom.' The essential wisdom that characterizes this path includes the qualities of self-transcendence, loving-kindness, compassion, profound understanding of the nature of the mind, the deep sense of the interdependence and interconnectedness of all beings, and the dedication to creating benefit and beauty in the world for everyone. The bodhisattva contributes to the awakened evolution of the collective into becoming an embodiment of the Sacred."
From *Buddha and the Art of Intimacy,* by Martin Lowehthal[53]

How did your Buddhist training progress?

I've studied Tibetan Buddhism in all the lineages, working initially with Kagyu and Nyingma teachers, and, in the last twenty years, with Bon teachers.

In 1991, at the year of Tibet celebrations in New York City, teachers from all the Tibetan lineages, including the Dalai Lama were present. There were also Bon teachers, which was my first exposure to them. Bon preceded Buddhism coming to Tibet and this is largely why Tibetan Buddhism looks so different from most other forms.

Shortly after that, I was leading a retreat in New Mexico and I was

---

[53] *Buddha and the Art of Intimacy* by Martin Lowenthal; Booksurge LLC, 2009

introduced to Tenzin Wangyal Rinpoche and then more extensively to Bon teachings. The practice of doing Dark Retreats[54] was part of that. Dark Retreats have been a major part of my practice and teaching.

Being Jewish, and never abandoning that identity, and then incorporating other teachings, I cannot take the view that there is one right way. I try to be inclusive and take the value of all traditions, including Christianity and Islam. This way one sees that there are different emphases in different traditions.

"I reflect on why I have been drawn to Buddhism and have it as my core spiritual lineage. Fundamentally, Buddhism is a path that opens to all spiritual traditions. Perhaps I might say I am a Jewish Buddhist Plus. It is about clarity, wisdom, the human design, and service to life and all people and beings. It also allows me to work with people of all religions, which is important to me in our heterogeneous society."
From *Dawning of Clear Light,* by Martin Lowenthal

Did you continue your spiritual quest while teaching at Boston College?

I began teaching at Boston College in 1970. I taught sociology and directed the Urban Affairs Program and ran a policy institute on the economy and its impact on low-income neighborhoods.

It was in Boston that I met Trungpa Rinpoche and other Buddhist teachers in the early 70's. I had started meditating before that, and with Buddhist teachers I became immersed in it. I was drawn to how Buddhism integrated spiritual practice with how our mind works with thoughts and feelings. I was always interested in psychology and Buddhism has a very highly developed psychology that I could relate to. It drew me in. I didn't see that in the Jewish world.

Over the years of working with various spiritual practices, I have

---

[54] Dark Retreats are meditation retreats of varying lengths experienced in complete darkness. Marty has written in depth about his own experiences of Dark Retreat in his book, *Dawning of Clear Light – A Western Approach to Tibetan Dark Retreat Meditation,* Hampton Roads Publications, 2003, and also *Writing in the Dark,* Dedicated Life Publications, 2009.

expanded my view of what the range of sacred practices are. My initial exposure to Buddhist meditation was primarily concerned with "the mind" or what I call the awareness dimension of being. This wisdom dimension of sacred work had been brought to the West primarily by teachers who had known a monastic life. I came to realize that mastery of what might be called wisdom practices did not necessarily bring maturity in other domains of life.

In addition to the awareness dimension, there are relational and creative dimensions of life. There are many examples of very developed people who follow a path that emphasizes love and connection, the relational aspect. There are other people whose path involves service in the world or who create beauty. The integration of these three paths can lead to both mastery and maturity, and they can be found in some form in the esoteric teachings of all the religious traditions.

In the Jewish Renewal world, there is an effort to integrate the spiritual, mystical development and the personal maturation work. Has it ever drawn you to "come back" to a more Judaic focus?

Oh, I've tried it. I have read a great deal and conversed with various rabbis and Jewish Renewal people. I used to go to some Jewish Renewal holiday services. At times I tried to immerse myself in it. But when I've gone to services, it doesn't resonate deeply with me. I have some familiarity with it, but after 40 years of working with the Buddhist tradition, I feel that more in my core.

Is it perhaps just the language, that you haven't studied Hebrew?

It's not just the language. The Jewish Renewal movement reinterprets much of what's there in Judaism, but I still feel uncomfortable with much of it. There is a very strong sense of God as Other. That doesn't work in my way, my practice.

Another issue is the content of the Biblical texts and prayers. Even translations that try to get at a more mystical or deeper meaning do not work for me. I can relate to the resonances of the chants and songs, but when it gets to the meanings it gets dicier.

You've heard the ways that some have reinterpreted or even rewritten the prayers to reflect a more immanent divinity and to eliminate patriarchal and even hierarchical messages. They say, let's go forward with a new vision of God or the stories of our past.

I agree with them, and I feel that that's for them to do.

You don't feel it's your calling?

At this stage of my life, that's not my calling. I don't even teach "Tibetan Buddhism." That's for Tibetans to teach. They come out of that lineage much more completely than I ever could.

You've said that you are a Jew.

And I would say that I am also a Buddhist, that I have many identities.

I hear you making the distinction; your Jewish identity doesn't call you to practice Judaism.

There is some calling and I've probably read more Jewish writing than anything other than Buddhist. I have shelves of Jewish books and use some of the stories in my teaching, much more than I use Christian or Islamic stories.

> *"In the temple of my heart*
> *the service has no sermon or announcements*
> *only hymns of longing, praise and love*
> *and the Sabbath lasts all week."*

"Daily Service," from *Writing in the Dark,* by Martin Lowenthal

Some make the point that the Jewish approach encourages more attention to human relationships and that Buddhism is more about leaving the worldly involvements behind.

The Jewish focus does tend to look more at the relational, such as the issues that would come before the rabbis, including how you personally relate to God. There is also more emphasis on the collective, the present and past community. Jews sacralize the history of the people and use sacred imagination which allows them to look at their history and have resonances that take them into sacred dimensions, just through the viewing or thinking about it.

The focus in Buddhism is more intra-psychic. In Judaism, styles of perceiving, and how we construct our internal world are not explored in anything like the systematic way that they are in Buddhism.

To say that Buddhism takes us away from the world is, I think, a misinterpretation and a simplistic way of talking about enlightenment from a Buddhist perspective. If you look at what they do in life or at tantric practice, it's all about engaging life, but in a different way. Buddhism asks, how do you become an embodiment of wisdom and compassion. Still, Buddhism is not relational in the same way as Judaism, perhaps that's one of its gaps. I've tried to write in ways to fill that gap.

Buddhism focuses on spiritual development, not psychological maturation. The Jewish focus is definitely on maturation, which may explain why Jews became so active in the developmental approaches of psychology.

What are the transmissions you take from your ancestry as a Jew?

Number one would be study as a spiritual practice. This is still very active in me. It is an important part of the lineage of the culture in which I grew up. Second, from my early meetings with Zalman Schachter, almost 50 years ago, there was a transmission of a sense of the ecstatic. This was different than anything I'd felt in synagogue. It was like what I'd experienced in Black churches, but it's clearly in the Jewish transmission. Buddhists have ecstasy, but it's more confined.

What is the consequence of these differences between the traditions?

From my point of view we exist in multiple dimensions of being, everything from physical to mental, emotional, and sacred dimensions. In terms of the sacred dimensions, different traditions will emphasize different aspects and center around them.

Practices in Buddhism emphasize the nature of mind; the awareness quality of pure being, often referring to it as ultimate. From my view, there is no real hierarchy to the different dimensions; one is not more important than the other. Rather, the emphasis may be there due to a need at a particular time in the context of culture or history. Some things get ignored and have been neglected and now may need emphasis. I don't privilege them, but see them in context.

I've come to appreciate how Judaism emphasizes certain dimensions not emphasized in Buddhism. The Jews take something like Tikkun Olam, repairing the world, and make it into a sacred process. One may relate to it as a kind of social service, but it really has a much deeper meaning in Judaism. It's really about repairing the tears that happen within us and between us, that keep us apart from the natural oneness and integration.

Would you say that the Jewish tradition places a major emphasis on healing, especially collectively, for the world?

Yes. You do see that in the Buddhist world also, with the notion of the Bodhisattva in service to the world, but it tends to be in the dimension of awareness. In the Jewish tradition, it's not just in awareness but it's in what I call "the relational dimension," the way in which we are creating the world now, and that's where the emphasis on justice comes in. It's very much about creating a better world now, in a sacred way.

I would also emphasize that there is a difference between secular justice and sacred justice. Sacred justice allows for much more nuance and complexity. Secular justice seems to see things in a binary way: this is right and that is wrong; these are the good guys, these the bad;

oppressors and oppressed, victims and victimizers. The sacred way sees that everybody needs healing.

Given the state of the world at this time, do you feel that the Jewish emphasis is more relevant?

It has a great deal of relevance and I do see my own path as helping bring out those elements in the Buddhist tradition. Buddha was in a sense quite a revolutionary. His view eliminated the caste system. It created a kind of social organization in which everybody is equal; all have Buddha nature. In the context of ancient India, that was pretty radical and was seen as radical. There is definitely this element in Buddhism. But the kind of Buddhism that we've tended to see in this country has been more monastic and concerned with the contemplative part of the teachings.

Buddhist study and debate talks about the nature of reality but also about what it means to be human and how society needs to be organized. As a result of this increased understanding, organizations of society would change. In this sense, karma can be seen not as the burden of our past, but as involved with the creative dimension: how our actions in this moment are creating the next moment. That is a major focus in Buddhism and relates to all dimensions of life.

Do you see it as your life mission to bring this emphasis that may come from your Jewish inheritance to Buddhism?

I try to bring a way of perceiving and thinking, and encourage what I call a heart posture about relating to life, whether coming from the Jewish or Buddhist tradition or Christian. I use the vehicle of the Buddhist tradition because I'm more known and knowledgable regarding that. I have more experience in using the practices which have been my base for decades. I haven't matured in the Jewish tradition of practices.

Did any of your explorations make you question your Jewish identity?

Not really. A Jewish identity was always just something I felt naturally. I would say that I have multiple identities. From my point of view, we have both our ancestry and our chosen communities. So, for many of us, we have multiple identifications. I still have a Jewish identity and connection. But it's not exclusive and it's not primary.

The Jewish identity involves the sense of ancestry, of being part of a people. My sense of responsibility to the Jewish people has grown more limited over time as I've felt more called to a sense of responsibility to a much larger community. I still care about and identify with Jews, tend to get passionate about the issues in Israel and my disagreements with the policies there in ways I do not with many other countries. Having worked with the Tibetans for so long, I get passionate about the way the Chinese mistreat the Tibetans. I care about the Tibetans as a chosen community.

Is it important to you that the Jewish identity continue in this world?

Yes. I care about that. I think it needs to change and evolve to reflect the reality of living in a global community, of numerous varieties of Jewish religious practices and affiliations, of Jewish communities in Israel and around the world. There is also a need to redefine Jewishness in light of contemporary life rather than an archaic tribal identity based in the conditions of thousands of years ago.

What other influences are you working to integrate?

Martin Prechtel[55] opened up a great deal, a whole lot of things. He's had a major influence on me over the years in terms of bringing nature to life as a spiritual reality. It's not so much emphasized in the Jewish or Buddhist world.

There are those who see Judaism as nature-based in its origins, such as Gershon Winkler and others who focus on the roots of

---

[55] Martin Prechtel is a writer and teacher. His books include: *The Secrets of the Talking Jaguar* and *The Disobedience of the Daughter of the Sun: Ecstasy and Time*.

the Jewish transmission and practice being very much immersed in nature.

Yes. That's what I'm doing in Buddhism too. I support the efforts to bring out these threads of the traditions and weave them into the fabric of spiritual practices today as part of an ongoing evolution of sacred teachings.

Among the Tibetans, this connection to nature is found most prominently among the practitioners of Bön, the indigenous religion that integrated with Buddhism after it came to Tibet from India. The Buddhist monastics often tend to get away from the nature practices. Yet there is also great respect for the yogis who live in caves, spend most of their lives in the wilderness, and make natural forces an integral part of their practices. This needs to be brought out more in all traditions at this time, because the religions have become more confined to the temple or meditation space instead of in the world.

How does that come into your practice and how you teach?

I practice a lot outdoors. One of my most important teachers was a tree. Many years ago, I meditated with that tree every day for years. This was not something my Tibetan teachers suggested I do. This came to me naturally, so to speak, and I learned and grew so much from that kind of spiritual work.

I have my students do a practice called Earth hugging. You lie on the ground, with as little clothing as possible, and entirely relax into that location until you can feel the vibration of the Earth at that spot and your body attunes and aligns itself with that vibration. You do it face down. Then you can turn over, lie on your back, open to the sky and experience yourself as the connection between the Earth and sky. This is a wonderful grounding practice.

I also teach a variation of the Taoist microcosmic orbit. In this practice you bring the energy from the heavens down the front of your body. When you reach the perineum, you move the energy down to the heart of the Earth and then draw it back up to the perineum again and then let it flow up your back up to the heavens. The orbit is a connection of Heaven and Earth.

We also do a posture of Bodhidharma, like the Ho Tai Buddha[56], in which your hands are taking in the energy of the heavens and through your feet you are taking in the energy of Earth and integrating them in your being.

As part of your own experience in nature, you did a Vision Quest[57] in the desert. Anything you want to share related to our discussion here? Did you have any visions or experiences that focused on your Jewishness?

My visions all related to my Buddhism. I was fasting near a cave in Canyonlands, Utah. I had envisioned this cave prior to going to Utah. The cave had probably been used by the ancient Pueblo peoples, the Anasazi, for hunting game because it looked out on a valley below and on the canyons. I was there fasting and practicing and as part of that, especially during the 24 hour vigil period, I received transmissions from Dilgo Khyentse Rinpoche and various other Tibetan teachers. I was getting this transmission in an altered state, with part of my mind trying to figure out what was being transmitted. A little voice came and said, "Shut up, just open and it will all be revealed over time." I sat there for hours receiving transmissions. Afterwards, the teachings kept unfolding over many years.

It's almost impossible to describe such a transmission in terms of ordinary experience. I experienced it as streams of consciousness and energy that became an environment that I tuned into, receiving a signal in large chunks rather than linear time. Later I became a vehicle for these teachings. As they came through me to my students, I was one of the witnesses to what I was articulating. I was experiencing the teachings in this way for the first time, even though they had been given to me during that time in the desert.

---

[56] A Chinese monk named Ho Tai, widely referred to by non-Buddhists as the "laughing Buddha" or "happy Buddha," depicted in statues of a large-bellied Buddha standing with arms reaching upward.

[57] A Vision Quest is a cross-cultural practice, usually involving fasting in solitude in the wilderness, during which one seeks direction, healing or spiritual clarity.

Buddhism is often associated with the idea of reincarnation. How does this fit with being Jewish? Are we Jewish before birth or after death? Do we have consecutive lives as Jews?

I don't have a sense of a personal soul beyond this life. My ideas about reincarnation don't line up with most exoteric versions of Buddhism. I think there are soul dimensions of life and the soul has certain tendencies at birth, perhaps a kind of spiritual DNA, but it's pretty open. It is possible that we have potentials that are influenced by ethnicity and ancestry and need to be activated by the environment we grow up in and live in. In the way this is commonly talked about, I don't have the sense of a Jewish soul.

I do feel that at death there is a physical death and that individual configurations of consciousness are released that enter into the field of consciousness, an invisible, yet important environment that we all participate in. These configurations may have more or less cohesiveness to them and yet are not permanent. Identity mostly dissolves.

Is there no Self that is beyond the personal that might continue to have existence after death?

The self that we experience as persisting through time I call the self-sense. This is definitely part of our life experience. This is not the same as the ego or any one identity. We can take on many identities and still have the same self-sense.

Is this different from the notion of a Higher Self?

Yes. The idea of a higher self tends to create a division, a split in who we are. I would suggest that the self-sense simply is. It is neither higher nor lower.

So this self-sense would be neither Jewish nor not-Jewish?

It's like clear Light or clarity. It has no inherent particular form. It has the openness and flexibility to take many forms. It has no inherent identity and its boundaries are permeable. It can go beyond this particular body and time and place.

How much importance do you place on the role of biological ancestors in this life? Is it possible that some spiritual seekers ignore the importance of ancestral influences as a form of "spiritual bypass,"[58] in order to see themselves as more universal?

For me, the question is not whether you become universal or stay within a particular cultural or ethnic framework, but how you metabolize what's there. One of the things I learned over time through tantric practice is not to deny emotions but to transform them. This also comes from my background in psychology, especially developmental psychology. I've developed a way of helping people outgrow what I call their reactive habit body and their personal archaic history. You work with the materials that are there, as in alchemy, and you turn the lead of those experiences into the gold of wisdom, love and beauty.

Many of our challenges come from patterns of thinking and feeling that have been passed along for generations and that you acquired from your parents. The more difficult patterns of fear and longing are often rooted in a deep sadness and sense of not belonging.

Unmetabolized grief, fear, and traumas can haunt people who do what you are calling the spiritual bypass. This includes griefs and fears that are based in your ancestry. If you're not metabolizing what you've inherited from your ancestry, then you may be haunted in significant but subtle and distorted ways. This is why I think it's important to confront the notions we have learned about being Jewish. If we don't confront what we have been taught about our relationship with Israel and metabolize the grief and rage related to the Holocaust, these things will haunt us and come out sideways.

---

[58] Spiritual bypass is a term often used to describe the tendency to adopt spiritual ideas without truly experiencing the nature of those spiritual realizations, using those ideas to rationalize the suppresson of feelings or thoughts that are uncomfortable.

Can you say more about what you mean by metabolize?

When we eat, the food goes through a digestive system that processes the nutrients. It separates what is useful from what is waste. It transforms the useful elements into forms that can nourish the organs and the body. This is the organic process that maintains life and enables us to grow. We also process emotional phenomenon, our history, current affairs and other experiences in a kind of psychological and spiritual digestive system.

What are Jews inheriting that needs to be metabolized?

It depends on what kind of Jewish community you come from. The kind that I came from was different from yours or many others. The process of metabolism involves finding what is of value in your inheritance and making it useful for your own development.

For example, when I read the stories in the Torah, I became interested in the study of mythology and how things operate at multiple levels. When you look at the story of the Jewish people, you realize that this is a story of a tribe that was very war-like. It's a story of a people who were at one point enslaved, freed, and then took over land from others claiming that it was given to them by God. Many of the figures in the stories can be found in even older mythologies. Learning how to understand that and learn from it is part of the metabolizing.

What do you make of the rabbinic approach to the story of our people?

One great feature of the rabbinic tradition is that a story is never fixed. In Judaism, there is an initial story and then there is forever commentary and elaboration and interpretation.

In terms of metabolizing a general Jewish story, there is the experience of being a people living in a diaspora and what that means regarding the core issue of where you find home, a sense of belonging. Any people in a diaspora have that issue and need to learn to turn it into a blessing. We learn how to metabolize it so that you become sensitive to the nature of belonging, the nature of home, finding a home in the nature of being, and experiencing the world as home.

The issue of persecution is an old one for the Jewish people and it takes an extreme form in the more recent dynamics of the Holocaust. This is very difficult to metabolize and is still going on right now. Many efforts of conscious and creative artists are striking and wonderful in the way that they are helping people to transform old wounds. At the same time other forces are arresting any authentic integration and movement forward by using the story of the Holocaust in some horrific ways.

For example?

Some of what's happening in Israel currently uses the Holocaust to rigidify a Jewish identification as a victim, and this becomes the justification for the victimization of others, namely the Palestinians. The ideology implicitly and explicitly argues that the Jewish people are always in a battle with the other. In this frame, the only humanity that counts is your own because you can't trust anybody else. That's part of what's happening now that's an example of un-metabolized process, something that didn't go through all the stages of grief and so got frozen into forms of fear and anger. The warrior themes from the Bible are resurrected in a modern way by contemporary stories about Israel. You can see this archaic imagery in the book and movie "Exodus," which is stuck in the victim/aggressor mentality.

How moved are you by your Jewish identity to be involved in what is happening in Israel, moving beyond awareness to action?

Since the time of my childhood, many synagogues have given a great deal of attention to the state of Israel. Even as an adolescent this seemed to me as having little to do with an authentic religious sensibility. So I have separated my religious and spiritual identity from my limited identity with the Jewish people.

I did live in Israel for a while in '63. I felt a connection to the land

and the people, but felt critical of the government policies. I also spent time with the Bedouin, which opened me in profound ways to new understandings of time and space. This experience helped break me out of my cultural mold. It also had the effect of opening me to understand and accept Arab people. I began to question the Zionist narrative that had been so much a part of my family. I started to really examine the dark side of Israel, the way Israel treated the Palestinians, and that was very difficult to integrate.

In terms of the kind of attention I give to Israel because I am Jewish, I would say that I have felt a connection to issues in the Middle East. For me the problem is not that we have these tribal connections, it is what we do with those connections. It is natural at various levels of social and cultural affiliation to feel drawn by and engaged in the struggles of groups we identify with. Like having a physical body through which we can grow and act in the world, we participate in one or more community bodies that can become deep vehicles for our caring and concern.

So do you find yourself drawn into actions on Israel/Palestine?

More recently I've been speaking out, particularly regarding the Occupation and what's happening in this country with its alliance with the right wing in Israel, which I find very problematic.

Speaking out on Israel can lead to problems with Jews strongly identified with Israel. And with my family, though there tends to be an acceptance of different points of view there. Debate was part of an accepted environment in my family.

How is it that people who have strong mystical experiences of oneness and unity can continue to be narrowly identified in political contexts?

It seems that religion and even mysticism don't always carry over. For Jews to forget that there is one God and it's the same for Palestinians and Jews is quite remarkable. Even with some connected to Jewish mysticism or Jewish Renewal, I think what happens is that when their mystical experience is brought back into everyday life, they conflate the dimensions of being. They wind up taking this spiritual experience and filtering it through a particular cultural identity and confining it within the limitations and attitudes of that identity. This happens for the Tibetans too. On certain kinds of subjects, such as homosexuality, suddenly all their cultural stuff comes flying out.

That's an interesting window into how cultural baggage can obscure spiritual insight.

I would call it a cultural filter. It doesn't have to be baggage. The culture can be a vehicle through which you express and manifest the spiritual. If you are not conscious enough of the biases in your own culture then it will come out in limiting ways.

Ken Wilbur argues that there are spiritual stages of enlightenment and there are psychological or cultural stages of enlightenment. It is possible to advance spiritually yet be in an early stage of cultural development. In such a case, certain aspects of the spiritual will not be held in a more universal way in the world of relationships.

Doesn't spiritual practice wake us from biases and help us develop culturally?

It's not that simple. One of the things we have in the West is the idea of psychological development and the stages of psychological development. I've met spiritual teachers who have had incredible spiritual awakenings but seem to have arrested emotional development, partly because they've never paid any attention to it. Sometimes monks come out of monasteries and get into sexual or romantic relationships, yet they're barely even adolescent in their relational development.

What has happened for many spiritual teachers is that they haven't learned how to integrate sexual and emotional development, so they wind up in what we call inappropriate situations. I don't judge them. I see them caught up in an undeveloped relational stage. Living life in the world is what develops that, but living it consciously and skillfully, not just from spiritual practice. Being willing to grow from life experiences, you don't remain a perpetual adolescent in relationship and commitments.

> *"Our reactive habit body has its own momentum and can continue in the tendencies of even highly developed spiritual people. The profundity of our realization does not mean that our body-mind is not affected by past experiences and patterns, and present habits, not to mention external situations. This simply is what is. We may change it to some extent but that is not an excuse for not being aware, awake and present right now with those patterns and everything else."*
> From Buddha and the Art of Intimacy, by Martin Lowenthal

Can you speak to the Jewish people from your heart wisdom in terms of today's reality?

As someone who has spent forty years immersed in spiritual practice, I feel it is important that Judaism continue to develop and evolve its spiritual practices and integrate the mystical elements of its tradition. For various branches of the religion this may take different forms. The primary concern should be to avoid the rigidity of a traditional dogmatism on one extreme and making the religion superficial on the other. What is going to make it vital and alive is to have the depth of spiritual practice that allows for many stages of development within it. It is not simply about having a sense of spiritual connection, but actually being able to grow in a spiritual way.

Also, the spiritual practice needs to be separated from the State of Israel. Many Jews may have personal connections, but the religion should not be tied to the politics of Israel. Such entanglements can lead to tearing within both the personal and collective soul because they tend to ignore our connections beyond the Jewish people. If we believe in "one God" then it's a God of all people. All people are our brothers and sisters even if they don't practice our religion. This connection to our global world is critical for our conscious development and is simply not addressed if we Jews become cocooned, self-absorbed and self-enclosed in simply what is Jewish.

We need to stay conscious and reflective and see what is beneficial for all, not just for the Jewish people. To ask, "Is it good for the Jews?" is a confining question. It's not an incorrect question, because it is worth exploring. But to treat it as a central or core question becomes much too limiting.

At a pragmatic level, what would you say to Jews about Israel?

Jews in the U.S. have a role to play to put pressure on Israel to make peace and not continue the Occupation which is a violation of many Jewish values as well as those of all the major religious traditions. The long-term sustainability of Israel, internally, externally and spiritually, is dependent on making peace with the Palestinians. To paraphrase Abraham Lincoln, they need to change their attitude, and rather than thinking of destroying their enemies, make them their friends.

Thank you.

"The embodiment of rapture radiates Aliveness and Love from the inside out, making our heart a source of light for all the world."
From *Alchemy of the Soul,* by Martin Lowenthal

Isaac Shapiro
ADVAITA TEACHER

A participant at one of Isaac's satsangs asks, "What does the name Isaac Shapiro mean to you?" Isaac responds, "Actually, not a whole lot. The translation of the Hebrew name for Isaac, Yitschak, means 'he who laughs.' And Shapiro, I have been told, means 'the beautiful.' . . . But ultimately, it is irrelevant."
From It Happens by Itself by Isaac Shapiro

Your path seems to involve not identifying with anything. Is it meaningful at all for you to say I am a Jew or I am a Jewish person?

Not at all.

At one time in your life that was a meaningful or true thing to say?

Yes, at one time in my life there was confusion (laughter). From that perspective, speaking would be from the perspective of identification, you could say, from some sense of me that was some thing. One of the things I invite people to explore, just to see for themselves, is the difference in saying, "I'm sad," or "I feel sad," or "sadness is coming up." Just noticing the difference between those three—I am sad, I feel sad, and sadness is happening—gives us a sense of different levels of identification.

So, is Jewishness ever happening for you?

Not at this point.

Well, does sadness happen?

Yes, sadness can arise, but not the Jewish identification. I think like any child, you're born into a circumstance and you follow along with whatever your parents are doing. For the first nineteen years of my life, that was the paradigm. There was this idea that I was supposed to marry a Jewish girl and that if anyone called you a "bloody Jew," you were supposed to fight them.

There were many ideas around it and you could just watch the pain and suffering that came from that. One of my cousins married someone out-of-faith (so-called), and his father refused to speak to him for the rest of his life. Imagine the difficulty that caused in that family. Growing up, my parents refused to buy anything German for many years. Then that softened and it was okay again to buy a Volkswagen or whatever. (Laughter)

Does your body react in ways contrary to what you know to be true? Do you sometimes find yourself having gut reactions to things in ways that are not consistent with your vision of what is real?

What windows do I look back at: the last year; the last two years; the last five minutes?

Right now.

Right now, all is well.

There's been a lot of peeling away of the old habits.

Absolutely.

Do you ever feel that you still have this reactivity, that it occurs in you, but you want to not have it?

This is where there's been a paradigm shift. It comes back to what I was referring to earlier: I'm reacting, I feel reaction, or reactivity comes up in me. When I see reactivity coming up in me, I can see that this reactivity has nothing to do with me; I see there's an opportunity there. Seeing it as an opportunity and not that "I am still reactive," it becomes a doorway into being able to penetrate it. I'm then able to be available to the transformation which not only serves this body/mind, but serves the whole field, because it's so connected.

So the reactivity that arises is connected to a collectivity that's larger than your personhood?

Yes, much larger then the individual, it could be the whole of humanity and beyond.

Some people feel that their expanded sense of collective connection is bounded by the Jewish world, their tribal connectedness.

One could look at it that way, but then we must ask where did the Jewish world come from? At best, the Jewish world is only five or six thousand years old. It's not that old in the whole history of life, it's a blip. Where did we come from before that? Why not include that in our sense of connections?

Do you find that what's happening with Israel and Palestine brings up more feeling than say, what's happening in China and Tibet?

No, it's the same ignorance that's playing out. It's just ignorance. When I look at it, I see that to the extent that there are beliefs or unconscious habits at play that are not seen, there's no choice whatsoever. There's nobody to forgive even. It's just like a program that's playing. It would be like blaming the computer for the program it has; it has no option, it just has to function like that. When it becomes conscious, then there's no choice then either, because once it's conscious, it would never do these things.

What can you say about your personal history? Where were you born and where is your family from?

I was born in South Africa. Both sides of my family came from Lithuania. My grandparents came to South Africa in the early 1900's. It was a time when there were pogroms in Lithuania. The families would send their kids off whenever they had enough money, anywhere but where they were. Then once they got there, they earned money and sent for others. My parents were both born in South Africa.

Did you grow up in a Jewish community in South Africa?

There were different perspectives on Jewishness. There were the really religious guys with the black hats. That was a very small fringe minority from my family's perspective. Then there were the reform Jews who ate bacon and such. We didn't keep kosher, but we didn't consider ourselves reform; we didn't eat bacon. My family would light Friday night candles, but we didn't go to synagogue every Saturday, just the high holidays (Yom Kippur and Rosh Hashanah). We celebrated Passover and had a seder, but didn't have the separate plates. There were these funny distinctions about what it all means. In any case, there was this identification with Jewishness.

The consideration is that someone is Jewish if they're born to a Jewish mother. It doesn't even matter who your dad is, just whether your mom is. But then what is it actually? It's not a tribe; it's not one religious belief; it's basically a mind trip, an identification basically.

When you were young, that was your identification and so it was true for you; that was your sense of yourself?

Yes.

Did you go to Hebrew school and have a bar mitzvah?

Yes, I learned how to sing the passages in the prayer book. I read the English translation, but I didn't really understand. I just learned how to do it and did it; that was the way.

Were your parents political?

I would say they were apolitical. That was interesting for me, because growing up in South Africa, it never occurred to me that it was different anywhere else in the world. You treated the dog a certain way, a cat a certain way, and black people a certain way. It never occurred to me that there was anything wrong going on with that. There wasn't TV in South Africa when I was growing up. The newspapers and books were all censored, and my folks never spoke about it. I just wasn't exposed to the questioning of the order of things.

I had a very strong and deep connection with our servants as a kid because my parents both worked. But it didn't even seem funny to me that they weren't allowed to swim in the swimming pool. They could serve you food and look after the kids. They had these rooms in the back of the house that were separated from us and I would never go into their rooms; all our interactions happened in the house. It all never got questioned, it was just as it was. When all of that stuff became apparent to me, it was so hurtful and shocking that my parents hadn't told me.

How old were you when you had that realization?

About 19. It was, "Wow, what's going on here?" I saw that it was like what happened to the Jews. I was shocked that my parents never said anything. They just went along with it, so it was really a big shock for me.

This was about 1969. I was a completely conservative guy and had not been exposed to very much. I'd been drunk once or twice in my life and I didn't particularly like it. Somebody smuggled a Playboy magazine in (they were banned in South Africa) and I was wanting to look at the intellectual articles. (laughter) There was an article in there by Timothy Leary talking about thousands of orgasms a second on LSD. That really appealed to me as a 19-year-old.

The next thing I knew, I met an American student who had some Orange Sunshine[59]. I really had no clue. All I knew about was aspirin. I took the acid with a friend of mine who also was clueless. We went to a friend's house when the parents were out for the evening. Suddenly, there was this experience of unconditional love. My mind was like a supercomputer where there was this huge download of understanding. I had never been interested in them, but I understood the philosophers. I could look at someone and know their past and their future; I could see what they were thinking. It was just like the veils parted for

---

[59] "Orange Sunshine" was the first largely available form of LSD after its possession was made illegal.

some moments.

I was studying medicine at the time, and I could see that I was in it for all the wrong reasons. I was in it because you're supposed to choose something to do and that seemed to make my parents happy. I suddenly saw, "Wow, I don't know a single happy person, not one, not one human being that's happy." I was seeing that everyone was caught up in the world of their thinking and that my thinking was completely convoluted. If I wanted to come out of that web, I had to re-examine everything. I didn't know anything about teachers or consciousness, but I experienced the oneness and the love of the universe. Even though it had been induced by a substance, I knew that what I was experiencing was REALITY. I also knew that what I usually lived in was a complete fabrication; it was so clear to me.

I could say that was the dropping point for me of Jewishness. I went and resigned from medical school the next day. That was also when I realized there was a political situation in South Africa. I hadn't even recognized that until then. It was like my life was going in one direction and it just took a complete turn. I saw that I had to reevaluate everything: what I thought about food; what I thought about sexuality; what I thought about marriage; everything. I dived into the deep end.

Had you ever in your childhood had any kind of openings of a spiritual sort?

No, not really. I didn't think much about all that. But when it hit, it hit big time; it was amazing. I went from being a nice Jewish boy studying medicine, my parents very proud of me, to being a hippie.

Was there a hippie culture around that reinforced these new understandings and explorations?

No. I was one of the first. I went from being protected by the South African system, to being an outlaw. In South Africa, when you walked down the street with long hair in those days, literally everybody rubbernecked and looked at you in a judgmental way that could easily turn violent. They were exciting times; people were very reactionary, like in the deep South of the United States. But, it was very exciting.

My parents had grown up, both of them, in very poor families. For them, the deal was that you had to get an education. They had watched what happened with the Nazis and said that an education is one thing they can't take away from you. They worked their entire lives so that their kids could have a better life than them. We were supposed to step into that. Being that I was the eldest, there were quite some expectations. When I didn't go down that road, it was not easy for them.

At that point, I started to look at what is Jewishness? What is it all about? Does it serve any useful purpose? It seemed to me I couldn't find anything substantial except a bunch of rituals, beliefs and identifications. As far as I could see it just caused difficulties. It gave some sense of togetherness, but in such a shallow sense. I watched the gossip and all the crap about people; it was very superficial to my sense of things at the time. It seemed to be a very superficial way of getting some sense of community or identity. It just didn't seem appealing to me at all. I couldn't see any benefit to it.

When I told my family that, it was upsetting to them. From their perspective, the program was for me to marry a Jewish girl and make my parents proud, be successful, make a lot of money.

Where did it go from there? Did you continue to take psychedelics and stay in a cultural sense involved with the hippie community? Was there any spiritual exploration?

For me, if it was possible to live in the way that I had experienced on LSD, I wanted to do that. If I could live in that consciousness, that was what was interesting to me. What also started to happen was getting visions of where the world is and where it was going. I could see that, like lemmings, we were going over a cliff; it was the blind leading the blind. I could see that there was going to be a huge financial crunch.

Did psychedelics continue to give you that kind of experience? Or did it become more recreational, hedonistic?

It was a mixture. At that time, there were the books by Carlos Casteneda, who was talking about meeting your ally and such. There was also this seeing into what was going on in the world. I was starting to see the craziness of the human psyche, how it was functioning, and I was recognizing the covert agendas and struggles. It was especially intense in South Africa where as soon as you stepped off the path you were targeted. I was followed by the police because I was very ideological; I wanted to wake people up. I wanted people to see what was going on and I thought the best way was to give them LSD. I gave lectures at the University that you should "turn on, tune in and drop out." For me it had been such a revelation.

Did you get involved with the anti-apartheid movement?

A friend of mine was publishing one of the only underground newspapers in the country. It was so repressive in South Africa that people were expelled from the university just for having a copy. If we were caught printing it or having anything to do with the production, it was definitely jail. There was no question about it. It was a wild time.

But for me what made the most sense was to try to get people conscious, to get people out of the narrow window that they were looking through that was about being asleep. I didn't see psychedelics as drugs anymore; I saw them as medicines. I knew there had been a tradition of people who had used them forever to pierce the veils. To me, that's what the opportunity seemed to be.

Do you find they still have value for you?

Not much at this point. Ingesting marijuana for example: it excites the nervous system and gives a certain buzz. But you have to deal with all the side effects of what it does. It seems too high a price to pay.

What about the more deeply shamanic medicines like Ayahuasca or mushrooms?

Definitely, they can give insights; there's no question about it. They can be a valuable tool. I did a lot of acid in my early days. What I see in people that have done a lot of acid is that it doesn't necessarily clear you up. You get certain insights, but there are ways in which crystallization happens in your system and there's a certain price to pay. They can be useful, perhaps if you are using it with a very experienced person that could assist you. You don't want to reassemble yourself in just another way that may be more expanded, but still identified. In the indigenous cultures, that's the way it's invited.

Why did you leave South Africa?

In the 60s, there was the birth of the organic movement. I had this idea, which was quite common in those days, of getting into a community and living on the land and growing our own food. It related to these visions of society having to readjust. Today, many people see that we are going to go through a big restructuring in the coming years and that it's kind of wise, if you can, to be as self-sufficient as possible.

At the time, my parents were putting a lot of pressure on me to get some kind of education. So I decided to study agriculture. But before you could study agriculture in college in South Africa, you had to have a year of experience. This was complicated, because I was living unmarried with a woman, and the very conservative farmers in South Africa would not let us live on a farm. So, I chose to leave South Africa and go to Israel to live on a kibbutz where I could work on a farm and get some agricultural experience.

Do you feel at all that, even though you were seeking the kibbutz as a communal farm experience, that you chose Israel because of your Jewishness?

For me, it was just practical. I knew I could go to Israel because they considered me Jewish and so I could slide right into a kibbutz. I grew up as a city boy without a clue about planting anything and I wanted to get some experience.

I idealized this whole idea of living on the land and what it meant. First thing on the kibbutz, I was given the job of sitting on this loud tractor spreading chemicals on the land. I thought, "God, are we going to eat that? There's something wrong with this picture."

Just seeing the way the animals were treated in Israel was too much. They had cages with three chickens in a tiny little cage with enough room for two to be on the floor at one time. They were constantly struggling to find some place to put their feet down. It was the same for the way the cows were treated. Everything was like that. They weren't considered as living beings; they were considered as some kind of factory product. To me, it was shocking. I didn't realize that was how it was. You could barely tell the difference between the yoke and the white from those chickens. Watching what we were putting on the vegetables and then going to eat made me lose my appetite.

I became more interested in growing foods naturally and organically. I went to the guys in charge and said I'd like us to grow and eat organically and they let me do that. I started reading books on growing organically and making compost. It was very useful for me. I got the hands-on experience I needed and met people and started to form friendships. But the kibbutz was as messed up as any political system I've ever seen.

During the year that you were there in Israel, did you travel to Jerusalem and other places of interest?

Just to buy hash, basically.

You continued to do psychedelics and smoke pot on the kibbutz?

When I first came there, it wasn't allowed. But for me it had become another identification at that point.

What was the identification?

Being a hippie: letting your freak flag fly, Bob Dylan, Woodstock,

Beatles, free love, checking out what was possible, trying to find my way. I wanted to live with people in a sane way where there wasn't a power structure, where we were meeting as equals.

Did the psychedelic experiences continue to move you in a more spiritual direction or was it more cultural?

The spiritual was very strong for me. I was reading spiritual books, but I'd never had a teacher, so I didn't really know what that was all about. I knew from my experience on that first LSD trip that I had just dropped into awareness, that there was this space that the whole universe was appearing in, that everything was all connected, that there was this vast intelligence of which this body was just a tiny manifestation. I could see that this body was not me. I could see that these identities had been assumed and they were not the truth of the matter at all. I'd had a taste of that and I wanted to get back, whatever it took. If it took taking all kinds of psychedelics, that's what was interesting to me.

When you decided that the Jewish trip was no longer relevant to you, did you still retain some of the imprints that came through that ancestry?

Yes, but for me I saw it as a hindrance. For example, having kids, the whole tradition of circumcision comes up. I'd been to a circumcision and to me it was barbaric, taking this little baby and cutting off the tip of his foreskin for tradition. I'm watching this baby screaming and everyone around going, "Mazel Tov, Mazel Tov." I'm going, "Oh my God! This is just not interesting to me at all." I lost track of Jewish holidays. I could say that there is a Jewish sense of humor that is inculcated into the system.

What is that?

I suppose it's certain words and certain traits that you could call the Jewish sense of humor.

Did you take on a new tradition

Later on, my journey took me to India where I met Papaji,[60] who was still following somewhat the tradition of Hinduism. But I wasn't interested in taking on any tradition at all.

At one point, I met this Tibetan who lived in California, and he told me his story. When he was very young, he was given to a monastery (which was the tradition). He learned the rituals and all that in the monastery. One day, he heard about a guy sitting in a cave near the monastery so he went there, and this guy transmitted beingness to him. He saw that the whole story that he'd learned his whole life in the monastery was rubbish. He just wasn't interested in it anymore. He was interested in the living truth. I can so recognize that in myself. It wasn't anymore about the dressing; it just lost interest for me.

Most of my family are fairly traditional. My dad and mom both had large families, so there were lots of cousins around the world. Some of them have gone the route of being really religious. Most of them still observe Friday night candles and all that. I don't have a problem with it; it's just not interesting for me.

Besides these ritualistic observances, there is often an inheritance of emotional or psychological traits that seem to come from the collective history of Jewish identity. How have these affected you emotionally or bodily?

Yes, I did inherit those things, but in seeing the bodily responses and paying attention to them, they started to quiet down. When I was asked by Papaji to be available for these meetings, one of the first places where I got invited was to Dachau. I was holding these meetings in Germany near the concentration camp and looking into people's eyes. People were telling me that their father was in the SS and different things like that. I was seeing the innocence of these people wanting

---

[60] Sri H. W. L. Poonja, (1910 - 1997) is also known as "Poonjaji" or "Papaji." A disciple of Ramana Maharishi. Poonjaji denied being part of any formal tradition, though he is considered by many to have been a teacher of the Advaita Vedanta and Bhakti traditions.

to be free; it had nothing to do with what their fathers or mothers had done. It touched me to see that it doesn't matter what our past was; at some point there is this deep yearning to be free.

At one point in my journey, I was traveling around and somebody told me about a very far-out Rabbi, world renowned. "He's very clear, come see him." I said okay. I'd visited Tibetan and Indian teachers, why not? I called this rabbi and asked to meet with him and told him I was a lover of truth. He was very forthright and said, "I'm not interested in truth, I'm interested in the Jewish tradition. I have my set of beliefs and I'm happy with them."

There are many different layers of this. People can say they are interested in truth but they hold onto some identification with their background. The truth in seeing who you are is that there is nothing. As long as there is some identification, there is still some mechanism of being connected to this body and seeing through some kind of filter. For me, there's no problem with that; it's just not true freedom, it's limited.

Isn't the issue one of attachment or identification, not whether one practices in a particular way? As you mentioned, Papaji worked within a framework of the Hindu religion, but he was not attached to it or identified with it.

It's hard to know where he was at with it. I just saw what he did, but who knows what was going on inside. He seemed very free of the whole thing, but at the same time something played out there. Yet for me, I didn't want to take in something else.

Did he encourage you to take on anything like a belief system or path?

He just did it and then the people around him did it.

How did you get to Papaji from working on a kibbutz?

There are a few steps along the way. I didn't want to go back to South Africa and I was looking to find my place. "Where can I go where I can live a simple life and be me?" It seemed to me then (and it still looks that way) that there is going to come a breakdown of our current economic structures particularly, but also political systems. With my interest in organic growing, I went to this little farm in Denmark where this guy was growing organically, commercially. After that, New Zealand became interesting to me. It was in the southern hemisphere, it wasn't a major power, it was away from the noise.

Did you continue as a spiritual seeker?

I continued to read about spirituality. But the way my system functions, whenever I met someone teaching a particular path, I would always find the holes in whatever they were talking about. Literally within minutes, and then they would be terribly upset with me and throw me out. I'd had a direct experience, and when someone was talking about it and it wasn't their direct experience, it was so glaringly obvious to me. It would become a challenge of belief structures, and since they were supposed to be the authority, it wasn't so well received.

Although you'd had that direct experience, would you say that you had some anger or anti-authority issues playing out?

Yes, all kinds of stuff, all of this. (laughter) That was all playing out too. (more laughter)

Anyway, I lived in New Zealand for four-and-a-half years when I met an American woman who had a community in California. We got together and would spend six months in California and six months in New Zealand. The community, in the Sierra foothills of California, was called Rainbow Ranch. We were a bunch of freaks living out in the country, building our own homes, birthing our kids at home, growing our gardens, eating organically, doing sweat lodges, taking psychedelics. They were folks interested in living in harmony with life; that was the predominant interest. Of course, there were different levels of maturity and wisdom, yet a common interest.

At one point, I ran into a guy who was doing "mind clearing," which was an offshoot of an offshoot of Scientology.[61] When I met this guy, the usual story happened of trying to find holes in where he was coming from. But nothing I did threw him. He was clear; he passed my test. I got interested in his methods, trained with him, and learned this biofeedback approach.

Meanwhile, in New Zealand, we had acquired 1000 acres of land and started growing a big garden. But in the middle of the growing season, there was a freak frost and it wiped out our gardens. After a second year of that, I started realizing that the climate is changing. So my friend and mentor from the mind-clearing work and a few other friends bought a small piece of land in Maui, about eight acres, on which we started a community. Over the years, I built my house with my own hands, planted gardens and fruit trees, had relationships and kids. It was a very laid back lifestyle.

At the community, my friend and I were looking at where we could take this mind clearing system. We were seeking to develop a technology that could show people in as short a time as possible how consciousness functioned. We eventually developed a very beautiful technology laying out the mechanisms of the mind, how the whole thing functions.

Still, I found that even though I could see all this about how the mind functions, things would still get triggered in me. I would watch these programs getting touched in me and I didn't know how to stop them. I could see that even wanting to come out of it was a drama. But I could also see that what was going on in me troubled me. I kept asking, regardless of circumstance, "why does my system get so upset if my lady wants to sleep with someone else, or if my kids don't listen to me?" Same for the millions of things that trigger violent responses or deep hurt.

I started to turn my attention towards attention itself. The qual-

---

[61] Scientology was developed by L. Ron Hubbard. Their most basic process involved measuring the stress around different ideas and working with it until the reactivity was discharged.

ity of attention that we give each other makes a huge difference. In family constellation work, which is now quite popular, they recognize that the quality of attention that happens in a family system can end up with somebody getting sick or committing suicide. The Hawaiians were onto that ages ago with "Oponopono." In the Hawaiian tradition, when someone was sick they would gather everyone who was involved with the person and would talk about how they had been holding this person in their minds. Very often, they would have spontaneous healings when the judgments were unloaded.

Ultimately, all that we have to give each other is our attention and most of us are giving a quality of attention that is, once you get sensitive to it, quite painful. It's based on fear and it's based on separation, and it is actually quite painful.

When I started to realize that, I wondered how to bring that into view? It's not something we do consciously, it's something we do unconsciously. It happens with our kids, with our partners, with our parents, it happens everywhere. It's like a filter that we look through that hurts everybody and everything, including ourselves. We just don't see it; we don't understand why our lives are the messes that they are. I realized that I was onto something and started to play and work with it, doing groups where we played just with attention.

I began to set up groups where we were giving feedback to each other that was as clean and clear as possible. It was super powerful; major transformation was happening in those groups. We can often see what's going on in someone else more easily than we can see it in ourselves, so I was using that capacity. The difficulty with that is it's so rare that there is ever any clear feedback. When feedback comes, it usually comes with some wanting it to be different. It's very rare that anyone says, "This is what I notice, this is what I see," without judgment or interest to change or fix anything, just recognizing information.

So how did this evolve into your meeting Papaji?

I was doing these groups and it caught on. I was doing this work in New Zealand, Denmark and around the world. In the midst of it, a friend who had worked with me in the past, visited. I saw this great energetic shift had occurred in him and I was interested in whether that happened to him in my group or where? He told me that he'd met this man named Papaji.

I didn't have a high regard for gurus; I'd seen that there was this thing of putting them on a pedestal and I could see that wasn't a useful paradigm. But I was deeply interested in transformation, and the more I questioned my friend, the more I could see that what happened for him was the real thing. So I made a plan to go see Papaji as soon as I could with the schedule that I had.

I went to see Papaji in India, went to his home and right away he said, "You've done very well, you've visited all the heavenly and other Locas" (referring I thought to some bad trips on acid). Locas is an Indian term for "realms." He said, "I can see that you've visited all these different realms and you've come here to finish your work. Very good, now just bring your attention to awareness itself." It just hadn't occurred to me. There was no big bang or anything, it was just, "Ah, of course." I was always interested in attention, but I hadn't considered just resting attention on awareness. So he immediately spoke my language. I was there for many years and I never heard him speak that way to anyone else. He was so tuned in; he saw.

Prior to that you had never meditated or done any spiritual practices?

No, never. Meeting him confirmed for me that all spiritual practice, in a sense, is postponement. It aims at getting somewhere else, other than here. You can't get here by trying to be here; trying gets in the way, and we can only know Truth in this moment. It was very interesting being in his Presence. I'd never met someone that was that expansive; he was consciousness personified, as we all are, and in him it was lived. There was something working in him that had nothing to do with anything I'd ever seen before.

I was scheduled to continue my work in New Zealand after the India trip. But after three weeks in India, I realized, "it's over; whatever I've been doing, it's over. I don't know what I'm doing next, but what I was doing is over." I had commitments, but I didn't know what was next. In that line of work it was required to book centers a year in advance and I had taken deposits from people. There was someone who made his living organizing for me. So it didn't seem fair to just walk away. I was in a predicament, so I said to everyone, "I'll give you your money back and I'll take my loss and do whatever I can to stay in integrity." They said to me, "Look, the changes that have happened to us with you have been so profound that if you've found something deeper, you have to show us."

I didn't think I was ready. I didn't know what to say. It's such a different dimension; there's no doing, no process or anything. But people insisted and said they would come and that started the first meetings that I had. I felt so unprepared, but it happened and people got value.

My plan was to go back to India and just hang out with Papaji and let whatever had started there, deepen. When I got there, he called me into his room and said, "You've found the diamond and I want you to be available for people who have this interest." Suddenly, I was asked to do what I had been totally insecure to do because while I'd had the direct experience of what he'd shown me, I didn't have any method. Also, I could see that there were still patterns playing in me that were confused. It was a strange paradox. He said to me, "Don't worry about it. You're just a finger pointing at the moon. You know where the moon is; just point at the moon. If you look at any finger, no matter which finger; they're always crooked. You don't have to trouble about it; you just point at the moon." So I said okay, and I started this traveling around and being available.

At some point was there a breakthrough for you, a sudden waking up, no longer needing to work on it?

There is a paradox there. To me, waking up is the recognition that the entire universe is perceived through five senses and those five senses appear in what we call awareness. That awareness is always here and is usually overlooked. Some try measuring awareness by the experience that's being had, which is a confusion because awareness can't be measured by any experience. I can't measure this cup by what's in it. This cup can have piss or the finest whiskey or tea, but that doesn't tell me anything about the cup. Experience is not relevant to awareness; experience has more to do with the habits of attention than anything else. That's what I call waking up: the recognition that it's all appearing in awareness, in you, that awareness is your nature.

Waking up starts a huge process, but many people stop there. It starts a huge process where, resting as awareness, a fineness develops where you can start to notice subtleties that you didn't notice before. We are dealing with habits that have been going on for generations. Ordinarily, there's no context to see them from because you are looking through them. It's only when you are resting as awareness that you start to notice the lenses through which you look at life. They make it seem that life is a certain way. Even though nobody sees the world the same way you do, everybody believes that the way they see it is the way it actually is.

At some point, you recognize that your way of seeing is just a perspective, not actually the way it is. There are certain habits, automatic and unconscious, that are being looked through. All of those habits consume a lot of energy; they require a lot of juice for which we pay a very high price. Instead of experiencing the unity of everything, and love, there is an experience of fear and separation; so the price is high.

After the experience of waking up, there are still these habits?

Absolutely, and they actually predominate.

Would you say the habits, or ways of paying attention, that you noticed in yourself, could be tracked back to the Jewish culture in which you grew up?

I could see that the conditioning I received from my parents involved a bunch of confusions. For my parents, there was this collapsing of caring with worrying. Their way of showing that they cared for me was to worry about me. This pattern may be more prevalent in the Jewish tradition than in other traditions. Every time I'd see my parents: "When are you going to get married? When are you going to settle down? When are you going to get a real job?" It felt like they were just totally encroaching on my space. The way my system would respond was by fighting and getting defensive. At one point, it dawned on me that it was actually their way to tell me they loved me. Once that realization came, they could do all that stuff and it didn't bother me; all I heard was, "I love you." Then I could say to them, "Is this the most efficient way to tell me that you love me? Is this fun for you?" After a while, it all fell away.

As life went on, my parents started to see that there was something that was happening for people around me. I started to be recognized in certain circles of people. My parents came to our meetings and were really amazed at how peaceful they felt and what they saw happening in people. They could see that something was going on. It was a shift that started to happen, and they began relating to me in a different way. Instead of relating to me as the problem child that had not met their expectations, they started to appreciate me and my work. They even came to retreats of mine. It was quite a shift.

Would you describe your work either in the mind-clearing phase, or currently, as spiritual teaching or more as psychological and personal development work?

I don't have such a strong delineation. I've been interested in peace on Earth and finding a way to live together on this planet. I've wanted to incorporate the recognition that this whole appearance appears in awareness but doesn't exclude the humanness, doesn't exclude the life experience. If you look at Advaita, there is one branch of it that just goes, "Look, all of this is illusion, why trouble with it at all? Your lifetime is a finger snap in eternity; just live your life and don't get involved in any way; don't touch any of it; it's all *maya*[62], it's all illu-

---

[62] Maya in Indian religions, usually translated as "illusion," refers to the fact that we do not experience the environment itself but rather a projection of it, created by us.

sion." I understand that perspective, but if I have a toothache, I can say, "It's an illusion," or I can get it fixed. If there's a way that a pattern of relating going on between myself and my kids or partners is troublesome, then I'm interested in what it takes for that to come to peace.

So the tendency within the Advaita tradition embodied by you includes a concern or interest in what's happening in the world politically, socially and ecologically, and you feel a sense that organic living and more cooperative living is important?

Yes, yes.

Regarding that element of concern or interest, do you feel it could be coming from a lineage in the Jewish world associated with the commitment to social justice and peace?

The Jewish paradigm that I grew up with was that family was very important. You looked after your family and maybe then your tribe. But family was the main thing.

Many people associate revolutionary activity and social involvement as strong themes in the Jewish collective consciousness.

You can also look at the strong stream in the Jewish world which is the strong urge to be successful at any cost, a strong egoic orientation. No blame or shame about it; it's just that there is a price that gets paid, and it's strong.

Well, okay, there are good and bad tendencies coming through. Isn't it work then, to dissolve these habits in order to be free?

Yes, however I wouldn't say it's work, it's a privilege. All of these habits, can only function unconsciously. For example, if I asked you to give a quality of attention that is painful to everyone that you love for the rest of your life, you could never do that consciously. But unconsciously, it will go on. It's only when it becomes conscious that there is a chance that it will drop. So this is the paradox. How does it become conscious? It's the lens we're looking through all the time and you just don't see it.

So how does it become conscious?

That's where you start getting into words like grace or luck and so forth. My experience comes from when I'm hanging out with people: I'm just resting, not doing anything, not trying to get them to see anything, no agenda whatsoever, just resting. What I notice is that what's going on in them becomes very visible both to them and to me. In that process of just hanging out together, transformation happens. As seeing happens, including seeing the ways that systems function to literally hurt not only ourselves but everyone around us, something happens. But it's not a doing, it's not a work. It's a love affair with reality, with what is.

Does the waking up process take us beyond the physical realm? Some people say that there are beings in the universe that exist at other levels of reality?

There are. (laughter)

I wonder if it's possible to sit in the present moment and not expand perception and see these other realms of the universe.

Sitting in the Presence, one does start to expand just naturally. It's not a practice about getting anywhere, it's about the love of being, and in the love of being, it starts to reveal itself to itself. That's how I would describe it.

Religions use the word God. Does that word speak to you at all? What would you say about that from the way you experience reality?

(Long pause) To me, it seems more like this vast intelligence that's manifesting as everything. You start looking into an atom and there's basically nothing there, and yet everything is made up of that. So what is it that everything's made up of? We say it's made up of atoms, and you go into atoms and there's just positive and negative forces, not even anything there. So this whole manifestation, this entire universe and galaxies are made up of something, and what is that? What is that? We're sitting here and these bodies are made up of these trillions of cells, and these bodies themselves are not separate from the totality. They aren't separate for an instant, because without breathing they don't exist. As far as I can see, it takes the whole planet to draw the next breath. Not only this planet, because if Mars decided to take a hike, the next breath might not be forthcoming. There's a whole cosmic dance going on just for the next breath. You start to go into it and you see that there is something that we can't wrap our minds around. You can't say what it is that's the mother of everything. It shows up as everything and it's inconceivable. The mind would love to grab it and put it into a concept and make it into a something.

How does this relate to an individual's relationship with that mystery? Do you see any meaning to prayer?

The first thing that I would look at is: is there such a thing as individuality? Is there any separation? One difficulty is that we communicate with language and language turns living processes into nouns. We talk about a tree, but that tree is not separate from the sun, from the earth, from the rain; it's more appropriate to say, "treeing." If you put that tree into a big bag and sucked all the air out of it, would it still be a tree? Obviously not, it would be wood; it doesn't exist separately at any level. It's the same with your body. What we call our bodies don't exist separately from the totality at all.

There's a lot of confusion around what people even call mind. If there's no thought, there's no mind; mind is just thought. That's how I use the word. I've been in a room and I've watched a thought cross the room. Everyone thinks it's their thought, but it's really an energy traveling through the room. It's the same for a feeling—anger, fear or disgust—that will also travel through the room. Everyone thinks it's theirs. We live in this field of information that we call the universe. What we perceive through the five senses are just different wavelengths of what we could call information. What we call the universe is this field of information informing itself everywhere.

Ask yourself what percentage of your body are you aware of? Even when you're really paying close attention, are we aware of what's happening in our cells, or in our bloodstream? There's this whole vast capillary system; how much of that are we aware of? We are only aware of a minuscule part of it even if we're being very conscious of our body. What I am to you and what you are to me is an experience, not more. What your own body is to you is an experience. For example, how do you know you have a body?

I sense it.

Which means it's an experience. Your body is an experience, and the universe is an experience. Everything is only an experience appearing in awareness. But through our thinking it appears as an object. We tend to assemble the data in a way that depends on what we're looking for and what makes sense from our point of view. It's very different when you are in the recognition that I'm an experience to you, that you know me in your experience; you feel something, you sense something. When we are objectifying, instead of noticing the experience you are having, you project it outside and think it's existing outside of yourself. That's a habit of attention, a habit of focus that produces the sense of object, when in actuality it's all an experience to us.

Just recognize that I'm an experience to you. Feel me and you, whatever that experience is at this moment. Now, see where the experience of me ends and the experience of the universe begins. See where the experience of you starts and ends. When you do that, you start to see that the sense of separateness is a fabrication; it doesn't actually exist. It only exists from the perspective of object consciousness.

I wonder how this relates to something like driving a car and knowing not to try to drive through trees, recognizing them as separate objects. In your book, you quote Papaji saying, "I realized everything there is to realize; I realize there's nothing here; I realize it's all a dream; why does this world still appear to my eyes?" Isn't it important to honor that things do appear to arise to our eyes and to our hands, that solidity exists and appears at certain levels that are important to us?

Our eyes, if we have eyes, are our most predominant sense. We are used to looking at objects. But there's another possibility where your eyes kind of get soft and they become holes where the light comes in. If you look at a young baby's eyes, you see that they haven't learned that habit of focusing outward and you can look straight into them. Play with that for a moment and let your eyes be holes. Seeing still happens, but a very different feeling sense opens up. The interesting thing is that you can drive like that. You can drive perfectly like that, with the eyes just being soft. It's actually more relaxing.

There's a tension when energy is used to produce a sense of reality that's object based. But object-based reality is not the only reality, by any means. There's a way of being where you're resting as awareness and all the senses are operating, including the sense of body as an experience just appearing in awareness. In this way of being, there is a sense of the different energy flows of things. It's not perceived as so many different objects anymore, but as vibrational frequencies and intangibles that we can't describe with words. Functioning can happen quite well that way, but it's more like the way a martial arts person or a healer would interact with something.

To me it's not a question of right or wrong, or good or bad. To me, it's that this is the only moment that we have, this is it. We're not conditioned to receive this moment as "the beloved." I often say, "This is as God as it gets. It doesn't get more God than this." But the way we usually relate to it is, "God, you made a big mistake; this isn't what I signed up for; I wanted it different." There's a way that we relate to totality that's jaded: it's not alive, it's not fresh, it's not drinking of this divine manifestation. We look through small blinkers.

Do you see yourself as offering a new philosophy or doctrine?

I'm not telling you to see it this way. I'm inviting you to your own knowing. I'm not trying to give you another belief system, or put something else in your head. It's more about, let's just see what's really happening. Look at what happens when your eyes get soft, when you shift out of object consciousness to a more felt sense. The moment that happens, there's no one to argue with; it's your experience. I've just invited you to your own knowing. The word educate actually comes from the word educe, which is to draw out, not to put on top of.

You talked about forgiveness at one point in your book. About the heart breaking open, being willing to absorb the pain of everyone. It didn't sound like that was exactly the kind of experience you were either sitting or working with in your days with mind-clearing. What kind of experiences led you to this kind of breaking open?

In the recognition that the whole universe is an experience to you, you are literally feeling what's going on in Japan, what's going on in Afghanistan, what's going on in Iraq. You're feeling everyone and everything in this moment. But what usually happens is that our system has a means of trying to shut out certain information. It's a protection mechanism because we don't want to be overwhelmed.

Isn't that necessary?

The awareness is ever open. Awareness is the whole shebang, all-time, all space, all matter is appearing in awareness. So awareness is never not available to that experience. But we're dealing with awareness and we are dealing with the capacity of the human nervous system. So for example, if the human nervous system has been severely traumatized, it doesn't have the capacity to meet the world easily. It needs baby steps to develop that capacity to meet this moment. So there's this paradox between awareness and this restriction of totality that shows up as this body. We honor where it finds itself.

What do you see as the causes of these restrictions or limitations in our ability to open?

We can ask where the condition of the body/mind comes from. You could say it comes from at least as early as conception. It's even earlier than that when you consider that all the eggs in your mother's body are formed while she was in the body of her mother.

Would you say that these conditions exist even prior to that, that there are non-physical aspects to us before birth, what some call the soul?

I would just say that this field that gets generated by the quality of attention that's going on, it's an intangible that you can't really put words to. It is powerful enough that it can actually produce illness or depression or suicide. Beliefs about reincarnation and such are means of trying to describe something that's not really describable. There's only one thing here; there's only one here.

To use the analogy of the ocean: a wave appears on that ocean, so we give that rising up the name wave. Then the wave crashes back into the ocean, but it never left the ocean to begin with; it's an expression of the ocean and it never left the ocean. Then another wave comes along; can we say that wave is a reincarnation of the previous wave? It's just the ocean expressing itself. Life is expressing itself from that substrate that we were talking about.

It's all in that field of information. Once the senses and the mind start getting quiet enough and you start tuning into that field of information, you see how people who are able to access that field can speak about things very accurately. It seems amazing until your own mind starts to quiet down and you see that it's pretty natural. When attention isn't fixated on perspectives, the information starts to come in. So, in my view, reincarnation is a way of trying to describe this process that's going on so that it makes sense to our minds. Once you start getting into time, and you look at what Einstein said about time, you start to see that the idea of linear time is just one particular perspective. Once you get into the quantum world the whole lot is out the window.

Yet, we have been talking about the story of your life as a child, a teenager and so on through time.

Whenever I or anyone tells their life story, it changes. Memory is just pictures and the pictures keep changing. I have a joke regarding the past: "The past isn't what it used to be." (laughter)

If I ask you to describe this moment, given that it's changing every second, how fast would you have to speak to describe this moment? It's an impossibility. You can't actually describe this moment. Yet we think we can describe what happened in the past. On a certain level, we can describe broad strokes that may make some sense or resonate in some way. But we could just as soon describe a completely different perspective of it. You see an old couple that have been together 40 years and they're talking about what happened 20 years ago. One says, "it happened this way," and the other, "no, that's not what happened."

I sit in a room with a few hundred people and I say, "Can anyone describe this moment?" No. How many senses of reality are there in the room at the moment? Everyone looks around and they go, "there's a whole bunch." Now who has the right one? Everyone starts laughing. They see that it's just perspective; it has nothing to do with what's actually going on. It's just thoughts that may seem meaningful or not. Drop a little acid, and you see that whatever perspective you had is suddenly vastly different. (laughter)

If you were to speak to the larger collective of the Jewish people, what would you say?

Look deeply and see what any identification does. Don't believe anybody, look for yourself, don't listen to anybody. Look very carefully at what the identification, including all the different strands of it, brings you in the moment. Does it bring a sense of kinship and oneness with everything? Does it bring a sense of separation? What does looking through that lens do? If you put on purple sunglasses, the world looks purple. What does looking through that identification of, I am Jewish, I'm black, or I'm anything, do?

There is a funny thing about people who have grown up white: they don't usually look through the perspective of, "I'm white." People with black skin grow up with the perspective that, "I'm black" (except if they're born in Africa). In an interesting study, they took a bunch of people and just before they took a test, had them answer on a form whether they are black or white. Black people, just with that action messing with their nervous system, did poorer on the test than if they hadn't been asked to answer that question. That was interesting for me to see. This relates to what identification does to us.

We have an opportunity here to meet this moment. In my language, I say we only have this moment; we never have more than that. There's two possibilities that I can see to meet this moment: we meet this moment with "ow" or with "wow." We've been conditioned to meet the moment with "ow." We take it for normal and as long as it's not too "ow," as long as it's an "ow" that we're used to, we don't complain too much. But the possibility is to meet the moment as a "wow," to truly meet it as if you suddenly came face to face with the beloved. Then, every cell in your system would respond to this moment as WOW!

Look at any identification with anything to see what it brings. See if there is any advantage to it; see for yourself; don't believe anyone else. There's an old saying: more people have been killed in the name of religion than anything else on the planet. I'd say it's pretty true. Same goes for, I'm Russian, I'm Chinese, or whatever belief systems. I once defined a belief as an idea that's taken to be true, that has a strong emotional conviction, and that we are willing to kill or die for. I'm American or I'm Jewish and then there's the Palestinians or whatever. It doesn't take much for us to go very far with it.

Does it have any meaning at all that there was an entry into this world into the particular collective identification of the Jewish people?

To the mind it would seem that way. The mind is very concerned with meaning. (laughter)

Thank you.

Victoria Amy Austin
SOTO ZEN BUDDHIST PRIEST

"My Hebrew name is Malkah. My Dharma name is Shosan Gigen, which means, Sunlight Mountain, Virtue Profound.

When I was 19, I was in a car accident and had a near death experience. Something happened that nothing had prepared me for. My mind opened up. When I recovered physically, I had to find out what that experience was, and who taught about it. It turned out to be a meditative spiritual awakening, and Zen masters and yogis taught about it.

While I grew up with the sense of the preciousness of human life, I had very few tools to deeply experience or enjoy life. The physical and physiological legacy of centuries of persecution was inscribed on my bones. Yoga and meditation practice transmuted the poison of my post-traumatic upbringing, maturing and developing the possibility of compassion and human enjoyment.

You've told me that you left home psychologically when you were very young to get away from the pain in your family home. You worked in a hospital as a teenager and enrolled in classes at Columbia in the Sixties. I imagine you were a little younger than most of the students at Columbia when all the action was going on?

I was a lot younger. I was in a program where you could go to Columbia and study science and physical chemistry as a high school student. So that's what I did.

What was your relationship to the rebellion and protests that were going on? Were you supportive or did you keep a distance?

I was totally intrigued, but scared by the shouting because of my post-traumatically sensitized family upbringing. The thought of riots was too extreme. On the other hand, I loved the idea of us students doing what we felt was right. I didn't see how the establishment was necessary, though I was put off by anarchy,

So you were really a child of the Sixties and somewhat swept up in it?

Yes. I hitchhiked out to California in 1975. I'd been busy putting myself through school before that. The night we finished school, some friends were sitting around asking, "What do you wanna do?" Someone said, "Let's hitchhike to California." So, we did.

Let's come back a little bit to an earlier time when you were living with your family as a child.

My sisters and I grew up completely identified with Judaism, particularly the suffering of the Holocaust. We all went to Hebrew school, and were bat mitzvah in the local Conservative community, though we identified as European rather than American Jews.

Were all of your relationships essentially with the Jewish community, Jewish people, Jewish youth?

Not at all. My family and many of my friends were Jewish. But my best friend was from a non- Jewish Czech family with immigrant parents, and I felt very close to her. We met at the school bus stop the first day of first grade and stayed friends. I was not allowed to go to her church; my parents taught us that something bad would happen if we did, maybe that God would punish us.

I also had friends whom I deliberately chose for their diversity. I was curious about the world and didn't want to live my life in a pre-defined, tiny, post-traumatic, Holocaust box out of inherited fear.

Were you given the view that Jews were the good people and you had to worry about other kinds of people?

My fear came from our family legacy of the European view. In the Vienna of my parents, Jews were a different race. Because of that, I became interested in knowing people of many races. Though my parents identified as white, our life was lived in the shadow of being racially different, and being unwanted. We would hear, "Are they Jewish? Is he Jewish? Is she Jewish?" both from Jews and non-Jews. When we were growing up there was a lot of anti-Semitism.

My best friend's boyfriend told her not to be my friend because I was Jewish. One of my biggest shocks as a teenager was when she stopped being close with me.

At what point in your life did you become aware of wanting to come out of what you call the post-traumatic mindset or box?

I'd say very early. I resonate with Maxine Hong Kingston's description of second-generation life in *The Woman Warrior: Memoirs of a Girlhood Among Ghosts.* She describes the cultural divide between her life at home and on the street. I felt that very strongly as a child. I also felt a real cultural divide between European refugee Jews and

American Conservative Jews, people I described to myself as privileged Jews who had never personally experienced what my family had experienced.

You've written that yoga and meditation helped you to transmute some of these fear imprints, and you came to realize that you didn't need to hold them anymore.

It is not that meditation and yoga get rid of the fear imprints. It's not a matter of pushing them away. It's about recognizing how my personality was formed with fear at the bottom, and developing a deep intention to develop a maturity that is even greater than the fear. We see this, for example, in mature Jewish humor, which acknowledges suffering and often plays with the idea of being a victim. This kind of humor acknowledges and transcends suffering. It is human, transcendent, and helpful for everybody. In short, I didn't want to live my whole life in a state of compensation for suffering, but rather to develop a personality that was big enough to hold it.

If you consider the difference between many of the Holocaust victims and, say, Victor Frankl, that was the maturation I wanted to build. I wanted to be like him. It wasn't just about intellectual insight, but about developing a sense of my body, a way of speaking, and an emotional life—a mind and a heart big enough to include my whole life.

So then, what happens to the suffering?

I would say it becomes composted and allows people to bloom in a different way.

It was through yoga and meditation that you did this composting?

Well, I don't say that I did it, but rather that the practices build maturity using the building blocks we already have. This is how we are. These practices are the human tools that allow integration to occur in a very deep way, at a cellular level. So it's not just pasted on or partial.

Would you say there remains for you a kind of deeper heart connection, a feeling of friendliness or identification with people that are Jewish, more than to non-Jewish people?

Well, Jewish people are family. For instance, you and I could be related. Though I don't know when your family came to America, chances are that we are related. We have a very small pool of people that have known each other for thousands of years. But at this point in the world, we have to be human first. We don't throw away who we are, but if we're not human first then humanity isn't really going to survive. I personally don't want to be the type of person who, when somebody else's family or tribe is threatened, doesn't care, that just stays in my own world.

The first time I was in Vienna to look at my family history was in the 60s. When we were there, we found the people who turned in my father's parents to the Nazis and it was shocking. Later, in the 90s, my sisters and I went to Austria and Italy and we found out about how it might have happened that these people turned in my grandparents after first hiding them. The betrayal occurred at the moment the Nazis came back over the Brenner Pass after an absence of years. I had to ask myself, what would I have done? What would I do if I were hiding someone and my family suddenly was threatened with death if I did not give up those people? Would I choose the refugees, or my family first?

I reluctantly had to answer, "I don't know." I could not know what I would do. But I can't condemn those people anymore. I can think they might have been weak. But I can't categorize them as bad people. I can't say they are not of my human family, not of me. So if Jewish identity means that other people are not of my tribe, I can't go there. But if Jewish identity is about history and family and what makes us spiritually and tribally unique, then I can go there. If it is about freedom then I can go there.

How does this relate to Israel and your feelings about it?

Same thing with Israel. If it's about hurting and killing Palestinians,

I can't go there. If it's about a cultural homeland and spiritual refuge, I can go there. By culture, I don't just mean some flavor, I mean a way of development, a way of life.

When did you begin to discover the tools of yoga and meditation that allow the processing to happen?

I would say in the Sixties when I was a teenager in high school. I was exploring yoga and meditation, but I didn't understand what it really was until much later, until the research I did after the car accident.

Would you talk about the car accident? You've described it elsewhere as a waking up experience?

I can try (takes a long pause). I was eighteen. I was in the car, it was dark, and there was sleet. My car was an older one. At a stop sign, when I tried to go again, the car engine cut out. The car was rolling with the engine unengaged. Because it was slippery, I didn't have much control. Another car hit mine. It was just lights and an impact. I became airborne and time stopped. I became aware that there was something at the side which turned out to be a telephone pole. I thought, "This is it," meaning this was the last moment of my life. It turned out, of course, that it wasn't; it was a pretty minor car accident. But the moment seemed to last a really, really long time.

Suddenly, it was as if the universe turned itself around and looked at itself through me. Not through the "thing" of me, or through the person of me, but through the structure of me. I could see exactly how I had come to be, exactly how I was made. I could see how small that structure was, how untrue, how false. Not that it was a lie—just that it was tiny in relation to how everything really is. It was a deeply, deeply embarrassing moment. Though it wasn't as if there was a me feeling the embarrassment, there was a sense of deep shame. At the same time, it was as if the whole universe held me with a giant warm smile and loving arms. It became clear that I had a choice. I could accept and jump in, or I could turn away.

Jumping into the warm smile?

Into HOW IT WAS. Yes, something happened. There was the Light, the sense of awe, all that was happening. But that wasn't the most important thing. This other part is what I remember as most important, but these words cannot do the experience justice.

I was given the choice to jump in or turn away, and I responded, "What the hell, I'm dead." So I jumped in. The next thing I remember was that there was something like a gray pattern above me. Then I realized that it was cold; then I realized it was wet; then I realized it was sleet falling on me, and that I was lying on the pavement looking up. My first words were, "Oh, shit." This was because I realized that I was going to have to follow through. There was nothing about my life that had built me that way, that I could follow through on such an experience. My personality structure was too little.

What did that mean, to follow through? Follow through with what?

The thought was, "I have to follow through." Just those words. At the time I had no further thoughts about what that meant; just, "Oh, shit, I'm alive. Now I have to follow through."

Back at school, I made the mistake of talking to the school counselor about this experience without knowing how to talk about it. Her response was to prescribe enormously high doses of Valium. At one point, I was lying in a dark room in a Valium state and said to myself, "This is ridiculous." I flushed the Valium and went through withdrawal.

When I was well enough to move again, I immediately went to the library and also started talking to my friends about what had happened to me. I needed to know what my experience was and who teaches about it? The answer was, "Zen people" and "yogis" teach about it. I thought, "Oh, no. I can't, I just can't!" That would be too far out, too strange, too disgusting, too weird for this Jewish-American princess to do. I had a prejudice about incense, chanting, and what I thought of as smarmy or precious. Then I had the thought, "I know! I don't have to do it. Instead, I'll just be friendly to everyone." I bargained with my conscience: "I'll just be friendly to everyone and then I don't have to do it, OK?"

So I vowed to be friendly. However, immediately after making my vow, I discovered my new toothpaste had been used by someone else, and worse, that they had squeezed it from the middle. There was toothpaste all over the bathroom counter. An enormous, spontaneous feeling of pure hatred arose in me. Then I realized, "Uh-oh, this friendliness vow is not going to work. I'm not a friendly person."

My next plan was to "just sit Zazen." I'd learn how to do it and just sit in my room behind a closed door so no one would ever know. This attempt lasted for about two days. I couldn't do it by myself. Next, I decided to go to a class, but just leave right after it. I went on and on in this way. I backed into it for years.

For years?

Yes. But the fact is, once such an experience happens, you can't undo it, minimize it or push it away; it has already occurred. The only way through it is to fulfill it. That's what I had to do, despite the many missteps and resistances that presented themselves along the way.

After the experience with the counselor, I made a vow to myself to be silent about the experience for twenty years. I decided to practice and try to incorporate what had happened before speaking about it again. The next time I spoke about it was in 1991.

You didn't talk about which part?

The whole experience. I simply practiced with it. After twenty years, talking about it was really different.

That was how I started to practice. My father had died in 1974. If he had been alive, I wouldn't have been able to take up a formal practice. I think it would have killed him. Everyone in my family was very upset.

They were upset that you were going to a Zen center?

Yes.

Were there other things that you did? Did you dress differently or bring Buddhist items home?

I cut my hair short, practiced voluntary simplicity, and wore simple clothing. I had donated my entire business wardrobe to Goodwill. I was dating a Christian.

What was worse, being into Zen meditation or dating a Christian?

I think it was dating a Christian.

I would think so. (both laughing)

But as far as my family was concerned, it was all bad. In 1977 my mother had me deprogrammed.

What did that mean? Was it a professional deprogrammer?

Yes. She had taken out a contract on me with a professional deprogrammer. My sister alerted me, which gave me time to respond. I called my mother to say, "No, you don't have to do this. You can save yourself the price. I'll do it voluntarily. If you call off the contract, I will do it for you.'"

How old were you at this point?

Twenty four.

Could they legally do this?

They certainly felt they could. I believe that this was before it became illegal to do such things.

It was a very long session, and very intense. But the deprogramming itself became a very interesting turning point in my practice.

The deprogrammer's office was all set up with a big chair for him and a little chair for me. There was a bright light focused on me. It was very intimidating. The door was locked and he had the power to commit me.

He started with questions that were markedly judgmental. He led with the tragedy of Jewish youth leaving and other such guilt-inducers. After a few hours of this, I was getting more and more uneasy. My early trust issues already made any confrontation into a major event for me. This was worse, with me in a small, exposed chair and my confronter in a big chair behind a massive desk. I was scared.

At a certain point I got very anxious, sweaty and cold. I started thinking about all the possible consequences. In my panic, I started looking around the room for relief. I saw that he had some beautiful Jewish objects, carefully tended and displayed. I said, "You've been asking me questions for a long time now. Can I ask you something?" He said, "Yes." I said, "It isn't often that I get to speak with someone who practices Judaism so clearly and thoroughly. Do you remember a moment at which you really began to practice, or did you always practice like this?"

At the time I was preparing to receive the Buddhist precepts and my question arose from truly wondering; is there a moment at which you really begin to practice, when you really take something on? He stopped completely. There was a silence, and then he told me his story. He told me that he had gone through the entire Jewish educational system, through Yeshiva and further as an adult as well. He said that he had gone through all his studies by rote. He didn't know that he was going through it by rote, even though he was.

One day, he was reading in a commentary, "You shall guard them and keep them and in keeping them, the treasure store shall be revealed." He said that the moment he read that sentence something happened, that God spoke directly to him. That was the moment that he really began to practice. Then he looked at me and said, "All that time, I guarded and kept them. All that time, I guarded and kept them and only then was the treasure store revealed!" It was like that.

I asked him, "Was it that all the time that you kept them, you just kept them, and then you got this perk of the treasure store being revealed? Or, was guarding them and keeping them itself the treasure store that was being revealed?" He stopped again, and we started having a real conversation. After a bit, he got up, unlocked the door and went out into the hallway where my mother was sitting. I heard him say, "She's sane." He asked her if she was willing to schedule some sessions about letting go.

That was the deprogramming.

It seems you deprogrammed the deprogrammer. Very powerful!

It was. But I think he deprogrammed me too.

Did you find that during it you were helped by remembering some of the Zen practices that you had begun to study?

No, I didn't remember any of it, I was too scared. (laughs)

I think what saved me was my intention. It was as if that first experience was pulling me towards itself somehow. The effective part of my response wasn't really conscious. My fear, not my practice, was at the top of my mind. But once something like my accident experience happens there is an unshakeable sense of orientation. It's like being outside and knowing what direction the sun is in. I didn't have to do anything. The impact of what had happened before was already changing me.

You proved to your deprogrammer that you were sane. Did your family then make the adjustment to accepting your path?

Not my whole family, only my twin sister. Different parts of the family declared me dead, disowned me, or stopped speaking to me. Even after the deprogramming it took about fifteen years for my mother to be able to speak with me. Many family members never spoke with me for the rest of their lives. Some spoke with me only after they had become really old and needed help. Then, somehow my meditation and yoga practice turned me into the person in the family they could most easily trust for help. Go figure.

It was all so painful. I can't even describe how painful it was. But, as I've said, once an experience like that has happened, you can't put yourself back into the box. You have to take care of it; it's not possible to ignore it.

That box that you came out of, that was the fear-based way of relating to reality. Did the box also include the Jewish religion or Jewish identity? Were you still a Jew after this? Is it a meaningful for you to say, "I am a Jew'?"

Yes, it is.

So, what is that for you now?

An example is that when I used to go and take care of my mother every few weeks in New York, I took her to services. That was when she was in earlier stages of Alzheimers. I just came back from Vienna, where I spent a few days with seven family members from four countries, researching what happened to our relatives in the Holocaust. Things like that.

I understand that you have an interest in your ancestry and family history. But more specifically, how it is for you? What does it mean to now say you're Jewish?

I think that the most fundamentally Jewish statement is when they say of the ancient people, "He or she walked with God." That is probably the most Jewish statement there is. I'm not Jewish to part of my family because I don't practice Judaism in a formal way. That's where all the disowning and declaring dead comes in; if you're not practicing in a formal way, you're dead.

You see the essence of Judaism as "walking with God" and you still see yourself in that tradition?

I think so. Jews say, "God and self, Know God and know self." Buddhism says, "No God, No Self." If you say "God" or if you say "Self," actual God and actual Self is not described or named by those words. If you say "no God" or "no Self," actual no idea of God and no idea of Self is not named by those words either. I just have to learn to live with the ambiguity of the form of my life and not get too concerned about labeling myself one thing or another. That way lies madness, or maybe not madness but all sorts of problems.

Do you retain any of the forms of Jewish practice such as the holidays, other than when you are with your mother?

Sure. Of course, I don't necessarily do them in a tribal way so that's a problem for my family. The last time I was in India was during Rosh Hashanah. There was a temple in Poona. An Israeli student and I attended together. It was very interesting because the men were all downstairs and the women were all upstairs, just like Brooklyn where some of my cousins lived when I was growing up. However, in India, some of the men were dressed Indian-style and some of them were dressed in European Hasidic garb. The women were in saris and gold. The Israeli with me was translating from Biblical Hebrew into teenage English: "Go God, you rule! You rock, God! Go!" We went downstairs for a post-Rosh Hashanah tea. Indian food was served. As I ate, one Indian woman turned to me and said in Marathi, "You're not eating! You're nothing but skin and bones! Come on, eat." (laughter)

These were Indian Jews?

Yes, Indian Maharashtrian Jews.

It seems like this was a very unique situation where you participated in a Jewish ceremony because of being in India.

But this kind of thing happens all over. That's what I'm saying. Am I or aren't I? You know? I don't know...

Have you had the experience of meeting up with any of the Jewish Renewal rabbis, or any of the people in the new forms of Judaism that have brought the feminine and meditation back into the focus of Jewish practice?

I knew Allen Lew before he died. He was a rabbi in San Francisco, not part of Jewish Renewal exactly. He was in the Conservative denomination, and a very interesting person.

I understand that he was very steeped in Eastern meditation, had a spiritual vision or revelation which caused him to decide to return to the Jewish religious path and become a rabbi. Did anything like that ever occur to you, something like, "Maybe I could do this within Judaism, Maybe it has the same essential truth in it and I could do this within the Jewish form?"

It wasn't the same for me. It wasn't like that. I read a lot of Jewish texts and I met a lot of other Jews. It didn't really strike me in the same way. The simplicity of the non-verbal meditation form was really what did it for me. The discursive study and analysis in Judaism played right into my habits. I couldn't get out of my habits of thought by using my intellect. My intellect was too strong. Though it did occur to me, it didn't strike me as a path for me when I explored it.

Do you feel as though there is any essential difference between the path that you've chosen, of Zen and yoga, and what you think of as Judaism?

Essentially, I think that they have the same aim. But, of course, there are differences. There aren't enough hours in the day to seriously practice the specifics of two religions. This is why my family was so disturbed by my Buddhist practice, and why several family members declared me dead in accord with the ancient practice of our tradition.

An adult has to be able to discern what is most necessary to heed the still, small voice within—and then to follow it. It's my understanding that in the Jewish tradition, when there is an apparent conflict between the law or tradition and necessity, health or conscience, that the voice of conscience is most important to follow. That is one of the spiritual definitions of an adult. We need to know that it is easy to delude ourselves about need and conscience, and to be willing to look deeply into both mind and heart.

Your choice led you to Zen and Iyengar yoga. Can you share how you became in involved with yoga?

In the first few years of Zen practice, I had a lot of physical difficulty with meditation. I was very restless and resistant and I didn't know how to be still. I didn't know how to settle with my legacy of suffering. So I would sit with too much force, suffer more, and then have to deal with the results. I knew that meditation was supposed to relieve suffering, but I realized I would have to go deeply into yoga practice to understand how meditation was supposed to work.

In 1983 I quit the monastery and came back to San Francisco to be trained as a yoga teacher. I had already taken some Iyengar yoga classes in the 70s after B.K.S. Iyengar came to the United States. I chose Iyengar yoga because it draws a link between physical actions and contemplation in a very specific way.

Are you involved with any kind of social action work on any particular issues?

Of course I've been involved in social projects. I taught meditation and yoga in the jails for a while. I worked with some interfaith groups against torture, and some for immigration reform.

Would you say that your way of practicing or experiencing and teaching Zen and yoga are influenced in some way by some aspect of your Jewishness? Is there some aspect of the transmission that you received as a Jew that is with you now?

Yes, certainly. There is the practical experience of suffering and also the emphasis on the personal relationship with the infinite. There is the idea of the sacredness of each everyday activity, the sacredness of nourishment and rest, the dedication to ethical principles as something to be lived. There are just so many things.

Do you feel you wouldn't have found those in the Eastern practices without your Jewish background?

I have no idea.

Coming back to the issue of social action; in the Jewish tradition we have tikkun olam (to heal the world). Is there something similar in the Zen world?

The whole point of Zen is that you don't practice just for yourself, you practice for the benefit of all beings. Benefit means healing. That's the point. I think of Buddhism as a collection of human practices that's not in conflict with religion. Buddhism and yoga both are collections of human practices that are about integrating all levels of ourselves, from the cell to the self and to the social universe too.

I'm sure the parts of Buddhism that I pick up on and can relate to relate to my conditioning and my early religious experience. I think that notions like tikkun, that's a place that the Eastern traditions have something to learn from Jewish practice.

Is it fair to say that you are one of those who are bringing that to the Buddhist world?

Yes, but especially by people like Alan Senauke,[63] who was also at Columbia. Alan is my dharma brother. That means that he's like a brother to me.

Are you in the same order or lineage of Zen?

Yes, Soto Zen, in the lineage of Shunryu Suzuki Roshi. Alan is my brother in that lineage. This means that we received transmission from the same teacher, Sojun Mel Weitsman. One of his parents also was Jewish.

Related to this question, I want to talk a little bit about Mel, Alan's and my teacher. In our lineage, you choose your transmission teacher. The teacher also has a choice about which students they want to receive the transmission. I picked Mel because he is a craftsman, a craftsman of life. One of my key experiences with Mel was watching him make soup. He would put in one ingredient, then taste, and then he would put in something else, then taste again. It seems like a simple story, right? But it is simple and deep. It comes from our life as Jews, and as humans.

Paying attention and sensing what is going on?

Yes, as a sacred activity, with awareness of the big picture when making an everyday soup. Mel gardens in the same way. He can make anything grow, including people.

I once got the chance to make such a soup. There was a woman who was my student, and around her 60th birthday her husband found her on the floor of their bathroom. She was then diagnosed with an aggressive adult-onset leukemia.

In her second month of very intense chemotherapy in the hospital, she started having immune system problems and a lot of physical pain. She hadn't eaten for a week and a half. During one of my daily visits, she said, "Vicky, I think I could eat something if it was chicken

---

[63] Hozan Alan Senauke is a Soto Zen priest, folk musician and poet, and serves as Vice Abbot of the Berkeley Zen Center in Berkeley, California. He is a former Executive Director of the Buddhist Peace Fellowship.

soup and if you made it." I went to the store, bought the chicken, brought it home, and here I was holding up this chicken. I was looking at it and I didn't know what to do. I'd been a vegetarian since I was seventeen and hadn't cooked meat in all that time.

Then a deep Jewish memory took over and I found myself making soup. A voice from the sky was saying, "Take out the paper, take out the paper." (laughs) So I did it, cut up the chicken and put it in the pot. My neighbors smelled the soup cooking. Since they knew I was a vegetarian they knocked on the door to ask what was happening. They started bringing ingredients—onions, garlic, stock, a carrot, celery, potatoes, fresh dill. Every neighbor brought something. I ended up with about a gallon of really, really excellent chicken soup. I strained it and gave all the chicken and vegetables to those neighbors. I brought the soup to my friend in the hospital. That's what she lived on for the last two weeks of her life.

This is tikkun olam, and it is also Buddhist practice. It's a part of my Buddhist practice and it comes very literally from my lineage. I don't know how to say it better than that, really. I wouldn't parse it out—this part of me is Jewish and this part is Buddhist, or this came from this or that. It's one picture, one package.

I think of myself in various ways: as a world citizen, a Jew, a Buddhist, a yogi, an Ivy League graduate, a woman, a Baby Boomer, and so on. In my life, all these have operated as tribes at one time or another. Can I allow myself to be a yogi without thinking less of the world of tai chi?

Some of the teachers I've spoken with make a distinction between spiritual awakening and human maturation. The idea is that it's possible to spiritually awaken in the sense of having expansive, cosmic states of consciousness, even to abide in them to some extent, but not be mature in the ways that human beings can develop.

Sure, you can be a jerk.

Yes, you can be a jerk. On the other side, you can develop a quality

of human maturity without a lot of spiritual practice and awareness of higher states of consciousness.

Sure, you can be a mensch without any conscious spiritual understanding.

Do you feel the emphasis of one or the other is more located in the Jewish or Buddhist paths?

Well I don't see it that way. I think you could be Jewish or Buddhist, be either spiritually awake or not, be humanly mature or immature. I think the whole range is possible in each.

Thank you.

Krishna Das
KIRTAN WALLAH (CHANT MASTER)

I was gazing at all of the beauty in the world. Can you imagine all of the beauty in the world condensed and shining brilliantly in one person? When we fall in love with someone, that's what we're seeing—all of the love in our own being is projected onto the screen of the loved one. Maharaj-ji merged with Infinite Love, so when his other devotees and I looked at him, we were looking directly into the light coming from the projector, rather than what was being shown on the screen. Then there was the feeling of being at home, so totally at home. My heart was at ease with itself.
- From *Chants of a Lifetime* by Krishna Das

What is your religion?

I never think about that. I don't think about religion much.

Would you say that you are on a spiritual path that doesn't have a name?

I don't know if it has a name. My guru was Hindu, but he never made us Hindus. We never were initiated in anything. He said to us, "Sub Ik" (it's all One), all paths lead to the same goal, all One. So at that point, I stopped thinking about it. That was 40 years ago. To try to get me to think about it now is going to be interesting.

But really, my experience with him is what my whole life revolves around. In him I found everything that I want and could ever want. He was the embodiment of the whole universe. In that Presence, which is not attached to his physical body, was the essence of everything I longed for. I had no questions after that. I had no doubts about what this is about, where I'm going. My only doubt is if I can get there myself, if I have the strength to walk on the path.

What is the path? How do you practice?

The path to me is: continually facing, moment-to-moment, day-by-day, life as it shows up in your awareness; trying to be kind to yourself and others; being patient with yourself and others; being compassionate with yourself and others; and trying not to use other people to serve your own selfish desires. In the meantime, on the other side, is to try to do some of what they call in India, Bhajan, which means remembering.

Maharaj-ji said, "Serve people and remember God." So that's what my life has morphed into, regardless of anything I might have thought it should have been or could have been or even wanted it to be. Looking at it from the outside, you could say that I serve people by going around and chanting, chanting in the remembrance of the Names of God. That is what they say in India is the practice of Bhajan.

So it's kind of mixed together for me, the internal moving practice, and the external moving and looking practice.

> *It is said that everything is contained within the sound of the Names. By repeating the Names as wholeheartedly as we can, anything and everything we need to know will be revealed from within; anything and everything that needs to happen will happen without having to think about it or understand it intellectually. All of the Names come from the same Source. By repeating these Names, we're directly invoking the indwelling Presence in our own hearts.*
> From *Chants of a Lifetime*

What does religion have to do with spirituality? I don't think it has anything to do with it. It just seems to separate people and cultivate hatred and anger and make money and power. Not that there aren't religious people who are saintly, but they seem to be the exception. The percentage is very low. Mostly it's keeping a lid on things and carrying on cultural tradition. It doesn't seem to have anything in it but worldly concerns; it's not related to removing the causes of suffering.

For the most part, I think of religion as a crock of shit. It's only been used to hurt people and destroy people and to serve the power desires of those people who find themselves in power. When I read about the lives of Saints from all religions, they are all the same life. The Baal Shem Tov is the same life as any one of the Indian Saints. You can read how they treated people, how they looked at people, what they thought of people, and you see the same thing. There are stories about the Baal Shem that say, "we knew he worked with the Goyim, but he never talked about it." He presented a Jewish appearance to the Jews that he worked with, but he was a Saint in the world for all people. He said things that were interpreted in certain ways that formed into an orthodoxy. Fine, that's what always happens. But it looks to me that he was also, just from his presence on Earth, a great blessing for all humans. That's the same for all the Saints: all the Indian, Sufi, Buddhist, Christian or whatever Saints, They are all the same and when they are in the room together, they all love each other.

The Saints often have a particular practice or teach within the form of a particular religion, and their followers all tend to use the particular practices or prayers and garments associated with those religions. Yet they themselves have a more universal acceptance of all forms or ways. Would you say that's how you see your path or tradition?

They call it skillful means in Buddhism. Maharaj-ji talked to us about Jesus. He said amazing things about Jesus whom I had never had any feeling for previous to that. He told us we should meditate like Christ. " What do you mean? How do you meditate like him?" we asked. He said, "He lost himself in love." What does that have to do with the Pope? Nothing. Nothing at all to do with all the murder and people slaughtering others in the name of Jesus.

Maharaj-ji pointed us towards the real Jesus. "He lost himself in love." A Jewish boy who made good, and they made crap out of it later. Ten seconds after a Saint is gone, it's over essentially, unless you have a direct connection to that Saint or you get an inner connection later, which is grace. But if you try to go through the establishment or religious form of what he left behind, forget it. That's for the people who don't know anything, who have no hope. People who know the Koran have told me it's about peace. It's not about slaughtering people in the name of this one or that one.

So this is human nature, this is the dark ages, this is what people do. Maharaj-ji talked to all people. He was born in India, but his spirit was completely universal, He didn't think Hinduism was better than any other religion.

He noticed the notebook in which I wrote down quotes and stories from holy books. He took it and started going through the pages. There were quotes from many different traditions: Hindu, Christian, Sufi, Buddhist. He stopped on one page and asked, "What's this?" I got very embarrassed. It was a hymn from the Tibetan Buddhist tradition, the Song of Mahamudra ... and represents the union between a seeker and the universe. Buddhists don't believe in "God," and here I was in a temple dedicated to Hanuman, the monkey god. I felt like I'd gotten caught with my finger in the spiritual pie or something. I sheepishly said, "It's Buddhist."

Maharaj-ji said, "Translate it for me." So Gurudatt, who spoke perfect English, translated the first few verses. Maharaj-ji stopped him and said, "Thik"(right, correct). I couldn't believe it!

He kept leafing through the pages and came upon a picture of himself. He asked, "Who is this?"

"Maharaj-ji, it's you."

"Nahin (no). It's Buddha!" Then he closed the book and gave it back to me.

From Chants of a Lifetime

I was shocked by his acceptance of non-dualistic Buddhist teaching, which was a reflection of my lack of understanding of Hanuman and that tradition at the time. So that's my tradition. It comes from beyond any particular religious affiliation. And I was once about as Jewish as the Pope is Catholic.

So let's go back to where you come from. What is your familial lineage?

Russian-Polish-Jewish on both sides; from the Minsk/Pinks, Russian/Polish area. I'm not sure about my family name, Kagal. It could have been Kougal or Keagal, I have no idea; no one seems to know. My father's side of the family lived in England for quite a while before they came to the States around 1900. My mother's side of the family, which was Fineberg, was more to the German side of that area, but I'm not sure, and they came later to the States.

So your family name is Kagal and you were given the name...?

Jeffrey. I was born in 1947 and was named after my uncle, who died in WW II as a pilot. My father was a lawyer and then became a psychotherapist. He was an intellectual. He had little use for religion. In our family, religion was cultural. We got together for holidays to eat turkey and what we called "the Pope's nose" (the part of the chicken that goes over the fence last). (laughs)

Was that a taste of how the family viewed the non-Jews, the Goyim?

Well, everyone in my parents' generation lived in Brooklyn; it was kind of a Jewish ghetto. There was definitely a lot of trouble with the surrounding communities over the years.

Growing up in the 1920s and 30s in New York, as my parents did, there was a lot of religious hatred. Jews were still seen as very different. The Irish were there as well as the other groups, and they all didn't get along.

Did you experience much of this yourself?

First we lived in Manhattan, then Brooklyn, then Queens, then Long Island. I really grew up not wanting to be Jewish. I saw that people saw me as strange and different because I was Jewish and I didn't want that. Being Jewish was something that separated me from people and I didn't like that. I still don't like to feel separate and different from other people. It made me feel bad that someone would look at me and not like me because of the family I was born into.

Did you experience this in school and in the streets.

I remember once in 5th or 6th grade, I came to school and all my Catholic friends weren't there. "Where is everyone?" It turned out that they were having their first confirmation class. So the next day they came back to school looking at me weird. I asked and they said, "You killed Jesus." They were taught in Catholic school that the Jews killed Jesus. They forgot to tell them Jesus was a Jew. They painted him with blond hair and fair skin. I don't know if they thought he was circumcised or not. From that moment on, in my head, I said I was no longer Jewish. "What did I do to deserve this? By accident or some karmic blip, I got born into this physical family and now I'm going to get hit on the head for it. Fuck that." (laughs) I didn't want any part of that.

What comes to mind as we talk is why as a young person I emotionally renounced being Jewish. There were few Jews where I was living as a kid on Long Island, though more and more came as time went on, and I couldn't stand being excluded from things. It was so painful to me. To be looked at as something different or strange hurt me so much. Also, I was doing a lot of sports and there weren't a lot of Jewish kids doing sports at that time. I was surrounded by non-Jews and I wanted to fit in. I wanted to be loved and it was very painful for me to be discriminated against. I pushed away any involvement with anything Jewish, especially after I was bar mitzvahed.

Obviously being Jewish didn't mean much to me if I could do that. Being Jewish wasn't giving me anything. Nobody in my family was happy. No one looked at religion as a way to find happiness. It was just something you did. You went to church or synagogue and then you screwed your secretary. You went to the club and screwed around with whores. There was no positive side to it. In my family, there was wonderful warmth but also great hatred. I have a cousin who actively hates me to this day. His father was my father's brother and they didn't talk for the last 20 years of his life, and it goes on. The other side of the family is at least as insane. As a youth I wanted to be accepted. I didn't want to be accepted as a Jewish person; I just wanted to be accepted as me.

Did something shift regarding these feelings?

Well, I'm more aware of the hurt that I experienced as a kid and how it figured into my life after that. I still don't like to feel like an outsider. Yet, I went to India where I was completely different from everyone and it didn't bother me. I felt good because I was so accepted and loved despite the difference. I wanted to be Indian. I loved Indian culture and I loved India. I didn't want to be Jewish, I wanted to be Indian.

Karmically, I can understand that because I feel that I have much stronger karmic ties to India than to any other place in the world.

How do you experience that?

I guess, philosophically, I believe that I've spent many lives there. But I don't really know that directly. What I can say is that emotionally, I'm completely at ease there, everything is familiar there. When I got off the plane and my foot hit the ground, I felt like I was home. I experienced a quality of being at home that I'd never felt in my life before, anywhere.

Is it a sense you have in your heart and body?

Yes, where I was completely comfortable. Also, Baba's spiritual teachers have told me that I was here or there in India. I take it with a grain of salt, but it is kind of fun to think about.

Did you go through a period where you dressed in Indian clothes?

Not for long. My friends tell me a story that right after getting back, I got off a bus barefoot in my red dress. But I don't even remember it. In any case, that changed very quickly and I've always dressed in jeans and western style.

Coming back to your earlier life with your family, was there any practice of the Jewish religion?

I went to Hebrew school and was bar mitzvahed. The primary memory of my bar mitzvah is that I had been given all these checks and my father came over and asked me for the money. I said, "What do you mean?" He said, "I have to pay for this." It seemed that the whole thing was just business, just a show. There was nothing of anything meaningful in it.

You want to talk about blood-lines and ancestry. I don't know, it never meant anything to me. Now as an adult, I can appreciate Jewish mysticism. But as a kid growing up in an environment that was 85% Christian, it wasn't a lot of fun.

Some would argue that what happened to you was very painful and it's understandable that you had strong feelings, but that your decisions involved running away.

I would say that perhaps those people were hurt so badly that they can't let go. They think I'm running away? (laughs)

Do you still consider yourself a Jew?

I don't consider myself anything. I'm trying to be human. Best human being I can be.

Well, you consider yourself a man.

Until recently, when my testosterone ran out. (laughs) Yes, I'm a man. I'm a human. I'm on Earth. That's about as much as I know.

Most people don't consider being a Jew necessarily accepting the religion of Judaism. They hold onto being Jewish despite adopting other religions or no religion at all. Is it your perspective that Jewishness is all about the religion, and if you leave the religion you leave being a Jew?

The world would say I'm a Jew because the world looks at bodies. But I don't consider myself a Jew or a Buddhist or a Hindu even though I do all these practices and work with teachers from many traditions. I don't consider myself one or the other.

If there was a chance of me joining any particular religion, it would have been Hinduism. But my Guru himself never made us do anything or intimated that it would be better if we were initiated as Hindus. He loved us as we are as human beings, and that kind of love I didn't find anywhere else until that time. That kind of love is God's love and that was the love I was looking for and it was that love I found in my guru. That opened me to all the other traditions, to finding it everywhere. I find it in Judaism and I find it in Buddhism. But I don't' see myself as one or the other. I've been initiated in Tibetan Buddhism because there are some practices in which you get initiated. I took refuge, but I still don't consider myself Buddhist.

There's a funny story involving the previous Karmapa, one of the greatest Tibetan lamas that ever lived. He was giving an initiation and two devotees of Maharaj-ji were there. They were going through the initiation which involved taking refuge in the Buddha, so they asked if they had to give up their guru. The Karmapa said, "No, you take refuge in your guru, Neem Karoli Baba. You don't have to take refuge in the Buddha. Do it with your guru." The real ones, they are beyond lines of separation. What's real is real and what's not is not, and they see what's real.

Incidentally, these same devotees were involved in the smallpox eradication program through Maharaj-ji's blessings. Smallpox was eradicated in India at the same time it was being eradicated in Africa by a different group. Maharaj-ji pushed this doctor who was there with us, Larry Brilliant, to get involved and keep going out with the UN health organization to eradicate smallpox. Now, there is no smallpox in the world except in little vials, thanks in part to the blessings of the great Saints.

How did your spirituality evolve after your bar mitzvah?

Nothing much happened spiritually for me until I took peyote in 1965. It was between my junior and senior years in high school in Long Island, and I did it with some friends. My mother was away for the day. We cooked it up, ate it, and I went, "Oh, this is the way it is."

That experience was a very direct experience and it had nothing to do with religions. It had to do with seeing things the way they are. Looking back, I can now say, that was the beginning of me recognizing that what I needed to be working on was how I see the world. I understood that everything I had been seeing was a projection, and that it is possible for the screen or curtain to open and see without the projection. I took the sunglasses off and it became obvious that the spiritual path is an inner path having to do with removing the screen in our subjectivity.

I imagine you couldn't have articulated that at that point.

No, definitely. My level of clarity was such that I almost killed myself listening to "Mr. Tambourine Man" on peyote and almost driving into the lake.

Can you describe more of what the experience itself was like?

Everywhere I looked, there was love and a sense of extraordinary freedom and happiness, something I had never tasted. Nobody was happy in my family, secrets and lies all over the place. Here was happiness that I had no idea existed, or I had forgotten. So this was a big thing. I felt free, free of all the burdens I was carrying. Even at seventeen, I had felt a tremendous burden, and at last I was free, let out of the cage. It was so extraordinary.

It led to a very tumultuous senior year in high school. I wanted to go back there, but didn't know how. I didn't have more peyote. I started reading *Autobiography of a Yogi*, *Zen Japanese Culture*, and *The Gospel of Ramakrishna* because they were available to me at that time. Bob Dylan was telling us what to think and what was going on through his songs. I was waiting for each record to come out to know what to think. It was a great time. Everything was exploding.

Where did it go from there?

I went to college at Stonybrook, playing basketball and taking drugs, mostly psychedelics. A friend had scored a pound of mescaline in a mayonnaise jar. You could just scoop some out, and sometimes we'd also take large doses of acid.

Were your experiences continuing to be spiritual or were they more recreational?

The mescaline was a wonderful loving, sweet comforting experience. But the acid was just beyond anything. It gave me great experiences, but I could not incorporate them into my life. I can still remember some things that I experienced. I would often get into play mode with my dog in the snow. I wasn't allowed to play as a kid and this was so wonderful.

One time, I was lying on my bed and I felt something far in the distance. "What is that?" I could feel it coming closer and closer and I realized it was ... a thought! I hadn't been thinking any thoughts and I saw this thought coming and it crashed over me like a wave, and then I was thinking again. Then it was me thinking, and then it left. I said, "No don't go," and it left. Then again it happened, and this whole cycle repeated itself faster and faster. Finally, the space between the thoughts was gone, and there was only this continual flow of me-ness and thought. That was such a powerful moment. Who are you when you're not thinking you are who you think you are? Who? What? You're pure awareness. That is all you can say if you have to answer that question. Not that I ever could have. Not that I'm even saying it from a very deep place right now; but I know.

Maharaj-ji said that acid experiences, "bring you into the room with Christ, but you can't stay." Love is the only way to stay. The other experiences I've had, the ones that have been really life changing, have included this (pointing all around). Acid didn't include this. Acid was another realm.

What is it that these other experiences included that you didn't find on acid, what you call "this"?

All this, the world (gesturing all around the room). I don't believe that acid experiences transform you. They give you a glimpse and they show you what's possible; they can even give you a good look at it. But it doesn't take away your anger; doesn't take away your fear; your greed; your selfishness. It doesn't do that. You have to figure things out and do the work.

As Maharaj-ji said, "it brings you into the room with Christ."

That's good. You get faith, you see there is something; but you have to leave.

I like the expression, peek experience, p-e-e-k, a glimpse.

Yes.

Did you continue to use hallucinogens?

I haven't in a very long time. I was addicted to cocaine in the 80s; freebase. Gone. I was saved by a devotee of Maharaj-ji who said, with great spiritual authority, "Stop now!" So I did.

How did you become involved with Eastern spirituality?

Once I'd done peyote and saw what I thought was the way things are, there wasn't a lot of help. I did go to Swami Satchidananda meetings in the City. There was someone named Bhakti Bagda, who was a disciple of Ramana Maharshi. We'd do asanas on the floor with roaches and mice running over us. There was a woman named Nina who lived in seclusion in Vermont who had been a disciple of Kirpal Singh. She came back to the States and people would seek to be with her. She had some juice and I met her.

But I was just fumbling around until I met Ram Dass. That's when everything changed. The minute I walked into the room I knew that everything I'd been searching for was real, that it was in the world and it could be found. Prior to that, in my mind there was always the thought that this whole thing could be just my fantasy drug experience or something I believed because of books I'd read. Who really knew if *Autobiography of a Yogi*[64] was true? Now, I've been to that cave a few times; then it was just a book.

It wasn't anything Ram Dass said or did. I just walked in and felt

---

[64] Autobiography of a Yogi by Paramahansa Yogananda was first published in 1946. It became very popular amongst spiritual seekers in the U.S. and around the world, especially in the Sixties.

it. It was Maharaj-ji's Presence I was feeling. It was a big moment. I don't want to say "waking up," because that's over-used. But I was definitely seeing something I'd never seen before. After that, I followed Ram Dass wherever he went. I followed him around the States, and I wanted to go to India.

I walked up to the house and knocked. A guy with a big beard opened the door with a funny grin on his face. He smiled and pointed up the stairs. I thought, Ah hell, this place is too weird. I should get outta here. But I walked up the stairs and into the room where Ram Dass was sitting on a mattress on the floor. He was dressed in a long white robe and was wearing lots of beads. The moment I walked into the room, something happened inside of me. Immediately, instantly, without a word being spoken, I knew that whatever it was I was looking for—and I didn't know what it was—was absolutely real. In every molecule of my being, I knew that it existed in the world and that it could be found. I didn't know if I could find it,
but this moment changed my life.
From *Chants of a Lifetime*

Was it in India that you took on the name Krishna Das? Did Maharaj-ji give the disciples their names?

I was feeling bad because everyone was getting new names but me. He was calling me "Driver." He was always playing with us. He called Ram Dass "Commander in Chief" and said he couldn't drive or touch money. He'd taken the keys to Ram Dass' car and so I was the driver. For a long time I was called "Driver."

I was Driver. Terrific. One night I wrote in my diary: "Well, I guess that's it.
I'm going to be Driver forever."
The next morning I got to the temple and was called into Maharaj-ji's room.
He looked at me and said, "Arjun…nay…Krishna….nay….Krishna Das!"
(servant of Krishna or servant of God)
From *Chants of a Lifetime*

You said that for a while you wanted to be Indian. But of course in this life, you can't be Indian. You've also detached from identifying as a Jew. Do you feel a need to have any kind of identity at all?

That's just what the ego does. The ego grabs on to anything to keep itself separate and compressed. I don't think you can call anything spiritual that doesn't help you get over that.

On a personal level, do you find yourself more comfortable being with Jewish people? Is there some kind of chemistry?

I certainly feel culturally Jewish. I grew up with it. But when I think of my closer circle of friends, there are both. Each is different. With my Jewish friends, we share a kind of shticking, a common sense of humor.

Many who have adopted a universal path and then discover the Jewish mystics have felt pulled to explore or immerse themselves more in the Jewish world. Did you ever feel that?

No, I never did. I don't feel pulled to immerse myself in Jewish mystical stuff because I feel that what I'm doing in my life includes all that. It could be that some people would think I'm wrong, and that's okay. I feel, as Maharaj-ji said, all paths lead to the same goal; so I honor all paths as best I can. But I don't have time to do more than what I already am doing. I'm already 24/7, 365 days a year on the road doing this chanting, which is my practice, which keeps me straight and which I need to do and want to do.

Some people ask, "Why don't you sing Jewish songs?" I say, "You don't understand. I don't make this program." People think that it's "me" doing this and I'm deciding what to do. It's just not that way, though I can't convince anybody. There are a number of rabbis in New York and Seattle who wanted me to come to their Temples. It was hard to get them to tell me what they really wanted. I told them, "If you want me to come and sing, I'll come and sing, but I'll sing what I sing. I'm not going to come and sing Jewish songs that I don't know. I'll sing along if you're singing, but don't expect me to come and lead Jewish chants, because I don't do that. If you want me to come do what I do, I'm happy to come do that. Happy! But don't invite me and expect me to do what I don't do." Now I haven't heard back.

You do an incredible amount of traveling and public chanting or kirtan. Is it also your personal practice to chant when you are alone?

I do. Mostly I sleep when I'm off the tour, but I have my own practices which includes chanting and repetition of prayers.

What is it that you feel you have inherited from the Jewishness of your family and community, both that which you value and what you needed to let go of?

There is positive stuff, certainly. There was a great humanism, caring about human beings, caring about people. My parents were left-wing liberals, involved in civil rights. I think the greatest thing they passed on was that we are all human beings; we all deserve to be happy and free and live the life we wish to live. When I was in my teens, all the civil rights activity was going on in the South. That was very big for us. I had a lot of Black friends because I was a basketball player and I was with these guys a great deal and there was a bonding. But we understood the difficulty of the culture. I had a Black girlfriend in high school that nobody knew about; it was a big secret.

A secret from your parents as well?

Definitely. My parents didn't know half the time that I was alive. They were busy with their own stuff.

They were liberal intellectuals. Did you inherit that?

My father was an intellectual and was different from most of the rest of the family, my uncles and cousins, etc. They were not really bad people, but not people you'd want to hang out with. My father was aware; he loved music and jazz. He became a psychotherapist and was involved in the life of the mind, which was a type of self-awareness. Nobody else in the family was; they were crazy people.

You inherited your father's ways then?

Absolutely. And my mother had great passion for civil rights and human rights.

On the negative, there was no love in my family. Well, there was love; my parents loved my sister and me. But there was a lot of tension and anger that colored the atmosphere in the house. Growing up wasn't easy. Trying to overcome that dark place was a difficult thing and still is.

Do you associate that with Jewishness; not necessarily the religion but the culture?

Not really. It seems everyone suffers. It's such a key thing in life; it's what triggers compassion and practice. It's a universal part of life. I have friends who are dying and some that are breaking down. Two friends died in the last few months. Life has suffering.

When I went to India, I saw the way people lived there. You would think they'd be suffering, except they weren't unhappy. That shocked me! Here I came from middle class Long Island where everyone had enough of everything, and I get to India and see people who have one *chapati*[65] a day. Yet, you look in their eyes and they are not suffering the way we suffer. They are suffering, but not the way we suffer. I began to think that Western culture breeds a very self-centered quality of suffering, perhaps because we tend to be isolated from each other. As for what I know of Jewish suffering in particular, there's no question that Jews have been persecuted. There is a quality that some Jews have of taking on that suffering from the Holocaust and other history and feeling it personally.

[65] An unleavened flatbread.

Was there any influence on you regarding Israel and Zionism?

My mother's brother fought in Israel. He was a frogman and blew up British ships and became a spy for Israel. Was he a hero? Was Zionism seen as a good thing? I thought it was strange. It seemed so intense and involved so much anger. I don't think I ever connected to it. I remember being somewhat repulsed by my uncle's intensity and anger. I knew he hated his father, my grandfather. He left this country for thirty years, swearing he'd not come back until his father was dead. I connected his anger about his father to his anger in the world and the Zionist movement. Perhaps I was wrong, but as a kid, it didn't seem right to me. The connection of my uncle and Zionism was very weird.

So as a youth you didn't have a strong bonding with Israel. But does your connection to the Jewish people make you more sensitive to the troubles there?

In India they would say it's puranibat, a big thing. They say this about the Hindu/Muslim conflict. Two or three hundred years ago, families became separated by religion. Even still, they usually live together pretty well until politicians start whooping it up for political purposes.

The conflict in Palestine and Israel is also a very deep, old, karmic thing. It's certainly very painful that it's going on. But personally, I don't have a big reaction or involvement with it. I don't see the Israelis as being "my people." They're not. First of all, I'm an American; I'm not an Israeli. I just wish they could live together.

So for you, personally, it's a conflict in the world and it's similar emotionally to the Irish Protestant/Catholic conflict or the Muslim/Hindu conflicts in India.

I'm not emotionally involved with it as different. The suffering is terrible and I ask, why? I understand, but I don't understand. This is real human nature. A big part of human nature; you can't say it isn't.

But one side is not "my people." It's two peoples.

Do you think in terms of reincarnation? It's certainly a major aspect of Hinduism.

I don't know if I have a particular personal experience of it, but it seems fairly reasonable.

Some who believe in reincarnation say that there is a choice we make when we enter this world.

You have to be careful when you say, "we make a choice." Your karma makes a choice for you. You, Alan, didn't make a choice to come here. You are the result of your karmic needs to be worked out. You got sent to this school because this is what you had to learn by becoming Alan. Alan wasn't sitting up there, saying, "hmm…." When you leave this body, you're not going to be Alan anymore. You're going to leave Alanness behind and the package will go on.

There's the karma that you try to work out in your life; it's a tiny little bit of the huge load that we're carrying around, so they say. So, people often say, "I made a choice." But why would you make a choice consciously to be born with no legs, to die when you're a month old? It's a different "I."

Have you accepted these beliefs as your own?

Well, I guess I do. I do believe, I do believe. I live with these people who are immersed in that.

Within your framework, what could be the karma involved in you coming into the Jewish tribal community?

I was supposed to be the first Jewish point guard to play pro basketball and I blew it! That was it. They transferred it over to the first Jewish kirtan wallah. I don't have to run around so much. (laughter)

Karma is something they say no one understands, nobody! It's such a complex web. You have to deal with it by just dealing with what is and never really knowing why. Some of the great Saints can see a lot of it, but they say that nobody can grasp the whole thing.

The stories of the Saints in this regard are extraordinary. There's a story of Nityananda, Muktananda's guru. One day, a car pulls up and a young couple comes out and the woman is carrying a newborn baby who is dead. She comes up to him and says, "Please Baba, bring my baby back to life. Open my baby's eyes." So Nityananda waves his hand over the child's face and the baby's eyes open. Then he waves his hand back the other way and the baby's eyes close and he says, "Now take him away and bury him." One of his devotees says, "Oh Babaji, how sad. Why didn't you let that baby live?" He said, "Do you want to take responsibility for that? Go ask her how many babies she has lost. She has lost three babies so far. Each time it was the same soul being born, trying to come into my presence to die in my presence. The first two times, they didn't get here. The third time he finally got here. You want me to bring him back to life? Are you going to take responsibility?" So the guy went and asked the woman and sure enough this was her third dead baby. So these guys can see a lot. Sometimes they can change things and sometimes they don't. This is the kind of world I've been living in, so it just kind of seeps into your brain.

Does looking at the world from such a vast or cosmic vantage point separate you from ordinary human life?

You feel at one with everybody. Everybody is your nearest and dearest. If somebody is hurting, you want to remove that pain. It's a natural compassion, you don't have to manipulate it. When you see someone, when the coverings are removed, you experience what is and you see we are all a part of the one body. Why wouldn't we do whatever we can to help someone who is suffering? Ramana Maharshi was asked, should I meditate or help this person? His response was, "When you see that everyone is a part of your own self, why wouldn't you help? What's to think about?"

So when people say that nothing matters, that's the neurotic taking over the spiritual truth. Emptiness is not empty. Emptiness means that nothing exists independently. Shunyatta, which is translated as emptiness, could have been translated as fullness. D.T. Suzuki, who influenced a great deal of the West's understanding, picked emptiness as the translation. The Beats took it from there because they were angry human beings and it suited their neurosis. They propagated that to everyone with the wrong understanding. His Holiness the Dalai Lama gives a different view of emptiness. It means the inter-dependence of all things; nothing exists independently of anything else, including the soul. The soul is not permanently separate from anything.

So there is more caring when you get this idea. It's not that you care, there's more caring. There's nobody saying, "I'm really compassionate today." It's the absence of the ego. Ego is the container that you need in this world to feed yourself and function, but it's not a real thing. It is very hard to talk about this. Words are inadequate, but they can point to something.

Even though you can't see the whole picture, do you have some sense of there being a meaning to incarnating as Jewish?

It's really easy to be seduced into thinking that we have some objective understanding of things because we are bright and have a lot of information at our fingertips, or because we've met a lot of people and taken some teachings from here and there. I don't think so. I don't think we have much objective understanding of things. We really don't even know who we are! Extending out from that, how can we possibly understand the whys and wherefores of such a complex issue?

Everything I could say about my Jewish friends who are practitioners, I could say about my non-Jewish friends, except maybe their lack of a sense of humor. (laughs)

How about from the personal side of it, do you feel a sense of meaning in your lineage?

My world has always been, right from an early age, a struggle with dealing with strong emotions. My mother was really angry, my father was always trying to get away from her. There were a lot of strong emotions, and I've always been pre-occupied with that particular angle of life. But maybe because I was born Jewish and there was a kind of tolerance for open thinking, I was able to grow in my own way and this is what has happened.

The way I see the world is certainly a result of many different things. A lot has to do with where I was born, who my parents were, my family, and all that. Not knowing any other life from the inside, it's hard to say. I'm just beginning to realize, after all these years, how differently the Indians see themselves from the way we do. How differently they see religion from the way we do.

When I first came to Maharaj-ji, the Indian devotee who we knew there said, "Do something for them, Baba." So he said, "They come from good families." Maharaj-ji said that. I wouldn't have said that. He saw something about my family that I didn't see about my family. I don't know how many generations back, tens of thousands of years back, who knows what he saw? But the point is, I am the product of a good family. I don't even know what that meant in his eyes.

Did that help you to accept your family?

I think so. It meant something. Something can't come from nothing. If there is goodness in my heart, it had to come from somewhere. I was brought up in a way where my parents cared about people; they were essentially good people, not wanting to hurt anyone. Those were the ideals I grew up with. But is that particularly Jewish? I don't know. There's a quality of being Jewish that's familiar to me, the humor, the shticking, the way of seeing the world.

Being immersed as you are in the universal path of the sacred, would you share something addressed to the Jewish people.

When I was in Cleveland, a guy came up to me after I sang "Jesus on the Main Line," which I do every night. This guy came up very upset and was telling me that he wouldn't give up his Jewishness, that we have to stick together and all this. I said, "Who asked you to?"

Of course, I know what he's saying. But as I see it, he's finding ways to hang on to his anger and that anger is going to destroy him and that's painful for me to see. I see a lot of people who identify with being Jewish hanging onto very dark, destructive emotions. I'm not saying they don't have reasons for that. There seem to be logical reasons; there's been a lot of suffering. But because they don't have a spiritual outlook, they don't see that the anger they are carrying around is blowing up their own hearts and destroying any possibility of finding real love.

When I sing the Jesus song, I regularly get e-mails: "Why do you sing that Jesus song with all the pain and suffering the Christians have caused?" I say: "Number one, Jesus was not Christian and never killed anyone as far as I know; number two, he didn't start any religions; number three, can't you stand to see a Jewish guy make good? Ask yourself, what does this have to do with your anger?"

I know it provokes or has the possibility of provoking people. I'm not doing it to provoke anyone. I do it because I love to sing it and I won't stop because they are provoked. As I see it, Jesus was just trying to get the Jews to clean up their act.

One time, a Tibetan Lama, after 20 years in prison, was released and came to see His Holiness the Dalai Lama. His Holiness said, "Were you ever afraid?" He said, "Yes, I was afraid I would get angry." That's how I see the spiritual path. The Tibetans have to deal with their Holocaust, with millions killed by the Chinese. Why hold onto the pain and torture yourself with the pain? Look at the difference at the way the Tibetans use all that negativity to confront reality and not lose a sense of truth and compassion and love. Why do many Jews stay in a circle of recreating that pain and suffering and never letting it go? I don't know the answer to that. I'm just trying to get through the day in a good way.

Thank you.

Calling out to hungry hearts
Everywhere through endless time
You who wander, you who thirst
I offer you this Bodhi Mind
Calling all you hungry spirits
Everywhere through endless time
Calling out to hungry hearts
All the lost and left behind
Gather round and share this meal
Your joy and your sorrow
I make it mine.
(Lyrics of Krishna Das's "The Gates of Sweet Nectar"
adapted from a Buddhist prayer.)

Allyson Grey
ARTIST

"God makes love to us through the Visionary experience. The Mystic Visionary opens their spiritual eye and beholds the conjunction of love and beauty as the basis and wonder of creation. Mystic Art provides a means for both artist and viewer to align with the creative force and unite with God through contemplation of Cosmic symbolism. We reflect on visionary art, in order to glimpse the Divine Imagination and align ourselves with God. Beauty attracts us by the shine of the divine – it's God that's the true magnet in Beauty."
    –from CoSM website[56] by Alex Grey and Allyson Grey

How would you describe your family background?

My parents eloped and were married by an orthodox rabbi with a *minyan* of ten men. Both my maternal and paternal grandparents were Reform Jews. I grew up in Baltimore, a major center of the Reform movement. Baltimore Hebrew Congregation (BHC) is surely one of the largest Reform Jewish temples, and my mother was confirmed there as

---

[56] Chapel of Sacred Mirrors website: http://cosm.org/

were my sisters, niece, nephews and I. My paternal grandfather, Murray, walked there every Friday night, and my maternal grandmother, Sedonia, got a ride there every Saturday morning. She belonged to the women's group that made the needlepoint ark cover which is still installed there. It is exquisite—four panels that must stretch at least twenty feet across.

My grandmother worked on the portion that symbolically portrayed manna falling from heaven. Considering the part psychedelics have played in my God realization and as a sacrament in my spiritual practice, recent speculation that manna could be associated with psychedelic mushrooms[67] seems an amazing synchronicity.

My parents and grandparents valued community and were joiners who participated and had many interests. They were original members of the temple and belonged to other Jewish organizations and clubs as well. I learned that Jews are "a people," which is truly the story of the Torah.

Would you say you had a religious upbringing? Did your family keep kosher?

Reform Jews are not required to follow kosher laws and we did not. I enjoyed Maryland crabs and bacon, though my family celebrated major Jewish holidays. Throughout my childhood we went to my grandparents for Shabbat supper. My parents attended shul only on Rosh Hashanah and Yom Kippur, and we had a big Passover with family every year. My parents were camp directors of a private girls' camp for 25 years and almost all of the children there were Jewish. Many of the counselors were not Jewish, so my parents, who led a Friday evening service every week, tried to make the services more inclusive by replacing all of the Hebrew with translations. They did a wonderful job and I was very influenced by their spiritual commitment.

I feel that my upbringing included a strong sense of Jewish identity. I went to Sunday school from pre-kindergarten, but my synagogue

---

[67] A number of writers have made this claim. See *The Mystery of Manna, The Psychedelic Sacrament of the Bible*, by Dan Merkur, Park Street Press, VT, 2000

did not offer Bat Mitzvah to girls so I waited until I finally went to Israel at age 61 to be Bat Mitzvah'd at the Wailing Wall.

Do you remember having any spiritual experiences as a child?

When I had high fevers from some normal childhood illnesses, I experienced frightening hallucinations. I've recalled these episodes when using psychedelics, and I see that the mind can create altered states of consciousness naturally under extreme conditions. But these cannot necessarily be considered spiritual experiences.

At age 15, I was confirmed from Sunday School, and I won books for high achievement. Comparative religions and ethics were the subjects that interested me most and still do. Jewish was a way of being, a way of living, a structure of special celebrations and social ceremony. In my early teens, bar and bat Mitzvah parties introduced me to young adulthood, and sanctioned socializing between girls and boys. Spirituality, in the sense of real contact with the Godself, did not occur until my breakthrough with psychedelics and the teachings of Ram Dass. I grew up in the midst of great beauty and love but did not contact true spirituality until I made personal contact with the Divine, the "primary religious experience."

Reflection is seeing as a spiritual practice. The Great Wisdom masters and traditions hold up a sacred mirror of the universal Light of love. Reflection is clarified attunement to the cosmic symbolism in life and recognition of the Godself in everyone. When sacred mirrors face each other, the infinite is revealed.

Did anti-Semitism have any impact on you?

I briefly experienced anti-Semitism attending a redneck junior high school in rural Maryland. After that, the Jews in my grade transferred together to the same private school, The Park School. Park was not a Jewish school, but was considered liberal at the time because it did not have quotas. Other schools only allowed a certain number of Jews, a certain number of Blacks or other races in each grade. At Park,

Allyson - '58

only grades and tests were used to determine admission. As a result the population had more Jews and Blacks than at other private schools in the area.

Would you say that you have inherited some specifically Jewish traits or values, healthy or unhealthy?

Sure. My grandfather was a self-made man, a hard working, hard-headed immigrant who scratched his way to wealth and success. I was a very fortunate child due to the cleverness and unstoppability of my grandfather. I know he smiles down from heaven seeing Alex and I pursuing our vision of building a sacred temple. My maternal grandmother, an all-American Jew, started her family in rural West Virginia where she butchered hogs, gutted fish, and prepared the dead for burial. Moving back to the city during the depression, she started her own beauty shop in her home and later made a living decorating hats with flowers and veils. Industriousness may be the trait of any immigrant, but adaptability, resourcefulness and recognizing opportunity could be seen as essential and ingrained traits in the Jewish psyche.

What were the stages or changes that brought you to your current spiritual path and what, if any, were the conflicts that you faced in terms of family or cultural reactions or rejections?

As a teen, I lost any faith I may have developed through my Jewish upbringing. In 1969, before leaving for my first year in college, I refused to go to services on Rosh Hashanah because my mother would not allow me to wear a mini-dress to shul. It all seemed so impossibly hypocritical.

My spiritual awakening happened in 1971 when, after reading Ram Dass' *Be Here Now*, I took LSD with an intention to see the "white Light" as Ram Dass reported. It was then that I had, for the first time, the unforgettable, undeniable experience of the presence of God. The results of Walter Pahnke's Good Friday experiment (1962), and Roland Griffith's mystical experience psilocybin study at John's Hopkins (2011), both concur with my personal experience. When Alex took his first dose of LSD in my apartment in 1975, I recognized that he had just shared that unforgettable, undeniable experience.

There has been no conflict with family about this. I'd been "experienced" with both of my sisters, and we didn't worry our parents about it for decades. By the time I spoke openly to my parents about these experiences, I had established myself as a responsible adult and clearly no harm had been done.

Would you describe your spiritual evolution or transformation as involving a change in your experience of your Jewish identity? Do you feel you stepped outside of or away from the Jewish community?

I have moved toward greater resonance with my Jewish identity as I've matured. After leaving home at age seventeen, living far from Baltimore Hebrew Congregation, it felt wrong to miss services on the High Holidays. I'd seek out a Hillel House or nearby synagogue to fulfill my obligation, but the experience always left me feeling like I didn't belong. When our daughter was born, we started going up to Woodstock during the summers and heard about Woodstock Jewish Congregation (a Reconstructionist[68] Synagogue) and their extraordinary rabbi, Jonathan Kligler. Attending High Holiday services at WJC has influenced Alex and my leadership and our creation of ritual and ceremony at CoSM. We have also had the honor to meet on several

---

[68] Reconstructionist Judaism, founded by Mordechai Kaplan, is the least well-known of the denominations of Judaism, the others being Orthodox, Conservative and Reform.

occasions the great rabbinic teacher and founder of the Jewish Renewal movement, Reb Zalman Schachter-Shalomi.

In my maturity, my heart has opened and more love and appreciation pours out. God is there. Alex says that love is God's secret name. In 2003, when Alex and I started trans-denominational Full Moon ceremonies in our loft in Brooklyn, I decided to represent the "Jewish beat." I started delivering the parsha (the weekly portion of the Torah read by Jews all over the world) as from an oracle. At each Full Moon ceremony for the past seven years, I have examined how the Torah story resonates with my life and the life of our community.

I've never missed a Passover or High Holiday. Alex always joins me. Passover 2010 came a few weeks after Alex and I suffered a terrible car accident. Confined to bed and unable to sit up at a table, I was emotional about missing Passover. Two of my Catholic friends asked for instructions to create a seder here at CoSM where Alex and I and all of the company (15 of us) reclined on the floor for the feast. We completed the entire Haggadah, and only two Jews were present.

Over seventy years ago, my grandmother, living in rural West Virginia, where there were no other Jewish families, became the head of the Women's Missionary Society. As there was no funeral parlor, she and her neighbors buried the dead. In a similar way, I am a Jew living in an interfaith world. All faiths are beautiful and I will always treasure my tradition and my ancestors.

It seems clear that you are comfortable with saying, "I am a Jew."

Certainly. Some people worship more fully than I do. Some may admit that their ancestors are Jewish but consider themselves atheists or have converted to another religion. Some people may not even consider me a Jew because I don't follow certain traditions. That's other people.

What were you seeking in choosing the path you chose? What were you leaving behind?

LSD catalyzed a spiritual awakening and my natural curiosity led me to read Ram Dass's book, *Remember, Be Here Now*, a book that drew me toward Eastern spirituality. I was a child of the Sixties, and the Beatles and the hippies were so enticing. Young adulthood is a time of experimentation. Nothing about Judaism sent me away from it. It was my Jewishness that made me want to explore. Israel means "God wrestler." Judaism was waiting for my interest and attention when I was ready.

I live into the future that I create and subscribe to Eckhart Tolle's recommendation to let the past die behind me. We learn from our past, of course. Letting the past die behind us means letting go of all negativities from the past and bringing into the present and future only what serves the greater good. Allowing negativities from the past to affect the present and future is like driving while looking in the rear view mirror. There will be negative consequences. Regret is the enemy.

Did you ever experience a pull to "return" or towards being more Jewish, religiously or otherwise?

There is nothing to return to. I've never left. I'm as involved as I want to be.

How would you describe your current spiritual path?

I am an artist and the co-founder of CoSM, a radically welcoming spiritual center that celebrates art as a spiritual path.

I am a teacher and co-founder of Mystic Artists Guild international, (MAGI), CoSM's core curriculum oriented to mystic artists and creative spirits. The purpose of MAGI is to form a higher social organism of inspired minds capable of building sacred space together.

Would you elaborate on how your work with psychedelics and your practice as an artist come together to form a spiritual path?

Psychedelics have influenced every aspect of my life including my art. My art is inspired by psychedelic visions but no claim is made that my art accurately portrays images I have witnessed when immersed in psychedelic reverie. The altered state can be quite beyond depiction. We can only point with a sharpened stick.

My Jewish heritage deepened me, making me present to "God wrestling." God is nameless and inexplicable, without a face. Fountains and drains of energy sucking and blowing Light in a vast endless vista, particles and waves flowing simultaneously, without conflict, over and through all beings and things—that more describes my experience of God. "No graven image" resonates with my experience of God and Judaism.

My current spiritual path includes leading Full Moon and Celestial celebrations, meditating, yoga, walking in the woods, and living my life in alignment with transformative possibilities, like building an enduring, radically welcoming spiritual center. All faiths, each one beautiful, are similarly initiated though God contact. Moses and the Burning Bush, Buddha's enlightenment under the Bodhi tree, Mohammed's ride on the back of a mule to the Seventh Heaven—these stories of God contact launched religions and a spiritual path for many. Many people have personally experienced the Divine. Few have shared their God contact in a way that inspires and organizes the allegiance of multitudes for eons. The story of the Jews is the story of a people synchronic with my experience of a growing global Love Tribe, which, having had personal contact with the Divine, now shares a soul purpose—peace on Earth and sustainability of the web of life.

Many spiritual teachers emphasize the primary importance of oneness, non-duality and non-attachment. How do you hold the meaning of "I am a Jew" in the context of "I am not separate from any-thing" or "I am no-thing"?

Jewishness is my ancestry and also my conditioned identity. It is a heritage and an archetypal psychic force.

The no-self of Buddhism means there is no independent arising. The central Jewish insight is that of oneness: "Hear O Israel, the Lord our God the Lord is One." The concept "God is One" represents the same truth as non-duality. This means that Jews and God of every tradition are not separate from each other.

How do you understand the relationship between one's essential nature and one's tribal or ethnic identity? Is there a part of you that is not Jewish?

Our essential nature is beyond any description or limitations, beyond gender, race, ethnic identity. Our essential nature is a higher dimension than our ethnic identity. The essential nature of all beings is goodness, purity and infinite love, the most powerful force. Ethnic identity honors the ancestors and offers a sense of belonging in a world where the illusion of separateness is very compelling. This is beautiful in its way, but it is not an expression of the unity of all beings and things, which is a higher plane of awareness.

If there is such a thing as an essential Jewish nature, could it be our receptivity to guidance from God? Abraham made a covenant with the One God. Moses was listening to God. God speaks to us if we listen. Judaism is all about Oneness. For Jews, God's name is unpronounceable. The Ain Sof, the highest realm of the Kabbalah, is beyond form and description; it is the absolute perfection in which there are no distinctions and no differentiations.

Some people talk about "being comfortable in their Jewish skin." How do you see this? Is it important to go beyond this to a more universal identity? Can a Jewish person "shed" their Jewish skin at all, even if temporarily? Or for their lifetime? Could this be part of the spiritual journey?

As a Jew, I am an ambassador aiming to represent the highest and noblest traits of my Jewishness to share with a wider world. There are people who are born Jewish and are atheists. There are non-practicing Jews and those who deny their Jewishness. But if they are born Jewish, we share a common gene pool—Abraham & Sarah, Isaac & Rebekah,

Jacob & Leah & Rachel were our ancestors.

In your understanding of birth and death, does being Jewish have any relevance before birth or after death? Is there a Jewish soul?

I believe the soul is beyond Jewishness. All borders are artificial and created by the human psyche. The choice I made to incarnate included choosing Jewish parents. After we die, our souls merge with God, and God is One.

The Torah and Talmud only allude to the concept of reincarnation; however Kabbalists embrace the notion and write a great deal about it. It is said that a Jew who dies without fulfilling every applicable commandment in his or her lifetime will return until completing them. One Hassidic story claims that a Jew who is martyred due to anti-Semitism can reincarnate to take revenge.

I see how that relates to reincarnation, but this Hassidic story also brings in the notion of revenge, which some people argue is a very negative aspect of the Old Testament.

Revenge and anger are definitely part of life. How could they be left out? The Torah is the story of a people, definitely not a perfect people. There is so much transgression and God-wrestling going on in those stories. Some stories may be there to warn us of dramas we should avoid. I do not mistake every act described in the Torah as an act condoned and sanctioned by the Divine.

In many spiritual traditions and teachings, great importance is placed on honoring our ancestors. How would you say your own path relates to that, and how does that affect the attention you give to things Jewish?

Honoring our ancestors means thinking and speaking kindly about them, looking for their best qualities in ourselves. I take the Jewishness that was born and bred in me and carry it into my leadership at CoSM, where all traditions and all faiths are honored. We can make exquisite music by bringing all the diverse tunes together in harmony.

Views on world affairs have colored the way people feel about Jews. When I represent the "Jewish beat" at CoSM Full Moons, I represent the story of an imperfect people that made mistakes that cost dearly. Jews are still in grave conflict with the Muslim world. Ishmael and Esau, according to the Koran, were both ancestors of Muhammed; both lost their birthright and were cast out of the houses of their fathers thousands of years ago. The vibrations of these brutalities, no matter how they are justified, ring through history and into present day resentments.

Of course the stories are used to manipulate people. That is what stories always do. Anything that is in the past is a story. We can make it mean whatever we want to make it mean, and that is why there are libraries of commentary on the Torah. I make it mean that enough is enough. Let's forgive each other for things that happened thousands of years ago and operate closer to the present and live into a future we desire.

It's likely that most Jews would say that they have a special relationship with Jewish people that is different from their relationship to other people: a greater affinity, sense of community, loyalty, or commitment. Is this true for you? If so, in what ways?

I love all people, but I do feel a resonance when I meet someone Jewish because we have a shared experience. Whenever I meet anyone, I look for the shared experience. Jewishness is an easy meeting place. Every Jew in every synagogue throughout the world is reading and studying the same parsha within the same week. No synagogue can exist without an authentic Torah, hand scribed on the skin of a lamb, according to rules that make each Torah unique and at the same time practically identical. This unity causes a vibration that rings the planet.

You seem to be saying that the common experience shared by Jews, that causes the resonance felt amongst Jews, is the reading of the

Torah. Yet, probably most Jews today in Israel or the U.S. don't ever do that and yet would describe a similar sense of resonance with the Jewish people. Are there other bonding agents at work?

The Torah readers, the most learned, are like the central engine that keeps the machine moving all around it. Some know more about the true workings of the engine, some know less. Jews often claim to know more than each other about Jewishness. This is because Jews have such respect for scholarliness, an inclination genetically programmed from eons of study and interpretation of this one scroll of stories. The bonding agent is like gravity pulling those on the outside, those who know little about Torah, to the center where the wheel is going around. Jews may feel connected even though they are far from scholarly regarding Torah.

Do you feel any special connection to the activities or suffering of Jews?

Life is suffering or perpetual unsatisfactoriness. That is truly the commonality of all beings. My special connection to the persecution of Jews reminds me to be kind to everyone without exception.

The mainstream Jewish community has come to identify strongly with the nation-state of Israel. How have you related to this in your life?

I am so grateful to have visited Israel in my lifetime. In synagogue nursery school and kindergarten we used to sing a song "Pennies, Nickles, Dimes and Quarters… Hear the merry clink, clink, clink…" It was time to collect for "Care In Israel." Our money would go toward planting trees in Israel. It was such a joy to visit my trees. I pray that Israelis and their neighbors will resolve their conflicts. Israeli's are brilliant and beautiful. We have met with a very strong and loving Egyptian community that includes both Moslem and Christian psychedelophiles. I'm working on a new Haggadah that is interfaith, gender balanced and mentions Egypt only historically, emphasizing liberation theology. Israel's breakthrough research into medical cannabis and forward thinking about mind-expanding sacraments will heal, make people more peaceful and open hearts.

All faiths are beautiful.

Can you describe what the experience of Torah study is for you? Does it give meaning to your life? Change or shift your state of consciousness in some way?

I love studying Torah and don't do it nearly enough. I read the parsha online like an oracle, as some people pull a rune or throw the I Ching. I do those things, too. Oracles give perspective on our life in the moment or concerning a specific matter or question.

I could not tell another person how to fulfill their life, but I'm sure Jewish religious leaders say that because of the tremendous value that they personally have gotten from their study of Torah. It is a wonderful study. I love the cyclical nature and structure of parsha reading and the infinite interpretation that is possible, down to the gematria[69]. No one in my family that I know of ever really studied Torah, so I cannot say it brings up emotional connections to my past. My maternal grandmother was a Kohen[70], however.

How does your spiritual path relate to that which people call "God"?

Alex and I are both very comfortable with the word God, which transcends concepts. In this we feel resonant with the Jewish respect for the Divine as the unpronounceable name. In our experience, God is beyond words. Artists of all kinds spend their lives attempting to portray God. God, the Creator, is a Divine Artist. We are the channels and as such, the co-creators.

---

[69] Gematria is a system of assigning numerical value to a word or phrase, in the belief that words or phrases with identical numerical values bear some relation to each other.
[70] A Kohen is the Hebrew word for priest. Jews with the name Cohen or Kohen are traditionally believed to be of direct patrilineal descent from the Biblical Aaron.

Do you hold other ways of understanding this than monotheism?

Non-duality, the concept of no independent arising, seems totally in concord with the One-True-God. If God is One, we all are praying to the same God. Krishna, Arjuna, Shiva, Parvati, Christ, Buddha and Mohamed, are all stories and, as such, works of art open to infinite interpretation, symbolic and not literal.

A beautiful example of this kind of interpretation that I've recently been hearing says that the manna in the desert was actually psilocybin mushrooms growing on the dung of the livestock wandering around with the people. The transgressors that created a Golden Calf were worshipping the physical beast that pooped out the dung onto which grew the mushroom that allowed them to commune with the Divine. The story tells us that God became very angry about this. The lesson being that we should not worship the sacrament and lose sight of the Source, the God within inspiring us to be a channel of the Divine.

Mohammed said, "To know oneself is to know Allah." Self- and God-knowing is very sophisticated mysticism with which the Kabbalah is aligned. Many religions, cross-culturally, have a sense of celestial hierarchy; speaking with angels and hearing the voice of the Divine happens in the stories of most religions.

"Love is the Universal Religion, Art is Universal Religious Expression."
–from CoSM website

What would you like to add as words to the Jewish people?

Albert Schweitzer said, "Dogma divides. Spirit unites."
The Dalai Lama said, "Be a good human being. Not a bad human being."
Alex says, "The secret name of God is Love."
I heard a voice that said, "Every moment is an opportunity for love and transformation."
And another voice that said, "Laugh more."

Thank you.

Tom (Tomás) Pinkson
Traveling Troubadour Cosmic Coyote Magic Mojo Medicine Man

"*At one point during the evening, I saw a rainbow-colored serpent crawling amongst the flames. It stopped in front of me. I thanked it for coming to me, then asked, Old one, what do you bring me? The serpent replied, Give me your beliefs, attitudes, identities, and behaviors that no longer serve you, that get in the way of your healthy growth and the blossoming of your flowers. I will take them into the heart of the Tatewari and he, the first shaman, will burn them up. I am always here, with the fire, to help you clean out your pipes – that way you will be able to stay in contact with Grandfather Fire and Kauyumari. Always respect Tatewari. Then he will help you in your life. Stay with the fire as much as you can. This is your Grandfather.*

You are an emissary for an ancient wisdom struggling to be heard in a culture that has lost respect for the sacred. You were initiated into the sacred way of the shaman over twenty thousand years ago. You are becoming who you are. This knowledge has been encoded in you ever since. Now is the time to bring it alive. You must use it to revise your life."

— From *Shamanic Wisdom of the Huichol: Medicine Teachings for Modern Times* by Tom Pinkson

(Joining Tomás in his office in San Rafael, California, we sit across a small cloth altar on the floor. On it is a feather and a shell with sage and copal. He lights the sage and brushes some of the smoke over the altar and over each of us.[72] He offers a prayer invoking the spirits of the four directions, our ancestors and guiding spirits and expresses his gratitude for my coming to talk with him. He offers prayers that this book project will help bring healing and light to all the peoples of the world.)

In your book, *Shamanic Wisdom of the Huichol: Medicine Teachings for Modern Times*[73], there was no mention in your description of your childhood of your family as Jewish. Were both your parents Jewish?

My mother, father and all my relatives were Jewish. Other than my non-Jewish looks from the Scandinavian that snuck into the woodpile generations back, I'm pure blood.

What was it like in your family? Were they religious with strong Jewish identity?

No religion, but very strong identity as Jews. Yiddish was spoken a lot so the kids wouldn't understand what the grownups were talking about. My Dad died when I was four years old. He had a number of orthodox people on his side of the family but it didn't pass on to him. My mother and father were both political radicals; I was a "red diaper baby." There was no spirituality. I didn't even know what the word spiritual meant. But Yiddish and Jewish culture were strong.

We celebrated Hanukah and Passover along with my grandpar-

---

[72] Burning sage and brushing the smoke over oneself or others is a form of blessing and a purification ritual commonly known as "smudging." It is a Native American practice that has been adopted by many who honor indigenous spirituality.

[73] *Shamanic Wisdom of the Huichol: Medicine Teachings for Modern Times*, by Tom Pinkson, Destiny Books; New Edition of The Flowers of Wiricuta, 2010. In this autobiographical book, Tom recounts his journey from atheism into mysticism, followed by his series of initiations with the Huichol Indians. He has journeyed numerous times with the Huichol on their pilgrimage to find the sacred medicine plant, peyote, and he has participated with them in their ceremonial use of this sacrament.

ents on my mother's side who were also from a progressive political background without any spiritual overtones. It was more historical and cultural; emphasizing the importance of the struggles for freedom and making this relevant to the injustices of modern times. That was the Jewish heritage passed on to my sisters and I that was most important. My parents were very active in the peace movement and the civil rights movement, taking part in many demonstrations.

We moved to LA for a few years after my dad died, and when my mother remarried we moved to Maryland with my new dad. He had the same orientation: no spirituality, a progressive activist. They got together with other progressives in the D.C. area to start a secular Sunday school.

Secular Jewish Sunday school?

Yea, for the kids of fellow progressives.

There were enough in Maryland to have a school?

Yes, the school had a pretty good-sized community that grew up around it. Carl Bernstein (the investigative journalist) was one year ahead of me in the Sunday school.

We would get a lot of historical and cultural stuff about Jewish life and liberation struggles around the world. We learned about oppression, slavery, prejudice, racism, discrimination and how Jews throughout time had stood up against these threats to human dignity. That was the Jewish heritage that was transmitted to me. That's what being a Jew was about: being concerned about injustice and freedom for everybody; be involved; be aware; pay attention; and do something about what's going on. That's what a good Jew does. That was the heritage that I got.

Did they use Biblical stories?

Yes. About being slaves and being freed and such. My mother's name was Ruth, so she'd tell us of Ruth and other heroines in Jewish history. Not from a spiritual, but from a political context; there were heroes standing up against oppression.

I never went into a synagogue until I was an adult, except one time when our Sunday school went on a field trip. I was ten or eleven and couldn't sit still, bored.

You were never bar mitzvahed?[74]

My biological dad, the one who died when I was young, his orthodox mother wanted me to be bar mitzvahed. So my mother came to me and asked me about it. At thirteen, I was a pretty disturbed kid due to the unresolved grief from my dad's death. I had shut down emotionally, was angry, acting out through alcohol abuse and delinquency. I said, "No way" to a bar mitzvah. I didn't even want to discuss it. But finally I said, "If they want to throw a party for me, I'll show up and collect the money. But don't ask me to say anything." I kept my word and that is exactly the way it happened.

Growing up I saw a great deal of hypocrisy amongst supposedly religious Christians and Jews which further turned me off to religion of any kind. I saw them having their religious holidays and I saw what kind of people they were on the other days. So religion itself was just bullshit and hypocrisy to me. On top of that, I was raised with the Marxist idea that, "religion is the opiate of the masses."

I was turned off to everything except sports and when testosterone hit, girls. For me, religion was just more hypocritical BS of society.

Jewish culture was evidently linked to leftist politics for you. Did you still have the sense of specialness of being Jewish, perhaps in a tribal, cultural or political way?

There was a sense of otherness. When we moved to Maryland,

---

[74] The term bar mitzvah is a noun and the correct way of using the term is to say, "he is a bar mitzvah," meaning he is one subject to the law. In common usage, the term is often used as a verb, such as "he was bar mtzvahed." The more common usage is found throughout this book.

after growing up in New York in a biracial community and then L.A., we were in the South, it felt to me like the deep South. Previously, I had never heard people use the word "nigger" before in my life. My mother had told me never to say that word. In Maryland, almost everyone used it all the time, along with discriminatory jokes about "kikes" and "Jews." I remember one day, when I was eight or nine, I was hiking with some friends in the woods and we got to a country club and saw a sign that said, "No Colored, dogs or Jews!" My dad told me about certain neighborhoods that had a "covenant" to not let in any Jews.

Because I didn't look Jewish, people would say anti-Semitic things in front of me. As a young, traumatized and insecure kid in a new neighborhood, I felt overwhelmed by it all. I just wanted to fit in. I didn't' have any Jewish friends. I didn't want to be identified as a Jew. I didn't want to be on the receiving end of the prejudice. I was trying to survive. It was a very tough junior high I entered when I was 11. I was thrown in with older kids who were pretty bad dudes, guys 16, 17, even 18, all in junior high. Almost daily fights in school, teachers were attacked. I had to get strong and tough myself to survive. I didn't have any space for being Jewish. Being Jewish was a component of my life that didn't feel safe. It's not safe out there, better pull in.

Did you ever process how that experience imprinted you?

Not until I was much older, in junior college, when I started to apply my self in school taking courses in psychology, sociology, philosophy, history, trying to understand why I had acted the way I did in my middle teen years. In my early twenties, I started to deal with my unresolved grief from my dad's death, going into therapy and other kinds of growth groups and activities that were the rage in the 1960s. This included psychedelics, which totally opened me to self-exploration and mysticism.

That feeling of not being safe ties into one of the powerful collective experiences of Jews?

I think that not feeling safe is in our gene pool because of our history and the violence directed against Jews around the world through the ages. I think it's in our collective unconscious as Jews.

Did your family get very involved with talking about the Holocaust or Israel?

My second dad's father was a Zionist, but neither of my parents were. They were idealistic communists in their youth, then socialists after it came out about the atrocities of Stalin. So I didn't grow up hearing much about Israel other than its ancient history and its struggle to become a nation after World War ll. My mother did gave me the book Exodus to read when I was a teenager. I heard quite a lot about the Holocaust and the relatives we had lost in it. But I was so lost in my own pain and grief, it was hard for me to take anything else in. My parents would talk about kibbutz life at times. But again, I was so closed down that not much entered my constricted mind.

What was the feeling about non-Jews?

I never heard my parents say a negative word about Christians, but somehow I got that they were the bad guys. I heard the word "Goyim" a lot from my grandparents. I'd hear lots of jokes disparaging the "Goys," as well as frequent stories about prejudicial behavior of Christians to Jews. I once heard my grandmother say a negative term for African-Americans, "shvarza,"[75] and I was shocked. It showed me that even though she was a progressive in her politics and for civil rights, she still had some prejudice.

My parents made me go to Sunday school while I was in elementary school. But around the age of eleven I stopped doing that. There were a couple of Jewish kids at school that I'd hang with a bit, but once I was in Junior High, I hung out mostly with the non-Jewish kids. In

---

[75] Shvarza literally means "black" in Yiddish, but when used to refer to Black people, it is mostly with a negative connotation, arguably the equivalent to the English slur, "niggar."

high school, I formed a street gang with some other hoodlum types and there was only one other Jewish guy besides myself in the group. He was also non-religious and not identified with his Jewish roots.

You crossed that cultural boundary as a youth and didn't feel a special affinity or need to be with the Jewish kids?

Part of that was that I was very athletic and the Jewish kids were more cerebral, not athletes or into sports. I saw them as bookish, square, not fun, not the ones I wanted to be with.

Were your parents oriented that way, cerebral?

My parents were both intellectuals, very cultured, avid readers, even though they were from blue collar and working class backgrounds.

Even though you were into rejecting everything, it sounds like you took in the Jewish transmission of focusing on the intellectual?

The prevailing notion that I got from my parents was to be smart. My mother told me that reading would open worlds to me and it did. I tended to read about sports and historical heroes. I loved reading through encyclopedias just for the joy of learning. My dad was a savvy businessman and dinner table talk was about politics and world events. Even though I was pretty closed off, I'd still hear it. My mother pushed education and learning. That was huge. I think part of why I was turned off with school was that it was boring compared to the things I was learning on my own. There was a lack of stimulation in school; I was bored.

Even though you were hiding from your Jewish identity, do you feel you inherited Jewish traits or values nonetheless, besides the intellectual focus?

Yes certainly. Most importantly, progressive values and world views that emphasized the Jewish tradition as people who cared about others. Throughout history, we had endured terrible violence and prejudice and thus we shared the importance of standing up against oppression and injustice of any kind. Get involved, help others, do something to make a better world for all. That's the primary value. Because we remember how we have been treated, we have compassion for others and always treat them with respect and dignity. It brings up tears, strong feelings. It's very deep in me.

Were you ever drawn to re-connect with your Jewish identity in a positive way?

Yes, through my opening via psychedelics and my healing process of examining my past, I became interested in that which I had rejected in my earlier years. I started to read up on Jewish religion, mysticism, history, culture, YIddish poetry, etc. I once attended a "World Work" session with Arnie Mindell[76] in which participants (200 of them from around the world together in one room for ten days) are encouraged to speak uncensored from their gut. There, I had an experience that brought me into my Jewishness with full force.

I was sitting on the outskirts of the group in a safe place, kind of hiding. There was this very dynamic and powerful Jewish woman sitting in the center of the circle with some other women around her and she was expressing her hurt and anger at prejudice directed at her and other Jews. At one point she became irate and screamed, "Where are the Jewish men? Where are the Jewish men here? I don't see them." I felt ashamed, totally busted. She was in there, taking the heat and battling for me and I was staying safe in the background. I felt totally busted by what she said and the next thing I knew, the tension inside me was so great, I couldn't stay where I was. I had to go into the center of that circle. I had to take the risk and be heard and be seen as a Jew. I was owning my identity as a Jew. Growing up, it wasn't safe to do that. I learned that in certain circumstances I wouldn't be public about that or I could be attacked. It wasn't safe.

[76] Arnie & Amy Mindell lead experiential process groups called World Work, which aim to resolve conflicts and build community. See http://www.worldwork.org

So in this situation, I just came right into the center and somehow I just erupted in there in the context of what was being addressed. I felt a combination of things. I felt my previously repressed anger from the hurt of anti-Semitic prejudice. Previously repressed feelings about issues that had long troubled me from mainstream culture burst forth: that we are a "Christian nation," that we're told to "be good Christians," that kind of thing. I realized that these messages marginalized my people and myself. Where does that leave us? So I felt this fury erupt in me that had been repressed all these years bursting forth and there I was in the center of the room with this rage.

I don't remember how, but I got to a place inside myself where after the anger was expressed I felt a deep inner peace. Later in the session, I ended up leading the whole group in the Hebrew peace song, "Shalom Haverim[77]" that I remembered from Sunday school long ago. Now, as I try to make sense of it, I see that after the rage and anger came out, then came the healing. I was not interested in trading violence and prejudice for more of the same, or attacking anyone. I turned to, "How can we come together as one human family?" Somehow, that song came up; the only Jewish song I knew. My mother was always singing Jewish songs. I was so alienated that I didn't let much in, but somehow that was in me and it just came out.

What was it that opened you up to a more spiritual orientation from your atheism?

I opened up my consciousness from the constricted state through LSD in 1966. After my LSD experience, I was so blown away that I felt I had to try to understand it. My initial view of the field was that Hindus, Buddhists and Taoists had some handle on it.

"My guides for the session considered LSD to be a sacred substance, "like a communion wafer." ... I had a full-blown, spiritually transforming mystical experience...and in many ways, my life since then has been an

---

[77] A popular Jewish song, meaning, "Go now in peace."

attempt to integrate what I saw….It took the form of three visions…. In the first, I watched in fascination as the forms on the ceiling turned into an undulating bas relief mosaic as seen in Meso-American stone-carved art … portraying a complete life cycle of a group of ancient Meso-Americans living and dying, making love, babies being born and nursed, parents working in the fields, children growing up, becoming adults, having children of their own, growing old, dying, new life coming through in the next generation, and so on. Mesmerized, I experienced, déjà vu, a memory of being a part of this very cycle that I was now watching. I knew I was watching myself in a previous lifetime! I also heard an internal voice: Not only did you live during this time, you will be returning to it in this lifetime as well.

The vision (then) took me into a vortex of time. I began to see the line of my ancestral heritage going back to the very beginning. I witnessed how each successive generation instilled its experience into the new generation all the way up to my parents doing it to me…. I watched the evolution of experience, values and concerns each generation had, and how it moved forward in time to culminate in me, shaping my very beliefs, values and personality, my raison d'etre. Simultaneously, I saw that the essence of my Being was something far beyond the conditioning of my ancestral roots. It was an energy force of Light that was connected with an infinite cosmic Light. I saw my soul and for the first time I understood the saying in the bible that we are made in God's image.

In the third vision, I saw Christ on the cross, his body being impaled, his shudders at receiving the blows. Then my awareness went inside his body, feeling what he was feeling, and I wanted to kill the bastards who were inflicting the torture. But a voice from within Christ said, 'Forgive them, Father, they know not what they do.' At that moment, I felt the presence of a kind of love that I didn't even know existed, welling up in Christ's heart and extending toward his abusers…. This vision was to come back to me in many forms in the ensuing years, but this was the first opening of the door."

— From *Shamanic Wisdom of the Huichol: Medicine Teachings for Modern Times* by Tom Pinkson

Your spiritual awakening came with an LSD experience and you looked for models and maps and saw these mostly coming from Eastern religions. Was there any thought at the time that it might come from a Jewish context?

LSD was the doorway to opening to the reality of the spiritual dimension. I sought out books and teachings on Hinduism, Buddhism and Taoism, and focused for a number of years with those. I had no awareness of a Jewish mystical tradition at the time. It was years later that I started to hear about the ancient mystical tradition of the Jews, and I felt cheated that I had never even known it existed.

How did you go from the Eastern religions to shamanism?

I did have some exposure in those early days of exploration. I recall that at the "Holy Man Jam" in San Francisco, where there were gurus from Hindu and Buddhist traditions, Rolling Thunder[78] was there. But it didn't really click because I was focused on the Eastern way.

Where it really got started was when I was working with adolescent addicts and I started a wilderness project modeled on Outward Bound. In the program, after challenging mountain climbing experiences, a participant would have a period of 24 hours of solitude in the mountains without any food. I went through the experience myself and it was very powerful. It was actually my introduction to meaningful ritual.

On my solo time during the day, I took off all my clothes and walked through the mountains feeling very peaceful. A small stick caught my attention and I picked it up and carried it with me, my fingers somehow feeling a connection with it. When I set up my tarp that night to sleep, I was terrified about bears that I'd seen around. So I

---

[78] Rolling Thunder, birth name John Pope, was a Native American medicine man. He was born into the Cherokee nation and later immigrated to Nevada and lived with the Western Shoshone. He is the subject of *Rolling Thunder* (1976), a book by the American journalist and author Doug Boyd, and *Rolling Thunder Speaks A Message for Turtle Island* (1998), a narrative edited by his second wife, Carmen Sun Rising Pope. He became a well known teacher and hero of the counter-culture and for those seeking the wisdom of the Native American people.

hung this piece of wood over me where I was sleeping and I thought maybe it would give me protection.

I didn't sleep well, worrying with every sound, and I thought, "Well, if I survive this night, I'll give thanks to that stick that it helped me in some way." After the long night, when I saw predawn light, I knew I'd survived and I felt this tremendous gratitude for the return of light and being able to see; I didn't have to be in the dark, I could see. I realized at that moment how significant that is. I could understand how indigenous peoples throughout the world get up and welcome that in. It's an amazing thing. How could any sane person not get up and do that, celebrate the sunrise?

I realized that I'd done this ritual with the stick, putting it above my tarp and saying that it would help me survive, and at that point, I saw the power of ritual. I took the stick off the cord and held it over my heart and to the sun and expressed my gratitude. That was an opening into ritual and understanding of the role it plays with indigenous people. I saw the underpinning of the why of ritual, that it is connected to life-giving and life-sustaining events without which we wouldn't be here; it's about expressing gratitude back to those powers that give us life.

When the guides came to pick me up, I knew that I had just scratched the surface. I knew that I needed to come back and do this again for a longer period of time. A year or so later, inner guidance told me that I needed to do that, and when I did, I had an amazing transformational experience.

On my return from that trip, I stopped at a bookstore and the book, *Lame Deer, Seeker of Vision*[79], jumped out at me. It told of Lame Deer's experience as an adolescent, being alone fasting in the mountains in solitude. I saw how his whole culture was predicated on giving young people the kind of experience I'd just had, providing it at a vital time of life for a rite of passage. I could see how my culture had given me nothing meaningful as a rite of passage, so I'd gotten involved in acting out as a juvenile delinquent. It was my way of testing myself in

---

[79] *Lame Deer, Seeker of Visions*, by Richard Erdoes & John (Fire) Lame Deer, Simon & Schuster.

an adventure without knowing the outcome. Clearly, the rite of passage I'd created for myself was an anti-social one and not constructive. But it was a seeking of that experience.

I saw that Lame Deer's culture recognized the importance of this kind of experience for the rite of passage of teenagers and it raised the question in my mind of other transitions in the life cycle. I guessed that his culture recognized the need for taking people through rituals at various points to help them come through to the other side strengthened and empowered. I wanted to learn more about indigenous cultures.

I recognized that I needed to find a teacher and as things work, two or three months later, someone introduced me to a Native American who was teaching art at a local college. After really testing me to see if I was worthy, he became my mentor. He told me that if I wanted to really learn about this, I would have to learn how to penetrate the "buckskin curtain" as he called it. Several months later, he invited me to a ceremony with a medicine man. So he lifted the buckskin curtain and introduced me to this medicine man and that opened the door to my introduction in a conscious way to learning about shamanism.

Coming back to the question of Jewish spirituality, when you did learn of Jewish mysticism, did it ever draw you to be more involved or take up a Jewish religious practice?

Once I became aware that there was a root in my tradition that speaks to me, I felt ripped off that I'd never been exposed to it. What a loss that was. I began to read as much as I could about Jewish mystics and met a few times with a progressive rabbi who I'd met who shared more with me about our mystical tradition. I even thought of going to rabbinical school to become a rabbi. I started to study Kabbalah and other teachings, but still did not feel drawn into synagogue attendance or Jewish practices. I did start to wear a Jewish star necklace and feel ownership of my Jewish roots with pride and gratitude.

Is there anything about the Jewish path that caused you to choose what you do instead of being a rabbi?

Quite a while ago, I was reading about the prophets and I realized that my ancestors did exactly what I'm doing with my vision quest work. I realized that I am carrying on part of that tradition. They went out in the desert and fasted up in the mountain for vision, guidance and communion with Spirit. That's exactly what I've been doing now for thirty-eight years. I feel that I'm carrying on a primal root of Jewish spirituality going back to the very beginning, the visionary tradition that went out into nature in solitude and sought communion with greater power, then brought the fruits of that encounter back to share with their people.

So I feel huge connections. I feel like I'm carrying on the deepest roots of my people and that's huge for me (tears). It's very important. Later on, I became aware of Gershon Winkler's[80] teachings about the shamanic roots of Jewish mysticism, and that confirmed what I'd been feeling.

You seem to retain that Jewish connection within yourself, yet it doesn't come out as Jewish forms of ritual and prayer.

Because I don't really know those; I wasn't brought up in them. When I read Winkler, it felt very simpatico to the way I do my prayers and rituals. He teaches that shamanism was a vital part of Judaism before the patriarchy got threatened by it and took things over. In my thanksgiving prayers to the Earth, the plants, the animals, the trees, the flowers, the Creator of All, I am doing a Jewish mitzvah of giving gratitude to and celebrating the animating forces of life and the Source from which they all come forth from.

When people ask me, "What religion are you?" I say, "I'm Jewish." If they ask, how do you reconcile it with this or that, I say that I'm carrying on the oldest tradition of my people, like the prophets. They went out and had their experiences and then came back and tried to share the fruits of what they received for the people, for their betterment.

---

[80] Rabbi Winkler is the founder of Walking Stick Foundation, devoted to the recovery of "aboriginal Judaism." He teaches a highly unconventional approach to Judaism, linking it to indigenous and shamanic spirituality.

Gershon Winkler's view that shamanism is the ancient way of Judaism is new to most people, including you. Did reading his ideas bring about a shift in your attitude about Judaism?

Yes. Reading his work made me feel an even deeper connection with the original roots of my tribal people, not what patriarchy later did with that. It's the spirituality that was brought back from the deserts and mountains by the visionary prophets. I had only previously known that certain prophets had gone out on what I'd call vision quests and that I was following in that root. His teachings make it clearer that most of the Jewish religion has its roots in similar ideas or experiences to shamanism. I felt and still feel very affirmed in what I have been doing, reclaiming indigenous mind and indigenous spirituality. That is what Judaism grew out of historically - people relating to the land and animating life forces of that land in a way of gratitude and celebration, honoring the Gifter and the Gifts and seeking to live in harmony with it and all of creation.

You seem to have an understanding that stretches the boundary of what it means to be Jewish in saying that you are on a Jewish path, even though you don't use the language, methodology or forms associated with that. Is that correct? Would you say that you are Jewish and practicing the Jewish religion?

Of course to the first. I'm a Jew. But I wouldn't say I practice the religion because I'm still suspicious of all organized religions. I think there are good things in Judaism as in Christianity. There is a light and shadow to whatever you look at. I wouldn't say I'm practicing the Jewish religion, but I'd say I'm a spiritual person in touch with the deepest reality. As a Jewish person, a Jewish man, looking back to the beginning of my people's experience, I'm continuing in that tradition. It's not that I'm practicing the Jewish religion. It's that I am a Jewish man trying to honor my spirituality in a way that feels right to me. It's interesting though, that when I pray by myself, I see that I am davening.[81]

---

[81] Davening is the term used for Jewish prayer. While praying in the standing position, individuals often rock back and forth, and this movement is commonly referred to as davaning.

> *"My religious heritage is Jewish. I lost relatives to Hitler's genocide and I lost relatives fighting against it. This history of prejudice, discrimination, persecution, and violence is a part of who I am. My roots also include a long history of standing up against oppression and supporting justice for all peoples, a tradition of which I am proud. ... My way is of the Earth, the way of listening to nature. I have found it amongst the shamanic people who still live according to the earth-based spirituality of their ancestors. It is these people who face an even greater holocaust than the one faced by mine, and it is still going on today. ...*
>
> *"We should not seek to copy Native people and be something we are not, but instead endeavor to learn from them, and with them in cooperative partnership, with sensitivity, respect, and humility, how to create a way of life that is in harmony with all the forces of creation and the spirit of the land."*
>
> From *Shamanic Wisdom of the Huichol: Medicine Teachings for Modern Times* by Tom Pinkson

A major focus of most religions involves prayer. How do you work with prayer?

Two thoughts come to me in terms of prayer. I have a group that's been meeting for 10 or 15 years, and we make a commitment to pray for each other every day. In that context, I would say that what I mean by prayer is bringing our awareness to our breath and following it down into our heart with the intention to use that fuel of breath and awareness to open our hearts to the presence of love inside of us. We don't create that love, just as we don't create the breath. Love is just part of the given nature of the universe that we inhabit and that inhabits us. So we open the doors to the vault of the treasure chest within, that energy of love, and send it out to some person; just send that love to that person. There is no intention to control them or to tell them how to use it, or to change them. It is just a free gift for however they need to use it. I call doing this practice, prayer.

So that's one way that I use prayer; opening the heart to send love to a person. You can't go wrong with that in any situation. It helps you when you do it and it does in fact send helpful energy to that person.

They may or may not be aware of it, and there is no expectation of something back from them. Just do it. When I say I'm going to pray for you, or when people ask me to pray for them, that's what I'm doing.

The other kind of prayer comes from the understanding of what physicists call "quantum entanglement," the recognition that on the deeper levels of reality unseen to the ordinary eye, everything is connected in mysterious ways like an invisible web. We all have the potential to access that web because we are living in the middle of it and it's living in us. We can learn to access that web with intentionality, consciousness, and focused energy, and "wiggle" it in precise ways where it then has the potential to activate other areas of the web in order to achieve desired outcomes. This is what shamanism is about, and this is one aspect of mystical practices in many traditions.

Who knows what's possible to accomplish in this life unless we show up and give it our best shot using whatever psycho-spiritual technology that might help us in the process? If we don't try something because of our thought forms of limitation and inadequacy, or the rational thinking mind that says, "it's not possible," nothing happens. But if we try, freeing our energy up, putting it out in a positive way towards an end that is not hurtful to anyone and is in alignment with the greatest good for that person or situation, then it can access a larger, deeper inter-connected, power or Presence that has the potential to do anything it wants to do.

The wisdom that underlies and is interwoven with that web is a manifestation of the intelligence, consciousness and creative power that creates big bangs, universes, the whole *mishpuchah*.[82] In this form of prayer, we access the web through genuine gratitude. When we genuinely feel gratitude in our hearts for the gifts of grace in our lives and for life itself, when we really feel it and send it into that web, it opens up the doorway.

For the person in our group who had major melanoma surgery, we joined together to give thanks for his life. We prayed for his health and

---

[82] *Mishpuchah* in Yiddish means family. "The whole mishpuchah" is often used with some humor to mean "everyone and everything." Interestingly, in shamanic circles, the phrase mitakuye oyasin derived from the Lakota language, meaning "all my relations," is often used.

well being to whatever degree we might be able to have influence on the outcome. We prayed for good results from the biopsy and that he would have a good, long and healthy life. We put all of our energy into accessing the web with that intentionality, without attachment to the outcome. When we are attached to the outcome, we tighten, and when we're tight, we're coming from fear and that obstructs the clarity of intention.

So interwoven in the prayer is not being attached to outcome, and if that outcome which we would like is not for his greatest good, we surrender to that. But we focus into the web with our intentionality for his greatest good and pray to activate that as an outcome. We never know when our energy is going to contribute towards reaching a critical mass in any given situation, and therefore there is always hope.

What about intermediate spirits, power animals, ancestors?

These are all different ways of accessing the grid, the web; these are all entry points. Different people, depending on where they are in their life experiences, have different access points. For instance, it could be your Aunt Ida or other ancestor who is now in the spirit world, or the unicorn or bear who might be a totemic animal. It could be a place of power like Mr. Shasta. There are infinite ways of accessing the grid for different people depending on their life experience, and power animals are the shamanic way of doing so.

Would you say that the grid is similar to what people call God?

The grid or web (I'm using the terms interchangeably) is a manifestation of God. God is the word we in the mainstream West call the ultimate source of all. The grid is a manifestation of God's mysterious creative power, what you might call the invisible reality underlying the world of perceived physical phenomenon.

Of what you know of the Jewish religion and how it has evolved, is there anything that you've come to see as problematic in the Jewish worldview as regards the wisdom and truths that are sacred to you? For example, how do you see monotheism as related to the shamanic path?

I see monotheism as a manifestation of patriarchal his-tory and worldview which is a relatively recent event in the scope of human history. My understanding is that in the original language of the Old Testament the deity was not expressed as masculine. That was a later occurrence formulated by a male-dominated priestly caste. My direct experience tells me that all of creation has consciousness within its energy form, and has spirit and intelligence as well. Human intelligence is relatively recent on the scale of evolution, but non-human intelligence is part and parcel of the interfaced universe or universes in which we are embedded. As a spiritual man who is Jewish, I worship both the Creator and the Created. What mainstream Jewish thinking and religious practice has to say about the matter does not set my course in life or in my beliefs; my direct experience does that.

Muslims, Christians and Jews tend to think of themselves as a higher evolution from the Pagan and indigenous peoples' ways. These religions evolved into what we know as monotheism and claim to have a covenant with the one highest God. Some see that as a disconnect between earth-based spirituality and Jewish forms of practice. You've immersed yourself with the Huichol and Mazatec. Your thoughts?

I don't have any formal Jewish religious practices, but I believe our historical Jewish roots were in fact based on sacred relationship to the land that our ancestors were originally living on. So I do not experience any disconnect for myself as a spiritual Jewish man involved with indigenous spirituality and practices. To me, real spirituality is all about respectful, right-relationship to creation, creator, and to all life, human and non-human. Right relationship is that which honors, protects and sustains healthy interaction patterns with the creative powers that create life, i.e., with nature and the animating invisible wisdom power—God, Spirit, Great Spirit, Holy Spirit, Cosmic Mother, Goddess, Shekinah—that underlies what we observe with our senses and ordinary consciousness. My time spent studying with indigenous elders around the world from various traditions for the past forty years takes me back into a remembering of my own indigenous mind, which connects me to my Jewish ancestors and my roots as a spiritual Being.

As for monotheists claiming higher wisdom and evolutionary status over nature-based pagan religions, just check out the violence committed against non-believers from the three monotheistic religions throughout their history and you'll find that the record is incredible. Whatever happened to "Thou shall not kill?" Moses goes up on the mountain and comes back with tablets that say among other things, "Thou shalt not kill." Then, in a few minutes, he's leading a slaughter of ten thousand of his own people who are practicing Goddess worship. That always blew my mind.

The male patriarchy of all the monotheistic religions does not want anyone going to God except through them. I see in history the influence of patriarchy shaping Judaism, and in that I have no interest. So there are parts of Judaism I accept and parts that I am against, such as favoring boy babies over girls. That's not okay with me, nor that until recently only men could become rabbis. Not okay in my book. My parents taught me to question authority, not take for granted what others told me, to go out and do my own research based on my experience of what is true and what is good, good for all. That is what I have tried to do with my life.

To me, the pure root of Jewish spirituality is our ancestors' vision-seeking and spiritual communion in the deserts and mountains of ancient Israel. That's the tradition I feel I'm still carrying on. As I've come to learn the mystical teachings of Judaism in my later years, I've sought to integrate them into my life. I try them out and see if they work for me in a meaningful way. These are not so much about religious practices, but about practical tools by which to access the realm of the divine higher consciousness and achieve union with the infinite Spirit that is the underlying reality of all creation.

You've evolved to an acceptance of your Jewish identity and seem to see our ancestral lineage as containing a universal truth. Sufis and other mystics also speak of a universal truth. So is it important to maintain a Jewish identity for the future? Do you see there being a negative side of tribalism?

I do believe there is a great importance to maintaining a Jewish identity for the future, as Jewish values have contributed a great deal to the progress of humanity in medicine, science, philosophy, the arts, philanthropy, in the power of faith, courage, generosity, humor, service and caring. But I've always had trouble with the notion of "the chosen people." It goes against the core values with which I was raised to say that one people is better or more deserving than others; herein is the danger of tribalism.

As I look at the Jewish religion and its role in the world, I see many wonderful things that it accomplishes and brings to people. But I also see many shadow aspects that I don't like, such as Israel's treatment of Palestinians and what's going on over there. Nevertheless, it is very interesting to me that this small group of desert wanderers, still a very small group in the world, has survived for all these years through so much and has contributed in so many positive ways to bettering the life of humanity. I think that we as Jews owe it to our ancestors, to all those who perished under the sword of the Nazis, the Cossacks in Russia, and others throughout history, to carry on a Jewish identity, a Jewish presence in the world community. We need to simultaneously honor our history, our story, our way of being in the world, while equally honoring the history and contributions of the other tribes that inhabit our planet. We need to recognize that beneath our cultural, religious and social differences, we are all one people, one family; we are all related, and what we do to the other we do to ourselves.

It certainly seems that the Jewish journey through the millennia has included powerful encounters with the shadow; some would say evil. What do you see as the lessons in that?

We are a part of nature and nature is in us. As much as I love the warmth of the sun, and the daytime, and being able to see flowers opening, there is also the night. So too in us, there are light and dark energies. We have the reptilian brain and we wouldn't have survived without that. When it perceives a threat, it's either going to run away or kill; that's in us. Mature, wisdom-based cultures that were in touch with nature, developed ways of initiating their young people so that those energies were used towards protecting and nurturing life rather than towards violence. So when our basic needs for love, caring, protection and nurturance are not met as human beings, and on top of that we are slammed by forces in our environment, raped and beaten and such, the system gets warped. Basically, you don't find people who are happy and well adjusted going out and being mean or violent to others. Those energies come up when we are frightened, or are running negative programs about ourselves that say we are worthless or bad, when we have been abused, violated, oppressed.

There are also historical forces that can push people into doing evil towards others. If I'm totally identified with being Jewish, looking at the thousands of years of violence that Christians have committed against Jews could bring up a lot of hatred. Then if my personal life falls apart, I might go to a Catholic church and blow it up in retaliation for what they did to my people. Would I then be evil? I don't think so. Was Hitler evil? You go back and look at the dynamics of what happened with him and his father and you get a better understanding of how emotional and physical abuse in childhood can lead to very sick and disturbed people taking out their pain on others. I have within me the full potential of the human experience from saintliness to evil.

Everyone comes in with that full range of potential. What comes forth in a person's life has to do with so many interfacing variables, ranging from brain chemistry to social and economic pressures to childhood dynamics. Anyone, under certain conditions, could grow up to be a raving psychopathic murderer, or a saint, and all points in between. It's not an external force of evil, the devil and such; hurtful behavior comes out of hurt people.

Energy fields play a role in human behavior as well. I had an experience on LSD once on a farm in Virginia. Horrible things had happened there to the Indians and I could feel it and had to get out of there. I think such energy fields exist, and a "person of power"[83] can create and access an evil energy field and use it for their purposes. People like Charles Manson or Hitler and others, who had charisma and personal power, knew how to manipulate the web in a way to create more power and to influence many, even millions, of people. But I don't see it as a battle between God and an external force, the Devil, making us do evil things.

I look at myself as a troubled teen and know I was doing all kinds of hurtful things to people. Someone could have died. I could be in jail for murder. Was I evil? No, I was hurting, and it was coming out as hurting others.

How do you work with people to transmit the knowledge and teachings you have acquired?

Wakan[84] is a spiritual community that grew out of my visionary work years ago, and it is still going. We do solstice and equinox celebrations and other events. We celebrate good times with each other and are there for each other in a supportive way in challenging times of crisis. It is a beautiful thing to see how community comes together to help each other when in need.

---

[83] In shamanism, a "person of power" is one who has learned to access spiritual forces or larger-than-personal energies to bring about changes in the physical world.
[84] WAKAN is a spiritually-based shamanic studies community dedicated to the sacredness of life. The word *wakan* means "sacred" in the Lakota language, and "heart of the sky" in the Mayan language.

My shamanic work includes group work, retreats and leading vision quests in the High Sierra. I see a small number of people individually but my primary work now is with a program I started in 2010 called "Recognition Rights for a New Vision of Aging, Honoring Elders."[85]

I want to ask you about the Trickster. You use "coyote," a Native American version of the Trickster, in your humorous but also serious description of yourself as "traveling troubadour cosmic coyote magic mojo medicine man." What is the trickster?

The Trickster is a cosmic teacher who busts us in our arrogance when we think we know more than we really do. It brings us into humility. "Don't get so ego inflated to think so highly of yourself so that you think your poop doesn't stink." The Trickster is always around, whether manifesting clearly or not; he's saying, "Respect mystery; it's sacred. Don't try to figure it out or control it. Be humble. Remember, it isn't all about you." The Trickster guides one towards humility, and opening to wisdom from spirit beings for guidance on how to go forward in life towards a win-win, which is the only real win in life. Some medicine men are Coyotes; they do their teaching through the Trickster.

Your work with elders seems to bring you through the full cycle, having worked with teens, adults and now elders. What else do you have energy for?

Well, I have not been gifted as a great singer or musician. I have an okay voice and can play somewhat decent sax, piano, guitar and harmonica. For many years, I would sing in retreats, mostly songs or chants from sacred rituals. However, I was coming back from an ayahuasca retreat and a song started singing through me and I pulled over and wrote it down. I was in ecstasy. I found that whenever my at-

---

[85] Through his program, Recognition Rights for a New Vision of Aging, Honoring Elders, and in his book, *Fruitful Aging*, Tom works to revision the experience of growing older in our society. See: http://drtompinkson.com/recognition-rites-for-a-new-vision-of-aging-honoring-elders/

tention went to something, a song started to come through regarding that. So, I've begun recording these songs and I'm filled with passion with the process.

I asked Spirit on a vision quest and was given the name for this work and that is where "traveling troubadour cosmic coyote magic mojo medicine man show" came from. I use it as a vehicle for what I do. It honors an ancient tradition of the troubadour storyteller and the cosmic Trickster. Sometimes I'm the Trickster and sometimes the buffoon being tricked, and it is a show about and with medicine.

What I have energy for is exploration of what is possible: listening and asking what do I have the passion to do, what do I owe myself, my family, and my community? This involves going slow, being present, letting go of yesterday's answers, and noticing what arises internally and in the field around and through me. Just like you coming in and bringing things up.

Music is the thing I love doing most and I love sharing it with people. One of the ways Spirit uses me in this regard is to give everyone out there encouragement to sing, even those who would love to sing but don't have a "great voice," like me. But I don't let it stop me from doing what I love to do. My work with song and music is not about entertainment; it's about inner-attainment of a state of consciousness based on loving connection with self, other, and Spirit. I'm being used to help that process with whomever is open to it. It's a way of dissolving the boundary between "ceremony" and "real life."

Would you express something addressed to the Jewish people?

Take pride in the good things of our people's history, our accomplishments and contributions. Face and own the shadow aspects of Judaism and work to change it. Stand up to be counted and do your part in carrying on the tradition of our ancestors throughout time who have worked to make this a better world for all. May it be so!

(Tom lights some of the sage, smudges us and the altar)

Let's open the doorway.

Thank you Great Spirit for this time with brother Alan and for the good man he is and the good work he does in the world; and thank you for calling him to do this book, for whatever ends it goes, it's wonderful. It's also wonderful to hang out with him today and talk about things that are meaningful to both of us. Thank you for this. Let him go home safely to his loved ones and keep going forth blossoming with what you've given him to do with this.

Thank you for our ancestors; we are remembering you here and all you've been through to pass on life to us. (Tom takes long deep breaths and tears fill his eyes.) I feel the tears coming out and the sadness with thinking about the strife and the violence that's taking place in the world, and the extent that my Jewish people are allowing with our thoughts and actions support of policies that are hurtful to other people. My sense of pain and sadness comes from seeing that and realizing that. I pray for us to come back to remembering how we are all chosen people; that we are all equally loved by Spirit; and that we are all equally important to be here and have contributions to make.

Help us to open and heal our hearts Creator so that we can live out the deepest values for what being a good Jewish person is about. Being a mensch, being a good man, a good woman. It's about being kind and generous and supportive and helpful and working peacefully with our brothers and sisters—Palestinian, Arab, Muslim, of every color and nationality. Working cooperatively and recognizing that in our essential humanity, we are all part of the same family. I pray for healing of historical hurts and fears and bitterness, all of that which closes our heart, so that we can see the Light in our Palestinian brothers and sisters and Muslim brothers and sisters and they too can see the same Light in us, in all of us.

I pray that we can come back to living in a way that God intends us to live: as brothers and sisters, in heart-felt partnership, addressing the human challenges of life, creating a new garden of Eden, living sustainably, living in harmony and balance with all creation, with all people. Not just two-legged people, but all people. I pray for this sacred, fragile world that we are gifted to be part of; I pray for healing of our hearts and our minds and coming back to the real roots and the real understanding of what it means to be a good Jewish person, to honor our sacred heritage, our spiritual heritage, remembering how we too were once in bondage and oppressed and it is our sacred duty to stand up for those who today are struggling for freedom and dignity. As one Hassidic mystic said centuries ago, we need to blow life force into the sparks of divinity in ourselves and others,[86] to come alive to the fullest realization of who we are, what we are, and why we are here, which is all about love. We are all sacred, worthy, luminous beings. We are love and our love is forgiving. May it be so, and so it is.

Thank you.

---

[86] The "shattering of the vessels into sparks of light" is a Kabbalistic metaphor as taught by Isaac Luria. It is part of a complex mystical cosmology in which God's creation shattered into sparks of divinity, which are found in all humans. It is seen as one of the primary tasks of human life to repair the brokenness of the original vessels, a process referred to as *tikkun*.

Padrinho Jonathan Goldman
Leader of the Church of the Holy Light of the Queen (Santo Daime)

"I'm a Jewish kid from Detroit who somehow ended up in the middle of the jungle, in this esoteric, gnostic, Christian, shamanic spiritual path."

(In what seemed like a beautiful synchronicity, I met with Jonathan less than a week following a special Santo Daime work (ceremony)[87] that he had led in which a number of Jewish rabbis participated. In this service, Jewish chants and songs were sung in addition to the traditional ones of the Brazilian church.)

---

[87] The ceremonies of the Santo Daime are known as "works." They include the singing of many hymns and the drinking of the sacrament, a specially prepared brew of ayahuasca which they refer to as the "tea." The overall religious orientation draws a great deal from Catholicism. Thus it is referred to as a syncretic church, blending Christianity and the indigenous spirituality of the people of the Amazon.

How did this special Daime ceremony with a Jewish twist come about?

The esteemed Rabbi Zalman Schachter was leading a special workshop in our town for his students that included 280 people from around the country. He had expressed interest in drinking Daime, and we had been involved in previous discussions with the Rabbi of the Havurah Shir Hadash congregation about the possibility of doing such a work. Reb Zalman's great heart and brilliant, open mind gave us the excuse for this energetic joining of spiritual lines. We held a Daime work on his behalf at the Havurah Shir Hadash. We called the work "One Light." There were eight or ten rabbis among the eighteen people from their community and thirty or so from our community. It was extremely beautiful. Reb Zalman loved it. This was March 9th, 2011.

We did the Daime work in three parts. I put together a collection of Daime hymns for the first part, then we had a section that was Jewish hymns or songs, many of which had come through Reb Zalman. The rabbi of the Havurah, David Zaslow, led that part. He and a few others from their community had participated with us before. One of the rabbis who was present is in fact now an initiate in the Daime, a Fardado (uniformed person).[88] There was a middle section of Jewish songs, then there was another section of Daime hymns.

It was truly beautiful on many levels to have that ceremony together, and it seemed that everyone loved it. The Daime itself, like all traditions, is just a way to organize and direct and give a particular slant on what is a universal spiritual experience. That direct, undeniable, palpable experience of Divine Light is what is usually missing, and certainly can raise the intensity, in many spiritual paths or investigations. We brought that Universal Master, that pure Light, into the context of the Jewish Renewal movement, which has at its heart exactly the same impulse as the Daime—to know God inside yourself, as you and beyond you. People are seeking to reconnect literally, viscerally, palpably with the Divine Forces. The Daime affords that. In this work

---

[88] Members of the Santo Daime wear white shirts, ties and blue jackets (for men) for their ceremonies referred to as uniforms

we investigated together the question of what is the possible place of the Daime in the Jewish tradition.

The idea for the session came from a conversation that Rabbi Zaslow initiated with Padrinho Alfredo, the leader of the Daime Church. It came about when we rented the Havurah space two years ago for his visit to Ashland from his home in the Amazon forest. So many people come to the ceremonies when Padrinho Alfredo visits that we can't hold them all at our own place. The Havurah has a big synagogue that can accommodate the more than two hundred people that come from all over to drink Daime with us in the atmosphere of freedom that we have gained. Since we've liberated the Daime[89], we can go anywhere and perform our ceremonies without worry. The Havurah is literally half a block away from the police station. I love that. I liked wearing my uniform and standing out there in front of the Havurah where anyone can see me.

Rabbi David, who is a brave man, an innovator, a *macher*[90], came and drank Daime in one of the ceremonies we held there, and afterwards he initiated a conversation with Padrinho Alfredo. It was a beautiful conversation. It was an honor to observe and translate for two spiritual leaders from two seemingly very different traditions having a respectful, truthful and deep conversation. David said he wanted to give Daime to his people and Padrinho Alfredo liked the idea. It took some time. Zalman, who is one of the rare ones, in his generosity said, "Let's do it."

I know that in the Daime expereince, there is often what is referred to as a rebirth in which you leave behind the old self and become a new man or woman. In your sense of new self, is it still meaningful to say you are a Jew?

For sure. I've always been clear about that. In the 60s, when I was very active in leftist, anti-war and revolutionary groups, in particular

---

[89] On March 18, 2009, a U.S. District Court judge, found that the U.S. Religious Freedom Restoration Act (RFRA) protects the Santo Daime's use of DMT-containing ayahuasca as part of their sincere religious practices.
[90] Macher means an important individual

the left-wing of Students for a Democratic Society, SDS, in Ann Arbor, it was very fashionable for many Jews who were involved in those movements to be what struck me as anti-Semitic. They were ashamed of and tried to deny their Jewishness and went out of their way to be particularly critical of Israel. But I never felt that way at all. I was always very clear that I was a Jew and I was totally comfortable with that. I didn't see what the problem was in evaluating things critically without having to totally reject them. I visited Israel in 1968 when I graduated from Hebrew school as the president of the youth group and was rewarded with a trip. I fell in love with the Israeli spirit of freedom and aliveness, which I saw and still see as independent of some of the policies that are not dedicated to making peace a possibility in that crucible of the Middle East.

When I came to the Daime, I was surprised to find myself drawn to what I now understand is an esoteric, gnostic, Christian path. It wasn't a plan or desire that I had. I had no hint that path, or any path for that matter, was in store for me. The first ritual I went to was in Brazil on a mountaintop in a remote community. I didn't speak any Portuguese and I really didn't know anything about it. I went on the recommendation of my therapist who was Brazilian. His name was José Rosa. He was my therapist and later became my mentor, partner, friend and brother in the Daime. He simply said, "In one month, we're going to do the equivalent of ten years of psychotherapy and ten years of meditation." I thought that was good deal so I agreed to go, being virtually clueless as to what to expect. I knew we'd drink some "tea," but I was very unprepared for what was going to happen.

The first ritual I attended was an all-night dancing and singing session with 200 people on a mountaintop in a remote valley in Brazil. Along with how strong the Daime was, how confronting the inner experience was for me of my most hidden pain and Light, I found myself in a strong altered state in the presence of this big cross in the middle of the altar table. I started to have thoughts about the pogroms my Russian ancestors had gone through, and I thought, "Holy shit! Here I am in this totally bizarre place and they're going to kill me." I had this feeling that I wasn't safe there. It wasn't intuitive, because it was in fact totally wrong, but it was a strong feeling. I was experiencing what Zalman calls Jewish PTSD, and it's deep, for good reason. I kept asking myself, "What am I doing here?" The combination of PTSD and Daime made me want to run away. Fortunately for my future self, I was on this remote mountaintop two hours walk in the dark from even a bus stop (not that I could have told the driver where I wanted to go). After a while, I managed to center myself, and then I saw that the cross on the table was sitting on a base of a six-pointed star. I looked at the star and said to myself, "The star I can deal with. I'm going to ignore the cross so I don't run out of here screaming." I was already deep into what we call the power of the Daime. It was super strong.

I understand now what took place then. When we make a true prayer, and when we are then linked to true Light, that prayer becomes the guiding energetic, the guiding paradigm within which our subsequent healing process takes place. It can take years for the prayer to work out. In that moment when I was looking at that cross, inside me there was a prayer, not yet conscious, but nevertheless deep in my heart, that I needed to resolve this conflict inside me between the cross and the star because I didn't want to live in fear any more. That prayer extended to not wanting to live in fear about anything, but in that moment the metaphor of the Christian/Jewish conflict was the focus. I looked at that cross sitting on a Mogen David[91] and I made a prayer to Whoever was listening to come bring peace inside me.

In the second vision I had with the Daime, a couple of hours after my initial freak out in this first ceremony, I saw a village green like in an old New England town. I saw a group of people standing around in a circle, and a straight beam of light was shining down on them from heaven. The people were holding hands, ecstatic, in bliss. In an instant, a church spire sprang up and completely blocked the light. I understood that the first thing the Daime was teaching me directly was that it was the structure of the Church, or any institution, that had blocked the universal, free Light. I saw that there is one Light and that Light is pure and for everyone, beyond ideology or religion or tradition or

---

[91] Mogen David translates to "Shield of David," also called the Star of David, familiarly known as the Jewish Star.

any other human made structure or thought form. It has nothing to do with the structures we build to contain it. In fact, the structure blocks it from touching us. The understanding that came from that vision has guided me since that day.

There is a logical question that comes with that understanding, especially considering what I went on to do after that initiation through the Daime. Why should we have any structures at all, particularly ones that are so vulnerable to the pervasive influences of the craziness we have seen done in the name of various churches and religious institutions? And yet, I have been clearly guided, both from "over there" and from "in here" (pointing to his heart) to form and guide a church for these last 20 years.

It would seem contradictory. But I relate to the form of a church in the same way I relate to the form of my body; they both are vehicles for experience. The trick is to know what is what. My body is not who I am, it is where I temporarily live. My church is a holding space for me and others to come and meet spiritual forces and get to know ourselves. The structure of our church could be anything that facilitates that encounter. There is nothing better about one body than another, nor about one structure than another. As Reb Zalman said in the work we did with him, "She comes wearing different clothes. Don't get hung up on the clothes."

To have an authentic experience in both arenas of body and church, I have to be able to sit within the form and then drop my attachment to it completely. At the same time that I love and honor and care for my body, I also care for the vehicle that has made the experience of truth beyond the form possible. It's one of the very cool things about being a human, that we have so many levels of consciousness to navigate at once.

That understanding of the difference between the essence and the form matched something that I've known from birth and that was reinforced by my Judaism. One of the things I love about being a Jew, at least the way I was raised, is that Jews are taught to only bow your head to God, not to any man. That's why we get in trouble. (laughter) I knew this truth from what I now see as coming from past lives. When I came to the Daime, in fact when I came into this life, I was looking for truth. Having a structure to investigate inside is just a convenient way to organize the experience of truth. But the structure, the institution, the body is just a convenience. It can be one thing or another. It doesn't matter what the form is. Some of us do better with boundaries to the path. So that helped me when I came to the Daime and was shown this vision. There was a deep knowing in me that if you are going to organize experience, you can organize it one way or another; that someone wears *payos* or a robe or a *keffiyeh* makes no real difference except as it helps the person focus their attention on truth.

Soon after that vision, I was given a dream that showed me this exactly. I saw myself going through many layers of the astral to do a healing. I looked to my left and I saw a lunch counter like in a junior high school. There were the fat ladies serving food and there were people lined up, organized by groups, and each group had on different clothes and especially different hats. There were Hasidic Jews with payos[92], Arabs with keffiyehs[93], Asians with Chinese hats, Native Americans with head-dresses, and on and on They were all receiving the same food!

Truthfully, even that didn't really solve the problem in me. I was still carrying the Jewish PTSD. When I was growing up in Detroit in the fifties and sixties, who was Jesus to me? He was that weird guy on that cross in agony. Worshiping agony never appealed to me. And he was the guy in whose name I got beat up on Ash Wednesday. When I was eight years old, I went to an elementary school that was on the other side of the Catholic school from my house. One Wednesday in April, I was walking home and saw two boys my age with dirt on their foreheads in exactly the same place on both their heads. I knew something was up, but had no idea what. So I asked them in my eight-year-old wide-eyed innocence, "Hey, how come you guys got dirt on your head?" They looked at each other and then at me, and one said, "Are you Jewish?" "Yeah," I said, like it was just a description, not an indictment. The next thing I knew, one guy was holding my arms and the

---

[92] Sidelocks or curls worn by Hasidic and other ultra-Orthodox Jewish boys and men.
[93] The cotton headress worn by Arabs.

other was punching me in the face, yelling, "You killed Jesus." And I'm thinking, "Huh? I don't even know Jesus." I ran home in tears more confused than hurt. My mother's response was that there are a lot of seriously ignorant people in this world.

That was my previous experience with the guy who was the big kahuna of the Daime. I came to the Daime with that engraved in me. But at the same time, I had made this prayer for total healing of myself and to know truth beyond the forms. I wasn't drawn to the Daime intellectually or culturally. First of all, the Daime is not an intellectual path. The teachings are all in the form of poetic songs that are received from divine sources. There is not a catechism, a Torah, no official writings beyond the hymns. People read and study whatever they want to. There are Buddhist Daimistas, Jewish Daimistas, Native American oriented Daimistas. New Age Daimistas, African Daimistas. While I fell in love with the Brazilian people and the Brazilian culture, it was not that which drew me to the Daime path. I fancied myself as someone who didn't need a path. I was somehow beyond that, whatever that meant. Paths were for lesser folks than who I imagined I was. I was drawn to the Daime from an unfamiliar place in me, from my heart. I fell in love with the Light that I saw and felt and that moved me and healed me in the way I fell in love with my wife. I felt that I have to follow this trail even though I couldn't believe I was doing it. It made no sense, was completely inconvenient and was so far outside the norm of my culture that all my concepts of how my life would look from then on were blown. I realized this a year and a half after my first experience with the Daime, when I went with my friend José to the center of the Santo Daime path in the middle of the Amazon jungle. I was in the middle of the jungle with these little brown people and I'm this six foot white gringo sticking out like a sore thumb. I was in love with the Light and was being called to a path. I could have said no. I said yes and stepped off the cliff.

I made a prayer in relation to the icons of this new path that my heart had put me on over the objections of my mind. For me, meeting the divine feminine, the Virgin Mary, wasn't a big deal. In the Judaism I was raised in, there was no feminine spirit. Now, in the Jewish Renewal world, they've reclaimed the feminine as the Shekinah. But I didn't have a thing one way or the other about it. I felt it was very comforting to have these prayers with Mary and the Queen of the Forest and all that. But Jesus? Forget about it. Which I conveniently did for a time. I spent five or six years in the Daime keeping a distance from anything to do with Jesus, even though there are a ton of hymns about him.

I've come to realize that if you don't have a connection with the divine feminine, you can't truly meet the masculine. It's just as children go from the mother to the father. Protestantism is an example, as well as mainstream Judaism where you deny the Mother, pretend she doesn't exist, and then you're lost because you don't really have the internal territory fertilized to meet the Father.

I found myself in a ritual in the same place I had begun my experience with the Daime, six years later. I was in the middle of the ceremony and sucking up my courage, I said, "Okay, I'm ready. I want to meet you." I expected some vision to appear in a blaze of glory, a flaming chariot to descend from heaven with a voice proclaiming the "Son of God has arrived."

At the moment I asked to know Him, I was dancing[94] in the characteristic way we dance in the Daime. I was lined up behind a guy that I didn't like (of course, because our personalities were very similar). So I had this feeling of dislike for this guy in front of me and I was praying to Jesus. I wanted to see Him but ignore the asshole in front of me. Instead of a chariot of fire, I heard a clear voice, a young man's voice, saying, "Open your eyes, I'm right in front of you." I had met a teacher who wouldn't let me off the hook. Ultimately that was more impressive and transformational than a fleet of chariots.

Still, that didn't solve the Jewish/Christian thing for me entirely. It was finally resolved when I saw very clearly in another ritual that there was a war going on inside me. Inside my own being I had the ancient war going on between Jews and Christians. I was embodying it. I began to see that I wasn't denying my Judaism by being on a Christian path. That dichotomy was the creation of ignorance, injustice and

---

[94] In some of the Santo Daime works, the participants chant as they move in a line formation in a very structured dance form.

arrogance, all of which I had plenty of in me and all of which I was praying to transform. I saw the dilemma, held it, didn't try any more to rationalize it, assign blame, or fix it. I found myself spontaneously declaring unilateral, unconditional peace, a peace inside me, whatever anyone else might choose as is their God-given right. From that day on there has been no conflict. I declared peace. I am a Jew and I am a follower of that Master who was known on Earth as Yeshua Emmanuel, who was also a Jew (in his body). He is a son of God the Father and so am I. So are you. He knew it, I'm learning it.

So what does it mean that you are Jewish now?

It means that Judaism is in my blood. The way I walk through the world and the way I see things has a Jewish characteristic to it, including the wounds. My sense of humor is definitely Jewish as well as my bluntness and my bullshit meter. I don't deny any of it. I'm not an active Jew in the sense of my practice. I'm a Daimista and I have a meditation practice. But I feel that I'm Jewish in the way that I'm a man. I'm Jewish in the way that I have memory, that Judaism is part of the heritage I am living. I've been on many different paths in many lives, all in the same ray. There are lines, sub-rays of spiritual Light on Earth. There's a Hindu line; that's not my line. There's a Buddhist line; I have visited that line. I have total respect for that line, but it's not my line. My line is the Egyptian, Aramaic, Hebrew, Christian, Gnostic, Daime path. It's a line of work on Earth. I've walked it in various lives in various costumes.

I've been a priest and I've been a monk and I've been a begger, an Egyptian, a Jew, a Catholic, a pagan. I've been a man and a woman. I've been a Jewish-Christian. I've been persecuted and I have committed persecution. There is an opinion held by some people that you are a Jewish soul and that's all you are. I am a Jewish soul, but Jewish soul doesn't mean the practice of Judaism in every life in the same way. Judaism is for me an essence, not a practice. The practice of Judaism today is not what they practiced in previous times. We don't sacrifice goats on an altar anymore. I'm a Jew and I'm a Christian and to me, truly, they are no different. When I was in the first century, I was a Jewish-Christian. I am today also. At least in me there is no more conflict. I don't relate to the idea that by following where my heart and my soul have brought me I am somehow traitor to Judaism. I haven't gone over to the enemy because I don't have any enemies left.

If you would, let's go back to your childhood. What was your family like?

My grandparents, my paternal grandparents were from White Russia. My grandfather came alone from Russia on the run from the Cossacks in 1907. He was a socialist, and he got out by the skin of his teeth when they started killing members of his party. My great grandfather, my grandmother's father, was the rabbi and *moile*[95] of the community in which they lived. My grandmother was one of ten children. Their whole family came to Canada, New York and Detroit. My father was born here, so I'm second generation American on my father's side.

My mother's family came an earlier generation back. Her people came from Hungary and Germany. My mother was raised in an upper middle class family, my father in a typical depression era working class family. My grandmother hocked her wedding ring to help put my father through college. He became a lawyer. My grandfather, who was really a scholar and an intellectual, ran a number of singularly unsuccessful businesses but managed to get his family through the depression. He always wanted to be teacher. Instead, he was a door-to-door shoe salesman.

I was born in 1950, postwar era, raised in a suburb of Detroit called Royal Oak, which at that time was a lower-middle-class town. We lived a middle class, upwardly looking life, typical of the era. That trajectory was waylaid because both my parents died when they, and I, were very young. They died within 14 months of each other when I was 10 and 11. My mother died when she was 34, my father when he was 41. They both had forms of cancer. In 1960, my paternal grandparents,

---

[95] A Jewish ceremonial circumcision practitioner.

who were then 69 and 72, took over raising my brother, sister and myself. I was the oldest, and being in a Jewish family, there were lots of expectations on me.

What was their religious orientation and how did you experience religion as a child?

My grandfather was a socialist and rejected his religious background. As he got older, he became more religious. My grandmother was bitter about everything, especially about a so-called God that would snatch her favorite son away before his time. When I was young, we belonged to a Reform temple in Detroit and I went to services every week. When I was in high school, I was the president of the temple youth group and a national officer. Sometimes I think I'm still the president of the temple youth group with the Daime. (laughter).

I was very involved in the social action side of things. That was also something about being Jewish, that sensibility. Today people still have it, but because of the confusion about Zionism it tends often to be a much more conservative-leaning sensibility. But when we were raised, Jews were communists, socialists, certainly liberals, and at the forefront of the civil rights movement. I was raised in that milieu.

We lived in an all-white suburb. My parents joined a social club that consciously brought black families into it. I remember the family picnics we had, and visiting the houses of the people in the club. I was raised in that kind of Jewish atmosphere. Jews were supposed to be helping others because we remembered what it was like to be oppressed. I participated in temple services all the time. But the most moving times for me would be on weekdays in the temple when sometimes I'd go into the sanctuary by myself, sit on the altar, stand in front of the arc and sneak a look. I'd open the Torahs, which you're not supposed to do, and just be in that vibration. Now I understand. For me that was the most moving time. The services were rarely moving, but the vibration that was always there waiting to be felt was what touched me.

There were prayers I really loved and I loved the music. Of course, we celebrated seders and such as well.

Would you say you had some sense of God, of the divine?

I had a sense of something bigger, something that I wanted to be connected to. Also, there was a huge amount of pain in my life from all that had happened with my parents. I was on the edge a lot. I was able to get by with cockiness and intelligence and charisma. Inside I was in screaming pain. I got really good grades and was really popular, but I needed lots of healing. There was this impulse, this prayer I didn't know how to make or who to make it to, "Help me!" which didn't really get answered for many years. But I had a sense of something. When I'd be on that altar on a Wednesday, standing with my hand on the Torah, I'd feel a touch of something, a slight vibration that gave me hope that there was maybe something beyond pain. I'd affirm inside me that I wanted that.

So the pain didn't take you in a rebellious direction?

It took me into political rebellion, and plenty of drugs.

Was that in your college years?

Yes. In high school I was emotionally rebellious, I'd be in your face and nasty with adults in general. I was arrogant. I was the first born Jew and I was used to being very smart and very successful and all that, so I had this typical first born, Jewish male arrogance. I'm surprised I didn't get slapped. The Jews felt sorry for me and the Goyim didn't know what to do with me except call me "Jonny Jew."

How much anti-Semitism did you encounter?

Relatively minor. I did get beat up on Ash Wednesday, as I said. In Middle school a girl whose chest I had a crush on, who was from the South, told me one day, "Ah hate Jews." "Oh yeah," I said, "Why?" "Because a Jew killed my cousin." I asked if the killer was a man and if so why didn't she hate all men. She looked at me like, "Huh?" I saw more anti-Semitism in college when there were Black radicals who didn't like Jews, and the anti-Semitism of Jews who were confused.

Did you experience what some have called "anti-gentilism" within your family?

For sure. We would never buy a German car. I suppose it was more anti-German. There would be jokes about the Goyim. But, when I was in high school I'd go to my friend's church on Sundays and found it interesting. I didn't think it was that different from the Jewish services, someone up front preaching. I thought our music was better. I liked the cantor better than the choir.

How would you describe what you inherited from the Jewish lineage, what you continue to value and also what you needed to let go of?

It's very important to me, this thing about not bowing your head except to God. I carry it over even in the Daime which is very hierarchical. I still respect people based on what they show me, based on what the Divine tells me, much more than any title or assumption. On the other hand, I have learned to respect my elders, one of which I have quite surprisingly become. I give people a certain amount of respect because of their position, but I don't accord honor except as it is warranted. I'm not a very good follower except of what I know to be true. This is something precious about Judaism. It's gotten me into trouble in the Daime, just like it did before I joined. It's something that's very important to me. I cherish the link, the ancient link to the line of Judaism, to know my origin, my path on Earth.

I believe there is such a thing as truth, but it isn't ideological, it is revealed. It can change as I grow in my ability to understand, and it comes through direct connection with the Divine Forces, not through someone's opinion, including mine. Somehow, my Judaism had that sensibility in it. "Quiet, I'm talking with God here." For sure, I'm going to give what I discern as coming from higher source a lot of weight in my considerations. How dumb would that be to ask for advice and then ignore it? But I also reserve my own sensibility, my own integrity. I don't just follow orders, even Theirs. I think that's something about being Jewish. You bow to God and you have the responsibility to access truth as it is to you, to follow that and accept the consequences. You get to say yes or no and then you have to deal with what happens from your choice. I am not a fan of people of any stripe who abdicate their responsibility for honing their own God-given right of free will to God, or the Devil, or society, or their mind, or their emotions.

Is there a sense in which this is about honoring your ancestors, their spirituality and sensibility?

That, but also I'm very glad that my people were Russian peasants. I like that. I like being connected to that. There is something very rich, very real about it. It's like being able to hold rich dirt in my hand and be linked to life on Earth through that grounded reality. I appreciate the sensibility of that connection with the salt of the earth, the oppressed people. They bled into that earth so I could grow in relative freedom. I don't take that lightly at all. The Daime has taught me that I don't identify with that oppression, even as I see it and honor the people who endured it. That's not who I am. That's not who anybody is. That's an experience. The Daime has given me a new orientation to all that, but I still hold it as very precious.

Would you say that you feel the connection and empathy with your ancestors, but are not identified with them?

The word I would use is compassion. Empathy and compassion are not the same thing. This is something that I've learned through the Daime and through my very deep resonance with the Dalai Lama. He is not my teacher, but he is a man who embodies something important for me. What I've learned from the Daime is that all paths have something to offer. We are all like the blind men and the elephant; everyone has a piece of the story.

The thing I reject about some forms of Judaism, and other religions, is the idea of them being the holder of the truth. There is one truth, one Light, and we are just all exploring it in different ways.

This speaks to the part of the question that is about what you inherited that may have been toxic or negative in some way, things that you've needed to let go of.

The thing that I inherited that is toxic is that, "the world is a dangerous place and you've got to be vigilant all the time or the fuckers are going to get you." On the one hand, it's true—there are a bunch of misguided and mal-choosing fuckers on Earth. There are people who are lost and blind and doing evil, both by addiction and by conscious choice. There is that and they are dangerous and need to be addressed straight on. We need to be aware of this and not be stupid. I'm not a New Age bliss ninny. But that constant vigilance and wariness and suspicion has been replaced for me with a connection to my authentic, grounded intuition, which will tell me who is doing what and what my posture needs to be in relation to it. That allows me to be open and relaxed when there isn't danger, and grounded and alert when there is.

So I'm not constantly monitoring everything. I'm constantly aware, but I'm not living in fear anymore. That unrelenting suspicion is part of the inheritance of Judaism, with good past reason. We can see this in many segments of the Jewish population. It turns people bitter, it turns them angry, it turns them fearful. It makes people very, very protective of their own territory, seek vengeance, which never works, and not see the bigger picture and have the courage to forgive.

So right now, people are liberating themselves in Egypt, people are liberating themselves in Tunisia and Libya. All over the world this is happening, and yet for some Jews, the only thing they care about is, "What's going to happen to Israel? Maybe we need to keep this madman dictator in power here or there because he's not invading Israel." That's PTSD, and that puts those people on the wrong side of history because it makes them anti-freedom.

In your formative years or teen years, were you identified with Zionism or Israel?

When I graduated high school, I was given a trip to Israel. This was in 1968, a few months after the '67 war, and Israel was a different place than today. I loved it. I loved it. "My God this is a Jewish place! Oh my God!" I felt free. I was 18 and I just had a blast. I was there for six weeks and participated in building a youth village. What I loved about Israel at that time was the spirit of newness and pioneering. In middle-class American life in the 1960s, there wasn't much pioneering going on. It was boring. I was living in suburban America and one of my first and most fervent prayers was, "God, don't let me be bored." In Israel, I met people who were on the edge and they were most certainly not bored.

Up until then, I was supposed to be a lawyer; I was to carry on and do what my father hadn't lived long enough to accomplish. But when I came back I thought I wanted to be a rabbi. Interestingly, in many ways I did, just not like anyone imagined it would look.

I'm still very supportive of Israel, of the heart of that dream. In some ways, I think it's a completely crazy situation; plunking down this European-based culture in the middle of this milieu of hundreds of years of Arab culture. There's a level that's absurd to even try such a mad thing. But I look beyond the surface, beyond the miracle of creation in that desert, beyond the conflict that is absolutely the result of everyone involved choosing from fear and suspicion and ideology and vengeance. I look at why this whole thing has been given to all of us on Earth. What are the opportunities and the invitation and the possibilities? Because the Middle East is the crucible for the whole world. It is the place of ancient birth, of archetypal conflict, and therefore of opportunity. We will all heal or we will all fall into the abyss based on what happens there. So I look at what we've all created, all us humans, in our collective unconscious prayer to heal. We've created this opportunity to transform something so deep and powerful that all humanity can progress from its positive resolution. And for sure, the jury is so far hung.

Can you clarify what it is you see as the potential for transforming or healing?

To transform this division, this false division among the tribes. To learn the power of true forgiveness. To learn that in fact there is enough of everything for everyone.

You see a higher purpose behind what's happening?

Through the heart is the only way that it's going to resolve. How else can you resolve this thing? There has to be forgiveness. People have to learn this. I know there are people doing this in Israel and on the Palestinian side. There are people in every place and every group on Earth praying to learn forgiveness. We need to find the people who get it, who get that underneath we are all one and that that reality is not just namby-pamby rhetoric. We are still fighting the battle of Jacob and Esau. Okay, there has been betrayal on all sides, hurt on all sides, a history of horror on all sides. There is also stupidity and brilliance and stubbornness and genuine heart on all sides. On one hand, it's a good thing to have everything so starkly on the table. What is going on there is not sustainable in the long run. Israel is a fortress that sees itself surrounded by hostile enemies. Those surrounding people give plenty of fuel to that paranoid fire. But in any arena, what is based on fear and the perpetuation of conflict will one day fall into total disarray. That is just energetic fact. In this case, that disarray may very well drag the rest of the world down with it. Or, we may all be redeemed by the choices those beloved people there can and may make. What's written is the chance, not the outcome.

What happened to your wish to be a rabbi?

When I got to college I decided I was a revolutionary. I don't remember any instances of practicing Judaism actively. I left formal Judaism for the revolution. That sounds a bit silly today, but at the time we were serious in a white middle class, clueless kind of way. I felt

Jewish, but I wasn't active in it. I was a Jewish radical; that was my religion so to speak. My practice on Earth was social change.

As you've said, that is a strong aspect of the Jewish cultural transmission.

For sure, and I completely related to that.

Were you introduced to the Daime when you were a radical?

I was introduced to acupuncture in 1971 and I started studying it in 1975. That was a radical choice at the time. I was among the first people outside of the Asian communities to practice acupuncture in this country. When I started there were no schools in this country, let alone any licensing or standards. My license number in Massachusetts was number 9.

Did this reflect a sense of something beyond the physical?

I grew into that sensibility and realized later that it was something I always had, the desire to see into the heart of things. Partly that was a reaction to the total shock of having my parents die out of the blue. Partly, like all karmic qualities, the shock stimulated something that was already there sleeping. Radical politics had that quality for me too. I wanted to know why things were like they were, not just accept them for their superficial explanations. But on the conscious level, acupuncture just seemed like a good gig. I didn't have to go to much more school, which I was already sick of. As well, nobody knew anything about acupuncture. I liked being on the far edge of something. I guess I still do. Avoid boredom at all costs, that's my motto.

Did your openness to acupuncture have anything to do with psychedelics?

I took a lot of psychedelics in college. I often say that I took my share of LSD and that of the Young Republicans. I think that those drugs, which I never related to purely recreationally, made me somewhat free from the bounds of my implanted cultural limitations. And they definitely reinforced my inherent need to see into things beyond the obvious.

That didn't take you out of the radical and put you into the more spiritual camp?

For me, psychedelics were mostly psychological; it was therapy for me. The explicitly spiritual thing started appearing at the end of the era. I was into a bit of hippy spirituality. I would cry at the song that said, "Come on people now, smile on your brother, everybody get together, try to love one another right now." When Che Guevara said, "At the risk of sounding ridiculous, a revolutionary must be guided by great feelings of love," he was speaking a truth that I knew even as I was marching and screaming at the "pigs" and fighting with cops in the street. I had so much pain, and LSD opened up layers of my consciousness to let some of it squeeze out. Now, I would interpret it as emotional-spiritual experiences. But I didn't have what some people report with LSD: being taken to another realm, having authentic spiritual awakenings. I wasn't ready for that level of experience. On a trip, I cried for the first time since my father died. At other times I felt myself as strong and free and wild, and even a slight bit happy. I am grateful for those experiences. I am also grateful that for reasons I can't accept credit for, I am not an addictive person. I never went as far as some of my friends who got burned out, brain damaged or died in Columbian jails.

These experiences didn't bring you to read spiritual books or study meditation?

No. It was the 60s and it was the music and a sense of liberation that was my spiritual connection. I read political books, or at least parts of a lot of them. I tried to be a good revolutionary and study the classics of Marx and Mao and all that. But truthfully, I found them plodding and boring. The liberation of myself from emotional bondage, that was my goal.

Where did it go from there?

My wife and I got together when I was 20 and she was 19. After we left the University of Michigan, we moved to Detroit, then to Boston, and set up our life there. That was '74. I started practicing acupuncture in 1976. For a few years I was involved in the pioneering stages of alternative medicine and doing revolutionary group activity at the same time. In '84, I made a shift. I realized that although I had framed natural healing as a way to support my work as a political activist, I really loved the healing work. I decided that even though it was probably selfish, and I was undoubtedly betraying the revolution, I would do what I loved anyway. So I dedicated myself full-time to the healing work and left political activism. It was a relief to all involved.

In '83, I met José Rosa, my Brazilian psychotherapist, and he helped me begin to transform the cache of pain in me. During the course of our therapy, he drank Daime in Brazil and came back and told me about his experience. After we ended therapy, he decided to take a group of his former clients to Brazil to drink Daime. I went because I loved him and because he told me it was a good deal. We had done sweat lodges and things like that, so I imagined I knew something about intense transformative processes. Not even close. He introduced me to Daime and I became an initiate in 1990. I've now been drinking Daime for 23 years. You'd think I'd be further along but some people are really stubborn. (laughter)

As I mentioned, one of the things that we've accomplished in my little corner of the universe that I feel very happy about is that we've liberated the Daime. It's now legal in Oregon and soon will be in the rest of the country. The accomplishment of doing that is, in a small way, contributing to human freedom. That's how I frame it. We've contributed positively to the universal movement for human freedom. Whatever adds to the manifesting of that universal and deep drive for freedom is a good thing. Even a small victory such as ours sends ripples of freedom across the world.

My understanding is that you were the principal agent of this case.

I was the catalyst, the leader of it. I got arrested in 1999 and that's how it eventually became a case where we sued the government. It took us ten years to do it. I have no doubt that part of the reason that I came to this life, born Jewish in that milieu, was to have that sense of social responsibility and to not be intimidated by authority. That's part of the Jewish thing and it gave me the fuel to keep at it for ten years in the face of many excuses to quit. On the one hand, they're out to kill us and on the other hand, we're not going to kowtow to anybody. I think that one of the reasons I came into the Daime at that time and place, was to hold that sensibility at the front of the movement; when it came time to do this small but important thing of freeing the Daime, I could do what I did.

My wife Jane and I, and the other people who stepped up and put themselves on the line, were able to step beyond the natural fear that facing guys with big bucks and big guns and big ideologies and no scruples brings up. We needed that courage and faith, not only in relationship to the government, but in relationship to internal processes within the Daime Church. In the community there were people who, out of their own fear, didn't want us to go and liberate the Daime. The ability to follow the truth that I knew in my heart, with lots of counsel and prayer, lots of Daime, and lots of agonized investigation, I attribute to my Jewish background. What could they do that hadn't already been done to us in other lives and to our ancestors? Nothing. So let's go and make some freedom.

You are saying that the boundary-crossing, revolutionary transmission that you inherited as a Jew is what you bring to the Daime itself, and so you are transforming the culture of the Daime?

The Daime, before liberation, was like the Muranos in Portugal or Spain. "I'm a public Christian, now let's close and put cloth over the windows and light a candle on Pesach." It's the same sensibility, but thank God the potential consequences were not so great this time around. They only put me in jail for a bit. They didn't slice my genitals off or burn me at the stake. But it's the same sensibility: "We're going to do what we're going to do because we are free in the eyes of our God." When we went to court, the prosecutors said, "Look, they've been practicing illegally." The judge said, "Well, of course they've been practicing illegally; what do you expect them to do? You were threatening them." I felt, "Yes! Take that you Spaniards!" That totally comes from my Jewish upbringing.

Can you talk about the Daime Church? Is there a cosmology, things that people study and learn besides what comes to them through their experiences in the ceremonies or works?

For sure. We call the teachings that have come through the various Daime practitioners, which we see as coming from the Divine Intelligence that we call the Daime itself, "the Doctrine." It's a tricky term, because "doctrine," in the common usage, is a set of stagnant, fixed rules, a dogma. It doesn't mean this at all in the Daime. The Doctrine is a living matrix of consciousness that reveals itself through songs. There are people in Daime who read the Bible, but we don't read the Bible in our church. There are people who are Buddhists. There are people who go and hug Mother Amachi. There are people who are more fundamentalist Christian types. But the center of the Daime is the Doctrine, whose teachings are contained in the many hymns that are sung in community. The Doctrine is revealed through the songs and there are teachings that are about both the more esoteric aspects, the more transpersonal aspects of spiritual evolution, and also the practical aspects of living on Earth.

The Doctrine teaches the golden rule, love yourself as you love God and all beings. But because of the confluence of forces—the vibration of the altered state, the communal experience of becoming one voice, the intensity of our prayers and intentions, and the living divine forces that come into the sacred and well-held space—that love for yourself and all beings is a palpable experience which can then be remembered and applied in your daily life. The Daime work is a laboratory in which we experiment with the teachings of humility, joyful celebration, courageous confrontation with both the light and dark within ourselves, and being obedient to higher callings than our own ego. The Daime gives you the experience of doing all that in a ceremony. Once you clean yourself of the weight of opinion and emotional baggage and learn how to navigate in the divine power, you can reach the state of loving yourself and all beings in the moment. Then you go out in your life and you realize that people piss you off and you have to pay a mortgage. You realize that you have to bring that vibration to bear on your lower self and on your daily life. You have to not just do it in ceremony, but on a practical level.

Like your experience of the man dancing in front of you that you didn't like?

Yes, the guy was in front of me and the Master says, "That's me; don't be looking for my golden face in the clouds." Learning to love is more important than seeing flashy spiritual pictures.

What else can you share about the Doctrine, the beliefs and so forth?

There are specific Beings that are connected to the Daime, by which I mean conscious entities who exist beyond my personal space and who choose of their own volition to interact with me on the inner planes. You need to understand that the Daime is not a hallucinogenic drug. It does not interrupt your synaptic firing and create visions that are the result of that random firing and nothing more. The Daime reveals what is there all along. Of course I would never expect someone to believe that just because I say it. But as my teacher José said to me, "It's a good thing that reality doesn't depend on your opinion." These

Beings and forces exist. There are many names they are given in various lines and many explanations for their existence. I am marginally interested in those various explanations, but extremely interested in learning from those entities.

We interpret the cosmology of the Daime as coming from the original Christian impulse. In other words, the Daime cosmology does a reverse leapfrog to 2000 years ago, bypassing the horrors and misinterpretations committed in the name of a person who came to Earth to plant the idea that death is an illusion and the heart is all that matters. But the Daime also comes from the natives of the Amazon forest and from the Black people who were slaves in Brazil up until almost the 20th century. The Daime is what is called a syncretic religion, incorporating harmonious aspects of all of those cultural perspectives. We say that the Doctrine of the Daime was "re-planted" through Raimundo Irineu Serra by his direct contact with the Virgin Mary, who appeared to him initially as a woman descending from the moon. She later revealed herself as the Queen of the Forest, the embodiment of the Divine Feminine among the Catholic people of the north of Brazil. Still later she was revealed in another aspect, the Queen of the Sea, who is called in the Afro-Brazilian religions, Lemanja. The One who we invoke and who is our main teacher, healer and comforter is the Divine Mother in all her aspects.

There is also the Master Jesus. There are hymns that talk about him as Jesus the Friend, the Master, God, all the different aspects of him, the teacher, the professor, the healer. We speak much less about the crucified, agonized martyr than the one who came to Earth to teach. He is seen as "planting" the Doctrine of forgiveness and compassion to replace the attachment to vengeance and domination. He teaches us here and now, not from a book but from direct communion with him and those who accompany him: love yourself as you love all beings; love your brothers and sisters; love the people around you; take care of your family; work on Earth; don't fear death or anything else. The Daime is very committed to right relationships, to family. All this is taught in the hymns.

St. John the Baptist is the master of our particular line of Daime.

He is a great Being, an archetypal Being, who also came to Earth in the person of Padrinho Sebastião to open the way for the Daime to become available to whoever needs it wherever they are on Earth.

One thing that's different in the Daime from some paths is that we have a conscious connection with levels of the astral plane. For instance, Judaism classically encourages us to talk to God and avoid intermediaries. Some Hindu paths want nothing to do with the astral plane. The Daime is more like Tibetan Buddhism in that you have layers of Beings that can be accessed through prayer, meditation and ceremony. If you study Tibetan Buddhism and you study the world of the Daime; there are many equivalent entities even though they may wear different clothes.

You mentioned that had you been alive at the time, you imagine you would have chosen to be a Jewish-Christian. You feel that Jesus brought to the Jews and to all people something different, something having to do with letting go of the past and being able to end suffering and vengeance, which had not been a part of the transmission up until that point. Is it vital that somehow Jews today need to accept Jesus? Or can they accept that message without accepting Jesus?

I gave a talk at a church in Oregon, a church that prides itself on being totally eclectic and open to everybody. They have no shading of any denomination at all. In my talk, I used the term, "the Christ on Earth." Afterwards, two Jewish women came up to me and they were pissed. "How dare you bring that danger, that sensibility into our safe space." I went home and I called Rabbi David Zaslow and asked him, "What do you call what I call the Christ?" He said, "We call it the Divine Essence."

The Christ is not that man, (Jesus). The Christ, the Divine Essence, is addressed by every religion, because it exists beyond all religion. I don't know what they call it in Islam, but I guarantee that it's the same thing as what I call the Christ and Rabbi David calls the Divine Essence. It's a vibration, a universal vibration that is the One that inhabits all life and motivates the homing impulse of all life forms. We all have that seed in us waiting to be watered by forgiveness. It can and wants to wake up and to take us to the universal experience beyond all designations.

My prayer every day is that I might be able to embody that essential truth. The question for me is not whether you or anyone else accepts the image of that particular Holy man as your savior or your teacher or your friend or your brother or your lover. What I want to know is what are we going to do here and now to heal the ancient wounds that keep us separate and scared and stuck?

According to the Doctrine, why are we born here?

Because this Earth is a school for us to learn in, and our bodies are the mobile schoolroom. This is a school in which rapid spiritual progress is possible. The Daime is a laboratory within the school. The hymns say that we are in a school of love on Earth, learning how to embrace everybody and learning forgiveness. If you distill the mythology about that Master whose name was Yeshua Emmanuel ben Joseph (Jesus), and who in the mythology was the embodiment of pure divine love, what did he come to teach? He came to teach forgiveness by the example of forgiving those who tortured and killed him. What are the historical facts surrounding that mythology? Marginally interesting as a conversation, not important at all spiritually. We can learn by that archetypal story to see into the heart of all people and access the divine spark that is in every being. Whatever they do to you, you know who you are and that only love is real. Forgive them and move on.

The Daime in its essence is the path of the Christ. The iconography is that there was a man who embodied that Christ, or as the Jews say, the Divine Essence. But the vibration of the Christ, the Divine Essence, is beyond that one iconic figure whose story got so twisted and who got used for such low purposes. The Christ is a living Presence that everyone can embody when they are ready. It's not exclusive to one guy 2000 years ago. The difference between Daime Christianity and standard Christianity goes this way: the line in mainstream Christianity is, "He's God, you're not. He will always be, you will never be. You're a sinner, feel bad about it." This then becomes the excuse to do all manner of horrific and greedy things to other people. The Daime says, "He's God, you're God. He knows it, you're learning it." That's the Daime. The Second Coming is seen in the Daime as the birth of that Christ, that Divine Essence, in the hearts of people. Drinking Daime, singing hymns in community and praying to heal myself and to be of service to the Divine Plan are the tools we've been given to make that birth happen a bit more quickly.

Are there other distinctions you'd make between the Daime path and the Jewish path?

In the Daime, I get to experience in my body viscerally, not intellectually. It is beyond all longing, beyond all ideas and ideologies, the actual vibration of Divine Light. When I came back from Brazil the first time, I was living in Boston. When the fall came, I thought, "I want to see if this Light is everywhere. I went to a havurah Yom Kippur service a few blocks from my office. I went in, sat down and meditated. Yes, it was the same Light. But in the Daime, people were feeling it and transforming themselves in its Presence. In that Jewish service there were some people feeling it, everyone was wanting it, many people going through the motions. There was way more longing than there was receiving going on. In the Daime, you get it straight on and along the way you get healed on all levels. That's the difference for me. As I said, I don't care any more about what form the ritual comes in.

If I'd come to the Daime and it was a Jewish form already, that would have been fine. I don't really care about the ritual. It's just a ritual; it could be a different one. We wear uniforms. Why do we wear uniforms? We do it because this is a ritual that is distinguished from our daily life. We could easily wear a different uniform than we do. This is my sensibility, it's not the dominant sensibility in the Daime.

How does meditation relate to the Daime? Are methods of meditation, working with the breath or focusing, taught in the church structure?

I teach it, but it's not the usual.

From the point of view of Daime Doctrine and your own impressions, what is the source of suffering in this world? Does it seem that there is some kind of evil entity in the universe that we need to be aware of?

It's an interesting question. The Daime is a school of self-knowledge, spiritual knowledge of intimate self, inner self, and universal self. So there are different answers to your question because suffering is what in the Daime we call a study. By a study, we mean that we look at the issue over time from different angles. One answer to the question is that the purpose of suffering is to purify for the spirit to learn and evolve. One of the ways that we learn on Earth is by the transformation of suffering, learning to embody faith in the face of all evidence to the contrary. That's one answer. Another answer is karma. We speak of karma in the Daime as well as the knowledge of past lives. Through our lifetimes we are learning to embody Light. Yet another answer is that we are learning forgiveness. If there was nothing to forgive we wouldn't learn to consciously embody it.

We also see some forms of suffering in the context of what we call mediumship. We each come to Earth and are given a portion of human suffering to transform; we are given a portion of the denser matter of earth to be active participants in the evolution of consciousness, which is going from denser to lighter, from contraction to expansion, from individual identification to the universal. We are each given a portion of the collective suffering and for various reasons some people are given a bigger portion. Some of us are given the job of helping others transform by taking in our own bodies the suffering of others. There are a lot of different angles.

Is there a conscious evil form? In the Daime we have perhaps 10,000 hymns. I can't think of one hymn that uses the word, "the devil," or "Diablo." There are mentions of demons. It's not that that doesn't exist, but the emphasis in the Daime is calling everything to Light. For instance, last night we did a service. I was leading the service and I'm a very active medium. One of the things I've learned in this life is to transform energy through my bodies; that's what I do. There was one moment when a woman with cancer was on the floor, someone over on the other side was discharging all kinds of stuff, and one of the guitar players dropped his guitar. All of a sudden, I felt coming from behind me, the energy of hatred that's happening on the Earth. It felt particularly connected with the Middle East, with all the fighting that's going on. There was so much agony, as there is so much agony going on right now on the Earth.

I felt it coming to me. It surprised me and for a moment I was kind of thrown off balance. But faith is much stronger than fear, and a Daime ritual is guided by faith. So I did what I've learned to do in the Daime: firm my heart on the cross that we have in the center of the alter table, open my heart, embody that cross in me, connect with the literal vibration of compassion that lives in the emotional body of my heart chakra, and give that contracted energy of hatred passage into Light without being involved and without thinking about it. And the moment passed. The woman with cancer started to feel better, the other guy stood up, and the guitar player who dropped his guitar got back into the rhythm.

When you say not being involved, do you mean that you are not identified with what is happening?

Yes, it's not me and I'm not fixing it, I'm not healing it. I hold the principle that nobody heals anybody. Healing comes from making oneself available to Light and embodying love. I'm just participating in the process. I'm a ladder, a conduit, a servant of Light. The point of the Daime is to call whoever wants to come to Light into the Light. That starts with those of us in physical bodies in the ceremony. There are many Beings and entities that show up that are embodying energies of hatred and committed to darkness. I don't actually care where they came from or what their previous actions were. If they want Light, here it is. If not, see ya' later, there will be another chance next time. We create a ceremonial space that is well tended. It isn't just wide open to anyone who wants to come, be they in physical bodies or not.

As for the existence of a chief of evil, I don't actually have a settled opinion. I've never met that Being, who people say exists, that is the mastermind of all evil. Maybe there is, I don't see why not. There are Dark Angels, why not a chief? I'm not making a prayer to meet him; I don't need to. I do know that there is a force that many people worship, that they even call God, that is dedicated to provoking division, promoting greed and war and misery. That force covers a portion of the Earth and many people are directing prayers to that. I've seen that. Many people are worshiping a different god than I am. I worship the Lord of Light, the Lord of Love, the Lady of the Heart. My God wants me to be happy and for all his/her children to wake up to their beauty and the magnificence of the world we 've been given. The other one doesn't want that. I suppose you can call that the Devil. The Gnostics called it the demiurge. I direct my prayers to the One beyond that, the Source of Light.

You've said that you're still a Jew. Are you still a radical?

I think I'm a very radical person. I also like to think I am a grounded person. I don't engage in the oppositional fight any more; I don't engage in the hatred. That space in me has been filled with something I like much better. I've learned that I can transform my own hatred and my own darkness and my own greed, and I can hold space for those who want to do the same. I can pray for those who are not quite ready yet.

Do you still see the world as it's organized as unjust and unfair? Are you invested or interested in the social change movements of the world?

I cheer all movements for freedom, no matter what they look like or the rhetoric they use. In reference to the previous question, if there is indeed a devil, ideology is his main tool. Ideology is evil. Ideology is awful. Ideology puts a mental picture on reality and tries to make reality bend to that picture. It is blind to other people's needs. I still carry vestiges of ideology in me but I am no longer ideological. That doesn't mean I am free from opinion, but I'm not defending an ideology anymore. I can listen to people from the Tea Party and see that some of what they say makes sense. I can understand the right wing militarists in Israel to some extent. The judge who helped liberate the Daime is a conservative, a strong conservative in the old sense of that word, before conservatism was taken over by radical ideologues. I fell in love with conservativism through him. I celebrate all expressions of freedom and I pray that the people who are working for freedom respect other people's freedom once they gain theirs.

Do you have any inclination to be involved with that kind of activity?

That's not my job anymore. I can't say that I would never do that kind of activism again, but I'm plenty active if you catch my drift. I bless the activists and I make allowances for their foolishness. Much better to be putting your stuff out there and stimulating change than sitting back and sneering at those who are motivated. I believe and experience that I'm doing my work when I help to call Light, help people join their hearts together, hold the space of charity for these beings, and help clean and scrub the inner planes. My work is to show that it's possible to heal pain, to open and live through the heart, to wake up while we are still in bodies, and then to help those who want to do that.

So you feel the Daime ceremonies are not only helping people who are present physically at the ceremony, but they are having an impact on the psyche of the world and helping to bring more peace, harmony and freedom to the world?

Yes, and not only the Daime is doing that. Many people on Earth are helping with that. There are Republicans who really want peace and pray for peace. There are sincere fundamentalists in every religion whose primary motivation is to help humanity receive Light.

I don't aggrandize what we do. I have been told in visions many times that we don't see the vibrational effects of our prayers and the transformation we allow. It's bigger than our little group. But how big? That's not my job to know that. The Beings will take our small bit of Light and add it to the mix of everyone praying on Earth and spray it where it will do the most good.

Some people say that there is so much evil and so much misery on Earth; they wonder what good is prayer doing? My attitude is, "imagine if people were not praying." The vision I've had is that there is a grid of Light on the inner planes that is holding the Earth. You can imagine thousands of hands, each with 10,000 fingers of crystalline light, holding the Earth. It is my view that all of these changes on Earth, the wars and the craziness, are actually being provoked by so much Light being infused into the planet and into us. So my job, and the job of many others, is securing those fingers so that the process can progress. Sometimes it's like holding onto the mast in a storm. But the more people who hold the ropes together, the better chance we have of making it through to calm waters.

The orientation to being on Earth that I've been led to is that as I align myself in my heart with the cosmic stream, with the way the universal energy is flowing, and with the Divine Plan, I'm taken care of. I have what I need and a good bit of what I want. Because what I most want is my heart to be open and to feel the love of those people and beings that my heart resonates with. The rest as they say, is gravy. As the Native American people say, "When the 300 mile an hour wind blows through the world, if it blows me, it will blow me into a good place." That's how I see it.

Do your experiences in the Daime ceremonies ever contain elements of your Jewish ancestry?

I have a very strong connection with the vibration of Moses. I have two hymns that I've recieved that talk about Moses. Moses was called the Justice Maker. Padrinho Sebastao, who is the Saint of our line of Daime, has a connection to John the Baptist, also the Justice

Maker. John the Baptist was also the Liberator, he liberated the sinners and stood up to the Romans. In our little way, by freeing the Daime, we are making justice. So I have a very strong connection with that Being, with that vibration of Moses, whatever the historical truth is. Also King David; I had a vision once of myself with King David.

How does the Daime fit in the framework of monotheism?

In the sense that there is one Creator, there is one Source, there is what is called by some, "God," there is one that is the One. Yet, there are also what in another context would be called Gods, though we don't use that term. Gods are Beings that embody archetypal power. Amongst Africans, there are the *Orixas*; they are the embodiment of natural forces. We honor angels and archangels and native spirits and divine messengers and saints. But there is only one Creator of all of this, one unified and unifying consciousness that holds all of us on all levels in its inexplicable huge heart and awareness. So yes, it is a monotheistic religion that also honors Beings that in relationship to us are gods.

In the Torah, there is the story of Moses who goes up on Mount Sinai and then he comes down and is told by his experience of God to kill all the people who were worshiping the golden calf, which was a symbol for the feminine in the Egyptian spiritual world. What do you make of stories like that, attributing wrath and anger to God?

It's one of those conversations. My own investigation is that there is a difference between anger and rage. Rage is destructive, coming from the second chakra, and is a distortion of passion. It comes through the liver and gets expressed hurtfully, destructively, blindly. Anger is what makes a plant in the springtime poke up through the earth instead of just lying there and waiting. I call that anger, aggression, positive individual assertion. I think that's good. I think that's positive. I think there's lots of use for that. Moses was right to be pissed off at his people acting from fear and with slave mentality. They needed to be slapped upside their heads. Was the One pissed also? Which One are we talking about? The God of love or the God of vengeance, who the God of love came to replace? A lot of what gets said in all the Holy books I don't relate to; I don't have to.

All things that come through humans are affected by historical circumstances and culture and ego, to varying degrees. That doesn't make them less useful. We need to be aware of our God-given responsibility to use our mechanisms of discernment. The Bible is a book of metaphorical legends that are meant to help us navigate the waters of living on Earth and waking up spiritually. Of course it's not in most cases historically accurate. Why is that important? We don't have anything better to do with our short time on Earth than argue about whether Moses really parted the Red Sea? How does that help us here and now to learn to forgive and open our hearts and find new ways to live on Earth?

I think you have to take all those stories and put them in historical context. We just put out a book called Essential Light, and it includes transmissions that have come through me in various settings. These are from my experiences with Beings who are beyond me, who give me words to say. The caveat is that it's coming through me, a vehicle that has an ego and a set of language skills and a certain level of spiritual awakeness. I do the best I can, praying on my knees to be a pure channel. Yet I guarantee that there is some distortion because it's coming through me and my language box. The filter of my ego, even as I try to get out of the way, is there. So I tell people to not abdicate your intuition and discernment to anyone, no matter how advanced you may perceive them to be. We are here to wake up and be empowered spiritual people. The time of sheep has passed. This is the time of co-creation.

I think it's the same way with books in the Bible which get tweaked and translated and changed in so many ways. You have to take it in a cultural context. I believe that one of the things that Master Jesus came to do was to change that paradigm; it's not about killing your enemies, it's about loving your enemies. So the myth is told in a historical context. The hymn I received doesn't say Moses had them killed; it says he called them back to Light. His wrath called them back to Light. The wrathful deities break the chains. There are moments when we need this anger. I have needed this many times. There were moments when people got in my face and said, "Look, you are not fulfilling who you say you are, you're a hypocrite." It's useful, even as it pissed me off. My experience of that One that I pray to is not that he/she/them/it is vengeful and petty. None of my experiences of that One has ever told me to kill my enemies. On the contrary, what I've been counseled to do again and again is to love them, forgive them and transform what they are showing me in myself. For sure, there are people on Earth who claim every day that their god has told them to kill and rape and destroy and dominate others. So maybe there are indeed multiple gods. I know who I'm with.

Would you feel comfortable addressing the Jewish people with a message from where you are now on this fantastic journey?

I don't think I have the right to speak to any people. I have my personal experience. For me, Judaism is a precious, precious gift. It is something on Earth that offers a link that goes back thousands of years. It links one to the heart of an impulse towards unity, towards one God. To have that huge gift was a revolution in human consciousness. It hurts me to see so many of my people living out of fear, living out of reaction, and living in what Reb Zalman calls PTSD. I believe and know that we can be relevant and strong and free of the past. To me, the essence of spiritual evolution, which to me is what we are here for, is to be free of the past. This doesn't mean free of the memory of the past. We become free of the filter of the past interpreting all present experience and causing us not to live here and now with the present moment's infinite possibilities.

We can have a new day, and the new opportunity is to affirm the essential principles that I learned in Judaism. All humans are equal in God's eyes; all humans have a direct connection with God regardless of what they've done and regardless of what they believe. This to me is an essential teaching of Judaism. So that's my experience.

I could be accused of being naïve. I don't think I am. Humans can choose. Because we make peace does not by definition make us patsies for another Holocaust. The Palestinians, what do they want essentially? Take away the people caught in ideology on all sides and what does everybody want? Everybody wants to love and be loved, to be respected and cherished and to live in freedom—everybody. So focusing on that common prayer with feet on the ground, that's how things are going to transform.

We need to understand that there is enough of everything for everyone. Things will not transform by staying in the fight. Eventually that leads to throwing nuclear weapons around. I know that there are many Jews who would just as soon take the whole world with us rather than give in. What if, based on our experience, we take the whole world with us into a new day of becoming what humans are meant to be?

Don't believe anything that I or anyone else tells you just because we say it or we claim some divine inspiration. You have a heart that has an unerring intuitive mechanism built into it. Go to where that intuition tells you to go and do what your heart tells you to do and have the courage to change your opinions and even your life if your heart tells you to. Don't believe anything I tell you, but I sure hope you will look in my heart and see the same spark that you feel in yours. Yeshua Emmanuel was a teacher and an avatar who embodied the Christ fully. He's not the only one who ever did it or ever will. You and I, me a Daimista and you a Jew, in our stumbling will get there one day in some life. A huge myth was built around that Holy man and that myth was then used by confused, greedy and even sincere men to, among other things, create pain and suffering among many people, including Jews. But if we can step beyond the human distortions for a second, beyond our own attachment to ideology as a shield against forgiveness, what's the essence of the myth? He embodied the Christ, the Divine Essence, completely. Therefore, a human can do that; that's the point. So Jews, Hindus, Jains, Native Americans, agnostics, atheists, everybody can embody that. Who cares what you call it? When you put yourself on the path to doing it, all that division gradually disappears.

Thank you.

Nettie Spiwack
INTERFAITH MINISTER

Touring Israel in 1973 with her family, a young Jewish woman stands in the Garden of Gethsemane. There, overlooking Jerusalem, with monks chanting nearby in the room reputed to be the site of the Last Supper, she quietly experiences a spontaneous spiritual revelation: "It all really happened. Jesus lived; His story is real and it is important to my life." She feels an overwhelming, awe-inspiring experience of the presence of God. In the following months, as she begins her freshman year at college, she meets Jews who believe in Jesus, yet still identify as Jews. Soon, she counts herself among them. This was the first of a series of "heresies" that later lead her to explore the world's rich trove of spiritual practices and religions, immersing her in many mystical experiences. Today, an ordained interfaith minister and Spirit-directed healer, she reflects on her relationship to her deep Jewish roots.

What kind of Jewish culture did you grow up in?

I was not raised religiously. I come from a very strong cultural tradition. My grandparents emigrated from Russia, where in revolutionary times there were Jews who felt religion kept them oppressed, so they abandoned the religious orthodoxy but wanted to keep their rich Jewish cultural heritage. In coming to America that cultural expression split off into many streams. One of those was the milieu in which I grew up, the labor and intellectual movements of the Workmen's Circle and Sholem Aleichem Folk Institute.

What were your parents' backgrounds?

In my family, my mother's background decided our practices. Her father arrived in America in the early 1900's from the Russian-Polish world. He worked as a pants-presser and became a very influential mediator in the International Ladies' Garment Workers Union. My grandmother was a seamstress. They were totally immersed in the world of the ILGWU/Amalgamated Clothing Worker's Union and they were among the first residents of the cooperative Amalgamated Houses in the Bronx. The Amalgamated was founded to give working people a decent place to live, near the greenery of Van Cortlandt Park. That's where I was raised. It was like being part of a great, loving, extended family, a multi-generational community. My mother moved there when she was five, and died there in her sixties, surrounded by the same friends with whom she'd grown up.

My parents did not practice religious Judaism. My mother often quoted her father on his disdain for Reform or Conservative Judaism. "Either be an Orthodox believer or nothing." My grandparents had chosen "nothing," and my mother followed suit. Yet they were very active in Workmen's Circle, in Yiddish education and preserving Yiddish culture. We lived in a totally Jewish environment, in what I jokingly call our "Shtetl in the Bronx." I didn't see a Christmas tree until I was seven.

My father came from Philadelphia where his parents had owned a small clothing factory. As former "owners," they couldn't work in the garment unions when they moved to NYC. So they opened a commission bakery in Harlem. My father's father and all the siblings of that generation, originally from Kiev, were a very intellectual and scholarly lot. My great-grandfather had been a *shoychet*, a kosher slaughterer. *Shoychets* needed to be well-versed in kosher laws, and they were highly educated. My grandmother, on the other hand, was from a theatrical family. At one point she took in boarders from the Jewish theater. My father literally grew up around a "cast of characters" and harbored unfulfilled desires to go on the stage. But the important part is that a great deal of intellectual, poetic, artistic and dramatic influences were passed down to us.

After their marriage, my father moved, physically and spiritually, into my mother's world. He'd been sent to a strict religious school (cheder) as a child and did not have good memories of it. My parents were in agreement about sending my siblings and myself to Yiddish schools, which were cultural but not religious. My father must have still had some feelings about preserving the religious tradition because he later told my mother she'd had her way with the three older kids, and insisted that my youngest brother go to a religious school.

So through your parents, the Jewish influences on you were primarily intellectual and artistic?

Yes, but there was a third very important influence: the Labor Zionist Youth Movement. My parents had met as teenagers in Habonim, an organization in that movement, before the war. By the time I came along, we were surrounded by and immersed in the community of post-Holocaust survivors and that too shaped me. Some of my Yiddish teach-

ers were survivors of the Warsaw ghetto and other harrowing experiences. They shared the belief in Zionism and re-building the Land of Israel as essential to Jewish existence in an anti-Semitic world. My parents had originally planned to make *aliyah* (move permanently to Israel), but circumstances didn't allow that to happen. My sister emigrated when she was 21, and still lives on a kibbutz in Israel with her husband, where they raised five children.

Was there any sense of spirituality in your family or in your childhood?

My mother considered herself an atheist. My parents lost a large number of relatives in the Holocaust. Mom used to say that the Holocaust was the proof that God did not exist. But then, she would add wryly, "but there are no atheists in foxholes." My father was more agnostic. He would go to the local orthodox synagogue on Yom Kippur and say Kaddish for his brother and father, both of whom died young. My mother was very uncomfortable around all religious observances, Judaism included, and avoided temple-going.

Despite all that, my parents were very insistent about keeping Friday night Shabbos dinner. We'd have a tablecloth and lit candles and blessed the challah. We were the only family I knew in our secular community who did. To my mother, it was a way of creating special family time, and reinforcing that we were a Jewish family.

For myself, I remember very clearly, as a child, lying in bed and talking with God. I remember looking out the window and being connected to a very personal sense of God. There was no precedent for that in my family.

So you had this deep religious sensibility and it seemed to you at the time that this had nothing to do with being Jewish?

Yes, there was an innate deeply spiritual sensibility. That it had nothing to do with being Jewish is probably inaccurate. I had no role models for a deeply spiritual Jewish life. Ironically, images from the

Christian world offered by the media set that tone. I saw Debbie Reynolds in "The Singing Nun" and Julie Andrews in "The Sound of Music," and I too wanted to be a nun when I was about eight. It all had an aura of romance! But it's not like I sat around wanting to be Christian— that was quite fleeting. I just sensed something attractive in what those nuns had, and looking back, I can recognize it as nascent spiritual longing.

Didn't you have any negative imprints towards Christianity?

When I was young, I didn't have to deal with it. Everyone around me was Jewish! Later I started to learn about persecution, pogroms, and the Holocaust. Yet in elementary school I remember being interested in the religious paraphernalia of my one Catholic friend. What little girl wouldn't be fascinated by dressing up as a bride for First Communion?

What do you think was happening? What was the attraction, as you see it now, to religion and the Christian message?

I believe that we as souls have many lives. I know that I've had significant lives as a Catholic nun. In a way I think that my soul chose this time, for karmic reasons, to put me in a situation where it would be difficult to repeat that again. Left to my own devices, I might unconsciously drift back to the same sort of life. So this time I was placed in a situation that would take away that possibility of ending up in a nunnery.

It's possible to imagine that if I'd been immersed in Jewish mysticism early on, my life might have taken a different turn. But I didn't have that exposure.

I was born with a soul-recognition that there is a God. My upbringing in the Jewish world excluded God. My parents' world did maintain one channel to the numinous through our community's strong participation in the arts. My parents and their friends had season tickets to the Philharmonic. We'd go to the ballet and theatre and the Young

People's Concerts. We were of modest means, but my parents spent their money on the cultural benefits living in New York offered.

Of great importance to me along those lines were my summers at Camp Boiberik. Our Jewish-Yiddish cultural camp did not mention God, but its profoundly moving cultural rituals and celebrations put me in touch with something higher and beautiful. Boiberik also had an elaborate yearly festival called "Felker Yontev" or "holiday of the people." It celebrated different folk cultures and countries throughout the world through music, dance and costume. I think its message of understanding and valuing other cultures played heavily into my later call to interfaith work. So, overall, I wouldn't say the sacred was ever really absent. It was always around me in different forms.

The words "Jesus Christ" and the symbol of the Cross tend to make Jews (especially Jews of your parents generation) extremely uncomfortable. You found yourself as a child being drawn to some Christian images, as you say of the nuns. But there still must have been a giant step to become a Christian.

In high school I had a Christian friend. When I went with my family on our second trip to Israel, I got it in my head to buy my friend a Maltese cross. We were in the Old City, and I had the excuse to look at crosses despite my mother's discomfort with my interests. I remember buying a cross near the Church of the Holy Sepulchre, ostensibly the site of Jesus's tomb. I went inside the church alone, down to the tomb, and felt a sense of the sacred that greatly moved me.

Later, in a moment alone at the Garden of Gethsemane overlooking Jerusalem and the Dome of the Rock, while listening to monks chanting in the "upper room" of the Last Supper, I had a spontaneous revelation, an instantaneous connection. "It all happened. Jesus really lived. The story of Jesus was real." I knew right then that it was vitally important to my life. It was an overwhelming experience of divine revelation, of connecting to the God-force. Awe-inspiring. And then the experience left—but seeds had been planted.

Didn't it shake you up?

It came with a deep sense of peace and wonder.

You didn't say anything to your mother?

Not to anyone. Within several weeks I went to the Kansas City Art Institute for my freshman year. At some point that fall, I was invited by two girls on my hall to visit a group of Jewish "believers," similar to "Jews for Jesus." It was the natural outgrowth of my experience in Gethsemane. I felt immediately drawn to the devotion and the teachings. It spoke strongly to me. Most forbidden—I was pulled by the notion of a personal relationship with God through Jesus.

Did you feel you were transgressing?

Absolutely! At first I put it in the category of, "I'm just visiting." Then it came to, "Do I accept that I actually believe in Jesus as the Christ (anointed one) and ask him into my heart?" I tortured myself at first. I did have to wrestle with it, deeply. I knew the seismic waves it would send through my world. Ultimately, six months after I'd stood in the Garden, I did pray that prayer.

Did you need to do it some public way?

No. Not like in the movies. It was a private and very sacred moment. Saying it to myself was more consequential than saying it to anyone else. Later, there were public expressions of that commitment.

I believe there are challenges at every new stage of psychological and spiritual growth, particularly at the onset of a great breakthrough. One night, when I was struggling with, "Do I believe in Jesus?" I fell into a dream state and had an experience that felt like it lasted for hours where I was falling back into a deep pit. There was an arm robed in white, and each time it would break my fall. When I woke up, I attributed it to Jesus or an angel. I knew that it was God's protection.

Soon after, I prayed and asked Jesus to come into my life.

I went home for vacation and kept it to myself. After Christmas break, I got very active in the Jewish-Christian community in Kansas City. It was a great time. We were networked into the greater "Jesus community." It was a period of learning. But in my new passionate enthusiasm, I also alienated other friends. I was evangelical. I sounded like one of those people you cross the street to avoid. (laughs)

Decades later, my mentor, Ron Roth, described what he called, "The Five Stages of Prayer and Healing." I had undergone the first stage, Awakening, and now in the second stage—Purification—I was fulfilling Ron's teasing description: "You get the biggest book of scripture you can find and hit everybody else over the head with it." That was me. I had all the wisdom of an 18-year-old convert, which is to say, none.

Was there ever a question of whether you were any longer Jewish?

In that belief system I became a "fulfilled Jew." The experience was that I had found "the answer"— and that Jews who didn't believe were missing half the story. But I always understood why Jews reject Christianity so vehemently because of the bloody history of Christian persecution of Jews leading up to the Holocaust experience. That can never leave you. That is why parents of my time were far less troubled by Jewish Buddhists and their teen's interest in Eastern religions. No Buddhist ever launched a pogrom. I was under no illusions as to why other Jews considered my choice to be the ultimate betrayal to Judaism! But I didn't need every Jew to believe what I believed, nor did I think that would happen.

You felt open to those Jews who rejected your path.

Yes, completely.

You've written that your family reacted very strongly when they did find out about your activities. They required you to go to

therapy and take six months without contact with the Jesus people. They had you meet with rabbis and get religious Jewish education just in case some base hadn't been covered. What was that period like for you?

It was one of the worst periods of my life, and I'm sure my parents and my younger brother would say much the same. This took place in the Jonestown cult massacre era, so my parents had good reason to be frightened, and I certainly didn't help matters by the way I spoke that made me sound like an automaton. But, for someone immersed in Christianity, a sense of martyrdom comes with the territory.

So you continued to hold on to your faith without real doubts?

I didn't have spiritual doubts. My doubts were about how I could live my life with this huge conflict in my outer world. I slipped into doing what I had to do to survive. I made those agreements with my parents. As time went on, I would listen secretly at night to Christian radio. Some months later I snuck away to a phone booth and I spoke to one of the leaders in our Jesus circle in Kansas City. He gave me sound advice that also proved to me I was not in a cult. He said a very beautiful thing to me: "Honor your father and mother. Stay with your parents. You always have a place here, but God is always with you." .

Looking back, I was being divinely guided in ways I didn't fully recognize. The therapist my parents found was a psychiatrist who was also a practicing Episcopalian priest. My parents surprisingly agreed to this arrangement and I connected instantly with him. He was smart, empathetic, gentle and completely non-threatening. They had a session with him where they expressed their fears that his religious vocation would influence me, but they trusted him and understood he provided a necessary bridge.

You stayed in New York and went through the required therapy. What happened to your religious fervor?

I met the man who was to become my first great teacher. He turned out to be a second divine intervention. He was my art teacher, Theo, my maestro. He gave me access to a new way to relate to divinity. I studied art with him for almost eight years.

During your period of intensive involvement in the art world, did the fervor about Jesus subside, go into the background?

Partly. My art teacher became the central figure in my world. He spoke in archetypal and spiritual terms about the tension between the Dionysian and the Apollonian in art and in life. He'd been educated in Greece by the Jesuits and he recognized my spiritual leanings immediately. Though he often teased me about them, he had them himself, albeit in his own way. So there was a new language and outlet for the spiritual through art. The numinous that had always been in my home became re-embodied in an acceptable, less-threatening form. My mother eventually saw me as more sane, even with her reservations about my major on Renaissance Studies, which she associated with Christian themes. But they were themes of High Culture! Who can argue with Miichelangelo and DaVinci?

My parents had given me a requirement of six months without contact with my Christian circle, and I lived in private desperation wondering what I would do at the end of the six months.

So when the six-month deadline hit, I took the advice of another art-student friend to simply go with the flow, as by then I was enjoying my self at school, and was just making my first breakthroughs in therapy. She somehow gave me permission to relax and remain in "I don't know." I made one very close friend early on, Julio, and when I told him about my secret inner world he chimed in with his own spiritual experiences—and now there was someone else in my world with whom I could share my deepest thoughts, and that broke my isolation. As a coda, more than 35 years later we're still friends and have been on several pilgrimage trips around the world together.

I got deeper into the art world. Christianity went to a very private place. I never lost my faith in Jesus, never stopped praying. Gradually,

I reclaimed my equilibrium to be able to live in the world of my family and friends whom I loved. Therapy was a major part of that. I'd come through a fundamentalist community, and fundamentalists by definition think in extremes. The world shows up as polarized: believer or non-believer, good and evil, saved or not saved. I had adopted that for a period of time and then my equilibrium returned, and with it came the "Middle Way." Although that's a Buddhist term, it fits. I like to say that I kept God but left the fundamentalism behind. I kept the spiritual truth, but dropped the man-made interpretations and form.

Then came the next decade or so of my life, which I call the transformational years. I did the EST training and advanced programs, (later Landmark Education) in which I became deeply immersed. From that time forward, I have always been on a path of expanding consciousness through a great variety of teachings and teachers. But the direct "God thread" did not re-emerge until my 40s.

Do you see your focus during that period as more psychological?

The word that comes to mind is consciousness, of which psychology, especially psychology of that era, was one piece. The work for me in that era was about consciousness: self-awareness, communication, integrity—all the things that are essential spiritual values but in another form. I call spirituality and transformation "the twin tracks." They are parallel and lead to the same result, to the same kind of consciousness. If you keep clearing up your integrity in the world, keep addressing and clearing your personal issues, keep taking responsibility for your life and the world around you, sooner or later you're going to end up at an experience of unity and union with people, with all of life. The spiritual path (not necessarily religious practice) has all those attributes, with the added element of worship and devotion to God. The transformational track appreciates wholeness, beauty and truth. In the Vedic traditions, those are just other names for God: Sathyam, Shivam, Sundaram.

Today would you say that you are a Jew?

When people ask me, I always say first that I'm Jewish. But I also add that I don't practice as an observant Jew. I consider myself to be on the mystic's path. A famous spiritual teacher has said: "a few mystical experiences do not a mystic make." But the path of the mystic is to see beyond limitations and forms into the heart of God. Not to know about God, but to actually know God. One of my primary teachers, Ron Roth, a true mystic, said that all mystics from all paths say the same thing. There is only One Truth, and the defining understanding of a mystic is someone who has reached that Truth —regardless of the road, they all end up in the same place. Ron, as well as Sai Baba, Mother Teresa and others summed it up using the same idea: "There is only one religion, the religion of Love."

Every faith has its fundamentalists at one end and its mystical branch at the other. There are Muslim and Jewish and Hindu and Christian examples. All true mystics experience that all is One, and are accepting of people of different faiths. You can't be a fundamentalist mystic; it's a spiritual oxymoron. But a lot of Christian mystics knew that they had to be very careful about how they languaged their experiences or they'd be burned at the stake. Cultural mores play a role in terms of what is acceptable.

So even Christianity is not your primary identification anymore religiously?

No. My primary identification is the mystic's path; and I view myself as a healer through an interfaith lens. Healing is ultimately about healing our sense of separation from each other and from God, whatever means we use to do that. There are others who are on that same path of mystical union with God who go through the doorway of a single religion, as did the saints of old and some of today. I'm an eclectic. Yet, when people ask me, what are you? I always start with, I'm Jewish, inextricably.

Secular Jews on the whole understand the part about being Jewish but not religious. We are both a culture and a race as well as a religion. And I feel that to a certain extent what my mother often said is true: "The world will make you Jewish whether you want to be or not." I accept that.

I'm sure that you now know that there is a rich mystical stream in Judaism. Many Jews who explored other faiths returned to Judaism in its more spiritual form. Did you ever feel a call or pull to that?

Sometimes I feel as if I should be more interested in things like Jewish Renewal and Kabbalah, but it just doesn't call me—or hasn't yet. I tend to like to explore everything, but you have to accept some limitations in life. I had a great deal of exposure and learning in traditional Jewish religious practices, but I practice it formally very little— though we do as a family have a seder, although our Hanukah has become more of a Christmas with latkes. My parents would not approve!

I have a rich prayer and devotional life that is informed by many traditions, and share with others like myself in a variety of settings. That's why being an interfaith minister was a natural for me.

Then what does it mean that one is Jewish? Does it mean anything more than that you are born to Jewish parents?

I wasn't merely born to Jewish parents. I was nourished in a very enriched Jewish community. I am at home with the fact that I haven't got everything resolved. I don't have a problem with having some conflicts, or with the fact that most other Jews would say I'm no longer Jewish. I know I am not the only Jewish person to have unresolved questions. Yes, there are things that are unresolved, but they are not painful; these are the enigmas of life. You don't get to have everything answered and tied up with a bow— and that's ok. I have a deep peace in my relationship to God that supersedes all the "what's your religious identity?" questions.

In the late eighties and into the nineties I studied with Fernando Flores and then with Arnold Mindell, the founder of Process Work psychology. I came to appreciate that however you are raised, you are born into existing cultural conversations that were there before you and will be there after you.

Being born Jewish, there is a long ancestral legacy that places a strong value on education—we are the People of the Book. Your Jewish parents may have been atheists, may never have had a whit of formal Jewish education, but somewhere there will be this emphasis on the value of education. You can't escape it!

So an attribute of what it means to be Jewish is to have an intellectual bent, a focus on education, information and analysis. What else? What are the transmissions that you value from your Jewish ancestral connection and that have been helpful and you want to pass on?

Many things. The transmission, the cultural inform, has the light side and the shadow. The light is education. The shadow is the culture of suffering, which I have worked within myself to put an end to in my generation.

Another transmission is questioning. It was a Native American friend who pointed that out to me after traveling with me for a month in India. "Jews ask a lot of questions," she said. I realized she was right! Questioning is completely embedded in our culture. The first thing you teach your child is the "four questions" for the Passover seder. I remember hearing a Jewish author say his mother always asked him, "Have you asked a good question today?"

Questioning is fundamental to Jewish discourse. That's part of the rabbinic, Talmudic stream, even if you don't know that is where it comes from: the discussion, the debate, Jewish lawyers! Jews aren't afraid to argue with God, or with anyone else.

You seem to be saying that there is a special kind of intellectualism in the Jewish world that's distinct, a kind of flavor of the mind of the Jewish intellect?

Yes. Number one: questioning. Number two: as with other oppressed peoples, you get comedians and artists. I believe that in the 20th century, Jews dominated many of the arts in America. Now, Jewish children are less likely to go there; there are more options, more choices.

There are many things we think of as "the Jewish transmission." But you point out that they may be temporal, related to events and changes of the time. So what is the long-lasting thread of what it means to be Jewish?

I think the transmission changes according to the container of the time and the limitations imposed by the society. Take money. For centuries in Europe, Jews were forcibly limited to a certain few trades. We got into managing money and banking because it was one of the few businesses allowed — it was considered too dirty for gentiles. So the gentiles gave "the dirty job" to the Jews, who by necessity and experience got really good at it. That set up that thought stream in our collective heritage, carrying with it both positive images of the smart Jewish businessman and the negative Shylock stereotypes about Jews and money.

Here's a societal example. At a certain point early in my career, a Strong-Campbell test suggested I be a rabbi. That's not an option that would have been open to me, a woman, even ten years prior.

Was that your 10 minutes of considering a return?

(laughs) The point is that times change and opportunities change. I didn't go that route then, but twenty years later I went to interfaith seminary.

Being a rabbi would have been a path for your spiritual inclinations.

And for teaching. A rabbi is an educator, not an intermediary between you and God. Rabbi means teacher, not anointed priest. It's a different archetype.

Is that the way you see yourself?

I think I'm a blend of the two.

Would you say you've crossed over into a more priestly role?

I think we carry certain archetypal imprints, and the priestly one is one of mine.

What are the elements of Jewish transmission you see as destructive?

The suffering.

So what is it about Jews and suffering? What have you learned about that?

I've learned that it's a legacy, and a set of conversations. Very real events, two thousand years of persecution culminating in the Holocaust, are going to develop a victim consciousness in a people. We all know that the suffering of the Jews is a conversation in our culture. That's why most Americans recognize: "Oy vey!"

When I was eight years old, at the same time God was emerging in my life, the local Community Center had a Holocaust exhibit. All of it: the pictures of mass graves, the bar of soap, the lampshade, the camps. That imprinted on me deeply. I never forgot that. In Israel, there are memorials everywhere you go, and I visited all of them by the time I was 16. I never watched "Schindler's List." I never went to the Holocaust Museum. I'm not the person who needs that education. I was raised and taught by people who lived that. I heard all those stories first hand. That's all part of the suffering legacy and there is good reason for that historically.

For myself, there were two memorable instances where I saw

the meme of suffering not as just my personal experience, but like a cultural entity living through me, and I was then able to transform it. Once was when I was in a two-year depression after a break-up. A friend's daughter said about me, when it was long past time for me to snap out of it, "There's six million Jews suffering in that body!" And when she said it, I got that part of my response to my personal loss was the archetype of suffering expressing itself in me with a life of its own. That helped me climb out of my funk.

Do you see a possibility of freeing oneself of that suffering in this lifetime?

I feel that I have freed myself. I've freed myself of the unconscious need to experience things through suffering. I've been around some rabbis, and in their sermons, even on some unrelated topic, there will emerge a dramatic story that has the theme and undercurrent and vocal intonation of suffering. You can hear it in their voice. It's being consciously or unconsciously used by an energy that's so much a part of your culture that you don't even realize that there are other ways of being. It's an archetypal energy. I've seen it with black preachers too—not the same suffering story, but the phenomenon of snapping into an archetypal energy that's part of your people's story. I sort of marvel that I don't have to do that anymore. I don't have to take that on unless I choose to. It's much like forgiveness—the story is still true, the memory is there, but the energy, the sting, is gone.

Freedom from that particular suffering for me came as a result of many things. It was the result of many years of work in awareness and consciousness. All of the studies that I've done in therapies, transformation, EST, Fernando Flores, Arny Mindell and Worldwork, ontological reconstruction of my stories—it happened piece by piece by piece.

The second notable event happened around the German/Jewish relationship. I realized in my 40s that this spiritual journey of my life meant forgiveness and letting go of any area in my life that still maintained a negative charge. That's my goal in life: equanimity—not having aversions or preferences. I know what still triggers me and where

I can still be polarized and lose my equanimity and make someone else into an enemy. At the individual level it almost never happens. It's more at the level of politics and society. That's where I wrestle.

At a certain point, I was asked to go to Germany to deliver a training. I was already deep into my adult spiritual journey. I'd been to India and I had recently been with Sai Baba. Yet, I had a hard time with the idea of going to Germany. My mother used to say she would never set foot in Germany; she would never buy a German product. So I was not free to be with Germans. I knew I needed to get over that. I knew intellectually that today Germans were not my enemy, but emotionally it was another story.

I went with an associate who was also a friend. I told her I needed support because I knew there would be times where I would be emotionally triggered. I turned it over to God and held this trip as an opportunity to rid myself of some of this. In the way that God laughs at you and the universe conspires to have things happen, I'll never forget this. We were met by a taxi driver who was the archetype of the jolly German housefrau. This was in 1999. East Germany and West Germany were still coming together economically and some of the people I met, including this driver, were still reveling in the opportunities the merging had given them as former East Germans to have a free and more prosperous life.

We were driving thru these picturesque German towns. First, in the middle of a field out of nowhere there is one of the rifle towers from war movies like "Stalag 17." What's that doing there? In these little towns we were going through, all I could imagine was the roundup of the Jews, like in all the movies I'd seen. Then all of a sudden there is a siren and we're pulled over and a large, imposing policeman comes over and in German (which I partially understand from Yiddish), he says to the driver, "Can I see your papers?" In that moment I went into an altered state. It was a complete hook for my Jewish nightmare: the rifle tower, the uniformed police asking for papers in German, and I went into a reactivated state. Then we get to this spa hotel in Baden-Baden and there is a blond guy at the reception desk who looks like the Nazi boyfriend in "The Sound of Music." I'm almost in a fugue state. I go up to my room and, unlike in most European hotels where everything is written in five languages, everything is printed only in German. I start to think, "I am in Germany and I am trapped." It was all a complete reactivation.

I just prayed: Please help me. That night I had a dream of my guru (Sai Baba), who shows up in my dreams from time to time. I just saw his orange robe, and I knew I was safe. When I woke up I was ok. I was at peace for the moment.

Over the course of the week, I met with East German people. At the farewell dinner, as I sat with one of the women, we were reading the menu together and I said, "Let me translate." She asked how I knew German. I suddenly recalled the story she had told during the week, of her very hard life under Communism. At that moment I had a choice: I could go into a story about the loss of our Yiddish language because of the murder of the Jews, or, I could have compassion, knowing this woman had a far harder life than I personally ever experienced. I chose compassion and simply told her that I studied a language similar to German and I left it at that. It was not just that I didn't pick it up with her to avoid conflict. I chose for myself not to go down that road and squeeze those memories for their painful juice, and I was left with a feeling of kindness and compassion. That was a sense of liberation. There was a huge amount of forgiveness in that for me.

Why do so many Jewish people, who had no relatives directly involved, attach themselves to the suffering of the Holocaust? Is it a conscious choice? And is that kind of identification different than honoring their memory or having compassion?

It's both a conscious belief and an unconscious choice. There's the feeling that if we don't suffer, we'll forget; the suffering means the people didn't die in vain, that you are not forgetting. There's also an unconscious transmission that suffering together is part of what makes us a people, and that remembered suffering is what has held us together and allowed us to survive. There's a lot of truth in that, too.

I no longer feel obligated to take on the suffering myself. That is different than not honoring the history and the memory; it doesn't mean you don't remember, or don't respect the horrible suffering. When you speak about releasing the suffering, it can be seen as a betrayal, and I already betrayed once, twice, remember.

You mean when you chose Jesus and.....

...forgiving the Germans.

And the third betrayal would be giving up the suffering itself?

Giving up suffering as part of a core identity.

So you are saying that we've been told, non-verbally, that if you give up the suffering you are betraying our people, our Jewish identity. Now you don't really see that as a betrayal but that this idea is a meme that we have been given.

It's like that beautiful scene at the end of the movie, "The Chosen." where the Rod Steiger character weeps and speaks of the suffering of our people and his role to carry the pain for all the Jews, and even to use it as a tool to create compassion in his son. I understand it, and it's very moving.

I'm not saying I'm complete about all these things. How can anyone be? Were I to visit the Holocaust Museum tomorrow, I would get triggered all over again. Who wouldn't? But I would not have to then carry that suffering energy forward for the rest of my life.

How important is it to you that in future generations there will be a Jewish people?

This time around, Jewishness is inextricable from my core identity. But one of the things I'm not complete with regards the future of the Jewish people. At the same time as wanting to preserve the culture, I recognize that all things in creation come and go, even us.

I'm not speaking of annihilation by enemies. I mean the gradual assimilation into the non-Jewish world that is considered a great or a greater threat to our continuation as a people. I am an example of that in my own life, and my daughter is also. Despite my interfaith background, I insisted that she go to Hebrew school and have a bat mitzvah (which I didn't have, by the way). The rich secular Yiddish world in which I was raised, in which simply living in the community and breathing was enough to imbue you with a Jewish identity, that world is gone. There are people who work hard to keep parts of it alive; some of them are my friends, but it wasn't my life. I wanted my daughter to at least know where she came from, to be familiar with the Jewish mainstream, to know her roots, and then, the choice would be hers.

As someone who is an interfaith minister and not a purist in any way, I have great regard for purists. They have a role in society and I value them, cherish them. They keep a particular stream pure and help it survive. Judaism won't survive because of me or people like me. It is far more likely it will be because of the Orthodox, and people like my sister, who moved to Israel to rebuild the Jewish homeland. Yet, I felt called to a different path, and I accept that it was the path for which I was born.

In the spiritual path there is a quest for the ultimate sense of "I." How does that relate to the "I" that says comfortably, "I am a Jew?" Does it exist before you were born and after you die? When you are immersed with spirit, how do you hold that? For example there is the "neti, neti" process.

"Neti, neti" is the Ramana Maharshi inquiry, the path to liberation through asking what is real, what is eternal. When you inquire, for example, is this body eternal? the answer is neti, neti, not this, not this. Eventually you arrive at the only truth: eternal divinity. The story of my name is that it came from Grandfather Nathan. My parents decided to call me Nettie, which I hated. When I later encountered the Maharshi story, and found out that neti, neti is a path to liberation, chills went up my spine. I knew my parents hadn't made a mistake.

Then at some point, don't you say, "I am not a Jew?" How else does one hold that this "I" that I truly am is beyond all those roles and beliefs and concepts?

In the highest levels of truth, there is no individual Nettie. It's all a temporal experience, including identities like being Jewish or Christian or whatever. However, in the practicality of living as a spiritual being in a "meat-bag" (laughs) there are certain things that help us live life. You have work to do in this dimension and one of those things is maintaining an identity and to feel, at the level of emotional and psychological health, integrated and functional and able to help others. So there's an awareness that you are not that identity, but it's useful to put a coat on when you go out in the cold. It's useful to have an identity: Nettie, Jewish, Bronx. Helps you to move around in the world.

It's not that I don't get trapped in my attachment to this particular skin bag. (laughter) I do, and I love playing around with this identity and I love being Jewish and all those other things, and I still live my life as if I am an "I" with a small "i". But I also know there is a higher truth, and certainly in times of crisis that higher truth has to come to the fore to help me get through.

Do you want to say anything about life after life in this form?

I believe that every life that we have lived is imprinted in our energy and is part of the expansion of our learning as souls. Whatever we have experienced positively and negatively before contributes to the soul's growth; and soul growth happens over eons. As for the afterlife, all the great spiritual teachers I admire say that a lot of what you experience after is shaped by expectations built here.

Returning for a moment to the Jewish/Christian issue: what is there about your belief in Jesus that's not Jewish? What is it that you believe that Jews don't?

There are two threads. The one that goes back to the time of Jesus is whether or not people believed that he was in fact the fulfillment of the scriptures as the Messiah. That was important to me when I was 18, but it's not really now. It is, of course, of critical importance to a great many Christians.

More important for me is that the Christian transmission, another variant of a transmission that's been in humanity for a long time, says that divinity embodies itself in a human incarnation for the purpose of giving human beings access to that divine vibration. Divine incarnations are a part of the belief systems of billions of people. I was a bit horrified to realize that even as a learned person, I could get to be over 40 years old before I understood that in India, in the Hindu tradition going back even further than the Jews, there were divine incarnations of God regarded in the same way as Jesus is regarded by Christians.

Christians believe that Jesus's life was the one and only time such a thing happened, and to say that about anyone else is a total heresy. Hindus believe that God incarnates on divine missions frequently, as in the minor avatars. Then there are the Great, or Poorna, avatars whose presence on Earth is more rare and effects all of us.

Is this the core difference that first drew you to Christianity in college?

Part of what drew me to Jesus was the notion that you could have a personal relationship with God. The Judaism that I had been exposed to had God as something more amorphous than that: impersonal, distant. You might beg Him or plead with Him, like Tevye in "Fiddler on the Roof." But what appealed to me was that God could be my friend. I'd already sensed that when I was a child, but had no Jewish models at that time to support it. Then there is the much deeper aspect of having been called on a karmic or mystical level, but that's more difficult to explain.

So now, knowing that Jews have a mystical tradition and that Jews talk to God in a personal way, often as HaShem, is there still a difference? Was there a breakthrough that Jesus brought? Did he say something new? Is there really a *New* Testament?

For me, at this point in my development, access to the divine is not confined to Jesus. It includes the Hindu avatars, saints of many traditions, and I am open to traditions I don't know of yet. Even with mystical Judaism, the place where the lines would probably diverge is where there are God incarnations, people who fully embody the God presence in the body. There are self-realized masters such as Sai Baba, Ammachi, and others. Sai Baba says of Jesus; "Jesus's life embodies the path of every seeker. First you believe that you are a messenger of God; then you believe that you are a son of God (a direct relationship); and lastly you realize that, "I and the Father are One." Experiencing that you and the Father are one is self-realization. So the difference in most Christianity is the belief that only Jesus could say or achieve union with the Father. The entire Vedic tradition says it is every person's path, though it may take countless lifetimes. I believe Jesus was an initiate who embodied this at the highest possible level of consciousness.

"All this and more ye shall do"?

Right. "All this and more ye shall do." Jesus also quoted the Psalms saying, "Know ye not that ye are Gods?" Nobody wants to deal with that quote! Jesus remains for me a bringer of overpowering love. The most immediate access I have to divine love is when I think of him. Same when I think of Paramahansa Yogananda.

Is the emphasis on unconditional love, rather than do the right thing and then you get the love, something different that he taught?

Yes, unconditional love: love that brings you to your knees because it's so overwhelming. For most people who identify as Christians, it comes in a package with "and he's the only one." So I appreciate that and try not to tread on people's toes.

You grew up in the Labor Zionist world. How do you feel about how American Jews relate to Israel?

That can be a very painful place because of what's happened in the press in recent years, Israel losing the public relations war. I have family there. What happens in Israel is of direct consequence to me. My sister lives 3 miles from the Gaza strip. When the Katusha rockets get fired they get fired into their area. I have a nephew in the Army. My parents' lives were committed to Israel, raising money for Israel; my mom belonged to the Pioneer Women. The existence of the Jewish state was of paramount importance to them and it is important to me. If I have one piece of guilt as a Jew, it's that I don't place enough attention on it.

If there were no Israel, would I feel more vulnerable in the world? As a Jewish person, I would feel more vulnerable. But it's sort of polarized in the Jewish world. Either Israel is always right or the opposite. The truth is far more complex. It's a terrible mess for which, as Einstein said, there is no solution at the level of thinking that created the problem. I'd like to believe there is one and I hold up a hope for that. It's a quagmire and forces well beyond my control influence it.

Do you see your path as heretical, but in a good sense?

Yes, in my life I'm the heretic. Do you know why? I think it's in part because I am an "old soul" with enough memories in my soul's energy field to know that I've been it all already: I've been Jewish, Christian, Muslim, Indian, Chinese, oppressor and oppressed, and on and on. If you have that knowledge in your soul, if you know that you've experienced life from all those perspectives, how can you then claim to identify with only one rigid identity? Choosing a single path, like Judaism, is an option, and I'm glad that some people do.

Sai Baba has said, "It is good to be born into a religion, but it is not good to die in one." I believe that means that spiritual growth is constant self-inquiry, which involves growing beyond believing something merely because it was handed to you. Religion is an appropriate place to start a journey. But I believe that true spirituality includes and also transcends form, and that is where we are headed.

I have a phrase that I use: "batting clean-up." In every incarnation we bring in a handful of former incarnations to clean up. We meet the people that we have met before, with whom we have debts to settle and so on.

I spent time immersed in reading the Mahabarata, the Bhagavad Gita, the Ramayana. They refer to vast amounts of time, of kalpas of hundreds of millions of years. In those terms there is a lot to cleanup! For myself, I take it that I am here batting clean-up. I'm here to complete those things that remain as karmic incompletions in my life. I've been with people where there seems to be animosity at first sight and we end up making peace. Each one of these as they present and resolve is "batting clean up." Sometimes, like when I think of the freedom from suffering, I feel a thrill when I realize I've "driven in another run."

Do you have a message, from your strong identification with the Jewish people, to your people?

The notion of a message to a whole people, and from one seen as a heretic, feels presumptuous if not preposterous. But, one thing would be about what we were discussing, the freedom from suffering—that you can discover that detaching yourself from the legacy of suffering does not mean detaching yourself from your history or your compassion for the suffering. It's important to make that distinction.

Suffering builds one of two things: hatred or compassion. The most remarkable person I know in this regard is my cousin in Israel who was saved from the Holocaust. She is now in her 80s. She watched her mother and father get shot, and yet she is not a bitter person. It's character, the same kind as in the film, "Invictus," about Nelson Mandela. Or Gandhi, who influenced both Martin Luther King and Mandela. These three brown men forgave their nation's white oppressors and changed the world for everyone. They came from centuries of enforced suffering and enslavement. And they forgave and brought spiritual and literal freedom to over a billion people. They are my heroes.

Being born Jewish in America, at my particular point in history, was a great gift; one that I treasure. It gave me so much, including my upbringing around God, which was essentially none. That cultural separation from religion saved me from having the poisoned God image that so many people have to heal. I never had to recover from a punishing God. There is so much I attribute to being Jewish, and a New York Jew at that. I received everything I needed to have what they call "privilege." I've had the privilege to develop, nurture and realize my artistic and intellectual talents, and to achieve psychological and spiritual health.

Every year at Passover we read a wonderful page in the "Haggadah for the American Family" that my father first brought home in the 1950s as a free giveaway. The page is about the legacy of deliverance: "In every age, we discover a new form of servitude from which we seek freedom." And I believe that it is our responsibility to pass on that freedom, whether spiritual, psychological or emotional, to the next generation.

My set of spiritual, emotional and psychological privileges has given me what I needed to live a life of service to others, to help them achieve some new freedom. To all my forbears, upon whose shoulders I stand, who didn't have these opportunities or freedoms, even those who would say that my life has been a rejection of everything they stood for, for all that their lives made possible, I say sincerely with all my heart, a *sheynem dank*. (Yiddish: a wholehearted beautiful thank you).

Thank you.

Ken Cohen
Taoist and Qigong Master

"When I was a child, kids used to bully me. One time, I was standing outside during lunch break wondering why these kids hated me so much, when all of a sudden I had this thought. I remember exactly how I framed it: 'It is because I know who I am and you're not supposed to know that; people object to that.' I immediately felt like I was an 81-year-old man. I don't know why that number came to me, but I felt I was an 81-year-old man inside and a 12-year-old boy on the surface."

(I met with Ken Cohen in a hotel in Queens, NY, where he was staying while visiting his mother. Just when we are about to start, he gets a call and has to take it; it's his mom. I hear him repeat himself many times, reminding her over and over of things they discussed when he was with her this morning. I get the picture that she has dementia. What strikes me is that he is never irritated or impatient, he remains completely relaxed, kind and gentle throughout the conversation.

Ken offers and prepares some tea and explains that this tea is organically grown and comes from a 700-year-old wild tea tree in China.)

Is it correct to say that you are a Taoist master?

Some people call me that. I consider such titles to be honorifics. People call me Qigong master or Taoist master, but I actually prefer the Chinese term Lao Shi, meaning teacher or professor. I consider myself an educator. I have also been described as a healer. In my opinion, titles that imply extraordinary knowledge of healing or spirituality, such as "medicine man" in Native American culture, should be bestowed by a community in recognition of good service. I think of myself as a teacher and educator.

You've had master teachers and have been in a lineage of Taoism, Qigong, and also Native American spirituality.

Yes, I have had wonderful teachers and mentors in these various paths. Let's start by focusing on the Chinese arts and on my multi-track spirituality, to allay suspicions I am a dabbler or that I am only looking for common elements. Americans tend to have a problem with dual expertise in the spiritual or theological realm, though not in the academic. We believe that one religion excludes the other, as though there were only one correct path to God. People might look askance if someone claimed to be a Jewish rabbi and a Muslim sheikh. Similarly, to be a Taoist as well as a practitioner of Native American spirituality, may seem odd. Yet I have equal training in both. They are both my life's passion.

In Qigong and Taoism, there are indeed lineages. I was the principle apprentice to a Taoist abbot from southern China, Dr. Huang Gengshi. From 1976 until 1981, I saw him a few times a week, and continued to visit with him yearly until his passing in 1999. In Qigong, I've had a number of wonderful teachers. The majority were from China. B.P. Chan, my first Qigong teacher, was originally from Fujian province and taught in the Philippines for many years. I began the study of Yang Style Tai Chi, which is actually a subset of Qigong, in 1968 with a student of Master William CC Chen. After one year, I began to study Tai Chi directly with Master Chen.

I also studied with Madame Gao Fu, who was a senior student of Feng Zhiqiang, in the lineage of the founder of the first style of Tai Chi, called Chen Family or Chen Style Tai Chi. Tai Chi was originally passed on like a family heirloom. If you didn't have the surname Chen, you couldn't learn it. Chen Style is like the ocean. It has strong crashing waves, slow retreating tides, high postures and low, slow and quick, hard and soft. There is a dynamic alternation of yin and yang. As you practice the exercise, you create a positive and negative polarity, and electricity—"the qi"—flows between them.

Hundreds of years ago one of the Chen family's students had the surname Yang. He developed Yang Style Tai Chi, which is more meditative than the Chen Style. (This is not yang as compared to yin. Rather, here Yang is simply a family name.) Yang Style is like a slow-moving stream, smooth and even, without the dynamic contrasts of slow and quick, high and low. So my first Tai Chi style was Yang Style, and then later I had the great blessing of meeting Chen Style Master Madame Gao and becoming one of her senior students and one of her translators when she first came to the United States.

I've worked with many teachers in Chinese healing, contemplation, and martial arts, but again the principal ones are: William C.C. Chen in Yang Style Tai Chi, B.P. Chan in Qigong as well as the Chinese internal martial arts and Taoist meditation, then Dr. Huang Gengshi, Taoist Abbot, and Madame Gao for Chen Style Tai Chi.

You have chosen a rich spiritual ancestry. What can you say about your biological ancestry? Is your family Jewish on both sides?

Yes, I'm a Kohaine[96]. The question is, would uncle Aarron, or Moses, be proud of me? (Laughter)

Before we get to those ancestors, who are your family and where did they come from?

---

[96] Kohen (or Kohain) is the Hebrew word for priest. Kohanim are traditionally believed to be of direct patrilineal descent from the Biblical Aaron.

My family came from Russia and Eastern Europe. My mother's mother was Rose Yahelevsky, but her surname was shortened to "Levine" by immigration officials at Ellis Island. So, I have some Levite also.[97] My grandmother was from Vitebsk and the St. Petersburg area and came to the United States when she was 16. My grandfather on my mother's side was born in the U.S., and his parents and grandparents were born in Austria, Russia, or Poland. On my father's side, my great grandparents arrived in the United States in the 1800s from Russia, Lithuania, and Austria.

What was their religious orientation?

I don't know what to call it, because I grew up without any Jewish education.

No Hebrew school?

I learned the meaning of various Hebrew words as an adult when I met a Jewish rabbi who wanted to study Tai Chi with me. Our association and friendship awakened an interest in Judaism, but I grew up ignorant of it. I knew nothing about it.

Did any of your family go to synagogue?

My mother's father started going to synagogue and became observant after his wife died. He certainly considered himself Jewish before then, but he became more involved and took up the study of Hebrew as an older adult. He had a second bar mitzvah at 83 when I was already an adult.

Did you grow up in a Jewish neighborhood or community? Did you even know you were Jewish?

---

[97] In Jewish tradition, a Levite is a member of the Hebrew tribe of Levi and works under the priestly Kohanim in religious practices.

I knew I was Jewish but I had no real sense of Jewish identity. There were kids in school who were Jewish, also Protestant and Catholic. I grew up in Fresh Meadows (part of Queens, near Flushing).

Were you and your family equally comfortable with Jews and non-Jews?

Absolutely. One thing for which I'm very grateful is that I never saw a hint of religious intolerance. My parents always demonstrated acceptance of people and welcomed my friends equally, whatever their backgrounds, religion or race. I never heard a racial remark of any kind except outrage against racism or other forms of injustice. Maybe that's a fundamentally Jewish attitude. Jews come in all colors. Linked by a common heritage and ethnic root, there are Ashkenazic, Sephardic, Chinese, and African Jews.

During the height of the Civil Rights Movement in the 1960s, when we saw on the evening news the violence against African Americans, I remember my father commenting, "That is disgusting. How can you act that way towards another human being?" This was beyond my family's imagination, that one race would demean another, whites against blacks, or any race against any other.

You never heard comments about Goyim, non-Jews or gentiles?

No, I didn't know the word Goyim until I was an adult. I married a non-Jew and this fact had no relevance or importance to my mother, father, brother, or grandparents.

It sounds like you didn't really grow up in Jewish culture.

Yes, that's true. I did attend a Passover seder one time in my youth. Other than that, the first seder in which I participated and that had any sense of meaning, was when I was in my mid-20s. When I was growing up, out of curiosity, I went to church several times, certainly more often than to Jewish events. And on Christmas I enjoyed singing with

a neighborhood group of Christmas carolers.

Was this pattern also true of your cousins and uncles and aunts as well?

My father was an only child. I only have first cousins on my mother's side. I believe that they went to Hebrew school. I don't know about my aunt and uncle; we never spoke about Judaism. My brother had a bar mitzvah, and I had a bar mitzvah; mine was a farce. Two weeks before the bar mitzvah, a middle-aged Jewish guy came over and gave me a Hebrew speech, written out by English pronunciation, of course. He told me to memorize it. I didn't understand what it was about. At the bar mitzvah, I wore a yarmulke and tallis, but didn't know why I had to wear such strange looking garments. Someone, I presume a rabbi, told me to use a metal pointer to point at some lines in a very large foreign language book. I honestly thought that the bar mitzvah was simply a very celebratory 13th birthday party designed for teenagers to receive savings bonds and other gifts.

I studied Christianity long before I studied Judaism, and I took a deep interest in the New Testament when I was about 20. One of my early Tai Chi students, a Greek man and member of the Greek Orthodox Church, offered to teach me New Testament Greek in exchange for Tai Chi classes. As I began reading more broadly, I soon realized that I had blindly accepted a common Christian interpretation and stereotype of Judaism as a tradition that worshipped an angry God through archaic rituals. Looking back, I see how ignorant I was. It later dawned on me that Jesus was not a Christian but a great rabbi. And so, through a study of the New Testament and mystical Christianity, I was led to Jesus' roots and, in the process, to my own.

Did you have any experience or understanding of anti-Semitism?

I knew that I was Jewish. I knew about the Holocaust. I knew there were people who had religious and ethnic hatreds and that atrocities had been committed against minorities. I was outraged against injustice. I felt some identification with Holocaust victims because I knew they were Jewish and I was Jewish. I was also aware of the pogroms. My grandmother told me that the Czar's soldiers had murdered her brother. That made an impression on me. I knew there was anti-Semitism in the world.

It sounds like you had a cognitive awareness of it. Did you take on any of the fear or have any experiences of being attacked?

No, not at all.

Many Jews grew up in families where judgments of politicians were based on whether they were good for Israel or the Jewish people.

The only thing I knew about Israel is that it was mentioned in the Bible. I never heard my parents comment on a politician's views about Israel or the Jewish people. If they ever mentioned Israel at all, it was only as another foreign country, no more relevant to us than India or Australia.

What were your parents involved with? Were they intellectuals or political radicals as were many other non-religious Jews?

Neither. Both my parents are still alive. I have a great relationship with my mom and dad, one that has improved over the years. I'm so thankful that my parents are goodhearted and have high integrity. My father was well educated. He was for a brief time a chemistry instructor at Columbia University and then became a public health officer for the New York City Health Department. Then, for many years he served as commissioner of public health for various counties in New Jersey, an occupational health editor for the Journal of the American Medical Association, and a Fellow of the World Health Organization. He was an expert on occupational health problems and a winner of the Dennis J. Sullivan Award, New Jersey's highest public health award.

My mother was a housewife with an artistic temperament and a love of poetry, music and piano. When I was 17, my parents divorced and my mother had to find work. She took a few years of college, learned stenography and became a full-time secretary for the Department of Social Services, commuting each day by subway from her home in Queens to Manhattan. Neither of my parents were political radicals or activists. Their only political activity was voting.

As I look back, I see that I never experienced any involvement with anything particularly Jewish.

How did your sense of religion or spirituality emerge?

I've always retained memories from infancy. I can remember when I was probably three to six months old, crystal-clear memories. When I was about six or seven, I told my parents about this and they said, "It's impossible, you can't remember that." But I remember when I was in a crib and being rocked and looking up at people's faces and hearing words but not being able to understand what they were saying. I still can remember very clearly my perceptions as an infant.

There were two significant spiritual turning points in my early childhood. One was when I was about six years old. There was a gang of kids that were "my enemies" in a kind of mock warfare game. Our "battles" consisted of throwing stones at each other, holding up garbage can covers for shields. My enemies had joined up with a Little League pitcher, quite a bit older, who seemed like a giant. He took a stone and threw it like a fastball right at me and I did a very bizarre thing. I dropped my garbage-can-cover shield and held my arm out in a rounded posture. The rock hit my arm and bounced off. I immediately went running home yelling for my parents. After telling them what happened I said, "He couldn't hurt me, because I was in my body."

I remember feeling this magical sense of expansive energy in my body as I deliberately threw down the garbage can cover and held up my arm in what I found out many years later to be a Tai Chi posture. There was this feeling of some kind of internal force that I knew would protect me. The stone that could have broken my arm, bounced off.

Another event that connected me to my spirituality occurred when I was about 12. I was at school and wondering why other children disliked me. There were a number of bullies and they used to beat me after school, taking turns punching me. I had many bad experiences with that in sixth grade. One time, I was standing outside during lunch break wondering why these kids hated me so much, when all of a sudden I had this thought. I remember exactly how I framed it: "It is because I know who I am and you're not supposed to know that; people object to that." I immediately felt like I was an 81-year-old man. I don't know why that number came to me, but I felt I was an 81-year-old man inside and a 12-year-old boy on the surface.

As soon as I said that to myself, that "I know who I am," everything became translucent. It was as though light was shining through everything and I had this magical sense that I could see and feel the light inside people, inside trees, in the sky, and everything around me. I not only perceived the light, but understood it. I felt that I was sensing the quality and intensity of spiritual light in all of the phenomena around me. The experience was a kind of kinesthetic direct knowing that involved all of my senses and was accompanied by a profound feeling of inner peace.

That feeling only lasted for a day. But in my teens, when I began practicing Buddhist meditation, I felt that I was in the same realm. I remembered the clarity of perception that I'd had as an infant, before words filtered or fragmented experience. The world was as luminous and filled with life force as when I was twelve. So for me, the real draw of Buddhism, and later Taoism, was an affirmation of the importance of these childhood experiences. They also gave me a kind of map to understand them, putting them into very meaningful context. To me that was the hook.

Did your experience at 12 have any effect on the bullies continuing to beat you or how you related to them?

I think so. Certainly over time my greater self-confidence made me a less suitable target for bullies.

When I was very young, I had felt estranged from other kids and I'd isolated myself from other people. I didn't have many friends. When I was in my teens and became more formally involved in Buddhist and Taoist studies, things changed. I met like-minded friends. Buddhism affirmed the importance of those childhood experiences and of spirituality in general. I realized that my memories and visions were not something that made me abnormal or bizarre, but that they were part of a path of self-realization.

So thanks to Asian studies and practices, I became more socially relaxed and experienced significant psychological and physical changes. I had poor health as a child—insomnia, bronchitis, and regular bouts of viral or bacterial infections. My health improved radically after learning Qigong and Tai Chi.

Was Tai Chi your first introduction to spiritual practice?

I was first introduced to Buddhism as a philosophy of life when I was fifteen years old. My brother, who is two years younger than me, had read a book about the life of the Buddha — *Gautama Buddha in Life and Legend* by Betty Kelen — and thought I would enjoy it. I told him that I was not interested in Buddhism, but he kept encouraging me. I read it and re-read it and re-read it and I thought, "This is it. This makes so much sense. What a beautiful philosophy." I saw how there is suffering in the world, that suffering is caused by self-centeredness, greed and attachment, by wanting what you don't have and not wanting what you do. Also, that there is a way out of this kind of suffering through the Noble Eightfold Path. The story of the Buddha's life made sense to me. When I learned about his enlightenment under the Bodhi tree, I thought, "yes, this state of mind, that kind of clarity and tranquility, is accessible to everyone. It doesn't belong to a privileged few. It's not something that requires a church or synagogue or a priest or rabbi, but is rather a state of being that can be discovered on one's own."

How did you proceed with your interest in Buddhism?

I started attending public classes and zazen (sitting meditation) sessions at the Zen Studies Society in Manhattan. I read voraciously, including all the English language works by D. T. Suzuki, probably about 20 books in all. I learned about the writings of Alan Watts because of his introduction to D.T. Suzuki's, "Outlines of Mahayana Buddhism." I thought Watts' books were fantastic; they really spoke to me. Watts and Suzuki are the ones who introduced the West to Asian thinking, Buddhism in particular. When I was 16, I went to a seminar with Watts in Bucks County, Pennsylvania at Bucks County Seminar House, one of the first holistic learning centers; it was like the Esalen Institute of the Eastern United States.

This was 1968. I was only 16 years old, the youngest person at this workshop, and I had to get my parents' permission to take the bus to Pennsylvania and stay two nights at the event. I had the chance to hear Watts' brilliant lectures on Buddhism as well as practice meditation with him. Watts had an extraordinary talent of using words to bring you to the origin of words—silent experience. During one of the seminar lunch breaks, I was sitting outside and watching a man do an eerie, slow-motion dance on the lawn. I didn't know what it was, but I was absolutely mesmerized. I asked what it was and he said it was Tai Chi. I immediately wanted to learn it. That was my introduction to Tai Chi. As soon as I saw it, I knew I had to study it. It was love at first sight.

At the same seminar, two other very life-changing things happened. Being so deeply involved in and enthused about Buddhism, I was thinking I wanted to go to Thailand to become a Theravada Buddhist monk. I shared this idea with Alan Watts in a private conversation. He knew I was just beginning my spiritual journey and needed some direction. Watts advised, "Why do you want to become one of those scrawny Buddhist monks? You should go to the Zen Studies Society and try Zen practice."

In a very strange way, Watts was also responsible for my interest in the Chinese language. One of the biggest influences in my life has been Western classical music. This was not because of any influence from my parents. My mother played a little bit of piano, but neither she nor my father owned any records or listened to the radio. For some reason, I independently developed a deep love of Western classical music. Even as other kids were listening to the Beatles, I'd be listening to Beethoven or Mozart symphonies.

In one of Watts' lectures he spoke about music and meditation. He was speaking on how to really appreciate music, how you have to be completely in the present and let the present unfold. You don't listen to the piece of music to reach the end; you have to have an empty, clear mind, get rid of all preconceptions, and just be present and appreciative. I thought, this is great, this is a link between Buddhism and the classical music that I love.

Watts recommended that everyone interested in this subject should get a particular book called, *Sound and Symbol* by a German musicologist named Zuckerkandl. He claimed that this musicologist, who knew nothing about East Asian spirituality, developed a philosophy that is almost the same. When I was back home, I took the subway to Manhattan and went to my favorite bookstore, Orientalia Bookstore. I thought I could find this book in a good Asian bookstore. I asked if they had *Sound and Symbol* and was told they had one copy.

Back on the subway, I started to read it and realized I had purchased another book with the same title but by a different author. This book was by a famous Swedish Sinologist (China scholar), Bernhard Karlgren, best known in academia as the linguist who rediscovered the pronunciation of Tang Dynasty Chinese. Thanks to Karlgren's research, one could experience the sound and rhyme of thousand year old poems. The book, that I had bought by "mistake" was Karlgren's very rare introduction to the Chinese language. I had been looking for a book about music and by mistake I had bought a book on Chinese language! As I started reading it and got into it, I thought, "Wow, if anything can disentangle me from the conditioning influences of language and help me reach the emptiness that I am seeking, maybe the Chinese language can help me get there." I thought that by learning such a different way of categorizing and looking at life, perhaps I could remove the conditioning influences of English in the process.

By the time I had finished the hour-long subway ride, I had decided to begin studying the Chinese language. So that first semester out of high school, I enrolled in an adult education program in Chinese at the New School for Social Research. My program was Tai Chi and Chinese at the same time, with Buddhism as the instigator.

Is this how you started college?

My college story is also unconventional. In my senior year of high school, I announced to my parents that I was going to withdraw the few applications I'd sent to various colleges. I had no intention of allowing formal education to interfere with my real education any longer. I had no interest in degrees or credits or transcripts, but I had a great interest in learning. I thought that a formal degree-based college education would be as much of an interference as high school had been.

Even though you were such an independent thinker and attuned to your own callings, do you think that you were influenced at all by the revolutionary spirit of the Sixties?

I bet I was. There was a sense of, "I don't want anything to do with the establishment." Though revolution was not my primary motivation, the milieu did influence me. I'd heard about Woodstock, but I'd never gotten into drugs or rock 'n roll or folk music, the songs of protest, that I only discovered many years later. The first time I finished a meditation session at a Zen Temple, I thought, "Talk about clarity of experience, about seeing the world made of crystal! This is it. Why would I ever need drugs? I can, through meditation, enter an alternate or underlying reality."

I'd already started developing a new, supportive group of associates who were also interested in the cultivation of consciousness. I also think I had some distaste or trepidation about being involved in the counter-culture because I associated it with the harmful effects of drugs on people I knew. One young man in particular, who was a neighbor, told me he was dropping LSD every day. I saw how it had affected him; he ended up in a psychiatric institution. I was looking for the potential in the human spirit and I didn't want anything from outside, like a drug, to interfere with that search.

Did that perspective continue over the years?

Yes and no. First of all, I now think that my tendency to associate the counterculture with drugs was unfair and a very limited perspective. Secondly, I now have great respect for people who use natural psychotropic plants, what indigenous people call "the teacher plants," in a good way, especially if they're doing it with the guidance of a spiritual elder and in a cultural context. Examples include the Native American Church, Peruvian ayahuasca healing, or the Huichol traditional use of peyote. The aim of such practices is not the sensation of "getting high" but rather transformation and revelation. I have deep respect for such traditions, but it just hasn't been my calling.

Did your parents have much of a reaction to your choices regarding education?

Oh, yes. My father told me that I was going to be "a bum on the streets." He had no clue about what I was doing. I remember one time I was doing yoga in my room and he walked in and saw me in the corpse position, a supine posture used to induce deep relaxation. He looked at me and said, "I now pronounce you dead." (Laughter) Until the 1990s, he would tell people I was a karate teacher. That was as close as he could get conceptually to anything I was doing. Now he has mellowed out and he's proud of my writings, what I do in my life and how I am as a parent and as a human being. We have a closer relationship then we ever had. He's developed some appreciation for the path that I've taken.

Was there negativity toward your study of Buddhism?

Not towards Buddhism, only the fact that I would not pursue a career that would bring me money and security. He didn't know Buddhism from Judaism. He was worried about what it would mean in my life if I didn't have a conventional education. My mother, on the other hand, was very accepting because she saw the changes in both my physical and mental health. She observed that I no longer had the chronic bronchitis and constant illnesses that I had as a child. She also sensed that I was calmer and more sociable. So she was accepting very early on. I think that my mother had an attitude that, as far as work and money, things would work themselves out.

But certainly it was difficult, especially for my father, when I announced I wasn't going to college to get a degree. For him, the degree was what was important, the piece of paper, not the education. "All you need is the degree." My view was the polar opposite. As a result, as soon as I was out of high school, I enrolled in an intensive not-for-credit adult education program in the Chinese language at the New School for Social Research in Manhattan.

It seems you were purely in the moment as far as education. Did you have any sense that this would lead to any kind of career?

No. I was with the unfolding process, like listening to music. I was motivated by love of learning, not by career goals. After my first year of study of modern spoken Chinese, I made an appointment to meet one of the leading professors of classical Chinese at Queens College, Dr. Bernard Solomon. He was a scholar, especially of Taoism, and taught courses on Taoist religious history, Taoist literature, and so forth. I tried speaking my broken, far from fluent, modern Chinese and told him, "I have no interest in degrees or simply being an auditor, but I would like to be your student. I'd like you to treat me as a student. I'm willing to take all the tests, but I want to do this off the record."

We spoke for a while and he said, "Yes, just don't tell anyone else." So I worked with him for two years, taking Classical Chinese, Chinese

History, and History of Chinese Literature. During that time he introduced me to other professors in the Chinese Language department and I became a kind of shared secret—a non-registered, non-paying student. They liked me because I was highly motivated.

In 1973 I took a break from my Tai Chi and academic studies to train semi-privately with Alan Watts. I won a summer scholarship to study Taoism with five other students at Watts' home and library on the slopes of Mount Tamalpais in California. Taoism was a natural progression from Zen, since, as D.T. Suzuki often noted, Zen is fifty percent Taoism, a marriage between Indian Buddhism and the earthiness and humor of Chinese Taoism. Taoism is also the philosophical and spiritual root of Tai Chi.

I returned to New York City after that glorious summer. Then, in 1976, I moved to Berkeley and continued my education. I had heard that the University of California at Berkeley had one of the first graduate programs in Taoism in the United States. Michel Strickmann, Professor of Chinese Religions at the Sorbonne in France, had just become a guest lecturer, and later a tenured professor. Other luminaries and scholars were there as well.

Did you feel that these scholars of Taoism had the experiential sense of Taoism you wanted?

Some did, some didn't. There is indeed a big difference between scholars and practitioners. I was studying Qigong, Meditation, and Tai Chi during the same period that I was attending Queens College, so I was involved with experiential and academic study at the same time. I was interested in both. In Chinese, it is a concept called "wen wu." Wen means scholarship, wu means knowledge gained through practice, especially in the martial arts. That idea of scholarship and practice has remained a constant theme throughout my life.

So when I arrived in Berkeley, I designed an academic program that matched my interests, as I did at Queens College. I visited Dr. Michel Strickmann during his office hours, told him about my background in undergraduate studies in New York City at the New School and at Queens College, and asked if I could continue graduate training with him in Berkeley. He agreed, as did Edward Schafer, the great scholar of Tang Dynasty literature, Wolfram Eberhard, scholar of Chinese sociology, and several other professors. I eventually took most of the masters and doctoral Taoist studies courses at Berkeley, though unofficially, with no degrees or transcripts. I was passed from one teacher to the other, professors essentially telling each other, "This guy really wants to learn, teach him." I participated in the classes, did all the paperwork, took all the tests, but ended up without a degree. Rather than "all but dissertation," I'm "all but degrees, transcripts and credits." I also continued practical, experiential learning with Taoist Abbot Huang, who was living not far from the UC Berkeley campus.

In the 1980s, after moving to Colorado, I taught for several years in the graduate psychology department at the Colorado Institute for Transpersonal Psychology in Boulder (later renamed "Boulder Graduate School"). I taught masters degree level courses in Qigong as Body-Centered Psychotherapy, drawing on the work of Alexander Lowen, Fritz Pearls, and others. The school was state accredited. One day in 1986, during the time when Boulder Graduate School was being considered for national accreditation, I received an interesting phone call from the Dean, Dr. Alec Tsoucatos. "We're reviewing the CVs of our professors, and yours is very impressive. But you neglected to include where you received your undergraduate and graduate degrees." I said, "I don't have any." He asked where I had gotten my bachelors and I told him that I only had a high school diploma. There was a long silence. I thought I'd be fired.

Dr. Tsoucatos asked me to submit a detailed portfolio documenting all of my academic and experiential learning, including names, dates, locations, with attached letters of reference. He called me back a few weeks later and to my astonishment declared that the faculty and Board of Directors had decided to award me an honorary masters degree in Holistic Psychology. I guess the hippies of my generation would've been proud; I'd beat the system. I'd gotten the masters degree without a bachelors, and in later years taught doctoral level courses and served on doctoral committees at several accredited universities without having a doctorate.

Do you see the qualities of character, the kind of orientation and sensibilities that you had in those periods of time, as kind of Jewish?

Yes I do. And it makes me curious if there is a genetic component to my love of learning, or if my passion for questioning authority and dogma is related to my Jewish ancestors' rejection of "graven images."

Since your parents were not oriented this way, nor the community you grew up in, how do you think you inherited these Jewish sensibilities or qualities of consciousness?

This is really the question of nature versus nurture. I don't have the answer. I can certainly trace a Jewish influence after age 25. I had just met Rabbi Burt Jacobson, a wonderful, brilliant man, and now a dear friend. He once posed an interesting comment and question, "It seems that the enlightenment of the Buddha represents a stripping away of ego and provides an essential model for Buddhist practice. Can you think of a similar example of wisdom in Judaism?" I told him I had no idea. He said, "It is Moses' experience at the Burning Bush. What did God first say to Moses? 'Take off your shoes, you are on holy ground.'" Then he explained that the shoes are concepts, belief systems, even a belief in God, any kind of belief. If you take off your shoes, the ground is holy everywhere. It's the shoes that are between us and the ground. I thought to myself, "This is the same teaching that I've been attracted to all along in Buddhism and Taoism. It's the same wordless realm I remember from my childhood. It's the same 'shoeless' state I enter when I do Tai Chi."

So, over time, I realized that there probably were some of what I now consider Jewish elements in myself or in these other traditions that drew me to them. A basic one is the unity of the spiritual and the mundane. Unlike the Christian view, or at least the post-Augustinian or post-Nicaean Christian view, that says that spirit and flesh are separate, in Judaism (and Taoism) the world and the body are manifestations of the divine.

The concept of Shekinah spoke deeply to me: the world as the indwelling Presence and feminine aspect of Hashem[98]. I also came to appreciate that Judaism is not a matter of belief. Rather, the Jewish path is a deeply spiritual, heart-full and physical way of experiencing the world in which prayer and focus releases the holy sparks that are in all things. That spoke deeply to me and still does.

Do you feel that these sensibilities were somehow transmitted to you by virtue of your being a Jew even though you hadn't been to a synagogue?

Is it my Jewish background that shaped my search or that made me want to dissolve boundaries? An interesting question. Remember Rabbi Gershon Winkler's work on Jews as boundary-crossers, as people who move fluidly between different realms. This is a very shamanistic concept, but also I think very Jewish and very Taoist.

How did you happen to meet Rabbi Jacobson?

When I was living in Berkeley during the late 1970s, Burt was writing a book on the Baal Shem Tov[99]. He felt there was a deep connection between the teachings of the Besht and the wisdom teachings of Asia, especially Buddhism and Taoism. He thought, very wisely, that the best way to learn more about those traditions was by exploring a related meditative practice, Tai Chi for example. So one day, he phoned and asked if he could learn Tai Chi from me.

Burt and I began to meet weekly, and the conversations we had after the Tai Chi sessions were fascinating. I realized that in my youth I had developed many false assumptions about Jews and Judaism. These were things I'd absorbed, not from my parents, but from society

---

[98] Hashem is the word most religious Jews use for God in ordinary conversation.
[99] Rabbi Yisroel (Israel) ben Eliezer, often called the Baal Shem Tov or Besht, was a Jewish mystical rabbi. He is considered to be the founder of Hasidic Judaism.

around me: that the Jews were "the people of the book"; they were rigid; they were ancestor worshipers; all sorts of bizarre stereotypes that I now see have nothing to do with Judaism. So I enrolled in Berkeley's Graduate Theological Union for three courses, two consecutive courses taught by Burt and one with the outstanding Zohar scholar Danny Matt. I also attended an inspiring workshop with Rabbi Zalman Schachter. Through these associations I met other wonderful people, such as Rabbi David Zeller and various members of the Aquarian Minyan. Some of the latter became my Tai Chi students, and one, Arieh Lev Breslow, later established a school of Tai Chi in Jerusalem.

On reflection, was there any sort of self-denial or what some people call self-hating Jewish feelings that were part of absorbing those kinds of stereotypes in your youth? Do you feel there was a sense of wanting to push this part of your self away?

I don't think that I had any self-hatred. Judaism was simply not relevant.

Did you feel you opened to a connection with your Jewish ancestors?

Yes. I began to sense and still feel a deep connection to Moses. When I sing a song connected to this lineage, it speaks deeply to me. (He sings in Hebrew and translates), "I lift up my eyes unto the mountains from whence cometh my help."

Burt taught me how to sing various Hebrew songs. I learned how to do Shabbat and offer the *brucha*[100] over bread and wine. I fell in love with the song "Shalom Aleichem" and Hannah Senesh's "Eli, Eli."

So you have a felt sense of connection to the Jewish transmission?

Now there is, absolutely.

---

[100] Brucha means "blessed" in Hebrew and is the word used for prayer.

How is it different from your connection with Taoism?

Well, it's a different tradition. It's like asking me if I feel different when I speak Chinese compared to when I speak English. Yes, I do. Language and landscape influence how spirituality is expressed. Taoism and Judaism are as different as China is from the Midddle East, or Egg Drop Soup from Matzah Ball Soup. Yet they are both delicious!

Well, a person with any religious identity might appreciate the beauty in Judaism. What I'm wondering is if your feeling relates to your connection to this tradition because you are a Jew?

I believe that there is an influence from one's ancestry. Perhaps there is a physical component to one's Jewishness preserved in the genes or perhaps it is more of an energetic, spiritual transmission through the generations. There is a Jewish teaching that all Jews were on Mount Sinai with Moses. It is possible that our ancestors are, in some mysterious way, always with us or at least ready to make themselves known when we acknowledge them or invoke them in prayer.

My love of classical music is, perhaps, also a Jewish trait. Consider how many great performers, especially violinists, are Jewish.

Do I identify myself as Jewish? Yes. Acknowledgment of my background is especially important in Native American circles, where I want to make sure that my Native American friends, colleagues, and relatives don't think I'm denying my own ethnicity, or that I'm trying to run away from something by adopting something else. So I make it clear that I'm not Native American by birth any more than I'm Han (ethnically Chinese).

Did your reconnecting with Jewishness bring about any of the fears or concerns of anti-Semitism that you didn't experience as a child?

No.

Have you felt a strong connection to the conflict in Israel as compared to concerns of other global issues?

Other global issues are equally important to me. Frankly, I feel a much stronger connection with the conflict between Native Americans or native peoples and colonial powers. That to me is much more personal.

Does that connect you to the Palestinian aspiration?

I feel connected to Palestinians as indigenous people, as people who should have their own country. I would love to see Jerusalem jointly managed as an international city if such a thing were ever possible: Jewish, Muslim and Christian at the same time. Why not create an autonomous city-state, like the Vatican, that is not part of Israel?

As regards the Jewish inheritance, what about on the negative side? Do you feel you've inherited any particularly Jewish neuroses?

A tendency to worry too much, to sometimes take things too seriously, to engage in *pilpul*, intellectual nit-picking. I have learned to manage or mitigate these tendencies with meditation and spiritual practice. I certainly relish good food, and ascetics might argue this is a negative inheritance. But I don't think so, and perhaps that also makes me Jewish.

From your understanding of Qi as energy or life energy, would you say that there is a particularly Jewish frequency or wave-length of Qi?

Yes, there is a particular frequency to each spiritual path; put them all together and you have a symphony of beautiful music. Yet, qi as life breath doesn't have a particular religious inflection to it. So the *ruach* that God breathes into the Earth person, Adam, is free of particularization. It's not a Jewish breath that was breathed into Adam, nor was Adam Jewish. Adam is just an Earth person (related to the Hebrew word *adama* meaning earth). We all breathe the same air, we are all infused by the same creative power. You can call it breath, prana, ha (in Hawaiian), qi, ruach (as it's called in the Jewish tradition), or any of a myriad of other similar terms.

Does reincarnation fit into your thinking?

Probably as much as it fits into Judaism. It's an old Jewish concept—*gilgul*, isn't that the term for it in Judaism? Yet it's never clearly defined. There are so many mysterious interconnections among every form of life, it's hard to imagine that there is one unique self that reincarnates or that sheds a body and puts on a new one, like putting on a new set of clothes.

I tend to think about reincarnation by using two metaphors. One is borrowed from Buddhism: if you have a candle that's lit, and you have another candle that's not, and you light the unlit candle with the first one and blow the first one out, is the flame on the second candle the same or different than the original? You can't really answer that question; there's a transmission, but the flame is neither the same nor different. The other way I understand reincarnation is to think of all of life as different vibrational states or waves on one great ocean of Being. The waves are each different; yet they are all aspects of the same ocean.

I would say that people can tune into a particular life-stream from the past and feel a deep connection with a particular person. But they could just as easily tune into another past life from the same period, as though they were simultaneously two people living at the same time. So I have a hard time accepting the popular view of reincarnation as a soul that jumps from one body to the other. Nor do I feel that reincarnation occurs only within the human realm. It could be that one was a stone or animal or plant or that one will become a stone or animal or plant. My view is that we are all mysteriously interconnected; I don't know much more than that.

What do you see as the cause of qi becoming polluted since it comes from a pure source? What are the causes of the degradation or distortions that we experience emotionally as envy and hatred?

Though the transcendent qi, the breath of Creator, remains pure, our choices and habits can influence the purity of our individual qi. One of my Native American elders said to me that no evil sorcerer can do as much harm to you as you can do to yourself through your own negative thinking. Still another native elder, Rolling Thunder, told me that pollution begins in the mind.

But what is it about our minds that takes us into this depth of negativity that some would call evil?

No one can ever fully answer that question because the mind that is asking is the source of the problem. There is no outside perspective. In addition to negative thinking, we can add categorization: the distortion that occurs when we put ourselves and others in boxes. Other factors that take us into negativity include having poor role models; excessive vulnerability to negative forces around us; identifying with negative attitudes or behaviors as children; and genetic as well as external factors that affect our brain chemistry and psychology, including environmental toxins, viruses, and bacteria. Still another perspective is that negativity may be a result of personal preoccupation, and disconnection from family, community, and nature.

Do you ask why that is there? Who started it? Does it come only from humans? I am interested in your thoughts on the source of evil?

Rabbi Nachman of Bratslav[101] was asked, "Where is hell?" He

---

[101] Reb Nachman of Bratslav was the founder of the Breslov Hasidic movement. He was a great grandson of the Baal Shem Tov and breathed new life into the Hasidic movement by combining the esoteric secrets of Judaism (Kabbalah) with in-depth Torah scholarship.

[102] As with most teachings from the Kabbalah, the notion of kliput is very subtle and paradoxical. In simple terms they are the masks or coverings over that which is true and real.

said, "It's wherever God is not." Or, I can paraphrase your question, "What are the *kliput*[102], the shells that separate us from God? (*Kliput* is also the Hebrew word for evil.) The answer is in the question. Although there are certainly gradations of evil, the root of evil is any hideout from the divine, whether it's a negative emotion, angry words, lies, or malicious behavior.

Does it remove the separation to simply be aware of it?

I'm saying that I don't know the answer to the why or the who, only something about the how. The Buddha had a parable about a man who is shot with an arrow. Before the doctor removes the arrow, the man wants to know who shot the arrow, where was it shot from, and how the arrow was made. The man will die before his questions are answered. Isn't it better to just remove the arrow?

One of my favorite teachings about evil is the Jewish philosophy of the *yetser harah* and *yetser hatov*, a pull or inclination towards evil and a pull towards the good. At every stage in our development, no matter how spiritual or advanced we are, even at the level of the *tzadik* (an enlightened master), we still deal with ordinary human foibles, we are still human beings. I remember reading a story about someone asking a Hasidic master, "What is the *yetzer harah* of a *tzadik*?" The answer was that the *yetser harah* of an enlightened being is an angel. It is as subtle as the person. The wisest sage lapses; no one can permanently maintain the state of *Echad* (oneness with *Hashem*). I think that's a beautiful teaching.

Is there an understanding within Taoism of this question?

I think so, but it's put in different terminology. In the first chapter of the *Tao Te Ching*, Lao Tzu says (Ken says this in Chinese and then translates), "Not-naming is the beginning of heaven and earth. Naming is the mother of all things." Lao Tzu is discussing the human tendency towards categorizing, labeling, putting ourselves or others in rigid boxes. In Jewish terms, it's qualifying the I Am. God tells Moses that His/

Her name is, "I am." Since the name of God is I am, as soon as we say, "I am stupid" or "I am smart," we are taking the name of God in vain. When we qualify and divide up that state of Being, we create the *kliput*, the shell, the onion we have to peel. In Taoism, the state of divine wisdom is referred to as not-naming. Naming is the mother of all things while it also gives rise to separation. A person who is stuck in the realm of words will always be in a battle of good versus evil or evil versus good. If you try to do good and act good you will probably repress your shadow and sooner or later turn into a scoundrel. Taoism teaches that good and evil arise together and give birth to each other. The only way out of this mess is through silence, the state of pure Being.

Lao Tzu continues in Chapter 1(again in Chinese and then translating), "Therefore, if you are without greed or grasping, you can see the mysteries. But if you have greed and grasping, you will be stuck on surfaces." In other words, a lack of grounding in a state of contemplative awareness (without greed and grasping) creates suffering and what we call evil.

Isn't there a healthy purpose for categorization?

Absolutely, and this is also in Taoism. Bai Juyi, the great eighth century Chinese poet, wrote a little poem in which the first two lines quote Lao Tzu (whose name, by the way, means "the old child"): "Those who know, do not speak. Those who speak, do not know. Then why did the old child (Lao Tzu) write 5000 words?" How is it that a tradition based on the indescribable Tao and that emphasizes the importance of inner quiet has a religious canon with more than 1100 texts? Taoists recognize that the intellect has its place. Let's use it but not be used by it; it is only one way of knowing.

I would add that there is more of an intellectual tendency and more recognition of intellect as a path of revelation in Judaism than there is in Taoism. If you asked 100 Jews, "Who or what is God?" I imagine you would get at least 101 opinions. But if you asked the same question of 100 Taoists, I doubt there would be more than 25 answers. The majority of Taoists would either sit silently or laugh.

How would you describe the emphasis of Taoism?

In Taoism, although there is a respect for the importance of intellect, nevertheless there is a clear and consistent emphasis on *bao pu jian su*, "Embrace the uncarved block of wood, see the unbleached silk." That is, "recognize your original nature; don't carve it up with rules and regulations; reduce selfishness and grasping." That's more the emphasis—simplicity and unity with nature.

Would you say that when it comes to suffering, different groups experience this in different ways? Is there a particularly Jewish form of suffering?

Like American Indians, many Jews suffer from intergenerational PTSD (Post Traumatic Stress Disorder), as well as stereotyping and racism by the dominant culture. There are different kinds of suffering, but I think that other peoples in similar circumstances would have similar suffering.

Are there different kinds of suffering? Of course. Does one kind of suffering belong uniquely to a certain people? I don't think so. All human beings experience a similar range of suffering and worries. Jews, Arabs, and Christians all worry about their children; they all flinch when pinched. Yet a culture's history and environment may make one kind of suffering predominant.

Is the experience brought about by immersion in Jewish spirituality any different from that which is brought about by Taoism or Buddhism?

On the surface, yes. Dancing to a Hassidic melody feels different from practicing Tai Chi or chanting *Om Mane Padme Hum*. Yet, one arrives at the same placeless place. Jews, like Buddhists, are taught to question absolutes. It is often said that to assume that one has a final answer is to make an ass of u and me. I feel that if a person is in a deep state of inquiry, so deep that one reaches a trust in that which cannot be known, he or she is in the same state as a realized Taoist or Buddhist or Jew.

Do you see questioning as one of the essential features of Jewish teaching?

Yes. It's the Jewish tradition of midrash, of multiple ways of interpreting the same Biblical passage. Great Jewish scholars, like Martin Buber or Abraham Joshua Heschel, encourage a questioning mind. Perhaps this was one of the historical sources of friction between Christians and Jews. Christians assumed they knew the truth and Jews were saying, "But what about...?" Of course many Christian mystics have also moved beyond dogmatic answers, as in Meister Eckhart's explanation of Jesus' admonition to be "poor in spirit."

What does it mean to be poor in spirit?

To want nothing, know nothing, and have nothing. To find one's fundamental connection to that which cannot be described. Then, out of this emptiness, Christ is born within. We can each experience the virgin birth.

Do you feel there was a purpose in your being born Jewish?

Oh, I'm sure there is a purpose. Maybe it has to do with having had the good fortune to grow up in a home that didn't provide rigid answers even about whether or not I was Jewish. (Laughter) My parents' lack of dogma and rigid beliefs may have given me the confidence to say, "let's see where the currents of life bring me."

Did you ever have a moment, after you discovered the beautiful things that you now see in Judaism, where you thought, "maybe I should be a rabbi, maybe I should really immerse myself in this and start regularly attending synagogue or Jewish Renewal activities?"

I've always wanted to spend more time with Reb Zalman, Eve Ilsen (his wife), Rabbi Joe Schultz, and other beautiful, holy people like them that I've met. Strangely, over the years, I seem to meet more and more rabbis. I count several rabbis among my close friends. Some have encouraged me to become a rabbi. I told them that it isn't my path, at least not in this lifetime. I love the tradition and I love the practices, especially the songs, but becoming a rabbi is not my calling.

There is the Jewish religion and the Jewish community. You are not married to a Jewish woman and not all of your friends are Jewish.

I don't really even think of people in those terms.

Can you talk about your journey with Native American spirituality and your introduction to shamanism? How did that come about?

My childhood experiences of luminosity and energy created a spiritual worldview that prepared me for both the Chinese and Native American traditions.

When I was in my early 20s, I went on a road trip with some friends who were deeply involved in Native American culture. We went to various holy places in the American Southwest, visiting sites of spiritual revelation that are important in native cultures. These experiences had a deeply transforming effect on me. Especially powerful was praying in a cave in Apache country that may have been visited by Geronimo. The whole cave was filled with quartz crystals; it was like being inside a geode. We asked for permission to enter the cave and made an offering of tobacco at the entrance. Once inside, we turned off our flashlights and sat in absolute darkness and stillness. We were in a realm of dreams, visions, and contemplation. I felt that when I emerged from that cave, I wasn't the same person that had entered; there had been a deep fundamental shift in my life path.

A few years later, I moved to California and began to teach weekend Tai Chi and Qigong classes in the parks. In a conversation with one of my students, I mentioned that I was doing research on the imagery and symbolism of semi-precious stones in Tang Dynasty (618-907 C.E.) poetry. Ancient Taoist poems described sacred caverns illuminated by crystalline stones; these caves were places for dreams and initiation, and, in other dimensions of reality, served as monasteries for departed souls. My student excitedly described one of her acquaintances, a Cherokee medicine man who used quartz crystals and other stones to heal patients and who had devoted much of his life to exploring their properties. "Please invite him to my class next week, and I'll take you both out to lunch," I suggested.

So on that day this old Cherokee man, wearing faded jeans and a turban-like hat with a big eagle feather sticking out the side (traditional head regalia for many tribes in the Southeast) walks across the park lawn to where I had just finished teaching my Tai Chi class. His name was Keetoowah. He was the great grandson of Ned Christie, known in Cherokee history as "the last Cherokee warrior." Keetoowah and I shook hands, and there was an immediate connection between us. It was uncanny; I felt I had known him my whole life. He invited me to his home in Santa Rosa, California. A week later, after coffee and conversation, while sitting across from him on a sofa, Keetoowah looked at me penetratingly and said, "I heard you're interested in stones. Let's find out if they're interested in you. Hold out your hand." He put a quartz crystal in my palm and continued, "Put your other hand on top of it and close your eyes."

I was sitting there in the home of this medicine man, wondering what was going on, if this was some kind of test. Would I be required to sit for days without food or water? After about twenty minutes, Keetoowah told me to open my eyes and describe what I had experienced while holding the crystal. In response to my answer, he said, "Okay, I want to see you here every week." That began a second apprenticeship—one with Dr. Huang, the Taoist abbot, and one with with Keetoowah. I visited Keetoowah weekly for the next five years that I lived in California and then more sporadically until his passing in 1987.

Can you describe what your experience was with the crystal?

I felt that the crystal became liquid and entered my bloodstream. I felt it flowing all through me, as though it had completely disappeared and was just inside my body.

What kind of teachings did Keetoowah share with you?

Keetoowah and I became very close friends. I studied with him and remained his apprentice for over ten years until his passing. I learned about "doctoring" (Native American healing), including prayer and plant medicines. He honored me with my first native name—Bear Hawk, Yonah Tawodi in Cherokee, and my first sacred prayer pipe. I learned pipe ceremony and, through his words and example, a great deal about native values and culture. Of course I also continued learning about stones and crystals and received teachings about the origins of the Cherokee people and their medicine ways. Interestingly, the Cherokee national symbol is a seven-pointed star, representing the seven clans of the Cherokee. Originally there were more clans, but some of them were lost at sea when they journeyed from their original home, their Sacred Land, or Elohi, in Cherokee. Keetoowah used to joke—or was it a joke?—that Jews were one of the lost clans of the Cherokee!

Towards the end of my stay in Berkeley, Keetowah introduced me to another medicine man, a close friend of his named Rolling Thunder. Rolling Thunder, though Cherokee, was considered "intertribal" because he was married to a Shoshone, lived on Shoshone land, and exchanged wisdom with people of many other tribes. I went to live at Rolling Thunder's traditional Native American community in the Nevada desert for two or three months a year from about 1980 to 1984. It was called *Meta-Tantay,* Shoshone for "Go in

Peace." There I learned how to live in balance with the land, including tending a large vegetable garden and milking and caring for goats. Rolling Thunder also trained me in traditional healing. I was one of his few apprentices and learned doctoring, native songs, herb gathering—many things. He tested me quite severely. He gave me a chance to back out before the last test, warning that I'd either be alive and practicing medicine or I'd be dead. He meant it literally.

Were these tests or ordeals physical or psychological?

Some of them were physical ordeals, some were tests of character.
Over the years, it seems that I was in the right place at the right time, where the healing powers or teachers would find me. I never sought any of them. I'll give you another example. In 1984, I was invited to a gathering in New York State of indigenous teachers from around the world, primarily North American Indian elders. The Ojibwe man who was hosting the event asked me if I would open the gathering by offering a prayer or blessing. He said that he recognized me as a "four direction person" because I was Jewish by birth; learned from Chinese people and spoke Chinese; trained with Native American spiritual leaders; and also had several teachers from Africa. He thought that because I had received "medicine" from the four races recognized by ancient Native Americans—the red, yellow, black, and white—I could help create a feeling of unity and harmony.

Although honored by the request, I offered a gentle reprimand. "I can't open the circle." "Why not?" he asked. I replied with another question, "Whose land are we on?" He said, "This is Iroquois land." I felt perturbed by his use of that word; I reminded him that Iroquois means "enemy." The correct term for this ancient Confederacy is the Haudenosaunee, the People of the Longhouse. I pointed out an elderly, white-haired Seneca Indian lady standing nearby. (The Seneca are one of the member nations of the Haudenosaunee Confederacy.) "This is her land. Go over there and ask her. If she requests that I offer opening prayers, I'll comply. But don't ask me first, someone not from this place."

So the Ojibwe man made the request, and the elder agreed. But when she finished speaking with him, she approached me and admitted that she had overheard the conversation. "I was glad somebody was paying attention!" she exclaimed. In other words she was happy that I knew about traditional protocol. We exchanged contact information, and she invited me to visit her at her home in Cattaraugus, Seneca Nation, near Buffalo, New York. The grandmother's name was Twylah Nitsch.

It turned out that the next week I was scheduled to teach a Tai Chi workshop in Rochester, New York, not far from Buffalo. I called Grandma Twylah and asked if I could come visit. She kindly invited me to stay in a guest room in her home. But when I arrived for what I thought would be a personal visit, there were about fifty people, mostly her students, waiting to greet me. She had set up a guest lecture and introduced me as someone who had knowledge of quartz crystals and stones. Interestingly, there was nothing in any published literature anywhere about my having studied with Keetoowah or that I worked with stones as healing helpers. I kept this information very private in those days. But somehow she knew.

I realized that this was set up as a test for both me and her students. Would I be driven by a need to show off, or perhaps demonstrate my own ignorance? Would the students be greedy, challenging, or patient in their quest for knowledge? They asked me questions such as "How do you use quartz crystals?" They were expecting a "how to" type class. Instead I told them about the lore of stones: that crystals are related to the moon and the moon in many ancient cultures is considered an orb of quartz. The moon controls tides of the ocean and controls tides of energy in our own bodies and minds. And because crystals can amplify the mind's power, I told them to be sure that they are in a good state of mind before they use quartz in ceremonies. Don't go out and buy stones, I advised. If you have a spiritual affinity with stones, someone will gift you one.

I spoke around the subject without directly answering their questions and without giving her students tools that they might not have been ready to use wisely. The next day, Grandma Twylah complimented me. She said that I had handled the situation correctly. After further conversations, she offered to teach me. From 1984 until about 1992, I traveled to Cattaraugus a couple times a year for brief intensives, and, a number of times to offer seminars myself. I was initiated into the Wolf Clan Teaching Lodge and received a teaching certificate from the Seneca Indian Historical Society that Twylah directed.

Not long after that initial meeting with Grandma Twylah, I also became involved with Cree culture in Saskatchewan. I had been invited to give a series of lectures at the University of Saskatchewan in Saskatoon. While touring the area during the following week, I met with various Cree elders and also facilitated a traditional Native healing for a well-known Cree activist. As a result, after continuing visits and cultural exchanges during the following years, I was formally adopted into a Cree family from Sturgeon Lake First Nation. Now I have a Cree dad and mom, a brother, sister and other members of a beautiful extended family. I've also developed a close friendship with other traditional healers in Saskatchewan and have offered and received healing in their lodges. You can see how one thing leads naturally to the other. I was neither on a quest to learn Native culture nor to avoid the culture of my ancestors.

There's a saying that you don't seek the medicine, the medicine seeks you. If you get out of the way, then the path you're supposed to be on finds you. It's a matter of having the courage to walk that path and making a decision to accept it. There are many people whose life purpose is presented to them and yet they say no because it's too threatening or it's not what their parents or peers would expect of them; it's not the way they were conditioned to believe in school; there's no money in it; there's no career in it. I have never felt driven by money—and that's not because I had it. Rather, I have accepted the sacrifices and often the poverty that this path has brought. Yet I am happy.

A central prayer for me is one that I learned from a Dakota friend that translates, "Creator, whether the path is easy or difficult, I will fear not." That is, we are not to pursue or avoid suffering, or pursue or avoid pleasure. Rather, we open ourselves to Creator's instructions and then have the courage to follow them.

You've spoken of the parallels of essential Judaism and Taoism. Does indigenous spirituality add something different to the mix of Judaism and the other spiritual paths you've studied?

It's the connection with the land. We are not in China or Israel, but here, on Turtle Island. Many Taoist practices are relevant because they deal with the common nature of the human body and spirit. Native American spirituality is a spirituality linked with place. My Native teachers and elders modeled how to be a good relative to the Earth, the river, the plants, the birds, the deer, the bear, all the animals. I have a feeling for them that I would not have had without their influence.

So the particular spiritual sources of this place, this continent, the animals and spirits are different than the universal that's everywhere and within everything.

That's right.

Is indigenous spirituality the same as shamanism?

I don't practice shamanism. I practice traditional Native American spirituality and healing methods. The word "shamanism," though based on a Siberian Tungusic term, is used by anthropologists to suggest common spiritual or religious elements among indigenous cultures. Today, many people are interested in "core shamanism." I have great respect for this branch of learning and for those who find practical ways that Westerners can apply shamanic wisdom. But my own training and interest is in contextualized indigenous spirituality, originating from specific cultures and tribal wisdom keepers.

The Jewish people are at a particular historical and evolutionary stage in which certain problems have arisen. There is something going on in the Jewish collective psyche. Do you have anything you would want to share with the Jewish people?

(Ken sings in a deep and powerful voice) "Return again, return again, return to the land of your soul. Return again, return again, return to the land of your soul. Return to who you are. Return to what you are. Return to where you are born and reborn again. Return again. Return again, Return to the land of your soul."

That's what I would say. Seriously and humorously.

Anything additional?

It is so easy for the victimized to turn into the victimizer. I pray that my Jewish and Arab brothers and sisters guard against this. I am not saying that we shouldn't protect our families, our homes and land. But we have to keep asking: Is this action just, compassionate, and necessary?

Do you feel that way about most social and political concerns, that your mission or message is to go to your soul and not to get too involved in the details?

We still have to fight against injustice, but we need to do it from the wisdom of our souls, not out of reaction to our past history. The Middle East question is so complicated, but I just don't get it. I see brother and sister fighting against each other, people who have almost identical worldview and philosophy. Meanwhile they ignore the real *jihad*, the war against personal ignorance and small-mindedness.

By all means, get involved in social and political details. Protest against nuclear power, against racism and stereotypes, against corporate greed, against patriarchy and any form of abuse. I consider myself an activist, but I'll only get involved in fights that I understand, and I try not to get so caught up in details that I lose the big picture.

How do you integrate all these different teachings?

These different teachings have all been an influence on me. I don't have to try to integrate them; they are aspects of who I am. Like anyone else, I am a product of my ancestry, my environment, my education, and my life experiences. The Native American and the Taoist path have been my calling. But as an educator, I keep the two aspects of my life work somewhat separate. I don't mix them up.

If I were teaching a class in French, I wouldn't want to throw in Chinese words. I don't sing Native American songs in a Qigong class any more than I would practice Chinese martial arts as part of a Native American healing ceremony. One of the things that I don't like about the New Age movement is a tendency to add a little of this to a little of that, a kind of chop-suey spirituality.

Anything else you'd like to say?

I know that some people who read this interview might wonder, "Who is this Jewish guy who speaks Chinese and was adopted by a Cree family? Chief Gefilte Fish?" I don't think that I am any more of an anomaly than anyone else. We are each unique, yet all connected. Do you know the definition of a "normal person"? Someone you don't know very well. In closing, when I ask myself what aspects of Judaism have spoken to me most deeply, I think of my passion for learning, my love of family, and my disdain for a path of denial or suffering. And then there's always the hot pastrami sandwich with a potato knish. L'Chaim!

Thank you.

Sat Santokh Singh Khalsa
SIKH

Born in 1939 in the Bronx, NY, the boy who was given the name Bertram Kanegson, decades later became Sat Santokh. He's been an activist most of the last 50 years, a teacher of Kundalini Yoga for the last 40, and for a while, the manager of the Grateful Dead. Speaking of the early development of his journey, he says, "At age six, I knew what the Holocaust was. I lost almost all of my large extended family except for two or three. I remember the Movietone news in which we'd see images from the concentration camps. They were burned into me and shaped my life. I spent much of my life being angry with God."

Was your family religious?

My parents observed the holidays and kept kosher. I grew up with plenty of exposure to my grandfather on my father's side, who was religious. We shared a two-family house in the Bronx. We did the holidays and I went to Hebrew school every day after public school for six years until my bar mitzvah.

Did the Jewish religion mean anything to you?

Hebrew school was abysmal. It was amazing that they could spend six or seven years and not talk about anything of substance at all. The community hired two old guys who were not qualified to be teachers. I learned to read Hebrew in the first year and after that, nothing. We heard stories but no real learning.

I had some Hasidic relatives. Their intensity made my father uncomfortable, so I was rarely exposed to them. They were quite possibly representing the only aspect of the religion that might have grabbed me at the time.

Did you continue with any Jewish practice after your bar mitzvah?

Until I left home for college, we observed the major holidays and would go to synagogue. But I considered myself an atheist from the time I was twelve. Later on, I had a philosophy professor who told me that if I was an atheist, I was really a religious man. His parting words were, "You will see."

What do you think he meant?

He said that if you care enough to be an atheist, then you care enough to be deeply religious. Most of my attention was fixed on trying to stop the world from being the way it is, which is still my major focus.

Was that something you associate with your parents or Jewish background?

My father was a New York Jewish leftist. He voted for Henry Wallace[103], and organized for the ILGWU (International Ladies Garment Workers Union) in his youth. I grew up in that milieu. But he wasn't an activist in the way I became.

How did activism start for you?

I went to City College in New York and had professors who were involved with the War Resisters League[104]. I was involved with the Committee for Nonviolent Action's anti-nuclear activities in the '50's. I had gone to Hunter College for two years, but when I got to City, from '58–'61, I became more and more engaged. In 1961, I became deeply involved in the War Resisters League and was a close follower of Bayard Rustin[105]. When I came out to California in '64, I started the WRL on the West Coast, and started organizing the first demonstrations against the war in Vietnam.

Through this period, did anything shift in your Jewish identity?

I considered myself a Jewish radical and I was in that tradition. Then, I got very involved with the Haight-Ashbury scene, the Grateful Dead, and psychedelics. There came a moment when I decided I didn't want to be a Jewish radical anymore. I didn't want to be uptight. I shaved my beard and we got into this rock-and-roll, cowboy thing. I transformed my identity.

Then I started to have experiences of God with LSD.

---

[103] Henry Wallace was the 33rd Vice President of the United States from 1941-1945, under Franklin Roosevelt. In the 1948 presidential election, Wallace was the nominee of the Progressive Party, and was supported by left-leaning Americans.

[104] The War Resisters League (WRL) is an American pacifist organization working against war and the causes of war since 1923. It considers war to be a crime against humanity

[105] Bayard Rustin, born in 1912, was an American civil rights activist and pacifist who is credited as the chief organizer of the 1963 March on Washington for Jobs and Freedom and an important counselor to Martin Luther King, Jr. on the techniques of nonviolent resistance.

Were your earlier experiences with psychedelics not so spiritual?

The first ones were personal transformations. After a while, they became very deep spiritually as I began to have experiences of God. One particular time, I realized I was done with drugs. I needed to build a spiritual practice from the inside, not from the outside as I was doing with drugs. By then, it was the late '60s and I'd been reading works that many were reading at that time: *Autobiography of a Yogi*, books about Tibet, Milarepa, and others.

As for Judaism, I felt no particular connection. For me, what I was looking for, didn't relate to the Jewish religion. I didn't see anything there that was attracting me. I was attracted to Eastern practices.

Then came the "Holy Man Jam"[106] at the Family Dog, which was a rock concert and gathering place on the Great Highway along the coast of San Francisco. Yogi Bhajan, Pir Vilayat, Swami Satchadananda and others were there. If I had seen Sufi Sam there, I probably would have wound up a Sufi.

So you were open to a number of possible paths if the teacher really called to you. What was it that drew you to Yogi Bhajan and Kundalini Yoga?

My primary stance in the world was how to best be of service—what's the work? That's still the question for me. I felt that I needed to be in a place where I could have a lot of power flow through me, to be a vehicle for that power. At that particular event, Yogi Bhajan spoke and led chanting. I said to myself that he's an example of what I want to be. I went to the first gathering that he held in the U.S. on the Summer

---

[106] One of the many Family Dog/Great Highway events was a seven-night gathering on October 3 - 9, 1969. The last three days of the event became known as the Holy Man Jam. On those nights, the stage was shared by rock bands, the Hare Krishnas, Middle Eastern music, Transcendental Meditation, lecturers including Timothy Leary, Alan Watts, and Lazarus, along with Golden Toad, Steve Gaskin, Michael Lorimer, Master Choy, Malachi, Afterglow, Sufi Sam, Chiran Jeev, Osceola, Allan Noonan, Asoke Fakir, Jim Kimmel and Jud, John Adams and Magana Baptiste, San Francisco's Radical Lab, Sebastian Moon, Floating Bridge, It's A Beautiful Day, Phoenix, Tup Fisher, Dr. Warwick, Swami Satchidananda, Pir Vilayat, Schlomo Carlebach, and many others, including Yogi Bhajan.

Solstice in 1970, and I've been with this practice ever since.

You were drawn by Yogi Bhajan's attributes of service and power?

Not power over others, but the strength to be able to lead people and speak to people. A lot of work needs to be done. Also, one of the things that made me want to follow Yogi Bhajan, as a Sikh, was that I didn't want to be a renunciate, I wanted to be engaged with the world.

Now I've been head minister for Sikh Dharma in Northern California for almost 40 years. I'm the regional director.

Did you at any point reconsider returning to Judaism as your spiritual path?

No.

Do your children have Jewish identity?

I have six children. Only one, from my previous wife before I became a Sikh, considers himself Jewish. The others were not raised as Jews and don't think of themselves as Jews. Some have very strong Sikh identity. My wife, who is a leader in devotional Kirtan practice, was also born Jewish. I often joke that while she was one of quite a few siblings, she is the only one who married a Jew.

Part of our exploration here is trying to understand what that means—in what sense are you a Jew?

I feel a connection to the

music. I feel a connection to the people. I like the literacy. I've always pondered what it was that happened after World War II with the explosion of Jews in all these different spiritual practices. I've read articles about it and still don't really understand it. It's been my own life. I understand where I've come from, but I don't know why it happened, or what it means.

Does being Jewish mean anything for you in terms of relating to Israel?

I find watching Israel very painful. I feel pain especially because in my work I help people deal with their wounds; mostly from abuse, but not only from physical and sexual abuse. Israel seems to me trapped in the collective identity of an abused person, trapped in the violence that came from the Holocaust and carrying that abuse.

It was fear and anger that gave birth to the Holocaust in the first place. Germans had 400 years of pedagogical beliefs involving "beat the children," and that produced what it produced. The anger and need to control things that were part of the German psyche sit on fear, and this fear was beaten into the children. Israel is now in that place. I would like to see it rise above that fear to the vision it first started with. But it has done some very cruel things out of that fear and anger.

Do you feel that the beginning of Israel was a good or necessary idea?

When it first began, I was still seeing myself entirely as Jewish. The whole notion of the kibbutz and another way of being in the world seemed a very lovely idea.

How do you feel about it now?

From what I've seen of what we are doing with Palestine and entangling with the whole Islamic world, it's a very hard situation.

Regarding your path as a Sikh, you seem to have come to a place where you are not so attached to the name given to your path and your practice. Do you think that the world would be better off moving in that direction, where people no longer hold to a particular collective identity?

Every religion has a beautiful and noble spiritual side. But most people are entangled with their pain and fear. For me, the different fundamentalists around the planet are all the same. There is no real difference between Hindu, Sikh, Jewish, Islamic and Christian fundamentalists. They are all full of fear and anger, and they don't understand at all what religion is really about.

I don't think people need to give up being Jewish, or Hindu or Christian or any religion. But if they understood and really followed their practices, the world would be a better place.

What about the tribal identity with a particular group? Does that create problems?

We all need some way to connect. In my path, there is the Sikh pantheon; there were ten people who were called the gurus. I relate to one of them who my teacher, Yogi Bhajan, related to. Although I now see this Being also as formless, it's easier to relate to this Being than to relate to the infinite-unknowable-beyond-everything divine. It's nice to have a little handle. I used to see what I am relating to as a person, but I don't any longer. The person died 500 years ago. I see it as a formless vehicle which I use to relate to the larger formless.

Some spiritual traditions place an importance on one's biological ancestors?

I don't relate to that. My teacher, Yogi Bhajan, spoke about the difference between lineage and legacy. He said he was more interested in legacy than lineage. In the Sikh path, when the leadership was passed from one to the other, it wasn't passed through biological lineage, but to that person who was most qualified. The legacy gets passed on, but not through the biological lineage.

Of course I feel a connection to my father and grandfather, but due to the nature of the world when they came over from Europe I have a very fuzzy connection beyond that.

You recognize the immediate psychological influence of family, but for you there is no spiritual channel related to your biological ancestors?

I don't feel any.

Your answer to the question, "Are you a Jew?" would it be "No"?

Unless I went to Israel for a visit. (laughs). I would say that I feel that I'm ethnically Jewish.

What does that mean?

I feel that I look Jewish, that I'm Semitic.

Does that include certain values or psychological tendencies?

I've grown up in a religion that places a lot of emphasis on family, on reading and being intelligent, on thinking. I majored in philosophy. I value those things.

When I think of alcoholism, I think that it is more uncommon in the Jewish world than in much of the rest of the world. Child beating, as well, is much more rare among Jews than in many other religious groups. Family is valued. Women are valued more than in many groups, even though some of the Orthodox practices are challenging in this regard. I value these things.

I was primarily raised in a secure and cozy environment, for which I am very grateful. In comparison to what most people experience in their childhood, I feel that I was very privileged, because there was so much love. I do feel that this home environment is an important example of Jewish culture.

Do you feel as though there were negative transmissions that you took on that you needed to work to liberate yourself from through your practice?

When I was six, in 1945, I experienced the nature of the Jewish Holocaust in a very deep way for one who was not there and never in danger. In the middle 1940s, kids all across America went to Saturday matinees at the local movie theater. In 1945, we would see Movietone News at these matinees that featured the concentration camps, at least monthly, and often weekly. I would see the same horrible images over and over again: Allied troops liberating Auschwitz, Dachau, Bergen-Belsen, Buchenwald, Chelmno, Belzec, Ravensbruck, Treblinka; these names always ringing inside me with their awful resonance: Auschwitz, Dachau, Bergen-Belsen, Buchenwald, Chelmno, Belzec, Ravensbruck, Treblinka. The images burned into the core of my being, always there under the surface. Since then, I have pretty much been primarily interested in how to change how we live on this planet of ours.

Did you experience any anti-Semitism directly yourself?"

Very little. I grew up in a Jewish community in the Bronx and then went to City College, where there were a great many Jews.

Was your choice to be with Yogi Bhajan and become a Sikh much of a challenge to your family?

It was a big challenge. Very big! I was 30 years old. I had been involved with the hippies and drugs. When I got with the yoga program, it was really an improvement from that point of view. I stopped doing drugs and got married. Yet, it was a big challenge for a long time.

What did they object to?

Not being Jewish, and changing my name. We worked it out over a long time. I think it took until my parents' 50th wedding anniversary, when I was 48. I remember my grandfather asked me why I grew a beard. I knew that in his own youth, he had been slated to be a rabbi, but chose to join the Russian army and shave his beard. I asked him, "Why'd you cut your beard off?" He seemed to get it.

They wanted me to be Jewish and become a doctor, lawyer or engineer. Actually, Sikhs are very similar in that way. They want you to follow a profession. Young people in the Sikh world are vocationally driven. I'm referring to the Indian Sikhs. Indians are now the wealthiest ethnic group in the U.S., mostly Sikhs or Hindus.

Would you say you have Indian identity?

I used to; not any more. I spent a lot of time in India. I have a lot of friends who are Sikhs and I feel a connection with India through the spirituality. I probably feel a stronger ethnic identity with Jews than with Indians.

What does it mean that you are a Sikh leader?

In my role as leader in the Sikh community, I would get called to speak for the community at events like multi-faith gatherings, such as in San Francisco in the post 9/11 period,.

What is the relationship of the Indian Sikh community to the Westerners who've have become Sikhs?

Relatively, there are only a small number of Sikhs who were not born Sikh but became that through Yogi Bhajan. In the U.S., there are about 1 or 2 million Sikhs from Indian heritage. In the world there are about 15 million, about the same number as there are Jews .

How does your sense of identity play out when you consider the conflicts in the world? Do you feel a sense of loyalty with the

Sikhs or the Jews in their conflicts with others?

I do feel a connection with Israel in that sense and also with Sikhs. But mostly my connection is in trying to see how things could be smoother and wanting them to be that way rather than the more conflictual way.

Does it help you as a peacemaker, to be able to empathize with those who identify with a particular side in a conflict?

I can understand the passion. I can listen and feel.

What do you think the medicine is for healing confilct?

Actually, I think one of the things that needs to change on the planet is the way we raise our children. There are 10 or 15 countries in Europe where it's illegal to beat a child. I'd like to see all religions take that stance. It's probably my next project. I don't expect to accomplish it in my lifetime. There are good people working on it, such as Alice Miller, who first wrote about the German experience and started the "Save the Children Foundation."

Also, we need to learn to listen and talk like civilized people and work out conflict. When you are sitting in fear, it's hard to do. Israel is like a powder keg of fear. The people may not go around thinking about it, but it's so small and vulnerable that there is not a single person who cannot imagine Israel just disappearing from some great act of violence. They want to hold on to their place, though it's a fear-based way, not in a long term, conscious way, of doing that. Even though we have fear, we need to learn to transcend the fear and look at what really needs to be done.

There's very interesting work going on in Israel related to all this, but it's not reached a position of policy making.

Have you participated in activism related to Israel?

I did some work with Rabbi Michael Lerner, and was involved in conferences on social change and spirituality; I appreciate the Tikkun movement. I also did some work with Michael Franti of Spearhead.

I've withdrawn from activist circles for several years while I've worked with my healing project focused on individuals. I'm now looking at bringing what I've been learning into the activist world.

What is it you do as healing work with individuals?

We all have been wounded, all of us. I like to say that we all have, by analogy, an "abundance meter." Most of us feel that we don't deserve all of life's abundance, all of life's happiness. We feel we need to prove ourselves, we feel we need to compete. We are fearful that things won't work out, that we can't be happy. People who've been abused sexually, physically, or what not, wind up choosing spouses and significant others where they get abused. We are all trapped in our stories and fears. I've learned how to get deeply into the subconscious where these fears exist and help people change their stories. One can stop living in fear, needing to compete. One can give up trying to prove that one is okay—which you cannot prove. You cannot prove it; it's not possible. You can only change your belief around it. You may conquer the world and still feel that you are no good.

You do experiential workshops?

Yes. Somewhat based on Kundalini yoga, but mostly based on listening to and opening the heart. When we are abused, when these things happen to us, we always figure out how to blame ourselves and feel ashamed. So we take on the shame and blame. I am able to be a vehicle for creating a very deep space in which we can open our hearts and get in touch with our wounds and shift the story we tell ourselves.

I've worked on this myself and continue to.

Would you say that part of your work on yourself has been healing those things that were transmitted to you as part of the Jewish

collective experience?

Yes, the feelings of fear and shame from the Holocaust and other things. To be able to say I accept myself as I am, that I'm okay as I am.

You plan to bring this work to a more social level. That fits with the goals you spoke of when you joined Sikhism. Some would say it's a very Jewish notion, to make the world a better place.

I still have that. There is a Jewish legend of the *Lamed Vuvniks*. The book, *The Last of the Just*[107], is a fictionalized account of the Jewish legend in which a certain number of just men (36), carry the basic goodness of God and take on the suffering of the world. For a long time I had the fantasy that I was one of those through whose eyes God judges the world. Even though I haven't really taken on the suffering the book depicts, I can relate to that.

It's said that their consciousness is so aligned with the world that whatever they do is connected to the repair of the world.

I actually believe that we are all contributing in every moment to positive or negative consciousness, and that's a decision we make in every moment in our lives. Whether we are contributing to the greater harmony, smoothness and love, or anger and hate. I could go on about that subject for a long time.

Would you say this is something you bring into Sikhi or is it inherent in the Sikhi tradition?

The problems with Sikhi is just like in any other religion. There is holiness, spirituality and beauty around which the religion was founded. Then there are people whose lives and practices involve calling themselves Sikhs, but aren't aligned with those truths. I remember my teacher, years ago in a very funny and powerful moment speaking at a Christian interfaith gathering. He stood up on the pulpit of the

---

[107] *The Last of the Just,* by André Schwarz-Bart was published in French in 1959; English edition by Overlook Press, 2000.

church and said, "None of you are Christians." These were all priests and ministers, so they were quite shocked. Then he added, "unless you have Christ in your heart."

Most people who think of themselves as Sikhs, just as most who think of themselves as Jews or Protestants or whatever, observe it only on holidays.

Do you feel that it is because of the social justice tradition in your earlier Jewish life that you are bringing this to the Sikh world? Or is it already there?

The Jewish heritage in the world is not just spiritual but revolutionary. Jews are at the forefront of many social change movements and philosophies, vastly overrepresented in terms of their numbers in society. I do see that and honor that.

Do you see yourself as one of those within the Sikh world transforming the tradition that you have chosen?

It's possible. I haven't been sharing my thoughts that much publicly lately. I've been doing this work of healing peoples' wounds and teaching others to do that. That's pretty much the only thing I've been doing for the last 5 years.

Do you feel there is a purpose involved in being born into a particular family or culture?

My teacher used to say that we choose our incarnation. However, in my work I've met so many people who have been abused in their families that the notion that they chose that is abominable. So I don't have any particular belief about that anymore. There is, in the overall Indian spiritual tradition, a belief that to be born into a spiritual household is a high birth. I can see that. So to be born into a loving family that valued thinking and education and love, those are good things and good values.

One of the jokes we would make with the folks who'd been abused was, "The stork made a mistake." I don't really know the answer. I haven't been there. Or, perhaps I've been there, but don't remember. One of my primary feelings about death is that I look forward to finding out what is there. My strongest feeling about death is curiosity.

You mentioned that four years ago, something significant happened in your relationship with God. Can you elaborate?

A friend in the Sikh yogic world held a gathering. While there, one of my friends said to me that it seemed kind of bizarre that I was a leader in what is essentially a Bhakti Yogic religion (a devotional religion, which is what Sikhism is), and I could be angry with the object of my devotion. "How can you hope to connect?" What he said made sense and we agreed that I should do something about it.

I was led through my own process in which I lead people on group journeys to heal their wounds. They lie down and close their eyes and I guide them. I've been training people in this for several years. At the time of this challenge, I had the first crop of people who were able to lead this process and I let myself be guided through it. I ended up stopping being angry with God.

God is so central to most religions. What does it mean to you?

In my LSD experiences and in my practice I've experienced the divine in a number of different ways. Now, every day in my practice, I sit in a space of connection to the divine.

I know that in the Jewish tradition, there are wonderful discussions involving the famous leading rabbis telling about God. One transition I made was that I went from my head to my heart. I think with my heart, not my head, about my practice. Practice is experiential, not intellectual.

When you say you sit in "a space of connection," what are you connecting with?

There is something or some "one" there, who I don't understand. Neither male, nor female, infinite. I'm still in a place where "worshipping" this Being or entity is beginning to be a real connection for myself. For a long time, I didn't have a real sense of this Being who I prayed to or thought about. In my practice, one is taught over and over again to sing the praises of the divine. I've done kirtan and I can get ecstatic chanting. But feeling the awesomeness is something that I haven't felt very often. Recently, in the past month or so, I've thought about the awe experiences I had on LSD and realized I could open myself to that, without the LSD.

My anger with God was very Jewish. I would argue with God, which is a very Jewish thing. It is one of the few traditions where that is part of the life of the practice. "Why did you do this? What were you thinking?"

You took on the transmission of this angry, arguing with God from your Jewish ancestry?

Yes. But now I've stopped that. I've decided, how can I know what's best in comparison to the divine. So I've given that up. I've become more comfortable with not knowing, moving in layers and layers outward.

Is Sikhism similar to other religions?

It's probably closest to the Jewish religion. Two of the major players in the formal worship service is the Grante (equivalent to the rabbi) and the Gyani (who is like a cantor) who sings and leads the kirtan. The relationship to the written word is worshipful, perhaps even more pronounced than it is in Jewish practice. It's very analogous to taking out the Torah, with a similar ceremony of reading from the scriptures. Those things are very similar. Sikhs also place great value on earning a living.

Does Sikhism have a mystical thread, such as is present within the Jewish world?

It's very devotional. The core of the practices are chanting and singing praises of the divine. To me, the people who represent what is most elegant about being Sikh are those who devote their lives to singing kirtan. Sikhism grew out of the Hindu Bhakti tradition and Sufism. It has the Sufi mysticism and the Hindu devotional aspect.

It seems that the Torah of the Jews is not really of significance in your life?

No it's not. It's not anywhere in how I connect with the divine. In any case, my spiritual life at this point is much more growing out of my own experiences. I don't have patience with, "These are my people and the others aren't my people."

Even with the Sikh?

Nobody, nowhere.

You've been an activist confronting some of the greed and hatred in the world. Does your spiritual practice give you insight into relating with evil?

I've been writing about this. The Zoroastrian tradition, which is about as old as the Jewish, speaks of the battle between darkness and light. I have a feeling that this relates to the struggle between love and hate. When people get enough brutality as children, they actually go through biological and chemical changes where they cease looking for love and start looking for hate and anger. That's one of the phenomena that's going on in the world right now, in the U.S. with the Tea Party and those groups that incite anger.

People doing that are not capable of experiencing love in the way we know love. They are only capable of experiencing anger, which is what happens when there is a great deal of suffering in one's life. That's partly what Israel is dealing with in the collective sense. So, evil is much more subtle than conscious intention. People don't intend or choose to be evil. That is not what is happening. There are people full of fear and anger, and that is the evil. It's a much more subtle thing to deal with than blaming people and casting them out as evil.

You've said you feel a sense of connection to the Jewish people. Is it possible to speak from that place to the Jewish community?

I have been trying to think about how to go about doing that. There was a time when I was thinking of attending a conference in Israel and I was wondering what kind of healing ceremony could one lead to bring people together. However, I'm not a strong believer in telling people what they should do. I don't find that useful. Some friends and I came up with the expression, "Don't should on me and I won't should on you." Mostly, telling people what they should do induces guilt but not change. So, what to do?

We are all fellow human beings. We need to understand that. I suggest we ask ourselves one question, not from any great spiritual understanding: If you want to imagine having dealt with the situation in Israel, imagine how it will be in 10 years, 15 years, 20 years, and ask yourself what needed to happen? What needed to change? What would allow that change to occur? How to deal with the fear? How to process the fear? Because anger sits on fear, there is no anger without fear.

One could totally support and honor that for victimized people, being strong and able to stand up for oneself is important. I felt pride that after the Holocaust we could see this in Israel, with the Hagannah[108] and other groups. Those things were moving to me

---

[108] Haganah (trans: "The Defense") was a Jewish paramilitary organization in what was the British Mandate of Palestine from 1920 to 1948, and later became the core of the Israel Defense Forces.

when I was young. But isn't it the Bible that says, "If you live by the sword, you die by the sword?" Guns are not going to solve the problem. It's the same for this country, the way we are dealing with Islam and also world terrorism. Take for example the controversy about the Islamic center in New York. It's a Sufi Center[109], one that seeks peace, and yet it's being attacked. The Sufis were just bombed in Pakistan because they are a threat to the jihad notion. We are not paying attention to whom to support.

How do you work for peace? When you breed anger and resentment, you are creating generation after generation of enemies. We have been doing this. How do you get out of that box?

How would you describe the core intention of Sikh practice?

The intention is to develop the consciousness of a monk in a cave while being a householder.

What is the consciousness of a monk in a cave?

Feeling one with the divine, free of attachment and desires.

And a householder?

You engage the mishagas of life.

Thank you.

---

[109] An Islamic community center, slated for construction near the site of the World Trade Center attack, became the focus of anti-Islamic attacks and a major controversy in New York City.

Heresy – The tale of Aher, Elisha ben Abuya

There is a tale told in the Talmud, the sacred set of texts which contain what are referred to as the oral tradition of the Jewish religion: "Four rabbis entered 'Pardes' (the Garden)—Ben Azzai, Ben Zoma, Aher, and Akiva. Ben Azzai gazed and died; Ben Zoma gazed and went insane; Aher entered and cut the root (became an apostate); Akiva entered, and exited in peace."

In referring to Aher, translations of this passage always include, "became an apostate." The phrase is added to be sure the presumed meaning of "Aher cut the root" is clear. The accepted meaning is that he cut himself off from the Torah; he rejected his religion and ancestry. Aher became the archetype of heresy for Jews.

Yet, the Jewish tradition has within it a deep emphasis on reexamination and reinterpretation, of opening to new and different ways of seeing words, phrases and stories, even from the most sacred texts. The tradition of such commentary is referred to as midrash[110]. Readers find hidden meanings that may have escaped the eye of even the most learned of their predecessors, meanings that may have been "hidden" from even the writers of the text themselves. It is part of the tradition of challenging and questioning that so many of those in this book report as a key element of their Jewish heritage.

At the end of Chapter 1, where I tell my story, I share a vision that offered another view of this tale. That experience, my desert vision, was what first motivated me to write this book. I felt a need to honor

---

[110] Midrash responds to contemporary problems and crafts new stories, making connections between new Jewish realities and the unchanging biblical text. (from the online source: "My Jewish Learning.com")

Aher, not as an apostate, but as someone who had made an enlightened choice to follow his soul's calling. I wanted to share my positive vision of the choice we are blessed with to find our own path, however different that may be from that of our birth community. My plan was to refer to each of the individuals interviewed for the book as a modern day Aher, someone who had experienced the Garden (a spiritual awakening) and had chosen a different path than Judaism on their return. I wanted to rehabilitate the notion of heresy, to see it as a positive force. The book was to be called, *Aher: The Way of the Jewish Heretic.*

However, my engagement with those I interviewed, hearing their deep love for their families and the Jewish community itself, led me to choose a different title less likely to be seen as disrespectful or rejecting of the Jewish path not taken. Though some may feel otherwise, the people represented in this book do not see themselves as heretics. They see themselves as simply following their truth and, in many cases, as very consciously aligned with their ancestral heritage.

That said, I continue to see the relevance of speaking about heresy, especially within the Jewish world, and giving some focus to the passage that inspired this book. In the Jewish religious and intellectual world there are contradictory opinions about all these subjects. What I offer here are my own interpretations from both research and reflection.

The above passage from the Talmud and a few other scattered references are all that exist to tell us of the one rabbi, of the hundreds cited in the Talmud, who came to be considered a heretic and whose name has been equated with heresy through the ages. His name was Elisha ben Abuyah. Excommunicated and banished, the religious authorities of the time determined that he would only be referred to as Aher (pronounced Acher, with a soft "ch"), "the Other." It was determined that since he "cut the root," and stopped following the rules and laws by which all religious Jews are required to live, he would be cut off from the community, his people. The Talmud tells us that after his death, lightning struck his grave and demolished his final marker as if God had spoken the last word affirming his banishment.

The story has attracted and inspired a number of writers in the midrashic tradition seeking to reinterpret its meaning. Like a myth, the tale of Elisha/Aher, especially in the past few hundred years, has seen new interpretations not only through exegesis, but poetry, literature and plays. In 1906, Yiddish playwright Yaakov Gordin wrote "Elisha ben Abuya," presenting him as a modern scholar of secular literature.

Though the name Elisha (or Aher) has become synonymous with heretic for Jews, the actual nature of his heresy has been the subject of a good deal of speculation. These speculations give us a sense of what might be thought of as heretical in the Jewish world. He has been thought or accused of being a Gnostic, a follower of Philo, or a Christian.[111] The very few other mentions of him in the Talmud connect him to minor transgressions of Jewish law that might be the source of his expulsion from the community. On the other hand, he is a kind of patron saint of Jews who have consciously veered from the religious path. Israeli Professor Nissan Rubin writes that after centuries of obscurity, "In modern times, Elisha ben Abuya rebounded to the public memory, in both Hebrew literature and ideology, becoming a figure of reference for authors and ideologues who found themselves on the border between the traditional Jewish world and the world of Western culture."[112]

In researching for this book, a rabbi friend recommended the novel *As a Driven Leaf*[113] by Reconstructionist Rabbi Milton Steinberg. Steinberg fictionalizes the life of Elisha ben Abuya in the context of the first century, C.E., at the dawning of Rabbinic Judaism. As both a man of faith and an intellectual, Steinberg felt a conflict between his love of Western philosophy and literature on the one hand, and rabbinic and Torah study on the other. He infuses his inner struggle into the novel, reframing the understanding of Aher's "cutting the roots" to reference the choice of pursuing rational Greek philosophy instead of a traditional religious life. In his sympathetic portrayal of Elisha/Aher, we see a tragic figure obsessed with finding strictly rational solutions to the problems of existence while struggling with his loss of faith in

---

[111] Wikipedia - http://en.wikipedia.org/wiki/Elisha_ben_Abuyah

[112] "Do not look at his deeds, look at the Torah he learned,' by Nissan Rubin, a review of the book, *He Went Forth into Evil Course: Elisha ben Abuya-Aher* by Nurit Be'eri, Yedioth Aharonoth Books (Hebrew)

[113] *As a Driven Leaf* by Milton Steinberg, Behrman House.

Jewish scripture and practice.

The few short references found in the Talmud are developed by Steinberg into the life stories of Rabbis Elisha, Akiva, (who entered and exited Pardes in peace), ben Azzai (who died), and ben Zoma (who went insane). Jewish history tells us that Akiva became a great leader in the development of modern day Rabbinic Judaism and was crucified by the Romans. As Steinberg tells it, although Elisha loved and respected Akiva, his obsession with Greek philosophy and mathematics brought him to play a Judas-like role, reluctantly betraying his dear friend and the Jewish people. He spent his final days in remorse and shame. It appears that despite Steinberg's resonance with Elisha's struggle, his book issues a strong warning against acting on "heretical" tendencies.

Isaac Deutscher, a Polish-born historian, political activist and Marxist, offers another perspective on Aher. Deutscher made his own exodus from Orthodox Judaism to become a self-declared atheist and humanist. In his essay, "The Non-Jewish Jew," he speaks positively of his identification with Elisha ben Abuyah/Aher, holding him up as a "prototype of all those great Jewish revolutionaries of modern thought: Spinoza, Heine, Marx, Rosa Luxemberg, Trotsky and Freud."[114]

Steinberg's novel had a strong effect on me. It resonated with my own life of following deep inner impulses or visions that took me on an alternate path from my Jewish roots. I was a heretic, but in a way that I felt was positive. It seems that the interpretation of Aher's heresy and what it means to "cut the roots" is like a Rorschach test in which each reader sees whatever divergence from religious orthodoxy relates to their own life experience. For Steinberg, it was attraction to Western philosophy; for Deutcher, involvement with social justice, and revolutionary political theory and action. For me, it was not about abandoning Judaism or spirituality, but moving in the direction of contemporaries who sought the mystical Garden by other-than-Jewish means. My speculation would be that Elisha ben Abuya's "heresy" was visiting the Oracle at Delphi or participating in the mysticism of

---

[114] "The Non-Jewish Jew," by Isaac Deutscher, from *The Non-Jewish Jew and Other Essays*, Oxford University Press.

the Eleusyan mystery schools of his Greek contemporaries.

This interpretation came out of my experience with the modern Judaism in which I'd grown up. It made perfect sense to me that someone having a mystical experience would not find resonance or openness to their questions or visions in the Jewish religious world. As I began my conscious spiritual journey, none of my newfound discoveries seemed to relate to what I knew of the Jewish religion. I couldn't imagine talking about my spiritual experiences to the men I remembered as my Hebrew School teachers and rabbis. To my mind, it seemed likely that Elisha's trip to the Garden had opened him to ideas and visions not acceptable to the rigid, rule-based mindset of the Sanhedrin or other Jewish authorities of his time.

We tend to see mythic stories through the lens or filter of our life experience. Perhaps Steinberg saw what he felt was a dangerous part of himself in Aher, that which craved the purely rational way of life. Deutscher agreed that Aher's "heresy" was to reject the religious life, but he saw this as a positive step, identifying with him as a revolutionary. I found in Aher a brother who, like many of my contemporaries, chose to pursue non-Jewish spiritual paths.

Heresy has a bad rap and is undeserving of its mostly negative connotations. I have come to think that all religions were started by heretics. The insights or revelations from which religions spring arise from experiences and utterances that challenge the orthodoxy of the time. Positive cultural transformations also come about as individuals or groups rebel and break from accepted norms of behavior—as they commit heresy. Like Luther to the Christian world or Marx to the capitalist one, whether those who profess religious breakthroughs or counter-cultural ideas are seen as heroes or villains depends on the perspective from which they are viewed.

In the Jewish tradition, Abraham heard the voice of God and was told to walk away from his family home and tradition and go on a journey. As the story is told, Abraham rejected the "idol worshipping" of the people of his time. This involved him in a conflict with his father who sold statues of the local gods and goddesses. Though the following account is written for children and does not represent the deeper insights of Jewish sages, it is the mainstream, normative tale which I heard as a boy:

According to Jewish tradition, Abraham was born under the name Abram in the city of Ur in Babylonia in the year 1948 from Creation (circa 1800 BCE). He was the son of Terach, an idol merchant, but from his early childhood, he questioned the faith of his father and sought the truth. He came to believe that the entire universe was the work of a single Creator, and he began to teach this belief to others.

Abram tried to convince his father, Terach, of the folly of idol worship. One day, when Abram was left alone to mind the store, he took a hammer and smashed all of the idols except the largest one. He placed the hammer in the hand of the largest idol. When his father returned and asked what happened, Abram said, "The idols got into a fight, and the big one smashed all the other ones." His father said, "Don't be ridiculous. These idols have no life or power. They can't do anything." Abram replied, "Then why do you worship them?"

Eventually, the one true Creator that Abram had worshipped called to him, and made him an offer: if Abram would leave his home and his family, then G-d would make him a great nation and bless him. Abram accepted this offer, and the b'rit (covenant) between G-d and the Jewish people was established. (Gen. 12).

from *Judaism 101, an online encyclopedia of Judaism,* http://www.jewfaq.org/index.htm

Abraham was a heretic to those who maintained the old ways, but he is the heroic founder of a new religious path for his followers and descendants, who now include Jews, Christians and Muslims. He heard an inner voice and broke with the path of his family and community. Jews honor him as the father of their people and universally accept the idea that he found the true God and left behind the superstitious, idol-worshipping pagan beliefs about many gods and goddesses. Ironically, now some Jews, such as myself, have the heretical idea that the early indigenous animistic and shamanistic traditions hold wisdom we need for our lives today. We don't think of statues of gods and goddesses as idols to be worshiped, but as windows to the spirits of higher consciousness.

In the story of the Buddha, Prince Siddhartha witnesses the suffering in the world from sickness, aging and death from which he had been shielded by his father. He reacts by renouncing his royal inheritance and the materialist worldview, and goes on a spiritual quest to understand the nature of suffering and how to find freedom from its seemingly inevitable grip. After years of exploring many spiritual paths and practices, he had the liberating experience of awakening to the "middle way," a path seen as heretical by the ascetic teachers and aspirants with whom he had associated after leaving his family.

Myths abound in which a man or woman steps away from what has been prescribed as *the way* by family or tribe. The journey takes her to new and different understandings that then become passed on as a *new way* for descendants or followers. On vision quests, the hero goes out into the desert, up on a mountain, or by a river, and returns to his people with visions for the benefit of everyone. If the vision too radically challenges some existing tribal dogma, he or she is branded a heretic.

It is unfortunate that heresy is seen mostly in a negative light. In some instances, where more fundamentalist thinking is prevalent, it is criminalized. Yet this need not be so. The word "heresy" comes from the Greek hairetikos, meaning, "able to choose" (from the New Testament Greek Lexicon), implying one has opened to an ability to look beyond the conventions of established thought.

Many visionary religious leaders have understood this. Rabbi Abraham Isaac Kook explores the necessity of heresy for awakening our religious understanding from a literal, fundamentalist or fixed viewpoint, to true depth and sacredness:

> *The crude complacency of imagining divinity as embodied in words and letters alone puts humanity to shame. Heresy arises as a pained outcry to liberate us from this strange, narrow pit, to raise us from the darkness of letters and platitudes to the light of thought and feeling. Such heresy eventually takes its stand in the center of morality.* [115]

[115] *The Essential Kabbalah: The Heart of Jewish Mysticism* by Daniel Matt, Harper, SF 1996

The issue of heresy is, of course, prominent in Christian history, notably in the atrocities committed in the name of maintaining orthodoxy of belief in the Church through the Middle Ages, especially during the Crusades. Even today, individuals associated with liberation theology[116] are silenced for preaching an interpretation of Jesus' teachings as advocating liberation from unjust economic, political, or social conditions. Cardinal Ratzinger (who became Pope Benedict XVI) was head of the Vatican's Congregation for the Doctrine of the Faith which issued official condemnations of certain elements of liberation theology that prohibited dissident priests from teaching such doctrines.

Matthew Fox was a Catholic priest in the Dominican Order until he was silenced and then excommunicated for his outspoken views on, among other things, feminism and creation spirituality[117]. Without doubt, his heretical views were treated far less drastically than in times past, reflecting both an increased flexibility in the Church and an enormous reduction in its political power and control.

The modern Jewish world is well known for its intellectual and religious tolerance, outside of the ultra-orthodox communities. But Judaism has its own history of controversies regarding heresy, which is reflected in the formation of the different Jewish denominations. Rabbi Isaac Mayer Wise was a principal founder of Reform Judaism in the United States. In the mid 1880s he held a rabbinic graduation dinner in Cincinnati serving clams, shrimp and beef in a cream sauce, a direct affront to the kosher rules of orthodoxy; efforts were made to excommunicate him. Conservative Judaism is considered heretical to some Orthodox sects. Mordechai Kaplan spent 50 years as a respected rabbi and teacher of Jewish theology. He believed that Jewish practice should be reconciled with modern thought; he was formally excommunicated by the Union of Orthodox Rabbis in 1945. He went on to be part of the founding of Reconstructionist Judaism.

Noted heretics from Jewish history who were excommunicated

---

[116] *A Theology of Liberation: History, Politics, and Salvation* by Gustavo Guiterrez, Orbis Books, NY 1988

[117] Mathew Fox, now a member of the Episcopal Church, founded The Institute of Culture and Creation Spirituality. He is the author of many books including, *Original Blessing: A Primer in Creation Spirituality*, Tarcher/Putnam, NY revised ed. 2000

include: Sabbatai Zevi, who claimed to be the Messiah in the 1600s; Jacob Frank, in the 1700s, who claimed to be the reincarnation of Sabbatai Zevi and King David, and accepted the New Testament; Baruch Spinoza, the renowned philosopher, who was accused of "evil opinions." Even Rabbi Moses Maimonides, now accepted as one of the greatest and most respected of Jewish teachers and philosophers, in the 1100s was accused of heresy and his followers and opponents attempted to excommunicate each other.

One of the longest-running heresy imbroglios is the 2000-year Christian-Jewish conflict which arose over the role of Jesus. Jewish leaders in the early centuries of the Common Era regarded Jews who believed Jesus to be the Messiah as heretics and prayed for their demise. After Christians gained the power of the Roman Empire they began centuries of persecuting Jews for the ultimate heresy of refusing to believe in the truth of the Lord Jesus and for being responsible for his crucifixion. Jesus, Mary and Joseph, of course, never saw themselves as anything but Jews, and were never heretical towards Jewish religious law. In *Rabbi Jesus*[118], Bruce Chilton offers a view of Jesus as an observant Jew whose teachings were largely within the bounds of Jewish law and practice of the time. Today, groups such as *Jews for Jesus* state as their purpose, "to make the Messiahship of Jesus an unavoidable issue to our Jewish people worldwide."

People with unconventional views often become a target for a group or culture who see feared aspects of themselves which are suppressed or hidden. Elisha ben Abuya was literally renamed "the other" and shunned by his people. Perhaps he was simply opening new gateways for exploration that challenged the collective fears of his community. Perhaps he was moving on to pathways that would have served not only himself, but the whole community – stretching the boundary of what it means to be Jewish, and to be human. Isaac Deutscher's reflections on Spinoza are telling:

"Spinoza himself, when he started out as independent thinker and as initiator of modern criticism of the Bible, seized at once the cardinal

---

[118] *Rabbi Jesus: An Intimate Biography* by Bruce Chilton, Doubleday, NY 2000

> *contradiction in Judaism, the contradiction between the monotheistic and univeral God and the setting in which that God appears in the Jewish religion—as a God attached to one people only; the contradiction between the universal God and his "chosen people." We know what the realization of this contradiction brought upon Spinoza: banishment from the Jewish community and excommunication.*
>
> *Spinoza's ethics were no longer the Jewish ethics, but the ethics of man at large—just as his God was no longer the Jewish God: his God, merged with nature, shed his separate and distinctive divine identity. Yet, in a way, Spinoza's God and ethics were still Jewish, except that his was Jewish monotheism carried to its logical conclusion and the Jewish universal God thought out to the end; and once thought out to the end, that God ceased to be Jewish."*[119]

It's hard to conceive of Spinoza's ideas leading to excommunication in modern times, and there were evidently political considerations that led to it in his own time. But Spinoza's heresy was truly a contribution to opening the Jewish mind-field to appreciate a deeper understanding of what it means to say, "God is One." What could be a more constructive role for a member of a tribe? The heretic, as in so many cases, was a true mensch.

In the final analysis, heresy involves crossing an imaginary line or boundary within which all the permissible thoughts and behaviors of a self-defined community are contained. Even the most orthodox of Orthodox Jews do not follow some of the commandments in Deuteronomy, such as cutting off the hand of a woman who grabs a man by his privates. Their community decides what is kosher and what is not, what must be done and what not, where the line of heresy is drawn.

Shalom Auslander, who grew up in an ultra-Orthodox community, gives a hilarious look at the inner life of a Jewish man raised in the Orthodox world, struggling with his inner conscience about his "heretical thoughts and actions." *Foreskin's Lament*[120] tells the story of

---

[119] "The Non-Jewish Jew" Ibid
[120] *Foreskin's Lament: A Memoir* by Shalom Auslander, Penguin, NY 2007

a man's daily decisions regarding what he eats and where he lets his eyes fall, struggling with what in his mind is the all-seeing, all-knowing presence of a God ready to punish him for his betrayals of the commandments. His journey culminates with the momentous decision about whether to circumcise his about-to-be-born son.

Though Auslander treats it with great humor, circumsicion is quite a serious matter. I couldn't finish this chapter without some comment on perhaps this most elemental aspect of Jewish tradition. One of the most significant controversies among the early Christians was called, "the circumcision heresy." As most of the early Christians were Jews, the controversy arose over whether non-Jews who wanted to come to Christ had to first become Jews, and therefore needed to be circumcised in order to be saved. This was, as we know, decided in the negative, which I am sure greatly facilitated the expansion of the Christian community.

The circumcision controversy continues even today amongst Jews, and it cuts (sorry) to the core of very deep feelings. I was once consulted by a young man who was expecting a child and had very uncomfortable feelings about circumcision. He wanted to raise his child as a Jew but wasn't sure if it would be okay to not circumcise him. I suggested the possibility of developing other meaningful rituals, and I asked several very progressive rabbis for their thoughts on alternatives. They all insisted that circumcision was necessary to be a Jew, that it was an elemental aspect of a man having a Jewish identity. The issue is often the cause of struggle in mixed marriages where even non-practicing Jews find themselves unable to bear allowing their son to be uncircumcised.

Where do we draw the line? My mom kept a kosher home, but would eat Chinese food when we went out. Many Jews will eat bacon, but never ham or pork. Some drive a car on Saturday, but fast on Yom Kippur. You may marry a non-Jew, but when you have a son, your parents and your ancestors are screaming in your head that it is heresy to not have that foreskin cut off. Aher, the heretic, has the courage to tell you, "You have a choice."

Drawing Conclusions - The Journey With Jewishness and Beyond

By focusing attention on Jewish identity, I sought to better understand the nature of identity itself. Identity is the core issue of the psychological and spiritual quest enunciated in the fundamental question, "Who am I?" and the related, "What am I doing here?" "Who are my people?" One could choose to focus on any ethnicity or racial group, but I began this life as a Jew, and that was the natural base for my exploration.

As I interviewed the fourteen spiritual teachers for this book, there were three primary themes: their personal life story, the relation of their Jewish identity to their current spiritual path, and the nature of a spiritually-based life. I found myself in fascinating discussions on the deep questions of life, death, service in the world, higher consciousness, reincarnation, good and evil, and more. It took a more focused effort to bring us to talk about Jewishness, not because of reluctance, but simply because, for most of them, it is not part of their current focus of attention (which says a great deal in itself).

Yet, as the window to the questions about Jewish identity opened, much came through, and in this final chapter I want to offer some reflections on the commonalities and differences of what was shared. Of course, each story in this book represents a unique life of searching and discovery. Each of those interviewed grew up in different communities with different parents and different exposure to religious, non-religious, or anti-religious sentiments. Some had direct experiences with anti-Semitism; some had little or none. There was a wide range of family attitudes towards non-Jews. Likewise, family responses towards their choice to pursue an alternate religious path ran the spectrum. For some, the process of awakening to their spiritual path was sudden, surprising and seemingly accidental; for others, it was a deliberate, gradual exploration that deepened into a life-long commitment.

So, what can be drawn from their life journeys that speaks to our core questions? Does Jewish identity endure regardless of the belief systems and practices a person adopts? If so, what are the core transmissions inherited by Jewish people that continue to influence their values and behavior? In my discussions, two primary themes emerged: tolerance for differing beliefs, associated with intellectual curiosity and ongoing questioning of dogma; and commitment and active involvement in transforming the world towards peace and social justice.

As might be expected, there were differing perspectives on whether these are, in fact, Jewish traits. Some emphasized that their present values and perspectives stem less from a Jewish ancestral connection and more from their particular parents and family, the place where they grew up, and their relationships with people within and beyond the Jewish world. What exactly constitutes the Jewish values that one might expect in a Jewish family when there is such variation in the way families relate to events? While many spoke of the intellectual openness of their family, others grew up in quite narrow-minded environments. There was, likewise, a wide range of family reactions to the choice of taking an alternate spiritual path. While some families responded with relative acceptance, others were furious and made strong efforts to resist or prevent it.

Yet, regardless of their personal family experience, most all felt that intellectual searching and argument is a strong part of Jewishness. In reflecting on this, it is a fact that the intense study of Torah and Talmud, which encourages questioning and debate of every story, phrase, word and letter, is deeply rooted in Jewish culture and carries over beyond religious discussions. Rabbi Gershon Winkler, an outside-the-box thinker and religious teacher who influenced several of

CONCLUSIONS — The Journey With Jewishness and Beyond

those included in this book, including me, uses the phrase, "boundary crosser"[121] as descriptive of the essence of Jewish tribal behavior. The tradition of intellectual rigor, debate and critical questioning has undoubtedly contributed to the proliferation of Jewish attorneys, judges and legal scholars, as well as writers, artists and intellectuals of all disciplines and schools of thought. Some of the folks in this book attributed the impulse to journey into an alternate spiritual path to their Jewish curiosity and the skeptical attitude that brought them to question their own family traditions.

Of course, Jews are not the only people to engage in debate and question established dogma. But amongst Jews it is not only a cultural norm, it is a strong element of Jewish religious tradition. Maimonides, perhaps the most highly respected Jewish philosopher, said "a person who is a Jew . . . can believe in Judaism and question anything. You can even question the existence of God and still be a person who believes in Judaism." [122]

The commitment to the pursuit of peace and justice was also a major aspect of the lives of the majority of those I spoke with. With some exceptions, they also see it as a part of their Jewish heritage. Many have been or continue to be active in movements for human rights, peace and ecological sustainability. Some see their spiritual teaching as a primary way of contributing to global transformation by shifting the consciousness of individuals as well as the collective mind of humanity towards kindness, compassion and love.

It's easy to find this commitment deeply embedded in Jewish teachings. The Jewish Renewal movement has revived the doctrine of Tikkun Olam, (repair the world) as the prime directive from God. For example, Rabbi Michael Lerner, founder and editor of *Tikkun* magazine and co-founder of the Network of Spiritual Progressives[123], speaks of God as "that force in the universe that moves us towards justice."

---

[121] *The Way of the Boundary Crosser: An Introduction to Jewish Flexidoxy*, by Rabbi Gershon Winkler, Jason Aronson, Inc.

[122] Norton Mezvinsky in *Radicals, Rabbis and Peacemakers*, Seth Farber (Editor), Common Courage Press.

[123] For more information on the Network of Spiritual Progressives and Tikkun: http://spiritualprogressives.org & http://www.tikkun.org/

Rabbi Lynn Gottlieb, author and activist, teaches the "Torah of non-violence,"[124] and connects the basic principles of Gandhi and Martin Luther King, Jr. to the teachings of rabbinic Judaism.

Several interviewees speculate that such teachings, as well as the personal and collective experiences of Jews as victims of prejudice and persecution, explain the very sizable presence of Jewish women and men in progressive and revolutionary social and political movements, including the labor, civil rights, anti-war and environmental movements. In the U.S. and Europe, Jewish people have been at the forefront of these movements for at least the past two centuries.

"For today every Jew feels that to be a Jew means to bear a serious responsibility not only to his own community, but also toward humanity."
— Albert Einstein (from *Prophets Outcast*[125])

It is not always clear how the urge to explore the unconventional or be involved in social justice arose in those I interviewed. Some spoke of the active discussions and intellectual arguments that were part of family life. Others spoke of watching the early films of the Nazi concentration camps with parents, or their family's emotional support of the Civil Rights movement as formative. Interestingly, for those whose family had no interest in or involvement with social issues, still there was often a sense of a collective Jewish transmission of such values from beyond their biological family or the particular Jewish community in which they grew up.

When asked about the negatives of Jewish identity, the most common response was 'fear,' fear of the other. Fear is a natural and understandable response to intense, multi-generational anti-Semitism experienced by previous generations of Jews. It would seem that fear would put a damper on crossing boundaries in general, closing minds to new ideas and limiting the inclination to take up activist or controversial causes. It would lead to non-involvement with people outside one's

---

[124] *Trail Guide to the Torah of Nonviolence*, by Rabbi Lynn Gottlieb, Editions Terre d'Esperance, Paris.
[125] *Prophets Outcast: A Century of Dissident Jewish Writing about Zionism and Israel*, Adam Shatz (Editor), Nation Books, NY.

own community. And most of these teachers are baby-boomers with parents who had direct experience with discrimination against Jews.

But in their younger years, the urge to free themselves of the fears of their family and community fueled the inclination to question the ways of their parents and associate with movements for personal and social liberation. Those who felt they inherited such fears, recognized the need to personally heal this within themselves, to process or metabolize this imprint. Through the work that they've done on their respective spiritual journeys, they now have loving and empathic relationships with their families and the Jewish community as a whole. I found a general sense of deep appreciation for the culture, humor, heart and spirit of the Jewish people. Still, it is interesting that while those in this book are exemplars of curiosity, experimentation, openness, and eagerness to contribute to the larger world community, many of their family members stayed in "safer" harbors. We are left with the question of which is the real Jewish way?

Fear and separative consciousness, however understandable, continue the cycle of suffering. As I write this final chapter, these patterns are being written on the world stage in fire and blood. We are in the midst of yet another massively violent episode in the ongoing struggle of Israel to maintain a Jewish state in what was recently a mostly Arab Palestine. This has become, in my view, the most pressing issue for Jews at this time in our history and calls up the core emotions and spiritual lessons of tribal identity.

Though it wasn't always the case, for most Jews today Jewish identity has fused with loyalty to the nation-state of Israel. Henry Seigman, former National Director of the American Jewish Congress, said, "If we make criticisms of Israel, it's not your politics in question, it's your Jewishness itself. One becomes considered a heretic." This fusion of Jewish identity with Israel occurred rapidly over several decades, instilled in the group consciousness through Jewish educational and religious organizations. Marc Ellis, Professor of American and Jewish Studies at Baylor University points out: "In the 1950s and 1960s neither Holocaust nor Israel was central to Jewish identity; today they form the core of our Jewishness. Without them, one wonders what

Jewish identity would look like."[126]

The British Jewish philosopher, Brian Klug writes: "The deeper issue is the tendency among Jews to define Jewish identity in terms of the State of Israel and the ethos of 'solidarity' to which this gives rise.... In the first place, it distorts Jewish identity, whether secular or religious, to collapse the distinction between being Jewish and owing allegiance to the State of Israel. The subject of Jewish identity, not least in relation to Israel, is complex, confusing and fraught with emotion." He goes on to say of Zionism, "There is a claim based on the idea that Israel, being a Jewish state, is my state and that its people, the Jewish people, are my people."[127]

Given this critical aspect of the Jewish experience and its relationship to Jewish identity, I probed for thoughts and feelings concerning Israel in my interviews and found a widespread set of responses. Some expressed a bond with the nation of Israel, and spoke of family and friends living there. Though pained by the conflict, they were reluctant to take positions that might sound critical. Others felt that as Jews they have an emotional relationship with Israel and a responsibility that called them to express their criticism of the occupation and the treatment of Palestinians by Israel. Father Paul Mayer, for example, took part in many vigils and actions protesting the occupation, and was quite frank in the shame he felt at the behavior of his "Jewish people." Starhawk was among those who participated in the Freedom Flotilla effort to enter Gaza by sea to challenge the Israeli blockade and she has been vocal in her solidarity with the Palestinian struggle. Several others spoke of how the actions of the Israeli government are contrary to what they see as "Jewish values."

On the other hand, there were those who said that Israel was like any other nation to them; the conflict there, though painful, was for them like ones in other parts of the world where ethnic strife was at the root of suffering. The fact that Jews were a primary part of the struggle did not create for them a greater emotional charge or need to

[126] Radicals, *Rabbis and Peacemakers: Conversations with Jewish Critics of Israel,* by Seth Farber, Common Courage Press, ME.
[127] *Prophets Outcast: A Century of Jewish Writing about Zionism and Israel,* Edited by Adam Shatz, Nation Books, NY.

be involved.

There is a Jewish joke that goes: if you have three Jews stranded on a desert island, you'll end up with three synagogues. Our explorations can be seen to take it a bit further—we have fourteen Jews, each with their own religion. But, while different religious practices and opinions are held by the Jews in this book, there is also a unity that underlies the differences. This unity continues to inspire me and give me hope, for it goes beyond political opinions and religious or metaphysical beliefs, and softens the boundary of group identity itself.

The common ground is the understanding that spiritual reality can be experienced through a wide range of practices and we need not privilege one over another. Further, there is the shared experience that we are more than our assigned identity and ideas about ourselves; we are all holy; we all have essential goodness, love and beauty; we are here to open our hearts to each other with kindness and compassion; we are not separate from the Earth or the universe of planets, stars and galaxies; and we have the opportunity to live in the embrace of our divine nature. I can say with confidence that all of those in this book agree with these basic truths.

Many, if not most of those I interviewed had not previously placed much focus on the questions about Jewish identity that I was asking. The issues did not weigh on them in the same way as they did with me. When I said this to Pir Shabda Khan, he gently suggested, "Alan, this is your work." He was right; these questions are an aspect of my personal quest. Yet, there clearly was an exchange in the interview process. Some of those I spoke with later told me that our interviews led to more contemplation of their history and involvement with the Jewish community and their own Jewish identity. The interviews and other conversations validated for me that questions about the meaning and role of Jewish identity lie deep in the psyche of even those outside the mainstream Jewish community.

For myself, I learned a great deal from the lightness with which these teachers carry their Jewishness. Being Jewish isn't a burden or a problem; it is simply an aspect of who they are, (or of how others see them). When seen as an either/or, the question "Am I a Jew or not?

can be troubling. Through my encounters, I've come to hold it differently. Sharon Salzburg's response to "Are you a Jew?" was "Sometimes." Perhaps this is a way to look at all instances of identity. As we move through different settings or different states of consciousness, we shift and change who we are, and that shape-shifting entity that we call me becomes something else.

I now see Jewishness as one stream or current in the oceanic flows of human consciousness; one can choose to swim in it or not. I am reminded of an incident that took place close to fifty years ago. I was living with my wife and newborn son in the redwood country north of San Francisco. It was at the height of the Sixties, and when a friend was visiting we took some LSD together (not uncommon in those days). We strolled amidst a small grove of redwoods, silently blissing out on the beauty and wonder of it all. Out of the blue, my friend (not previously religious) shared his realization that he is a Jew and needed to be on the "Jewish trip." I could not in the slightest relate to what he was talking about, and my response at the time was something like, "Whatever."

After my friend went home, he became an Orthodox Jew, learned Hebrew and took up the prayers and practices of Judaism. He joined the Jewish religious stream. In a similar vein, I've heard of Jews meditating in Hindu ashrams or apprenticing with a shaman in the Amazon, who had visions of Hebrew letters or heard the singing of the Shma.[128] They interpreted these experiences as messages from a higher source telling them to return to Judaism; some even became rabbis.

Though raised with Jewish identity, those in this book made different choices out of their experiences of spiritual reality. They attest to the idea that while a disciplined spiritual practice is important, you can choose whichever practices and disciplines help you on your journey regardless of the ethnic tribe of your birth. You can choose to swim in a different stream than your father's and mother's.

As human beings we have physical bodies, unique psyches, and networks of alliances with others, all of which make up aspects of our

---

[128] *Shma Yisrael Adonai Elohanu, Adonai Echud.* This is perhaps the most essential prayer of the Jewish religion, asserting that God is One.

personal identity. Yet, our essential nature, that which we are, is not separate from all that is; in some mysterious way, it is one with everything. Though this confounds the thinking mind, it is the experience of countless individuals from all parts of the world. Spiritual teachings guide us towards living a life with awareness of both the personal and the essential or ultimate aspects of identity. A spiritual life involves what my friend, the Basque teacher Angeles Arrien, called, "walking the mystical path with practical feet," aware of the unity of all life while able to navigate relationships with its manifold forms. This is what Christians refer to as, "being in the world but not of it," and it seems to be the path chosen by those I interviewed.

Jews honor the biblical Abraham as the father of the Jewish people. He left the ways of his father, journeyed to another land, and opened to a different religious understanding. Like Abraham, Buddha or Mohammed, those who do this and become leaders or founders of a new tradition are revered as prophets or scorned as heretics depending on who is telling the story.

Those in this book did not start new religions, but they are helping to shape the evolution of their chosen path. Whatever conscious or unconscious residue of Jewish transmission they embody has entered into the way they walk the road they are on. When they took up a home in a different tradition, they brought a new outlook to the practices and teachings they engaged. Having emerged from their own ancestral lineage, they brought a Jewish lens for seeing the world to their new community.

Indeed, many of those interviewed see themselves as bringing what they consider to be core Jewish perspectives and values into their new spiritual community. I also feel that through their continued relationships with family and friends in the Jewish community, they are enriching that world as well. Their discoveries of new perspectives and practices have sometimes been incorporated into the evolving Jewish worldview. A clear example of this is meditation. Many individual Jews and even some congregations continue with their traditional religious practices but find that Eastern forms of meditation enrich their experience and understanding of Judaism. This has inspired the rediscovery of Jewish forms of meditation and contemplation that were relatively unknown in normative Judaism.

Perhaps those who cross a boundary by being bilingual, bi-cultural or bi-sexual, have a stronger awareness than most of us of the commonalities between those whose differences they bridge within themselves. Those who cross a boundary of religious identification are likewise perhaps more able to see the essence beneath the rituals and outer forms of both traditions. They are able to find deeper understanding of the meanings and experiences towards which the surface forms point. They may be more likely to see the universal nature of spiritual experience and reality.

Whatever the outer forms of a spiritual path, it must relate to universal concerns: the relationship of the individual to the whole, of form to formlessness, the nature of the ultimate source of life, who we are and why we are here. Likewise, it must offer a way of relating with or experiencing the Source from which we obtain the wisdom to answer these concerns. The "perennial philosophy," an ancient idea popularized by Aldous Huxley[129], offers the image of the world's religions as many paths leading toward one mountaintop. It posits that all religions and spiritual paths have the same essential experience for their ultimate aim—the oneness of all that is, the sacredness of all life, the unifying force of love, the practice of kindness and compassion.

These universal understandings exist in Jewish spirituality and have found their way into numerous aspects of Jewish literature, art, and political activism. However, to use the metaphor previously discussed, Jewish spirituality is but one of the many rivers that can carry us in this way. As we've seen, some Jews have found the healing waters of Allah, Christ, Quan Yin, Tara, Buddha or Krishna to quench their spiritual thirst. We are blessed to have so many streams of wisdom and healing as part of our human inheritance, and doubly blessed to have the opportunity to find those that suit our unique calling.

In living a spiritual life, where the rubber hits the road is when we face suffering, our own or that of others. While spirituality illuminates

---

[129] *The Perennial Philosophy*, Aldous Huxley, Harper & Row.

our lives with inspirational, at times transcendent experiences, it must also aid us in facing heavy times and the fact that there is greed and hatred in the world and in ourselves. The collective, multi-generational history of the Jewish people has given rise to Jewish wisdom teachings to guide us in living a holy life in a world with great darkness as well as beauty. But trauma has a way of limiting our ability to open to such guidance.

Many of the teachers in this book share the view that there remains a deep wound in the collective heart of the Jewish people, a wound that offers a fundamental challenge for every Jewish person regardless of their religious choices. There are many ways to respond to this wound, but fundamentally, the choice is between two basic alternatives. We can embrace protective and defensive strategies that separate us and elevate us in relation to others, (the distorted version of the "chosen people" idea). Or, we can choose to recognize that all humans, in fact all beings, are equally "chosen," and embrace them in respectful and mutual relationships for healing and awakening. I believe that the teachers in this volume have found a way to face the times of great darkness and yet stay aware and connected to the joyous and beautiful reality of divine Presence. Their lives are committed to offering this teaching to all who seek it.

This book has focused on my meetings with remarkable men and women who crossed and also expanded the boundaries set by their ancestors. There is evidence of something in the Jewish tradition itself that lends power to such inclinations. Then again, perhaps it is simply an aspect of the human spirit. Whatever the motivating source, the courage and truth-seeking revealed in their stories and teachings give me hope that we humans have the potential to find our way through our seemingly insurmountable crises with wisdom and grace.

Bibilography

Armstrong, Karen. *Mohammad – A Prophet of Our Time*. San Francisco: Harper Collins/Atlas Books, 2006

Auslander, Shalom. *Foreskin's Lament – A Memoir*. New York: Riverhead Books, 2007

Badiner, Allen and Alex Grey, ed. *Zig Zag Zen: Buddhism and Psychedelics*. San Francisco: Chronicle Books 2002

Berry, Thomas, *The Dream of the Earth*. San Francisco: Sierra Club Books, 1988

Boyd, Doug. *Rolling Thunder*. Illinois: Delta, 1976

Buxbaum, Ytzhak. *The Light and Teaching of the Baal Shem Tov*. New York: Continuum International Publ. 2005

Chilton, Bruce. *Rabbi Jesus: An Intimate Biography*. New York: Doubleday, 2000

Cohen, Kenneth S. *The Way of Qigong – The Art and Science of Chinese Energy Healing*. New York: Ballantine Books, 1997

Das, Krishna. *Chants of a Lifetime – Searching for a Heart of Gold.* New York: Hay House, 2010

Dass, Ram. *Be Here Now.* New Mexico: Lama Foundation, 1971

Deutscher, Isaac. *The Non–Jewish Jew and Other Essays.* Oxford, England: Oxford University Press, 1968

Farber, Seth, ed. Radicals, *Rabbis and Peacemakers – Conversations with Jewish Critics of Israel.* Maine: Common Courage Press, 2005

Ferguson, Marilyn. *The Aquarian Conspiracy – Personal and Social Transformation in Our Time.* Los Angeles: Jeremy Tarcher, 1980

Forman, David J. *Jewish Schizophrenia in the Land of Israel.* Jerusalem: Gefen Publishing, 2000

Foster, Steven and Meredith Little. *The Roaring of the Sacred River – The Wilderness Quest for Vision and Self–Healing.* New York: Prentice Hall, 1989

Goldstein, Rebecca, *Betraying Spinoza – The Renegade Jew Who Gave Us Modernity.* New York: Schocken, 2006

Gottlieb, Rabbi Lynn. *She Who Dwells Within – A Feminist Vision of a Renewed Judaism.* San Francisco: Harper, 1995

Gottlieb, Rabbi Lynn. *Trail Guide to the Torah of Nonviolence.* Paris: Editions Terre d'Esperance, 2013

Grey, Alex with Allyson Grey. *Net of Being.* Rochester, VT: Inner Traditions, 2012

Huxley, Aldous. *The Perennial Philosophy – An Interpretation of the Great Mystics, East and West.* New York: Harper Perennial Modern Classics, 2009

Jacobson, Burt. *Teaching the Traditional Liturgy.* New York: Melton Research Center, 1971

Ka–Tzetnik 135633. *Shivitti – A Vision.* New York: Harper & Row, 1998

Kamenetz, Rodger. *The Jew in the Lotus – A Poet's Rediscovery of Jewish Identity in Buddhist India.* San Francisco: Harper, 1994

Kaplan, Aryeh. *Jewish Meditation – A Practical Guide.* New York: Schocken Books, 1985

Kushner, Tony and Alisa Solomon, ed. *Wrestling with Zion – Progressive Jewish–American Responses to the Israeli–Palestinian Conflict.* New York: Grove Press, 2005

Lame Deer, John and Richard Erdoes. *Lame Deer, Seeker of Visions.* New York: Simon & Schuster, 1972

Lerner, Rabbi Michael. *Healing Israel/Palestine – A Path to Peace and Reconciliation.* Berkeley: Tikkun Books, 2003

Lerner, Rabbi Michael. *Jewish Renewal – A Path to Healing and Transformation.* New York: G.P. Putnam's Sons, 1994

Lowenthal, Martin. *Buddha and the Art of Intimacy – Weaving Sacred Connections of Love.* U.S.: Dedicated Life Publications, 2009

Lowenthal, Martin. *Dawning of Clear Light – A Western Approach to Tibetan Dark Retreat Meditation.* Charlottesville, VA: Hampton Roads Publications, 2003

Lowenthal, Martin. *Writing in the Dark – Unseen Poems.* U.S.: Dedicated Life Publications, 2009.

Matt, Daniel. *The Essential Kabbalah – The Heart of Jewish Mysticism.* San Francisco: Harper, 1996

Merkur, Dan. *The Mystery of Manna – The Psychedelic Sacrament of the Bible.* Vermont: Park Street Press, 2000

Merton, Thomas. *Seven Story Mountain.* New York: Harcourt Brace Jovanovich, 1948

Metzner, Ralph. *Maps of Consciousness. I Ching, Tantra, Tarot, Alchemy, Astrology, Actualism.* New York: The Macmillan Company, 1971

Metzner, Ralph. *The Well of Remembrance – Rediscovering the Earth Wisdom Myths of Northern Europe.* Boston: Shambhala, 1994

Metzner, Ralph, ed. *Sacred Vine of Spirits – Ayahuasca.* Vermont: Park Street Press 1999

Metzner, Ralph, ed. *Teonanacatl – Sacred Mushroom of Visions.* Vermont: Park Street Press, 2004

Metzger, Deena. *What Deena Thought.* New York: Viking, 1989

Meyers, Wali Ali, Bilal Hyde, Faisal Muqaddam and Shabda Kahn. *Physicians of the Heart – A Sufi View of the 99 Names of Allah.* San Francisco: Sufi Ruhaniat International, 2011

Michel, Gregg. *Struggle for a Better South – The Southern Student Organizing Committee, 1964–1969.* New York: Palgrave Macmillan, 2008

Neihardt, John G. *Black Elk Speaks – Being the Life Story of a Holy Man of the Oglala Sioux.* Lincoln, Nebraska: University of Nebraska Press, 1961

Nisargadatta, Sri, *I Am That.* North Carolina: Acorn Press, 1973

Pinkson, Tom. *Shamanic Wisdom of the Huichol: Medicine Teachings for Modern Times.* Vermont: Destiny Books; New Edition of The Flowers of Wiricuta, 2010

Pinkson, Tom. *Fruitful Aging – Finding the Gold in the Golden Years.* CA: Wakan, 2013

Prechtel, Martin. *The Secrets of the Talking Jaguar.* New York: Tarcher, 1999

Salzberg, Sharon. *Faith – Trusting Your Own Deepest Experience.* New York: Riverhead Books, 2002

Schachter–Shalomi, Rabbi Zalman. *First Steps to a New Jewish Spirit: Reb Zalman's Guide to Recapturing the Intimacy and Ecstasy in your Relationship with God.* Woodstock, VT: Jewish Lights, 2003

Schachter–Shalomi, Rabbi Zalman. *From Age–ing to Sage–ing – A Revolutionary Approach to Growing Older.* New York: Warner Books, 1997

Schwarz–Bart, André. *The Last of the Just.* New York: Overlook Press, 2000

Silberstein, Laurence J., ed. *Mapping Jewish Identity.* New York: NYU Press, 2000

Shapiro, Isaac. *It Happens by Itself – Satsang with Isaac.* Haiku, HI: Luechow Press, 2001

Shatz, Adam, ed. *Prophets Outcast: A Century of Dissident Jewish Writing about Zionism and Israel.* New York: Nation Books 2004

Sheldrake, Rupert. *A New Science of Life: The Hypothesis of Morphic Resonance.* Vermont: Park Street Press, 1981

Starhawk. *Dreaming the Dark – Magic, Sex and Politics.* Boston: Beacon Press, 1982

Starhawk. *The Spiral Dance – A Rebirth of the Ancient Religion of the Great Goddess.* San Francisco: Harper, 1979

Steinberg, Milton. *As a Driven Leaf.* New Jersey: Behrman House, 1996

Tart, Charles, ed.*Transpersonal Psychologies.* Oxford, England: Harper & Row, 1975

Tatz, Akiva and David Gottlieb. *Letters to a Buddhist Jew.* Southfield, MI: Targum Press, 2004

Tolle, Eckhart. T*he Power of Now.* Vancouver: Namaste Publishing, 2004

Vermes, Geza. *The Religion of Jesus the Jew.* Minneapolis: Fortress Press, 1991

Waskow, Arthur. *Down to Earth Judaism – Food, Money, Sex, and the Rest of Life.* New York: William Morrow & Co., 1995

Winkler, Rabbi Gershon. *The Way of the Boundary Crosser: An Introduction to Jewish Flexidoxy.* Maryland: Jason Aronson, 2005

Yogananda, Paramahansa. *Autobiography of a Yogi.* New York: The Philosophical Library, 1946

Reader's Comments

"In an age in which increasing ethnocentrism has given rise to increasing violence, Alan Levin's Crossing the Boundary provides us with a model of intercultural/interreligious encounter. While acknowledging our roots in tribal identities, Levin's work marks out sacred space between and among a wide variety of spiritual traditions. His interviews with fourteen Jews who have found their spiritual home elsewhere shed light on a phenomenon that has sometimes been called "heresy" but which, in these moving accounts, is correctly portrayed as a journey of the spirit from which each tradition—indeed, each individual--learns from the other. This is a masterful work that deserves to be read by all who seek the light of the spirit in our troubled, divided world."

> LEONARD GROB, Professor Emeritus of Philosophy, Fairleigh Dickinson University and co-editor of *Encountering the Stranger: A Jewish-Christian-Muslim Trialogue* and *Anguished Hope: Holocaust Scholars Confront the Palestinian-Israeli Conflict*

"This book is an engaging, illuminating discussion about spirituality and how it intersects (or doesn't) with religion."

> SYLVIA BOORSTEIN, Insight Meditation teacher and author of *That's Funny, You Don't Look Buddhist: On Being a Faithful Jew and a Passionate Buddhist*, and *Pay Attention for Goodness' Sake: The Buddhist Path of Kindness*

"Shakespeare said, 'Know thyself and to thine own self be true.' The root of our personal and world dilemma is the fact that we don't know who we are. The ego and wego (collective identity) is a lifetime study, and Alan Levin demonstrates his skills of writer, student and teacher herein."

> SISTER DOROTHY MAXWELL, OP (Dominican Order of Preachers)

"For those of us who have become ever more aware, decade by decade, that migration is the story of human beings, in our time across borders of faith and community, this is a guided meditation to the heart of the experience. Exclusively focused on Jews who have crossed boundaries, or taken up residence in more than one house of spirituality, it still reads like a universal story. Alan Levin demonstrates a special knack for interviewing by listening closely. Though common themes weave their way through each exchange, themes of being Jewish, of experiencing anti-Semitism, wrestling with the occupation of Palestine, of using psychedelic enhancements to religious experiences, it is the interviewee who finally structures the report because the interviewer listens deeply. In the end Levin and his subjects answer the fundamental identity question, 'Is it ever heresy to be who we are?' In one word, 'never.'"

    MARK C. JOHNSON, Executive Director, The Center and Library for the Bible and Social Justice

"In Crossing the Boundary Alan Levin has assembled a group of spiritual teachers who show us that the deepest way to become authentically ourselves is to build connections with the variety of spiritual and religious traditions that we previously thought of as 'other.' A boundary crosser himself, Levin has much to teach all of us who seek to deepen our own spiritual lives."

    RABBI MICHAEL LERNER, editor *Tikkun* and chair, the Network of Spiritual Progressives. Author of *Jewish Renewal* and *Healing Israel/Palestine*

"In Crossing the Boundary, Alan Levin presents and demonstrates the restless spiritual curiosity and courage that distinguishes Jewish people everywhere. The 'God Wrestlers' interviewed here are not content with simply repeating prayers of the past but are part of the on-going struggle to discover the deepest highest truth alive today and imagine a sustainable tomorrow. Each unique personality, following their heart, discovered divinity that both altered and affirmed their original faith. Although meant as a study of identity, Crossing the Boundary is an affirmation of spiritual intelligence, resistance to easy answers, and universal love that renews the world."

    ALEX GREY, Artist, Author, Co-Founder CoSM, Chapel of Sacred Mirrors

"Alan Levin has written a thoroughly absorbing account of his interviews with fourteen spiritual teachers in a variety of traditions and how they have connected with as well as separated from their ancestral Jewishness. In our contemporary world men and women of Jewish family origin and religious upbringing have become not just practitioners but also teachers of Catholic, Sufi, Buddhist, Hindu, Wiccan, Shamanic, Taoist and Sikh spiritual doctrines and practices. These individuals have not rejected their Jewish tradition but built on it and integrated its essence into their chosen life-way. Surely this is a 20th century phenomenon: from the often gruesome persecution history of European Jewry has emerged a synergistic rainbow of spiritual teachings that honors the ancestral wisdom and devotion embedded in traditional Jewish religious life. This book offers rich and moving testimony to this unique historic process."

RALPH METZNER, Ph.D. Professor of Psychology, Emeritus, California Institute of Integral Studies Author, *The Unfolding Self* and *The Well of Remembrance*

www.ingramcontent.com/pod-product-compliance
Lightning Source LLC
Chambersburg PA
CBHW051358070526
44584CB00023B/3208